D1173966

Samuelsonian Economics and the Twenty-First Century

Samuelsonian Economics and the Twenty-First Century

Edited by
Michael Szenberg
Lall Ramrattan
Aron A. Gottesman

Foreword by Kenneth J. Arrow

OXFORD
UNIVERSITY PRESS

OXFORD
UNIVERSITY PRESS

Great Clarendon Street, Oxford OX2 6DP

Oxford University Press is a department of the University of Oxford.
It furthers the University's objective of excellence in research, scholarship, and education by publishing worldwide in

Oxford New York

Auckland Cape Town Dar es Salaam Hong Kong Karachi
Kuala Lumpur Madrid Melbourne Mexico City Nairobi
New Delhi Shanghai Taipei Toronto

With offices in

Argentina Austria Brazil Chile Czech Republic France Greece
Guatemala Hungary Italy Japan Poland Portugal Singapore
South Korea Switzerland Thailand Turkey Ukraine Vietnam

Published in the United States
by Oxford University Press Inc., New York

First published 2006

British Library Cataloguing in Publication Data
Data available

Library of Congress Cataloging in Publication Data
Data available

Typeset by Newgen Imaging Systems (P) Ltd., Chennai, India
Printed in Great Britain
on acid-free paper by
Biddles Ltd., King's Lynn, Norfolk

ISBN 0–19–929882–3 978–0–19–929882–2
ISBN 0–19–929883–1 978–0–19–929883–9 (Pbk.)

10 9 8 7 6 5 4 3 2 1

B'H

Dedicated to the memory of my sister, Esther;
to the memory of my parents, Henoch and Sara
to my children Naomi and Avi and
their spouses Marc and Tova;
to my grandchildren
Elki, Batya, Chanoch, Devorah, Ephraim, Ayala, and Jacob;
and to my wife, Miriam
-M.S.

To my wife, Noreena;
to my children Devi, Shanti, Hari, and Rani;
and to my grandchildren Soham and Lakshmi
-L.R.

To my wife Ronit, with adoration, and to my children
Libby, Yakov, Raphael, and Tzipora
-A.A.G.

Acknowledgments

We are deeply indebted to Terry Vaughn, the Executive Editor of Oxford University Press in New York who demonstrated early faith in the project and directed us to Sarah Caro, Oxford's publisher for Finance and Economics books. We extend profoundest thanks to Sarah Caro for shepherding the volume through the three anonymous referees and Oxford's delegates.

We would like to acknowledge the cooperativeness of the contributors to this volume. We thank them deeply for their congenial partnership. Deep gratitude and thanks are owed to the members of the Executive Board of Omicron Delta Epsilon, the Honor Society in Economics, for being a source of support: Professors Mary Ellen Benedict, James Bradley, Kristine L. Chase, Robert R. Ebert, William D. Gunther, Shirley Johnson Lans, Charles F. Phillips, Jr, Robert S. Rycroft, and the Secretary of the Society, Irene Gunther. We would also like to thank Rod Cross for reviewing the introduction.

The kind assistance of Amelia Lacey, our devoted editorial assistant, now with Workman Publishing Company, Lesley Sajdak, Jonathan Shapiro, Scott Sibbald was vital in the processing of the text through several drafts.

The librarians at Pace University—Adele Artola, Elizabeth Birnbaum, Amerene Denton, Michelle Fanelli, Eileen Gatti, Alicia Joseph, and Sanda Petre—provided unfailing assistance in the best tradition of their profession.

As for material support, Lubin School of Business offered us a grant to speed up the production of the volume. We are grateful for this gesture extended to us. Special thanks to Joseph Baczko, Lubin's Dean who sets for us highest possible standards for managing a business school.

The collegiality at Lubin of Lynette Wailoo an associate dean, William C. Freund, P. Viswanath, Jouahn Nam, and Lew Altfest, was a constant source of affection and care. We also want to recognize Irina Marutova, the department's student assistant, Nicola Simpson, the secretary of the Center of Applied Research, and Carmen Urma, the coordinator of the

Finance and Economics Department for their hard work and assistance. Finally, we owe the greatest thanks to Jorge Pinto, the publisher of our Samuelson biography. Writing about Samuelson's life and accomplishments sparked the idea for this edited volume.

For us, being fully aware of Faraday's dictum "work finish publish", editing the volume has been done for pleasure and, in Samuel Taylor Coleridge's words, "the gratification of knowing."

The simplest things are often the most complicated to understand fully.

It is better to have a model with inexact foundations that gives you a good grip to handle reality than to wait for better foundations or to continue to use a model with good foundations that is not usefully relevant to explain the phenomena that we have to explain.

Paul A. Samuelson

Foreword

Samuelsonian Economics and the 21st Century

Kenneth J. Arrow

I first encountered the work of Paul Samuelson during my graduate studies (1940–42) when my interests were changing from statistics and mathematics to economics. My mentor, Harold Hotelling, who was President of the Econometric Society, informed me that I had to join the society (at a student rate), and so I started reading *Econometrica* (Those early issues have a remarkably high fraction of papers that still resonate.) There I encountered several papers by Paul, particularly those defining and applying the concept of stability of economic equilibrium.

I was largely an autodidact when it came to economics, and, of course, having the skills and inclinations I did, economics to me meant economic theory using the tools of mathematics. Like Paul, I had profited greatly by happening on J. R. Hicks's *Value and Capital*. This work gave, like no other since Walras, an overview of the economic system, including, most importantly, its time dimension. For me, at least, it provided a map of the economic system into which individual issues would find their place. But it did not provide many specific results. My teacher, Hotelling, was primarily interested in statistics. His few papers on economics did deal deeply with a very limited range of special issues (the economic meaning of depreciation, nonrenewable resources, and spatial competition, most notably). Curiously, his own course dealt only with the theories of the consumer and the firm, the former one of several rediscoveries of Slutzky's ignored classic. (Considering its place of publication, an Italian actuarial journal, it is surprising that it was ever found before the modern technologies of retrieval.)

Paul's work combined breadth and intensity. On the one hand, his structures were grounded in a very wide knowledge of the nature of mathematical systems used to describe natural phenomena. On the other, he studied individual questions in economics, sometimes at a very detailed level.

The first underlay his pioneering and piercingly clear statement of the meaning of stability of competitive (or other) equilibrium in a world of many commodities and the relativity of the definition to a dynamic system of adjustment. The second was exemplified by his lengthy analysis of the meaning of constancy of marginal utility of income or, perhaps more usefully, by the multiplier-accelerator model.

The publication of *Foundations of Economic Analysis*, probably the most famous economics dissertation ever written, in 1948 was eagerly seized on by the growing community of young mathematical economists. I still have my well-worn copy; the much more elegantly printed expanded edition doesn't have the same resonance. But in fact it was only the beginning of Paul's contributions. The volume to which this is a Foreword contains detailed studies of the work of his long and stunningly productive career (the five volumes of *The Collected Scientific Papers of Paul A. Samuelson* contains 388 entries, but they carry us only until 1986), and there is no point duplicating them here.

In a review article (1967) on the first two volumes of *The Collected Scientific Papers*, I listed six categories of analyses which I thought to be his most vital contributions: (1) consumption theory, especially the revealed preference approach and the accompanying work on index numbers; (2) capital theory, both the pioneering work on intertemporal optimization and, even more novel and influential, the overlapping-generations model, which has been so stimulating to empirical work; (3) non-substitution theorems, both static and intertemporal; (4) factor-price equalization or, perhaps better put, the determination of factor prices by commodity prices, also a great inspiration for empirical studies; (5) stability analysis, especially of competitive equilibrium, which was followed by a great flowering of literature; and (6) formal analogies between dynamic systems and economic models. (Paul's knowledge of mathematics as applied to physical problems is clearly deep and acquired early; it has informed a significant body of his work throughout his career.) His subsequent work has added at least one more category of the same extraordinary level; the probabilistic analysis of securities prices and, more generally, reactions to uncertainty under repeated trials. The observations that there was little predictability of securities price changes worked powerfully on Paul's analytically-sharpened imagination. It led through a series of steps to a theory of warrant prices, which, in turn, inspired Fischer Black, Robert Merton, and Myron Scholes to the complete rethinking (or perhaps, first clear thinking) of the evolution of the prices of securities and their derivatives and, with that, a move to practical application unprecedented in the history of economics. Related to this was his challenge to naïve applications of the law of large numbers to willingness to undertake risks; it is by no means necessarily true that one should be more willing to take risks if one has many future opportunities to take the same risk. This line of study, in my judgment, is as important as Paul's other accomplishments.

There are a few remarks one can make about the character of Paul's writings. One is its pedagogical character. He frequently gives the feeling that he is concerned with explaining a point clear to him to a somewhat backward student. He remarks somewhere that his ideas were usually clarified by arguments with his teachers, so I assume they are still his target student audience.

Another outstanding characteristic of Paul's work is his strong and scholarly interest in the history of economic thought. This attitude shows up not merely in the many papers devoted explicitly to analysis of the doctrines of earlier economists, but even in many papers on new propositions in economics. Indeed, sometimes one has the feeling that earlier economists are among those in need of Paul's pedagogy, as he carefully explains their errors. But the pedagogy works very well for those of us listening in on the lecture.

In particular, Paul has devoted much attention, in fact fifteen of the *Collected Scientific Papers*, to the economics of Karl Marx, in particular, to the "transformation problem." This does seem a bit excessive. It is certainly not based on admiration for Marx as an economist. Perhaps it is another reflection of Paul's pedagogical ambitions; he has to repeat and expand his expositions because the audience has proved so obdurate.

Finally, I mention one interesting characteristic not only of Paul but of most, though not all, of the economic theorists in the second half of the twentieth century: the minimal influence of John Maynard Keynes on his and their work. Paul has repeatedly paid tribute to Keynes: "John Maynard Keynes was scientifically the greatest economist of this century. Only Adam Smith and Léon Walras can be mentioned in the same breath with him." Yet I look in vain in Paul's work for any serious studies of income analysis along Keynesian lines (the multiplier-accelerator model is the best that I can find, and Paul has ascribed the basic idea to Alvin Hansen). While, of course, others, like James Tobin, did construct rich models in which quantities played a central role in equilibrating savings and investment, I think on the whole the evidence is that Keynesian theory, for better or worse, is not a model rich in the kind of implications that competitive equilibrium theory has led to in the hands of a master like Paul. (Anyone brought up, as Paul and I were, in the Great Depression, may wonder whether analytic richness is a decisive criterion.) Indeed, the theoretically most interesting studies that emerged subsequently are those designed to criticize Keynesian conclusions, the new classical economics and the rational expectations theories (about which Paul has some kind words), as pursued by, among others, Robert Barro, Robert Lucas, Edmund Phelps, and Thomas Sargent.

Since I still have the floor, let me conclude by expressing my gratitude and that of the economics profession and of the world to which we have done a little good for all that Paul has created. Modern economics is inconceivable without his accomplishments.

Preface

The underlying notion in this volume is to spotlight, critically assess, and illuminate Paul A. Samuelson's extraordinarily voluminous, diverse, and groundbreaking contributions that encompass the entire field of economics through the lens of most eminent scholars. All this in honor of his ninetieth birthday celebrated on May 15, 2005 in Fairmont Hotel in Boston in the company of hundreds of scholars and their spouses. Samuelson, the first American economist to win the Nobel prize in 1970, the foremost voice in the second half of the twentieth century economics, set himself the task of creating a new way of presenting economics making it possible for it to be cast all in mathematical terms. He thus single-handedly transformed the discipline. What does it mean to transform a discipline? Wolpe inquires "What does it mean to follow the path of one's teacher?" A Hasidic story that Wolpe tells enlightens us. "Two students were disciples of the same rabbi. Years later they ran into each other. One had developed his own interpretations with their own nuances; he had even developed some of his own practices. The other had slavishly followed every word the teacher had spoken. The meticulous follower was angry with his less punctilious colleague. "How could you do this?" he asked. "How could you violate the way of our teacher?" The other responded, "Actually, I followed his way better than you. For he grew up and left his teacher. Now I have grown up and left mine."[1] In other words, distinguished teachers breed distinguished students who blaze new trails.

Sir Hans Krebs reports on a chart exhibited in the Munich Museum of Science and Technology summarizing the teacher–student genealogy of the Nobel laureates descended from Justus von Liebig, the founder of organic chemistry. The chart contains sixty individuals, all with important discoveries, and includes over thirty Nobel Prize winners.[2] A similar genealogy is unfolding in economics. As of now, five of Samuelson's students, George Akerlof, Thomas Schelling, Lawrence Klein, Robert Merton, and Joseph Stiglitz won the Nobel. The last three acted as his graduate research assistants. Samuelson's Harvard teacher, Wassily Leontief, received the Nobel in 1973.

Thomas Schelling tells us, "In 1946 I was enrolled in Joseph Schumpeter's 'advanced theory' course at Harvard. Half way through the semester Schumpeter asked whether Mr. Schelling was in attendance. I raised my hand to identify myself, and Schumpeter embarrassed me by suggesting I correct him whenever he made a mistake. Everybody looked at me, as perplexed as I was. I later visited him at his office to find out what it was all about. He said that my response to an exam question, a few weeks before, had been so professional and so superior to anybody else's that he figured he could count on me to keep him straight. I couldn't tell whether he was serious. Then he asked me how I'd learned so much about dynamic stability conditions. I answered that I had read Samuelson's *Foundations*. He said, 'Oh.' "[3]

Adrian Leverkuhn in Thomas Mann's *Doctor Faustus* declares, "There is basically one problem in the world and it is this: how do you break through? How do you get into the open?" Paul Samuelson not only broke through with singular virtuosity but he is being in Henry James' words "someone upon whom nothing is lost." Paul Samuelson serves as the secret and open inspiration for the generations of economists who follow him. He continues to weave new strands in economics without let up. As Frederico Fellini said, "If you do what you were born to do, you will never grow old."

Notes

1. Wolpe, D. J., Floating Takes Faith: Ancient Wisdom for a Modern World. Springfield, NJ: Behrman House Publishing, 2004.
2. Krebs, Hans, "The Making of a Scientist" Nature, Volume 215, (September 30, 1967), 1443.
3. Personal correspondence, 2004, as previously quoted in Szenberg, M., A.A. Gottesman, and L. Ramrattan, Paul A. Samuelson: On Being an Economist. New York: Jorge Pinto Books, 2005.

Contents

List of Contributors xxi
Ten Ways to Know Paul A. Samuelson xxiii
Introduction 1

PART I. Analysis of Samuelson's Specific Contributions 33

Overlapping Generation Models

1. Overlapping Generations 35
Robert M. Solow

2. Paul Samuelson's Amazing Intergenerational Transfer 42
Laurence J. Kotlikoff

3. Social Security, the Government Budget, and National Savings 54
Peter Diamond

Expectation, Uncertainty and Public Goods

4. Prospective Shifts, Speculative Swings: "Macro" for the Twenty-First Century in the Tradition Championed by Paul Samuelson 66
Edmund S. Phelps

5. Paul Samuelson and Global Public Goods 88
William D. Nordhaus

Preference and Consumer Behavior

6. Revealed Preference 99
Hal R. Varian

7. Samuelson's "Dr. Jekyll and Mrs. Jekyll" Problem: A Difficulty in the Concept of the Consumer 116
Robert A. Pollak

Marx

8. Paul Samuelson on Karl Marx: Were the Sacrificed Games of Tennis Worth It? 127
Geoff Harcourt

Stability

9. Paul Samuelson and the Stability of General Equilibrium 142
Franklin M. Fisher

Keynes & Post Keynesians

10. Paul Samuelson and Piero Sraffa—Two Prodigious Minds at the Opposite Poles 146
Luigi L. Pasinetti

11. Paul Samuelson as a "Keynesian" Economist 165
L. R. Klein

12. Samuelson and the Keynes/Post Keynesian Revolution 178
Paul Davidson

International Economics and Finance

13. Paul Samuelson and International Trade Theory Over Eight Decades 197
Avinash Dixit

14. Paul Samuelson's Contributions to International Economics 212
Kenneth Rogoff

15. Protection and Real Wages: The Stolper–Samuelson Theorem 224
Rachel McCulloch

Finance and Portfolio Theory

16. Samuelson and the Factor Bias of Technological Change: Toward a Unified Theory of Growth and Unemployment 235
Joseph E. Stiglitz

17. Samuelson and Investment for the Long Run 252
Harry M. Markowitz

18 Paul Samuelson and Financial Economics 262
Robert C. Merton

PART II. Samuelson's Relevance 301

Relevance to Mathematical Economics

19. Multipliers and the LeChatelier Principle 303
Paul Milgrom

Relevance to the Natural Sciences

20. The Surprising Ubiquity of the Samuelson Configuration: Paul Samuelson and the Natural Sciences 311
James B. Cooper and Thomas Russell

21. Paul Samuelson's Mach 330
Rod Cross

Index 343

List of Contributors

Kenneth J. Arrow is a Professor Emeritus of Economics at Stanford University. He won the 1972 Nobel Memorial Prize in Economic Science.
http://www-econ.stanford.edu/faculty/arrow.html

James B. Cooper is Professor at the Institute for Analysis at Johannes Kepler University at Linz, Austria.
http://www.tn.jku.at/tninstitute/index_ger.html

Rod Cross is Professor Emeritus at the Department of Economics at the University of Strathclyde.
http://www.strath.ac.uk/economics/staff/cross_r.html

Paul Davidson is the Holly Chair of Excellence in Political Economy, Emeritus at the University of Tennessee at Knoxville.
http://econ.bus.utk.edu/Davidson.html

Peter Diamond is Institute Professor at the Massachusetts Institute of Technology.
econ-www.mit.edu/faculty/download_cv.php?prof_id=pdiamond

Avinash Dixit is the John J. F. Sherrerd '52 University Professor of Economics at Princeton University.
www.princeton.edu/~dixitak/home

Franklin Fisher is the Jane Berkowitz Carlton and Dennis William Carlton Professor at the Massachusetts Institute of Technology.
http://econ-www.mit.edu/faculty/?prof_id=mullain

Geoff Harcourt is Professor Emeritus at Jesus College at the University of Cambridge.
http://www.jesus.cam.ac.uk/contacts/fellows/profiles/harcourt.html

L. R. Klein is the Benjamin Franklin Professor Emeritus of Economics at the University of Pennsylvania. He won the 1980 Nobel Memorial Prize in Economic Science.
www.econ.upenn.edu/cgi-bin/mecon/bin/view.cgi?id=18

Laurence J. Kotlikoff is Professor of Economics at Boston University.
econ.bu.edu/Kotlikoff

Harry M. Markowitz won the Nobel Memorial Prize in Economic Science in 1990.
http://nobelprize.org/economics/laureates/1990/

Rachel McCulloch is the Rosen Family Professor of International Finance at the International Business School at Brandeis University.
www.brandeis.edu/global/faculty_detail.php?faculty_id=26

Robert C. Merton is the John and Natty McArthur University Professor at Harvard Business School. He won the 1997 Nobel Memorial Prize in Economic Science.
http://dor.hbs.edu/fi_redirect.jhtml?facInfo=bio&facEmId=rmerton

Paul Milgrom is the Shirley and Leonard Ely professor of Humanities and Sciences in the Department of Economics at Stanford University.
http://www.milgrom.net/

William D. Nordhaus is Sterling Professor of Economics at the Cowles Foundation at Yale University.
http://www.econ.yale.edu/~nordhaus/homepage/homepage.htm

Luigi Pasinetti is Professor of Economic Analysis at the Faculty of Economics at the Università Cattolica del Sacro Cuore in Milan.
http://www.unicatt.it/docenti/pasinetti/default_eng.htm

Edmund Phelps is McVickar Professor of Political Economy and Director, Center on Capitalism and Society, Earth Institute, at Columbia University.
http://www.columbia.edu/~esp2/

Robert A. Pollak is Hernreich Distinguished Professor of Economics at Washington University in St. Louis.
http://economics.wustl.edu/faculty/faculty.php?id=12

Thomas Russell is Professor of Economics at Santa Clara University.
http://business.scu.edu/economics/faculty/trussell/default.htm

Robert M. Solow is Institute Professor, Emeritus at the Massachusetts Institute of Technology. He won the 1987 Nobel Memorial Prize in Economic Science.
http://econ-www.m/_it.edu/faculty/?prof_id=mullain

Joseph E. Stiglitz is University Professor at Columbia University. He won the 2001 Nobel Memorial Prize in Economic Science.
www-1.gsb.columbia.edu/faculty/jstiglitz

Hal R. Varian holds the Class of 1944 Professorship in the School of Information Management and Systems, the Haas School of Business, and the Department of Economics at the University of California at Berkeley.
http://www.sims.berkeley.edu/~hal/

Ten Ways to Know Paul A. Samuelson*

> I do not know what I may appear to the world, but to myself
> I seem to have been only like a boy playing on the seashore,
> and diverting myself in now and then finding a prettier shell
> or a smoother pebble than ordinary whilst the great ocean
> of truth lay all undiscovered about me.
>
> —Isaac Newton

In his lectures, Paul often opens with anecdotes that serve as a light introduction for the substantive analysis that follows. In the spirit of his lectures, my talk will be a warm-up for the main event. I will present selected vignettes that portray Paul's personality and character with, I hope, insight and humor. To quote Nigel Rees: "An anecdote can often say more about a person than pages of biography" (1999, p. ix). An historian once noted that in time the legacy of any individual can be distilled into succinct sound bytes. Think of Presidents Washington, Lincoln, and Franklin D. Roosevelt.

10. Paul Samuelson is a Great Maestro

While Paul describes himself as having "an important role in the symphony orchestra," we see him as the conductor for the economists of the second half of the twentieth century. A first-rate university is neither made by brilliant students nor by brilliant teachers alone, but by the cheerful and fruitful interaction between the two. Paul's visible hands, gifted mind, and heart succeeded in not only attracting exceptional teachers and students to MIT, but in orchestrating a superbly-tuned ensemble which takes true interest in one another.

A Version of this talk was delivered by Michael Szenberg at the birthday celebration for Paul A. Samuelson on May 15, 2005 in Boston Massachusetts.

*Reprinted with permission from *Economics of Education Review* (Spring 2006).

A conductor's wife once asked Alexander Kipnis, the Russian basso, "What is it about Toscanini? What is it he does that my husband cannot do? Does he do something with his hands? Or with his eyes? Does he conduct faster? Or slower?" And Kipnis answered by quoting Gurnemanz's reply to Parsifal's query: "Who is the Grail?" The answer was: "That may not be told, but if you are chosen for it, you will not fail to know" (Sachs, 1991, p. 159).

In the world of music, it is a rarity to find a person who is both a gifted composer and a top conductor. So it is in economics as well. Paul is that rarity. When Paul is writing, the sun is always out. His writing—ever eloquent, ever stirring—is done with the kind of verve that one seldom finds today.

9. Paul Samuelson Lives a Balanced Life

There is a widely exaggerated and stereotyped notion shared by many that superior scientists can neither live a balanced life nor be paragons of virtue. Consider the words of William Butler Yeats, the poet: "The intellect of man is forced to choose perfection of the life or of the work," or those of David Hull: "The behavior that appears to be the most improper actually facilitates the manifest goals of science. . . . As it turns out, the least productive scientists tend to behave the most admirably, while those who make the greatest contributions just as frequently behave the most deplorably" (1988, p. 32). In other words, aggressiveness and selfishness are associated with superior performance by scientists. But my experiences and observations of eminent economists do not support these assertions. In Paul's case, not only does he know how to maintain a balance between scholarship, family, and play, but he exhibits a high degree of humanity and kindness. The term *mentsch* aptly describes him.

8. Paul Samuelson Knows How to Disagree Agreeably

The Houses of Friedman and Samuelson disagreed on both methodology and policy. Nevertheless, the intellectual battles never encroached upon their personal respect for and friendship to each other. In fact, Milton told me of how Paul influenced him in a long telephone conversation to accept the offer to write a column for *Newsweek*.

In ancient Israel there were two houses of learning, Hillel and Shamai, which fiercely disagreed with each other on most issues. We are told that, although they opposed each other, they respected each other; and their children married one another (*Yevamot*, Mishna 4). For my analogy to be complete, the grandchildren of Samuelson must marry the grandchildren of Friedman.

7. Paul Samuelson is Politically Savvy

Theodore Schultz, then chairman of the Economics Department at the University of Chicago, sought Samuelson as a counterbalance to the school's laissez faire philosophy. Schultz's argument to Paul was enticing: "We'll have two leading minds of different philosophical bent—you and Milton Friedman—and that will be fruitful." Paul tells us that he verbally accepted the offer initially, but changed his mind twenty four hours later, fearing that the position would force him to counterbalance Friedman by adopting leftist opinions that he didn't fully agree with.[1] Samuelson clearly defined himself as a centrist, rather than an advocate of a right- or left-wing philosophy. Also, he resisted requests by former Presidents John F. Kennedy and Lyndon B. Johnson to join the Council of Economic Advisers. As he said, "in the long-run the economic scholar works for the only coin worth having—our own applause" (Samuelson, 1962). Also, by distancing himself from politics, Paul can call the "shots as they really appear to be."

In 1952, Albert Einstein graciously declined the presidency of Israel. He later remarked "equations are more important to me because politics are for the present, but an equation is something for eternity" (Gelb, 1999, p. 323).

6. Paul Samuelson is Piercingly Witty

Einstein had this to say about fame: "Yesterday idolized, today hated and spat upon, tomorrow forgotten, and the day after tomorrow promoted to sainthood. The only salvation is a sense of humor" (Gelb, 1999, p. 322). Alan Brown tells us that when Paul was asked how many children he had, he responded: "First we got one, then we got two, then we got three, then we got scared."[2] Avinash Dixit recalls Paul's humorous description of Joan Robinson's visit to the United States: "She was taken in a sealed train from coast to coast—from Paul Baran to Paul Sweezy."[3] Jagdish Bhagwati relates a story about Paul's encounter with the British economist, Lord Thomas

Balogh. Paul "once traveled from Heathrow airport to a party in Oxford; he walked up to Balogh and said: 'Tommy, I have just been reading the *Financial Times* and I find that someone has signed your name to a terrible article; you must do something about it!' "[4] Indeed, Paul's capacity for irreverence and wit is true to the John Maynard Keynes maxim: "Words ought to be a little wild, for they are the assault of thoughts on the unthinking" (June 1933, p. 761).

5. Paul Samuelson is Human

Paul has no problem with wealth, yet he advocates positions that work against his personal economic interests. He notes that, while advocating the closing of tax loopholes, he has no difficulty taking advantage of those that remain. Fundamentally, Paul represents a middle path, as expressed in the ancient dictum that "men with vision walk in the middle."[5]

Paul once remarked that the only fault of a certain person was that he had a loose string on his coat. One of the most famous loose strings on Paul's own coat has to do with his 1944 prediction in the *New Republic* that foretold of greater unemployment following the end of the Second World War, a prediction that subsequently was proven incorrect. This is reminiscent of Nathan Milstein, the famous violinist, who was approached by an admirer and asked to play a false note, only to prove his humanity.

4. Paul Samuelson is Unique

In ancient times, sages argued whether vast knowledge and erudition take precedence over brilliant depth and sharp dialectics. The argument was inconclusive and ended in a draw. Archilochus, the pre-Socratic philosopher, expressed this enigmatically: "The fox knows many things, but the hedgehog knows one big thing." There are economists who are hedgehogs, who search for scientific insights by turning their critical lens toward a few selected areas. Others, being more fox-like, drive their talents into many directions. Paul has reached immortal stature in the history of economics by being both a hedgehog and a fox. He possesses a genius that covers in its depth and breadth many areas within economics. Will Baumol describes him as a jack of all trades and a master of every one.[6] It is rare, indeed, to find conversation, correspondence, and scholarship so well blended in one person.

In contrast to the natural sciences, where Isaac Newton and Albert Einstein made their major contributions, most economics masterpieces were written when the authors were middle aged. Adam Smith, Karl Marx, John Maynard Keynes, and Milton Friedman come to mind. However, Paul started much earlier, in his twenties; and, even now, his new articles influence the fields of economics and finance.

Furthermore, not only is he a master of economics, his vast knowledge is far-reaching. For example, János Kornai tells us "He *knows* history. If he had a Hungarian sitting at his side at the dinner table, he would quote easily names of politicians or novelists of the Austrian–Hungarian empire of the late nineteenth century. He also *understands the significance* of the history of a country. This is a rare quality at a time when the education of economists has become excessively technical."[7]

Similarly, Bengt Holmstrom recalls a dinner at his house for a group of young faculty members, which Paul attended as well. "Between meals I arranged a light, informal trivia competition. Had answers been counted, he would have won hands down. He even knew the third president—of Finland—a question I threw in as a joke."[8]

With so much encyclopedic knowledge at his disposal, there is one challenge left for Paul: to appear on *Jeopardy* or *Who Wants to be a Millionaire?* His appearance, however, would probably bankrupt the American television network (American Broadcasting Company) ABC.

3. Paul Samuelson is a Mentor

When Paul's *Foundations* was published in the 1940s, readers experienced a kind of revelation that created a sensation. This brings to mind the post-First World War public's similar reaction to Marcel Proust's *Remembrance of Things Past.* Critics compared Proust's prolific writings to those of Homer, Dante, and Shakespeare. But, what a difference in Proust's and Paul's dispositions!

The attitude and the embrace by Paul of younger scholars lead to the nurturing and development of great minds, many of whom are seated in this hall. It is revealing to contrast his actions with those of Marcel Proust. Whenever Proust was asked to evaluate a manuscript, he always enclosed the following letter: "Divine work. It is a work of genius. I would not change a word. I take my hat off for you. All the best, Marcel Proust."[9] The novelist wrote the same laudatory note to all potential writers who contacted him. When confronted about what he was doing, Proust said that he did not have time to read the submitted material because it interfered with his writing. By telling young authors that their work was that of a genius, he made sure that they would not return their revised papers to him with changes. Interestingly, when Proust first wrote *Remembrance,* his monumental seven-volume tome, no one would publish it. In fact, he had to use his own funds to publish the first volume. Yet, this experience did nothing to fill Proust's heart with empathy for young writers or to enhance his reverence for the human spirit. Proust's behavior, though amusing and seemingly innocent, illustrates the gross impediments the turn of the century classical author was willing to place before fledgling writers and thereby violate an important moral principle, "Before the blind do not put a stumbling block" (Leviticus 19:14). Paul would find such a deceitful act abhorrent.

Perry Mehrling of Columbia University told me a characteristic story of Paul. "[Paul] mentioned that he had heard about a piece I had written on Irving Fisher. I have no idea how he heard about it, but I offered to send him a copy and within a few days I got back a letter. [Paul] read the paper and wanted to set down his own interpretation, but then he closes the letter with a remarkable line that I treasure: 'Do disregard my heresies and follow your own star.' "[10] It is remarkable that you, Paul, extended the same type of support and nurturing to me and other economists who occupy the back benches of the academy.

2. Paul Samuelson is a Pioneer

André Gide remarked that "I will maintain that an artist needs this: a special world of which he alone has the key" (1948, p. 77). In the world of the physical sciences, it was Isaac Newton who used mathematics to unravel the mystery of the universe. So did Paul in economics by moving economic methodology from Marshall's diagrammatic presentations to the present-day quantitative approaches. He single-handedly and fruitfully rewrote the theory of many branches of economics. Among his greatest contributions is his neoclassical synthesis. As such, he broadened the discipline, deepened it, and opened the doors to others. As Paul said to the students present at the Nobel banquet, "You are the posterity we work for. I can assure you that we are bestowing on you the most glorious gift of all—plenty of difficult problems still unsolved."[11] As a pioneer, Paul adhered to Ralph Waldo Emerson's tenet that one should not "follow where the path may lead, [but] go, instead, where there is no path and leave a trail." To rephrase what Cicero wrote of Socrates, Paul called down modern economics from the skies and implanted it in the universities throughout the world (Gelb, 1999, p. 15).

1. Paul Samuelson Continues to Contribute

What is amazing about Paul is that his life's work continues even today. What trumpet player Clark Terry stated of Duke Ellington applies equally well to Paul; "He wants life and music to be always in a state of becoming. He doesn't even like to write definitive endings to a piece. He'd often ask us to come up with ideas for closings, but when he'd settle on one of them, he'd keep fooling with it. He always likes to make the end of a song sound as if it's still going somewhere" (Hentoff, 2004, p. xix).

We are drawn to thinkers, musicians, and scientists who are in a constant state of becoming. When Pablo Casals, the famous cellist, was asked why he continued to practice four hours a day at the age of ninety-three, he said, "Because I think I can still make some progress" (Szenberg, 1998, p. 17). Similarly, Michelangelo frequently used the phrase *Ancora Imparo*, I am still learning, as he continued in his old age to perfect his masterpieces.

Because there is this tension between striving for perfection and never truly reaching it, no scientist or artist is ever satisfied or ever stops working. We owe to Martha Graham the following central insight on the subject: "There is no satisfaction whatever at any time. There is only a queer, divine dissatisfaction; a blessed unrest that keeps us marching and makes us more alive than the others."[12]

Acknowledgments

We would like to thank Bengt Holmstrom and James Poterba for organizing the event. We also wish to thank Victor R. Fuchs for graciously reviewing these remarks and offering his invaluable comments. We would also like to thank Irene Gunther, administrative assistant at Omicron Delta Epsilon, and the Omicron Delta Epsilon Executive Board for their continued support: James Bradley, Jr; Mary Ellen Benedict; Kristine L. Chase; Robert R. Ebert; William D. Gunther; Charles F. Phillips, Jr; and Robert S. Rycroft.

Notes

1. Interview, July 1, 2004.
2. Personal Correspondence, 2004.
3. Personal Correspondence, 2004.
4. Personal Correspondence, 2004.
5. Tosefta: *Baba Kama*, 2.12.
6. In his unpublished essay, "Generalists' Generalissimo".
7. Personal Correspondence, 2004.
8. Personal Correspondence, 2004.
9. *Maariv*, "Literary Supplement," weekend edition in the 1990s.
10. Personal Correspondence, 2004.
11. Paul A. Samuelson, Nobel Banquet Speech, December 10, 1970; available at http://nobelprize.org/economics/laureates/1970/samuelson-speech.html
12. From a letter to Agnes de Mille, undated.

References

Gelb, M. J. (1999). *Discover your genius*. New York: HarperCollins.

Gide, A. (1948). *The journals of André Gidé (Volume I: 1889–1913)*. Translated by Justin O'Brien. New York: Alfred A. Knopf.

Haggin, B. H. (1967). *The Toscanini musicians knew*. New York: Horizon Press.

Hentoff, N. (2004). *American music is*. New York: Da Capo Press.

Hull, D. L. (1988). *Science as a process: An evolutionary account of the social and conceptual development of science*. Chicago: University of Chicago Press.

Keynes, J. M. (June 1933). National self-sufficiency. *The Yale Review* 22, 755–769.

Rees, N. (1999). *Dictionary of Anecdotes*. London: Cassell.

Sachs, H. (1991). *Reflections on Toscanini*. New York: Grove Weidenfeld.

Samuelson, P. A. (September 11 and 18, 1944). Unemployment ahead. *New Republic*.

—— (March 1962) Economists and the history of ideas. *American Economic Review* 52, 1–18.

Szenberg, M., ed. (1992). *Eminent economists, their life philosophies*. New York: Cambridge University Press.

—— (1998). *Passion and craft, economists at work*. Ann Arbor, MI: University of Michigan Press.

Introduction: The Significance of Paul A. Samuelson in the Twenty-First Century

The contributors to this volume had unambiguous foundations upon which to build, due to Samuelson's use of mathematics as a language, "physics as the science for economics to imitate" (Hayek, 1992, p. 5), and reality over theory as a paradigm. Samuelson's early and later writings are consistent and somewhat invariant, and in harmony with Adam Smith's maximizing individual in society. Samuelson asked: "What is it that the scientist finds useful in being able to relate a positive description of behavior to the solution of a maximizing problem? That is what a good deal of my own early work was about. From the time of my first papers on 'Revealed preference' . . . through the completion of *Foundations of Economic Analysis*, I found this a fascinating subject . . . my positive descriptive relations could be interpreted as the necessary and sufficient conditions of a well-defined maximum problem" (Samuelson, 1972, p. 3).

Samuelson developed broad frameworks such as the neoclassical synthesis, a mixed economy, and the surrogate production function, which provided practitioners with a vision for research. His contributions to economics are rich, complex, heavy with facts, consequential, and relevant to the ordinary economics of life. Because of the quality of Samuelson's output and methods, the contributors to this volume see a near complete success for his theories in the twenty-first century.

Many of the contributors have defended Samuelson's work elsewhere. Now they have gathered to appraise the relevance of his work in the twenty-first century. Robert Solow explicitly states that Samuelson's Overlapping Generations Model (OLG) had slipped through the cracks in a previous work, which he now seeks to remedy in this volume. Luigi Pasinetti demonstrates elements of similarity between Samuelson's and Piero Sraffa's writings to explain why they were friends and not enemies, as would be expected. Geoff Harcourt discusses Samuelson's repeated and vexed interest in Karl Marx's approaches, and identifies an "Aha!" moment about how Samuelson treats the transformation problem.

Appraising Samuelson: Units of Appraisal

As "Archimedes' lever is useless without a fulcrum to rest it on, and . . . angels need the point of a needle to dance upon" (Samuelson, 1978, p. 790), so too do we need a template against which to appraise the significance of Samuelson's writings for twenty-first century economists. Samuelson provided some insight when he argued that in order to appraise Alfred Marshall's originality we must take into consideration economists such as John Stuart Mill and Antoine-Augustin Cournot, whose contributions Marshall knew well (Samuelson, 1972, p. 22). If we were to sample the writings that Samuelson knows well, then mathematicians such as Henri Poincare, Frank Ramsey, and John von Neumann, scientists such as Albert Einstein, James Clerk Maxwell, and Henri-Louis Le Chatelier, philosophers such as Ernst Mach, Karl Popper, and Thomas Kuhn, and economists such as Adam Smith, David Ricardo, Karl Marx, and John Maynard Keynes would be included.

In awarding the Nobel Prize to Samuelson in 1970, the Nobel committee identified works that were worthy of appraisal. They were "*scientific work through which he has developed static and dynamic economic theory and actively contributed to raising the level of analysis in economic science.*" These include Samuelson's novel view that "under free trade both parties are better off than under no trade at all, but are not necessarily in the optimum position" (Samuelson, 1966, p. 779); his Le Chatelier principle that explains how an economic system that is in equilibrium will react to a perturbation; his Samuelson–Bergson utility function that measures welfare gains; and his factor price equalization theory, which as John Hicks pointed out, "if there is a removal, not only of the obstacles to free trade, but also of the obstacles of factor movement . . . the two economies then become virtually one economy" (Hicks, 1983, p. 235). Those enumerated novelties are in addition to his neoclassical synthesis, revealed preference, multiplier-accelerator, and surrogate production function models. These novel contributions have already withstood the rigorous tests of coherency, consistency, falsification, and pragmatism, and have become objective and valid scientific achievements because they are open for revision and criticism. For over half a century, Samuelson's contributions have held up well with much cross-fertilization from other areas. In sum, as Kenneth Arrow puts it, "Samuelson is one of the greatest economic theorists of all time" (Arrow, 1967, p. 735). He should, therefore, be appraised as such.

An appraisal is different from a mere description. It appraises why a theory is superior and does not bother about how to construct an even more superior theory (Latsis, 1980, p. 3). Samuelson's hypotheses fit in this appraisal schema because they are scientific. Karl Popper draws a separating line between the "empirical sciences on the one hand, and mathematics and logic as well as 'metaphysical systems' on the other," and called this separation "the *problem of demarcation*" (Popper, 1968, p. 35). The fact that mathematics is included in the nonscience side should not be perceived as having a negative implication for economics and Samuelson's work. T. W. Hutchison cites Popper as saying that "The success of mathematical economics shows that one social science at least has gone through its Newtonian revolution." He adds that "surely such an outstanding post-Newtonian salient would deserve the closest analysis and appraisal from philosophers of science" (Hutchison, 1980, p. 187). Popper fuses the idea of "corroboration" with the idea of "appraisal" when he notes that "corroboration can only be expressed as an appraisal" (Popper, 1968, p. 265). Mark Blaug states that "By the degree of corroboration of a theory, I mean a concise report evaluating the state (at a certain time *t*) of the critical discussion of a theory, with respect to the way it solves its problems; its degree of testability; the severity of the test it has undergone; and the way it stood up to these tests. Corroboration (or degree of corroboration) is thus an evaluating *report of past performance*" (Blaug, 1983, p. 26).

A "corroborative appraisal" establishes a fundamental relationship between accepted basic statements and the hypothesis (Popper, 1968, p. 266). Hypotheses "are 'provisional conjectures' (or something of the sort); and this view too, can only be expressed by way of an appraisal of these hypotheses" (Popper, 1968, p. 265). "From a new idea . . . conclusions are drawn by means of logical deduction. These conclusions are then compared with one another and with other relevant statements, so as to find what logical relations (such as equivalence, derivability, compatibility, or incompatibility) exist between them" (Popper, 1968, p. 32). Therefore, Popper's demarcation criteria are the "standards for appraising competing scientific hypotheses in terms of their degrees of verisimilitude" (Blaug, 1983, p. 10). Hypotheses must be subjected to a severe test and found compatible, that is, not falsified. The testing procedure is fourfold: (1) A test of the internal consistency of the system by comparing conclusions among themselves, (2) A test of the logical form of the theory to see if it is empirical or tautological, (3) A comparison of the theory with others to see whether it truly is a "scientific advance should it survive our various tests," and (4) A test of the theory "by way of empirical applications of the conclusions which can be derived from it" (Blaug, 1983, pp. 32–34). The overall implication is that if Samuelson's theories are incompatible, we can regard them as falsified. If they are compatible, then we might give them some degree of "positive corroboration," but that will depend on the "severity of the various tests" that the hypothesis has passed (Blaug, 1983, pp. 266–267). A positive degree of corroboration is like a nested function: Positive corroboration = f [severity of test = g (degree of testability = h {simplicity of the hypothesis})].

Although Samuelson has some grand unifying scientific theories such as the neoclassical synthesis, he has also made particular scientific contributions to many subdisciplines in economics that need to be appraised as well. Fortunately, appraisal methodology comes in "units" as well as in bundles of "units." Imre Lakatos, a student of Popper, called units of appraisal in science a "research program" or a series of connected theories, rather than a single theory (Lakatos and Musgrave, 1977). A single theory can be falsified when only one instance of refutation appears. However, a research program is not easily falsified. It has theories in its "hard core" that practitioners are not willing to abandon, and theories in its "protective belt" that practitioners are interested in improving. The Duhem–Quine hypothesis also embraces units of appraisal. It holds that the incompatibility of one consequence does not falsify all of the antecedents (Quine, 1990, pp. 13–14). For example, if one finds that the paradox of thrift hypothesis is incompatible, one does not have to give up the neoclassical synthesis. For Samuelson, such units of appraisal are exemplified in the roles that mathematics and facts play in economics. Building on Pareto's idea that mathematics represents complexly interacting and independent phenomena, Samuelson adds that "after mathematical notions have performed the function of reminding us that everything depends upon everything else, they may not add very much more—unless some special hypothesis can be made about the facts" (Samuelson, 1966, p. 1758).

Besides the above broad methodological perspectives, Samuelson can be appraised as a "craftsman" using his personal knowledge to improve economic science. A "personal appraisal" holds that "in every act of knowing there enters a passionate contribution of the person knowing what is being known" (Polanyi, 1958, p. viii). As Jerome R. Ravetz (1979, p. 75) frames the problem, we are interested in how "objective scientific knowledge can result from the intensely personal and fallible endeavor of creative scientific inquiry." On the craftsman's side of appraisal, Samuelson has certainly demonstrated high "morale" defined as "any positive and energetic attitude toward a goal" (Bateson and Mead, 1941, p. 206). The contributors of this book are living proof of successful "morale transfer," and good "morale resonance" among colleagues and students with Samuelson's craftsmanship. But besides craftsmanship and good morale, Samuelson can be appraised from the perspective of "universally valid appraisals" (Polanyi, 1958, p. 22), "systems of appraisals" (Polanyi, 1958, p. 43), and "appraisal of order" (Polanyi, 1958, p. 36), the criteria of which include "(1) a correct satisfaction of normal standards, (2) a mistaken satisfaction of normal standards, and (3) action or perception satisfying subjective, illusory standards" (Polanyi, 1958, p. 363). The neoclassical syntheses and intergenerational models are objective and valid scientific achievements because they are open for revision and criticism from everyone, and have had significant and verified progress thus far.

Samuelson should further be appraised for his adoption of successful epistemological viewpoints in his scientific approach to economics. The big "M" approach of Rod Cross places Samuelson's works beside those of Mach. Samuelson's method is also consistent with the epistemological approach of Poincare and Einstein. Poincare would build up science from lower level hypotheses, such as Galileo Galilei's one-dimensional to two-dimensional motions of falling bodies, ending up with Isaac Newton's laws. Einstein would make inference statements from axioms, but in moving from axiom to inference statements one has a clear link with the empirical world of data and experiments, including mental (*Gedanken*) experiments (Miller, 1984, pp. 39–46). Such research programs are geared to find novel facts. "Einstein's program . . . made the stunning prediction that if one measures the distance between two stars in the night and if one measures the distance between them during the day (when they are visible during an eclipse of the sun), the two measurements will be different" (Lakatos, 1980, p. 5). As Popper indicates, "stars close to the sun would look as if they had moved a little away from the sun, and from one another" (Popper, 1963, p. 37). This is indeed a novel prediction of Einstein's program. For Poincare, "facts outstrip us, and we can never overtake them; while the scientist is discovering one fact, millions and millions are produced in every cubic inch of his body" (Poincare, 1908, p. 16). We must therefore select facts. "The most interesting facts are those which can be used several times, those which have a chance of recurring" (Poincare, 1908, p. 17). Recurring facts are "simple" such as the stars, the atoms, and the cell. In short, simple facts lie "in the two extremes, in the infinitely great and in the infinitely small" (Poincare, 1908, 18–19). One is reminded of Samuelson's Simple Mathematics of Income Determination, Surrogate Production Function, and simple 2×2 trade models. To sum up, in Samuelson's own words, "we theorists like to work with extreme polar cases, what is the natural model to formulate so as to give strongest emphasis to external effect?" (Samuelson, 1966, p. 1235).

On the empirical side, Samuelson is primarily appraised for his study of the mixed economy. "The mixed economy is not a very definite concept. I have purposely left it vague, in part because that is its intrinsic nature and in part because increased precision should come at the end rather than at the beginning of extensive research" (Samuelson, 1966, p. 632). Further, "A mixed economy in a society where people are by custom tolerant of differences in opinion, may provide greater personal freedom and security of expression than does a purer price economy where people are less tolerant" (Samuelson, 1972, p. 628). Even though "History oscillates, backtracks, and spirals" (Samuelson, 1972, p. 612), in the end the mixed economy emerges because it is based on reality. We know that Samuelson nourishes his foresight with strong doses of the reality paradigm, for he said that "I would take aid from the Devil if that would help crack the puzzle of economic reality" (Samuelson, 1986, p. 873), and that "it is better to have a model with inexact foundations that gives you a good grip to handle reality than to wait for better foundations or to continue to use a model with good foundations that is not usefully relevant to explain the phenomena that we have to explain" (Samuelson, 1986, p. 295). In short, "A good economist has good judgment about economic reality" (Samuelson, 1972, p. 775).

On the theoretical side, Samuelson is also most appraised for how his theories explain reality. For his theories to survive in the twenty-first century, they must solve and explain problems and anomalies in a normal scientific way. Normal science will require us to: (1) unearth economic values; (2) compare theories T_n with T_{n-1} to see which one performs better; and (3) overthrow or re-specify degenerating theories.[1]

Samuelson's neoclassical synthesis can be used to appraise different theories to see which is better. Take the demand versus supply-side theories of the 1970s and 1980s for example. The demand-side theory was well tested in the 1970s against the stagflation problem, and some economists charged that it was weakening. Other Keynesian ideas such as the paradox of thrift were eliminated from some of the newer editions of Samuelson's own book, *Economics*. Some major principle textbooks dropped the Keynesian IS/LM and the Keynesian-cross diagrams. However, the hard-core elements of the demand-side system such as the mixed economy, wage rigidity, and interest inelasticity remain intact, and its future seems assured: "the underlying framework for a new period of creative consensus in economic thought . . . will be a newly appraised balance between the public and private sectors in which the role of the former is considerably elevated over its earlier status" (Heilbroner and Milberg, 1995, p. 119). Newer policy problems such as targeted interest rate policies and monetary policies within the EMU saw the need to keep the Keynesian modified paradigm within the Mundell–Fleming BOP/IS/LM model, and its implied Keynesian-cross framework. This example underscores the fact that the Keynesian paradigm has a strong heuristic power to suggest ways of solving a wide variety of problems; that it is theoretically progressive in that it will yield more testable content in T_n than in T_{n-1}; and that it is empirically progressive, for at least some of its additional testable consequences can be confirmed.

As an appraisal of Samuelson's ability to re-specify a weakening theory, let us consider his improvement of the Heckscher–Ohlin theory. As a criterion for a better theory, one may be content to accept von Mises' "Science and Value" concept, "a situation in which a given amount of capital and labor was able to produce a definite quantity of material economic goods 'better' than a situation in which the same amount could produce only a smaller quantity" (von Mises, 1960, p. 36). But Samuelson would not settle there: "What Samuelson did was graft Ohlin's trade theory and the problems connected with its rigorous articulation and generalization onto the mainline research tradition concerned with the conditions governing the existence, uniqueness and stability of general competitive equilibrium" (De Marchi, 1976, pp. 112–113).

To sum up, we have been very restrictive in our appraisal of Samuelson's work for the twenty-first century, limiting our examples to only the mixed economy and policy combinations. The contributors to this volume are more impressive in their predictions and explanations of their topics, which include ideas, theories, and facts.

Samuelson Appraised Through His Own Methodology

In at least two articles, Samuelson uses the word "appraisal" explicitly in the title. In one, "Economics of Futures Contracts on Basic Macroeconomic Indexes: An Economist's Appraisal" (Samuelson, 1986, p. 557), he reaches the conclusion that "Economists' theories will be better when they can perceive what the *expected rate of inflation* really is.... What is infinitely more important, the players in the economic game... will be better off when the exchange institutions evolve that help to signal risks, reduce them, and allocate the residual irreducible risks optimally"

(Samuelson, 1986, p. 558). In the other, "2 Nobel Laureates' Theories on Trade: An Appraisal" (Samuelson, 1986, p. 831), where, after his appraisal of the contributions of J. E. Meade and Bert Ohlin, he reaches the conclusion that "Each man has demonstrated that those who are best at pure science are often outstanding policy advisers and public servants" (Samuelson, 1986, p. 831).

One can surmise that Samuelson uses the term "appraisal" broadly in accordance with the methodologies described above. It could include his way of appraising two competing paradigms, such as when he writes: "The two paradigms seem to tell different stories. Which is the relevant story, the correct one for the case of competitive capitalism? There can be no doubt as to the answer. The bourgeois paradigm of Smith, Ricardo, Piero Sraffa, and Leon Walras correctly predicts that the new invention will displace the old technique under ruthless competition" (Samuelson, 1986, p. 365). It could also mean finding necessary and sufficient conditions, and logics to appraise a theory: "Here I provide necessary and sufficient conditions for price invariance in the presence of exponentially depreciating durable capital goods. The result is a surprisingly simple criterion: price ratios are invariant to interest rate changes if and only if all industries have . . . the same capital-to-labor ratio" (Samuelson, 1986, p. 375).[2]

Fritz Machlup distinguishes three streams of Samuelson's methodology: (1) theories, antecedents, and consequents that must be mutually implicative, and identical in meaning; (2) strong simple cases like the 2×2 trade model that bring out elements of truth in a complex theory; and (3) methods as advocated in his *Foundations of Economic Analysis* that emphasize the derivation of "operationally meaningful" theorems (Samuelson, 1972, p. 758). We look briefly at these three streams below.

Mutually Implicative Theories

Regarding mutually implicative theories, Samuelson wrote that "after mathematical notions have performed the function of reminding us that everything depends upon everything else, they may not add very much more—unless some special hypothesis can be made about the facts" (Samuelson, 1966, p. 1758). Again, "mathematics is neither a necessary nor a sufficient condition for a fruitful career in economic theory" (Samuelson, 1966, p. 1760). Furthermore, "Marshall in his own way also rather pooh-poohed the use of mathematics. But he regarded it as a way of arriving at the truths, but not as a good way of communicating such truths" (Samuelson, 1966, p. 1755).

2×2 Trade Theory

Nowhere is the process of scientific appraisal more clearly demonstrated than in the trade theory of economics. Trade theory, from mercantilism to Adam Smith's absolute advantage, and from Ricardo's comparative advantage to Heckscher–Ohlin's factor proportion–intensity assumptions, have been now standardized in a 2×2 form (two goods and two factors). Samuelson's place in this research is secured when he demonstrates that "Both the classical and Ohlin versions of the explanation of trade may thus be viewed as adaptations of a common general equilibrium framework" (De Marchi, 1976, p. 112). Samuelson has shown that "the assumptions sufficient to yield factor price equalization also suffice . . . to yield the Heckscher-Ohlin theorem" (De Marchi, 1976, p. 112). In scientific parlance, Samuelson has shifted the research in trade theory from "before Samuelson" to "after Samuelson." This shift has made it possible for "rigorous articulation and generalization on the mainline research tradition concerned with the conditions governing the existence, uniqueness, and stability of general competitive equilibrium" (De Marchi, 1976, p. 113). Therefore, under the idea of appraisal that asks "Is theory A better than theory B?" (Latsis, 1976, p. 3) it is fair to say that Samuelson's research on the 2×2 trade theory is poised for scientific conjectures and refutations in the twenty-first century.

Operationalism

A byproduct of Einstein's Special Theory of Relativity is that it allows us to define a term by the physical operations the agent performs in order to observe the object. Any concept corresponds with a set of operations. Samuelson seeks "the derivation of operationally meaningful theorems" in economics (Samuelson, 1947, p. 3). One aim of meaningful theorems is that we can ascertain their truth values, the likelihood that they will occur in reality, and that we can attempt to verify them (Machlup, 1978, pp. 165–166). Another view is that through these operational theorems, we may not "verify" but "infer" the object.

According to Machlup's argument, operationalism purges a theory of its assumptions, and therefore of its theoretical and mathematical framework. Friedman's F-twist theory emphasizes the independence of assumptions from prediction. Others, such as Bateson and Mead (1941, p. 55), think that "whenever we start insisting too hard upon 'operationalism' or symbolic logic or any other of these very essential systems of tramlines, we lose something of the ability to think new thoughts. And equally, of course, whenever we rebel against the sterile rigidity of formal thought and exposition and let our ideas run wild, we likewise lose. As I see it, the advances in scientific thought come from a *combination of loose and strict thinking*, and this combination is the most precious tool of science."

To cut through the hurdles of the various brandings of his methodology, Samuelson reminds us that he is a truth seeker. On the one hand he argues for reality as the paradigm, but on the other hand he holds that "observations are not merely seen or sensed but rather often are perceived in gestalt patterns that impose themselves on the data and even distort those data" (Samuelson, 1993, p. 244). Here we have the interplay between theory and fact. We know that his basic paradigm of facts is not based on dialectic but on the cumulative method.[3] As Samuelson puts it, "in the language of [Thomas] Kuhn, knowledge in economics accumulates, and paradigms can be commensurable only if the 'black' in one paradigm can be considered as the 'white' in another paradigm" (Samuelson, 1993, p. 244).

Analysis of Samuelson's Specific Contributions

In this section, we look at some of Samuelson's specific contributions to highly specialized topics in economics. The idea is to underscore the essence of the contributions in relation to the respective authors' appraisal as to why the material will be relevant for the twenty-first century.

Overlapping Generation Models

The first section of this book contains three chapters:

- "Overlapping Generations," Robert M. Solow
- "Paul Samuelson's Amazing Intergenerational Transfer," Laurence J. Kotlikoff
- "Social Security, the Government Budget, and National Savings," Peter Diamond

Samuelson introduced the overlapping generations model (OLG) to "develop the equilibrium conditions for a rational consumer's lifetime consumption-saving pattern" (Samuelson, 1958, p. 104). Since that time, the OLG has become a strong rival theory to the Arrow–Debreu general equilibrium model, extending theoretical and empirical research to areas that previously could not be reached.

Solow's description of the original Samuelson model invites the distinction between theoretical and practical uses of the model. Essentially, OLG has an overlapping generation structure, which operates in infinite time. Although no generation can step into the same time twice, a person in one generation, G^t, can trade with a person in another generation, G^{t-1}, G^{t-2}, etc., where a "household born at *t* will be said to be of generation *t*, or simply G^t" (Hahn and Solow, 1995, p. 13). For example, a person in a three-period model that wants to save for retirement in the next period can lend to a person in the first period. This is essential because the model deals with generations which are defined in terms of age, and people have different tastes and preferences over different age cohorts.

A similar model is found in the appendix of Maurice Allais' book, *Économie et Intérêt* (1947). Both Solow and Malinvaud (1987) essentially agree by implication. They agree that time is infinite in both cases, but Allais uses two periods and Samuelson uses three periods. In Allais' model, the presence of Government is as a wealth holder and/or a debtor, say of land and financial assets, following a variety of hypotheses (Malinvaud, 1987, p. 104). According to Kotlikoff, in Samuelson's model, "government can redistribute across generations." The interest rate in Allais' model "is not fully determined by the individual's preference for the present and by technical feasibilities" (Malinvaud, 1987, p. 104), and, according to Samuelson, it can have a biological dimension that results when a correlation between prices and population changes leads to equality between the interest rate and population growth rate.

The interest rate as a bridge between current and postponed consumption appears as a time cohort model. To turn this into a real OLG model, we have to layer it with people in different age cohorts. Using the didactics of Samuelson's three-period model, the middle generation may want to lend excess current income (savings) to the younger generation, but not to the old, for when the middle generation becomes old, it wants to consume its savings plus earned interest. Therefore, consumption, c, and savings, s, cannot exceed wealth, w, that is, $c + s \leq w$. Solow's chapter continues in this line of symbolic generalization, originating in his joint paper with Frank Hahn, to illustrate market imperfections (Hahn and Solow, 1995, p. 13).

Kotlikoff's work has given rise to a new term in the expansion and articulation of the OLG model, particularly in generational accounting. Both Kotlikoff and Diamond take up current and future concerns of the Social Security problem, a good indication of the relevance of the model for the twenty-first century.

Expectation, Uncertainty and Public Goods

The second section of this book contains two articles:

- Prospective Shifts, Speculative Swings: "Macro" for the 21st Century in the Tradition Championed by Paul Samuelson, Edmund S. Phelps.
- "Paul Samuelson and Global Public Goods," William D. Nordhaus

Edmund Phelps appraises Samuelson from the point of view of expectation and uncertainty. Although his multiplier-accelerator contribution to Keynesian modeling became famous, his interest in macroeconomics ran deep and spanned the perspectives of theorists before and after Keynes. Ever interested in real-life economies, Samuelson was alert to the occasional sea change in the American economy. In the 1970s, he invented the term "stagflation" to stand for the ratcheting down to slower growth and increased unemployment amidst no lessening of inflation. Evidently parametric shifts were occurring, from the world price of energy to the exhaustion of the stock of unused ideas. Comparing this history with the stationary rational-expectations models becoming fashionable in the 1980s, Samuelson concluded that "[a]s a description of what happens in the real world and as a tool for intermediate-run macro predictions, the Lucas-Sargent-Barro model is a poor tool" (Samuelson 1986, Vol. V, 294).

Samuelson's concepts pertaining to a business economy – its orientation toward the future, the uncertainty of future prospect and the non-stationarity of its demographic and technological environment – were tools, Phelps argues, that Samuelson used and are tools we need in this century for an understanding of the secular shifts and big swings in the American economy. Samuelson does not see rational expectations as taking root in an enterprise economy. Samuelson, Phelps acknowledges, was "a pioneer of rational expectations theory" and willing to postulate rational expectations for the purpose of explaining differences in share prices across categories over a given period; and the "micro efficiency" he sees in those markets, if he is right, may justify the postulate for that purpose. Yet Samuelson finds "macro inefficiency" in the index of share prices. Thus rational expectations appear not to describe the ups and downs of the values entrepreneurs in aggregate put on new projects (and the values that retails investors place on the shares financing those projects).

Phelps, supporting Samuelson's views, points out that an enterprising economy is driven by the "visions" and "fears" of entrepreneurs, financiers and speculators. The postulate of rational expectations, Phelps argues, is simply inapplicable to the expectations of entrepreneurs peering into the unknown. Furthermore, an outsider in the public has no way of forming rational expectations of the expectations of the entrepreneurs: Their knowledge is importantly "personal knowledge," which the public cannot access. And the public infer from its data available what the entrepreneurs must be expecting, for to suppose that their expectations could be the subject of unbiased estimates by the public would be to imply that entrepreneurs have no special knowledge and play no special role.

This piece recalls Keynes's point of view. In its essence, Samuelson's brand of expectation and uncertainty subscribes to Chapter 12 of Keynes's *The General Theory*. Keynes exposed a disequilibrium paradigm, in contrast to the rational expectation models that exposed an equilibrium paradigm.

Following Phelps' presentation, we need to understand the effects of the "visions and fears" excluded by the now-standard paradigm theory. Phelps examines the effects of expectations regarding three future events – future "debt bombs," future productivity surges, and war prospects. An economy continually pinged by such expectations is "never 'vibrating' up and down its saddle path"(Ibid.). Samuelsonian economics of the 21st century will emphasize that "macroeconomics must incorporate future prospects if it is to capture the big swings in economic activities." It will preserve the perspective that the rational-expectations movement excluded.

The distinction between public and private goods follows from concerns about market efficiency concepts. Nordhaus' piece fits in with the appraisal of polar cases of fact from an epistemological appraisal point of view. A public good, "for which the cost of extending the service to an additional person is zero," is "a polar case of an externality," says Nordhaus. Externality, nonrivalry, and nonexcludability are budding research programs, which will be of great concern for the twenty-first century because "private markets generally do not guarantee efficient outcomes." The "stock externalities" concern for public goods, particularly with regard to nuclear energy and greenhouse gases that have a firm hold in the twenty-first century policy concerns, and have implications for the course that international laws will take.

Revealed Preference and Consumer Behavior

There are two chapters in the third section of this book:

- "Revealed Preference," Hal R. Varian
- "Samuelson's 'Dr Jekyll and Mrs Jekyll' Problem: A Difficulty in the Concept of the Consumer," Robert A. Pollak

The explosion of research on revealed preference still builds on the foundations which Samuelson constructed. One foundation is the weak axiom of consumer behavior, another is the strong axiom, and a third is the fundamental theorem. While these axioms still support the model for empirical work, the empirical work now relates the strong axiom to Afriat's "cyclical consistency" criterion. Varian found that testing consistency with utility maximization requires a general axiom as well. The three axioms performed well, that is, "aggregate consumption data easily satisfied the revealed preference conditions." Besides consistency, Varian investigates the form, forecasting, and recoverability criteria. He concludes that the strong axiom is necessary and sufficient for utility maximization, and rich in empirical content.

Samuelson foresaw all the possible progressive birth signs of the revealed preference model when he initially proposed it. First, he gave it a twin feature (which he later integrated into a more single condition): (1) a single-value function on prices and income, subject to a budget constraint, and (2) homogeneity of order zero so as to make consumer behavior independent of the units of measurement of prices. Consider two batches or vectors of goods, ψ and ψ', with their respective price vectors, p and p', and denote their inner product by $[\psi p]$, and $[\psi' p']$, respectively. Now, we can observe the following: (3) "If this cost $[\psi' p]$ is less than or equal to the actual expenditure in the first period when the first batch of goods $[\psi p]$ was actually bought, then it means that the individual could have purchased the second batch of goods with the price and income of the first situation, but did not choose to do so. That is, the first batch (ψ) was selected instead of (v')" (Samuelson, 1966, p. 7).

A third proposition deals with consistency. "If an individual selects batch one over batch two, he does not at the same time select two over one" (Samuelson, 1966, p. 7). In a later note, Samuelson compacts the first two propositions with the third; "Postulates 1 and 2 are already implied in postulate 3, and hence may be omitted" (Samuelson, 1966, p. 13).

At its inception, Samuelson had the foresight that the revealed preference model had some virtue: "even within the framework of the ordinary utility- and indifference-curve assumptions, it is believed to be possible to derive already known theorems quickly, and also to suggest new sets of conditions. Furthermore... the transitions from individual to market demand functions are considerably expedited" (Samuelson, 1966, p. 23). But the revealed preference theory matured into an even more powerful rival research paradigm. Samuelson wrote: "I suddenly realized that we could dispense with almost all notions of utility; starting from a few logical axioms of demand consistency; I could derive the whole of the valid utility analysis as corollaries" (Samuelson, 1966, p. 90). The corollaries followed from axioms of consumer behavior noted above, which Varian has cast in more up-to-date symbolic form. But the way Samuelson stated them shows that he could be as eloquent in prose as in mathematics. The axioms as originally stated are as follows:

Weak axiom: If at the price and income of situation A you could have bought the goods actually bought at a different point B and if you actually chose not to, then A is defined to be "revealed to be better than" B. The basic postulate is that B is never to reveal itself to be also "better than" A (Samuelson, 1966, p. 90).

Strong axiom: If A reveals itself to be "better than" B, and if B reveals itself to be "better than" C, and if C reveals itself to be "better than" D, etc . . . , then I extend the definition of "revealed preference" and say that A can be defined to be "revealed to be better than" Z, the last in the chain. In such cases it is postulated that Z must never also be revealed to be better than A (Samuelson, 1966, pp. 90–91).

Samuelson then elevated the revealed preference theory to the empirical domain: "consumption theory does definitely have some refutable empirical implications" (Samuelson, 1966, p. 106), or we can "score the theory of revealed preference" (Samuelson, 1966, p. 106). Samuelson required a benchmark to allow refutation/scoring, for which he postulated this fundamental theorem: "Any good (simple or composite) that is known always to increase in demand when money income alone rises must definitely shrink in demand when its price alone rises" (Samuelson, 1966, p. 107). He then proceeded "to show that within the framework of the narrowest version of revealed preference the important fundamental theorem, stated above, can be directly demonstrated (a) in commonsense words, (b) in geometrical argument, (c) by general analytic proof" (Samuelson, 1966, p. 108).

How good a rival theory is the revealed preference theory? As Hildenbrand puts it, "Instead of deriving demand in a given wealth-price situation from the preferences, considered as the primitive concept, one can take the demand function (correspondence) directly as the primitive concept. If the demand function *f* reveals a certain 'consistency' of choices . . . one can show that there exists a preference relation . . . which will give rise to the demand function *f*" (Hildenbrand, 1974, p. 95).

Pollak's chapter describes a rich number of cases in which Samuelson distinguishes between the individual and the family as the consuming agent. On the theoretical side, he considers a Bergson–Samuelson type of social welfare utility function, with implications for Arrow's impossibility theorem. On the application side, he features Becker's "rotten kid" model problem, holding out the possibility of a solution with a family member as a possible dictator.[4]

Marxism

There is a single chapter in this section on Marx:

- "Paul Samuelson on Karl Marx: Were the Sacrificed Games of Tennis Worth It?" Geoff Harcourt

Is Samuelson a Marxist? The late Adolph Lowe said in one of his lectures that if Samuelson would say that Marx was right, then standard/orthodox economics would collapse. In Samuelson's words, "John Maynard Keynes was scientifically the greatest economist of this century. Only Adam Smith and Leon Walras can be mentioned in the same breath with him. Karl Marx can be mentioned in the same breath with Mohammed and Jesus, but it is of scientific scholarship that I speak and not of political movements and ideology" (Samuelson, 1986, p. 262). Again, Samuelson wrote: "I regard Marx as a scholar deserving of analysis on his objective merits and without regard to the deification or denigration meted out to him in various regions and ideologies." "I appraised Marx as a mathematical economist, . . . hailing Marx's most original contribution in *Capital*'s Volume II *Tableaus of Simple and Expanded Reproduction*. Marx's critics have missed this achievement, while at the same time his partisans have been praising his sterile paradigm" (Samuelson, 1986, p. 263). Also, "I follow Marx's portrait with Table II, which is what he and his followers wrongly think makes him great" (Samuelson, 1986, p. 273).

Harcourt challenges us to look at Samuelson's ideas from an eraser's point of view. When we look, we find Samuelson saying: "Contemplate two alternative and discordant systems. Write down one. Now transform by taking an eraser and rubbing it out. Then fill in the other one. *Voila*! You have completed your transformation algorithm" (Samuelson, 1972, p. 277). Here is a question and Samuelson's answer on this idea applied to Marx's transformation problem: "*The 'algorithmic transformation' from the 'value' model to the 'price' model (or vice versa), is truly a process of rejection of the former and replacement by the latter?* Here is my true crime. I pointed out the blunt truth. And this has been construed as an attack on Marx, covert or explicit" (Samuelson, 1978, p. 284). Naturally then, if Samuelson's idea is appraised as the truth, it shall prevail.

Stability

There is a single chapter in this section on Stability:

- "Paul Samuelson and the Stability of General Equilibrium," Franklin Fisher

Franklin Fisher wishes to attract attention to the topic of stability in the twenty-first century, for it has not yet reached a "satisfactory conclusion." Why is stability important? Not because it attracted the attention of Walras and Marshall (Walker, 1983, pp. 276–277). Stability is about "the determination of equilibrium values of given variables (unknowns) under postulated conditions (functional relationships) with various data (parameters) being specified" (Samuelson, 1966, p. 539). When rummaging into the equations of a theory, be it simple supply and demand equations, one always wants to know its stability properties, for if no more than equilibrium can be found, then "the economist would be truly vulnerable to the gibe that he is only a parrot taught to say 'supply and demand'" (Samuelson, 1966, p. 539). There would always be a need for stability analysis, even of a comparative static nature, to unearth the predictive power of models for scientific appraisals. Samuelson likened stability behavior to the soul and mind of business. "Since this competitive industry's comparative-statics can be shown to behave as if the industry had a soul and an integrated mind, expediency urges us to pretend it has" (Samuelson, 1986, p. 103). Those are, therefore, reasons to expect that this model will attract attention in the twenty-first century.

The sequel of statics versus dynamics also deserves unique treatment. Samuelson wrote: "For comparative-statics analysis to yield fruitful results we must first develop a theory of dynamics" (Samuelson, 1947, pp. 262–263). "Statics concerns with the simultaneous and instantaneous or timeless determination of economic variables by mutually interdependent relations . . . It is the essence of dynamics that economic variables at different points of time are functionally related . . . functional relationships between economic variables and their rates of change, their 'velocities,' 'accelerations,' or higher 'derivatives of derivatives'" (Samuelson, 1966, p. 354). There is a "formal dependence between comparative statics and dynamics . . . the *Correspondence Principle*" (Samuelson, 1966, p. 565). But there is a "two-way nature: not only can the investigation of the dynamic stability of a system yield fruitful theorems in static analysis, but also known properties of a (comparative) static system can be utilized to derive information concerning the dynamic properties of a system" (Samuelson, 1966, p. 565). "The nature of dynamic processes can best be appreciated from a study of concrete examples" (Samuelson, 1966, p. 593), and "in the field of pure theory, the important problem of the stability of equilibrium is wholly a question of dynamics. For it involves the question of how a system behaves after it has been disturbed into a disequilibrium state" (Samuelson, 1966, p. 613). How then do we involve facts and reality? George Feiwel (1982, p. 7) has a simple answer: "The growth of general equilibrium has given increased focus to static concepts." No theory can be more static than Keynesian. "All sciences have the common task of describing and summarizing empirical reality. Economics is no exception" (Samuelson, 1966, p. 1756) and "no a priori empirical truths can exist in any field. If a theory has a priori irrefutable truth, it must be empty of empirical content" (Samuelson, 1966, p. 1757). Stability concerns are here to stay. All models of reality call upon them to assess their compatibility. Samuelson has grounded stability in dynamics, which is promising for the twenty-first century economics.

Keynes and Post-Keynesians

There are three chapters in the sixth section of this book:

- "Paul Samuelson and Piero Sraffa—Two Prodigious Minds at the Opposite Poles," Luigi Pasinetti
- "Paul Samuelson as a 'Keynesian' Economist," Lawrence R. Klein
- "Samuelson and the Keynesian/Post-Keynesian Revolution," Paul Davidson

Luigi Pasinetti appraises the source of Samuelson's interest in Piero Sraffa's work. He finds that the two authors were attracted to each other because their works are of "equally foundational character." Samuelson's *Foundations of Economic Analysis* (1947) is on the side of maximization under constraints, with the use of mathematics as a language, while Sraffa's *Production of Commodities by Means of Commodities* (1960) tries to weed out ambiguities in solving analytical problems, starting with a prelude and advancing to a more constructive stage. Although their approaches are different, "they reached the same analytical conclusion, though with different nuances, accentuation of details, or shades of emphasis" as it is illustrated by the debate on reswitching.

Where Samuelson and Sraffa differ is in methodology. Samuelson defends the "exchange paradigm," while Sraffa defends the "production paradigm." This disagreement is evident in Sraffa's work (1960), which Samuelson sees as a defense of Ricardo's labor theory of value. Pasinetti appraises Samuelson's labor theory view along with two other propositions, reaching a somewhat different conclusion in answer to the question, "Why has Samuelson been so interested in Sraffa?" Pasinetti argues that Samuelson's stated desire "of formulating a general theory of economic theories . . . , would seem to imply the absorption and inclusion also of Sraffa."

Klein's chapter "Paul Samuelson as a 'Keynesian' Economist" traces the development of Keynesian economics in the United States from the early days. Although Keynesian economics came into the United States in fragments, Samuelson views it as a unifying principle. "What made Keynes different . . . was the fact that . . . He tackled the whole thing in one brilliant analytic formulation and provided economists with a new way of looking at how the entire gross national product is determined and how wages and prices and the rate of unemployment are determined along with it" (Samuelson, 1986, p. 280).

One of Samuelson's first attempts in Keynesian economics is the simple mathematical formulation: "$Y = C + I$, and $C = C(Y)$, $I = \hat{I}$" (Samuelson, 1966, pp. 1197–1219). Klein traces the development of "Paul Samuelson as a 'Keynesian' Economist," and also appraises the econometric foundation of Keynesian economics. Paul Davidson considers a different stream of post-Keynesian economics. Samuelson writes: "In . . . contrast to monetarism is the mainstream of modern economics today which . . . I shall call 'Post-Keynesian Economics.' Modern economics, as represented by men like James Tobin, Franco Modigliani, and myself, basically believes that changes in the money supply engineered by Federal Reserve policy have important effects upon the level of money, Gross National Product (GNP) and, depending upon the state of slackness in the employment market, upon real output and the price level" (Samuelson, 1978, p. 765). He then gives three post-Keynesian propositions "Even when the money supply is held constant" (1) Changes in thriftiness and the marginal propensity to consume can affect output, prices, and production; (2) An exogenous burst in I or investor's instinctive behavior has a systematic effect on GNP; and (3) An increase in public expenditure, or a cut in the tax rate has a systematic effect on GNP (Samuelson, 1978, p. 765). Davidson appraises the many versions of Keynes—Old Neoclassical, New Keynesians, Old Classical or New Classical Theorists—as adopting Keynesian general theory as their basic framework. As long as those research programs last, Samuelson's input into Keynesian economics will be followed.

International Economics and Finance

There are three chapters in this section of the book:

- "Paul Samuelson and International Trade Theory Over Eight Decades," Avinash Dixit

- "Paul Samuelson's Contributions to International Economics," Kenneth Rogoff
- "Protection and Real Wages: The Stolper–Samuelson Theorem," Rachel McCulloch

Avinash Dixit provides an appraisal of Samuelson's work on trade theory. He explains the scientific importance of starting with the Ricardian 2×2 model, and the current literature on comparative advantage. Samuelson rests this model on the shoulders of giants, whether we want to explain gains from trade by swapping bananas for steel, or from the modern theoretical points of view.

Samuelson has picked up this model without any rigorous proof and has given it many "operational" assumptions so that one can test—or falsify—its predictive or explanatory powers. He provides this intuitive proof: "Anybody can see that the tropics are capable of producing bananas while the temperate regions cannot produce bananas but can produce steel. Thus there would be profitable interchange between the cold, northern region, and the tropical region. That's the theory of comparative advantage" (Samuelson, 1986, p. 52).

In modern times this cannot be improved too much from the intuitive side. Dixit and Norman (1980, p. 5), for instance, argue that "the concepts involved are imprecise," and therefore "it is far from trivial to establish them rigorously." More advanced proof led to the welfare gain concept that Samuelson advanced from the classics, and anchored squarely on the First and Second Welfare theorems. With these theories, we can now model trade to assess who gains, for instance, in the formation of a Free Trade Agreement (FTA). This kind of research has only just begun.

Rogoff's chapter, which addresses the contemporary policy debate, appraises Samuelson's trade contributions such as the Stolper–Samuelson and factor–prices equalization theorems as "vital in today's globalization debate." The idea that gains from trade can be modeled through side-payment, that Samuelson added intuitive understanding and easy testing of the Stolper–Samuelson theory, and that his simple "iceberg-cost" metaphor helped our understanding of transit cost and friction in trade, are very active in the modern scientific and development views of modern trade theory. Rogoff's chapter spans a wide range of thought, from the "iceberg-cost" concepts to a Ricardian "continuum of goods" trade model. In between are financial analysis models such as the Harrod–Balassa–Samuelson theorem that the exchange rate increases faster for growing countries, which has led to the development of the Heston–Summer database for world comparison of income and prices. In between is his contribution on the "Transfer Problem," which at that time proved Keynes correct in his prediction of the cost of Germany's postwar reparations, and is still used today to assess the effects of a trade deficit on trade.

McCulloch appraises the Stolper and Samuelson (1941) theorem under varying conditions and assumptions. The model predicts that a country will export commodities produced by its abundant factors, and will import commodities produced by its scarce factors. The consequence is that trade will lower the real wages of the scarce factors.

In the current milieu of free trade, factors can move from import competing to export industries. In that movement, the factors including labor may lose real income, independent of taste and spending patterns. Using Jones' reformulation of the theorem, McCulloch demonstrates that when the relative prices for labor-intensive goods fall, real wages will decline in that sector, and the returns to other factors will increase, resulting in a redistribution effect.

The model had been robust in its predictions. When the number of goods and factors are increased, at least one factor is likely to gain or lose. The model is relevant for modern policies such as the Trade Adjustment Assistance (TAA) and unemployment insurance programs that assist distressed industries, where compensation can make a difference for individuals or firms that are hurt from free trade. The model is also relevant in the political arena where owners of factors vote or lobby. It has shown strength in explaining patterns of protection across countries. We see that the model had a long life in explaining distributive shares of factors, an area that will undoubtedly occupy social scientists in the twenty-first century.

Finance and Portfolio Theory

There are three chapters in this section:

- "Samuelson and the Factor Bias of Technology Change," Joseph Stiglitz
- "Samuelson and Investment for the Long Run," Harry M. Markowitz
- "Paul Samuelson and Financial Economics," Robert C. Merton

Stiglitz's chapter appraises a simple model Samuelson enunciated over 40 years ago on the liberalization of the capital markets. The model finds a home in the globalization of modern capital markets, indicating Samuelson's anticipation of free trade ahead of its time. The story is that unlike the situation of OLG where capital markets without liberalization but with technology shock will transfer over to another generation, with liberalization the shock may be dissipated in the current generation.

Stiglitz appraises the capital liberating model first from the traditional equilibrium points of view, and then from his new paradigm of disequilibria or market imperfection points of view. In the equilibrium version, some ambiguity exists as to how technological progress would augment capital or labor. Kaldor's stylized facts approach had assumed away the problem. The standard Harrod–Domar model did not include the effect of technological change, and when it was added, the disequilibria between exogeneous labor, and adjusted warranted growth rate becomes clear. Solow's modification did improve the analysis by making capital and effective labor grow at the same rate, but at the price of diminishing the concept of a job.

Stiglitz's appraisal of the capital liberating model now points out that wage adjustments with given capital and technology can support only maximum employment, and not necessarily lead to full employment. He provides two versions. A fixed coefficient version that extends Samuelson's paradigm to include wage effect through technology and capital accumulation on employment, and a version based on agency theory or efficiency wage theory where the wage rate must be adequate to induce labor to work. By integrating efficiency wage theory into the capital liberalizing model, Stiglitz has shown that Samuelson's model will be significant for future research in explaining dynamic economic problems.

Markowitz appraises a debate with Samuelson regarding which criteria the long-run investor should maximize in their portfolio. Markowitz provides the example of receiving either 6 percent per year with certainty or a lottery with an equal chance of 200 percent gain or 100 percent loss each year. The expected value returns criteria yields a return of 0.5. The expected log of 1 plus the returns is negative infinity ($-\infty$). Therefore, the investor would choose the certain prospect.

Markowitz considers whether the long run investor should follow the arithmetic mean or the log arithmetic (geometric mean) criteria in maximizing its portfolio. Markowitz makes the case for the log model. Samuelson argues that "It is a mistake to think that, just because a w^{**} decision ends up with almost-certain probability to be better than a w^{*} decision, this implies that w^{**} must yield a better expected value of utility"

(Samuelson, 1986, p. 246). He complemented this argument with an intransitive rule of odds: "You may well pick A(N) from A(N) and B(N), and pick B(N) from B(N) and C(N), and yet still pick C(N) from A(N) and C(N)" (Samuelson, 1986, p. 554). Nevertheless, the Markowitz chapter continues to present the case for the log model.

Merton's appraisal identifies essential and substantive gems from Samuelson's original contributions to financial economics. He selects financial facts that form a synthesis, implying that some conflicts have been resolved about them. Merton found that much of Samuelson's contributions, which he had appraised 25 years ago, are even more significant today.

Merton's appraisal places models of time and uncertainty in household allocation of resources at the center of the Samuelson contribution. He assesses Samuelson's contributions to the areas of efficient market theory and risk analysis, portfolio selection, and option and warrant pricing. Samuelson found that efficient markets do not allocate resources the way casinos do. Rather, asset prices vary randomly around an optimal path that can be discerned mathematically. The theory links space (spot price) with time (current future prices) in order to forge a solution (current futures prices = future spot prices), where spot prices are determined by optimal control theory. Can a George Soros, for example, provide superior performance? The answer depends on whether he can explain variation around expected returns. Operationally, that depends on the amount of information he has. The ranking of information produces strong, semi-strong, and weak versions of the efficiency hypothesis. Technically speaking, the matter of superior performance requires explaining the difference between a random variable and its conditional expectation, a difference with martingale properties. Researchers today are testing for these properties, and will continue to do so in the future.

Prior to Samuelson's works, options pricing centered mainly on European options, defined as options exercised on their expiration date. Samuelson introduced the American option that can be exercised before that date, and he considered longer-term horizons as well. For long-held or perpetual options, he discovered that the option would sell for more than the value of the stock. To correct that anomaly, he introduced log values that eliminated negative terms in stock pricing calculations. In short, Samuelson's work in warrants and option pricing provide a bridge between early and later option pricing models, thanks to his insights on hedging and mathematical analysis that were incorporated into subsequent theories.

Merton further appraises Samuelson's financial contribution for some other long-run issues. Samuelson introduced very specialized utility functions to address age-dependent and risk issues relating to, for instance, the notion that stocks are not risky in the long run. The argument for that proposition was based on some empirical fact on returns over 15- or 20-years horizon, and the argument that people become more conservative with age. Samuelson reached the conclusion that stocks are risky in short, intermediate, and long runs, and therefore, he leans toward the rejection of that hypothesis. Not heeding Samuelson's advice, retirement investment during the 2000–2002 period has experienced much loss.

Samuelson's Relevance

There are three chapters in this section:

- "Multipliers and the LeChatelier Principle," Paul Milgrom
- "The Surprising Ubiquity of the Samuelson Configuration: Paul Samuelson and the Natural Sciences," James B. Cooper and Thomas Russell
- "Paul Samuelson's Mach," Rod Cross

Milgrom appraises Samuelson's LeChatelier principle of how the market responds to a change in parameters of demand and supply curves. He uses examples in demand theory, economic policy, and empirical research to illustrate the principle. He also stresses the flexibility of the principle to adapt to changing assumptions. We notice changes from the optimizing agents to equilibrium systems whose primary use is to "provide a foundation for understanding multipliers."

Milgrom evaluates how the principle performed when it was confronted with local optimization problems as in production function settings, and in positive feedback systems as in gaming situations. The principle is found progressive in that it is able to capitalize on symmetric relations among substitutes and complements. In that regard, the principle has extended research into multiplier analysis, a research area that would continue into the twenty-first century.

Cooper and Russell appraise one aspect of how Samuelson adopted the methods of physics for economics. Samuelson is considered a leader in adopting the concepts of optimization with constraints to economics.

Cooper and Russell grasped the source of this principle in the "little used" and "amazingly obscure" writings of the physicist James Clerk Maxwell.

Cooper and Russell's appraisal delves deeply into the areas of physics and mathematics. "Classical thermodynamics is the subject that deals with such interactions of mechanics and 'temperatures' . . . my formulation . . . is idiosyncratic in that the formal relations that are important in analytical economics have motivated my choice of physical axioms and the order of their introduction." In thermodynamics, Samuelson "utilize[s] the area of a closed curve in the (pressure, volume) plane." In economic analysis, we use the terms price and quantity to replace pressure and volume, respectively. In such a diagram, equivalent areas between level curves can be interpreted as solutions to the maximization of profit subject to input constraints problems. From the area of classical mechanics, Samuelson borrowed "the law of conservation of (mechanical) energy for a (frictionless) system." A frictionless pendulum has the greatest kinetic energy (squared velocity) at the bottom of its swing, when its potential energy is minimal. The sum of a conservative system's kinetic and potential energies is constant along any motion, conserving the initial value of that sum (Samuelson, 1986, pp. 231–232). This conservation model has been a workhorse in modern economics in optimization problem, and shows no sign of weakening in the twenty-first century.

Cross appraises Samuelson's methodology through the work of the physicist, psychologist, and philosopher Ernst Mach, categorizing such thoughts with a big "M". The range of thought of Mach is from sensory observation to phenomenology, including other disciplines such as psychology to the extent that such disciplinary thoughts are in harmony with the stability of the concept.

Cross appraises Samuelson from the Heraclitus dictum to the effect that one cannot step into the same river twice because of changes that have taken place. The river has essential properties that do not change, and substantive properties that do change from an Aristotelian viewpoint. For Samuelson, "Science, even inexact science is public knowledge, reproducible for analysis by everyone" (Samuelson, 1986, p. 564). Cross locates that reproducibility in the "action and reactions" of the elemental qualities of a river, or relationship among economic variables. When the qualities such as a, b, c satisfy a functional form such as $F(a,b,c\ldots) = 0$, then they come together at that point, forming a state between appearance and disappearance. States have recall properties that allow association of past observations with current observations, enabling scientific discovery to take place. Cross appraises how Samuelson meandered among the thoughts of his teachers, colleagues, theoretical and empirical concepts to place his final allegiance on facts as the pivot on which to gauge scientific economic theories.

Cross ventures that Samuelson's methodology arises from the consideration of many views of Science. Faced with a blurred distinction between facts and theory that was highlighted by W. V. Quine, and the argument that economics deals with the world of social phenomena, Samuelson maintains a firm foot in reality, letting the facts tell their story. Samuelson also acknowledges how new thoughts such as Thomas Kuhn's paradigm, regarding the notions of cumulative knowledge, and incommensurability brings to the theory of science. He accepted that facts are numerous and therefore must be carefully sampled for their economy. But his goal remains that we should be able to tell the "how" and the "why" of things and phenomena of the economic world.

Samuelson's relevance starts with his curiosity for finding simple facts. He wrote that "The simplest things are often the most complicated to understand fully." He suggests an approach that treats simple things with: "(1) A literary discussion; (2) A mathematical treatment, and finally; (3) A history of the subject" (Samuelson, 1978, p. 3). Even in the area of mathematics, which has the reputation of being precise, he reminds us that "When mathematicians, like Debreu, speak of a competitive equilibrium, they do not insist that it is to be the only one but merely that it be self-warranting in the sense of satisfying all the conditions of the problem" (Samuelson, 1978, p. 143). In the same vein, he writes that "If the solution is simple, the assumptions must be heroic . . . Assumptions would not be heroic if they could be easily taken for granted as being exactly applicable" (Samuelson, 1978, p. 150). In one sense, we can think of the term "generalist" as a polymath—that is, one who has an umbrella of concepts under which to predicate particular concepts. From this point of view, Samuelson reaches for infinity as the limit. His search for the truth is far reaching. It is worth repeating his famous quote: "I would take aid from the Devil if that would help crack the puzzle of economic reality" (Samuelson, 1986, p. 873). Again, he is willing to look at the recesses of the subconscious to find the truth if need be: "We are eternally grateful to Henri Poincare for his detailed exposition of the role that the subconscious plays in the discovery of mathematical theories: how one wrestles consciously and unsuccessfully with a theorem, then puts it aside, as if out of mind, but apparently not really out of mind; for suddenly . . . the successful solution arrives" (Samuelson, 1978, p. 846). From Samuelson's generalist point of view, the truth can be approached from anywhere. "A mathematical theoretical Walras–Debreu system would find a full-employment equilibrium path even if it started out from initial conditions like those of 1933" (Samuelson, 1978, p. 915).[5] To appraise Samuelson as a generalist is to put him in the heart of research for the twenty-first century. In the twentieth century, the physical scientists could tell what to do and where to go if some object was hurled at you, needing only Newtonian laws. As we enter the new millennium, we are bombarded with more uncertainty in science. Just think of such phenomena as global warming, parallel universes, antimatter, and spin theory.

Samuelson's "generalist" approach seems to be right at home with the general view of the physical sciences.[6] In his *Foundations of Economic Analysis* (1947), Samuelson looked for similarities among the various areas of economics. He then proceeded as a "generalist" to bind them together. This is in the time-honored canonist approach to scientific discovery extolled by Bacon and Mill, of which we list the First Cannon according to Mill: "*If two or more instances of the phenomenon under investigation have only one circumstance in common, the circumstance in which alone all the instances agree is the cause (or effect) of the given phenomenon*" [Italics original] (Mill, 1970, p. 255). To do that for economics, Samuelson prescribed the tools of a precise language, which he found in mathematics. He also prescribed and invigorated concepts such as maximization, minimization, equilibrium, efficiency, stability, and multiplier. With these generalized concepts came new ideas in the areas of cost, production, consumer demand, revealed preference, and trade in their static and dynamic points of view.

Samuelson is explicit and conscious about his position as a generalist, for he notes "I can claim that in talking about modern economics I am talking about me. My finger has been in every pie. I once claimed to be the last generalist in economics" (Samuelson, 1986, p. 800). Without proper appreciation of Samuelson's "generalist" perspectives, many analysts who have attempted to appraise Samuelson's work, not necessarily for the twenty-first century, have not been able to contain their analysis to the scientific domain, but rather were led into directions dictated by their own partiality. For instance, in reviewing the contribution to utility theory, Hayek was led to the view that "refinements suggested by P. A. Samuelson are hardly in the Austrian tradition" (Hayek, 1992, p. 54). But even Hayek too sought the general, not reasoned, approach, which he found in the theory of evolution. How democratic socialism can evolve into totalitarianism is the thesis of Hayek's *Road to Serfdom* (1945). Even though the Austrians are apt to argue that Samuelson has adopted the wrong method, "establishing physics as the science for economics to imitate," (Hayek, 1992, p. 5) their sympathizer, Robbins (1970, pp. 40–41), had this to say of Samuelson's methods: "It is difficult to argue that . . . the comprehensive treatise of Dorfman, Samuelson and Solow have not deepened our insights in many directions . . . in the raison d'etre of the price mechanism as something inherent in any maximization process within the restraints of different degrees of scarcity."

Conclusion

In this introduction, we reviewed the significance of Samuelson in the twenty-first century using the scientific criteria of "unit" and "units of appraisal." Our appraisal suggests continued success for Samuelson's specific and general studies for the twenty-first century. His work on trade is finding applications in the modern global economy. While his writings on the neoclassical synthesis were put to severe tests (and some parts shaken) during the 1970s and 1980s, they have an increasing role to play in the modern global economy. A mixed economy and public versus private goods with their associated externalities are very much twenty-first century concepts. Samuelson's theoretical contributions, when given operational meaning, are increasingly being confronted with facts and reality, and are performing well. Overall, the appraisals place a high value on Samuelson's vast output from a scientific point of view, which supports their endurance in the years ahead.

Notes

1. To appraise Samuelson, consider his preference for mixing fiscal and monetary policies. Samuelson wrote: "Now, I will very briefly summarize my view on the subject. The late C.O. Hardy said, 'Fiscal policy really has not independent importance. It is just a complicated way of getting the banking system to create some extra money. It is like burning the house in order to roast a pig' " (Samuelson, 1972, p. 552). This story falls in with Dewey's *Propositions of Appraisal*, where an "examination of these appraisals discloses that they have to do with things as they sustain to each other the relation of *means to ends or consequences*" (Dewey, 1939, p. 23). One interpretation of this "means to ends" model is that one should skip fiscal policy and get to where the action is—monetary policy. This will be an instance of "the end justifies the means"

(Dewey, 1939, p. 41). Samuelson thinks, "this view is profoundly wrong . . . that the mixture of fiscal policy and monetary policy we actually use was absolutely crucial in this and other regards" (Samuelson, 1972, p. 552). Such policy mix has already made its way into the current economic thinking that argues for monetary targets when the IS curve shifts about, or fixed interest rate policy if the LM curve shifts about (Dornbusch, 2004, p. 426).

2. Samuelson appears to substitute the term "audit" for "appraisal" at times: "What does an audit show for these opposite-line claims? Does it confirm any hope to explain the trends toward deterioration of the double factorial terms of trade of the Third World vis-à-vis the affluent nations by means of the concept of unequal exchange?" (Samuelson, 1986, p. 477). Also, he used the synonym "analyze" from time to time: "Here in this brief investigation I hope to analyze what the effects are on the welfare of different regions of a great burgeoning of productivity in the Pacific Basin" (Samuelson, 1986, p. 484), or: "I shall be analyzing the merits and demerits of protection" (Samuelson, 1986, p. 493), and the synonym "evaluate" as well: "To evaluate the question of how different the classical paradigm was from today's mainstream economics, it is worth sketching briefly the consequences of replacing f (Min [L,K]) by smooth constant-returns-to-scale technology" (Samuelson, 1986, pp. 606–607).
3. Note that Popper (1962) says that to appraise is not to accumulate knowledge but to replace one paradigm with another.
4. The longevity of Samuelson's model is assured in the twenty-first century and beyond. For as long as marriage and divorce will be around, the need for utility function inside and outside of family relationships will be needed to assess benefits and losses. The paper also appraises the pitfall of Samuelson's model, indicating the pros and cons of various empirical applications that are currently being carried out.
5. This should not be taken to imply that economics is all about common sense. Samuelson was clear about this matter when he wrote that "While it is true that few with advanced training in economics can be trusted to use common-sense economics, fewer still, and maybe no one, without advanced training in economics, can be trusted to use common-sense economics . . . experience does show that the best economic policy-makers have spent years studying economics and doing scientific research . . . Common sense, and folklore generally, lack empirical content . . . I would liken common sense to the hands of a watch, hands so short that they lie in every direction; lying in every direction, the hands cannot point in any direction and such a watch can tell us the correct time only after we have already learned it elsewhere" (Samuelson, 1962, pp. 16–17).
6. We see this as compatible with Adam Smith's intention when he set out to do for the social sciences what Newton did for the physical sciences, and predict that the foundation that Samuelson laid for the twenty-first century is a progressive one.

References

Allais, Maurice, *Economie et intérêt*, (Paris: Imprimerie Nationale, 1947).

Arrow, Kenneth, "Samuelson Collected," *Journal of Political Economy*, Volume 75, No. 5, (October 1967), 730–737.

Bateson, Gregory, "Experiments in Thinking about Observed Ethnological Material," *Philosophy of Science*, Vol. 8, No. 1, (January 1941), 53–68.

Bateson, Gregory, and Margaret Mead, "Principles of Moral Building," *Journal of Educational Sociology*, Vol. 15, No. 4, (December 1941), 205–220.

Blaug, Mark, *The Methodology of Economics*, (Cambridge University Press, 1983).

De Marchi, N., "Anomaly and the Development of Economics" in *Method and Appraisal in Economics*, Spiro Latsis, editor, (Cambridge University Press, 1976).

Dewey, John, "Theory of Valuation," *International Encyclopedia of United Science*, Volume II, Number 4, (The University of Chicago Press, 1939).

Dixit, Avinash K. and Victor D. Norman, "Theory of International Trade. Cambridge", (Cambridge University Press, 1980).

Dornbusch, Rudiger, Stanley Fischer, and Richard Startz, *Macroeconomics*, Ninth Edition, (New York: McGraw-Hill Irwin, 2004).

Feiwel, George F., *Samuelson and Neoclassical Economics*, (Boston: Kluwer-Nijhoff, 1982).

Hahn, Frank and Robert Solow, *A Critical Essay on Modern Macroeconomic Theory*, (Cambridge, MA: The MIT Press, 1995).

Hayek, F. A., *Collected Works*, Volume 4, (The University of Chicago Press, 1992).

Heilbroner, Robert and William Milberg, *The Crisis of Vision in Modern Economic Thought*, (Cambridge University Press, 1995).

Hicks, John, *Collected Essays on Economic Theory: Classics and Moderns*, Volume III, (Harvard University Press, 1983).

Hildenbrand, Werner, *Core and Equilibria of A Large Economy*, (Princeton University Press, 1974).

Hutchison, T. W., "On the History and Philosophy of Science and Economics," in *Method and Appraisal in Economics*, Spiro Latsis, editor, (Cambridge University Press, 1980).

Lakatos, Imre, and Alan Musgrave, eds., *Criticism and the Growth of Knowledge*. (Cambridge University Press, 1977).

Lakatos, Imre, *The Methodology of Scientific Research Programmes: Philosophical Papers* Volume I, Edited by John Worrall and Gregory Currie, (Cambridge University Press, 1980).

Latsis, Spiro, "Situational Determinism in Economics," *The British Journal for the Philosophy of Science*. 1972, Volume 23, 207–245.

Latsis, Spiro, *Method and Appraisal in Economics* (Cambridge University Press, 1980).

Machlup, Fritz, *Methodology of Economics and Other Social Sciences*, (New York: Academic Press, 1978).

Malinvaud, Edmond, "The Overlapping Generation Model in 1947," *Journal of Economic Literature*, Vol. 25, No. 1, (March 1987), 103–105.

Mill, John Stuart, *A System of Logic*, (London: Longman, New Impression 1970).
Miller, Authur I., *Imagery in Scientific Thought: Creating 20th Century Physics*, (Boston: Birkhauser, 1984).
Poincare, Henri, *Science and Method*, (New York: Dover, n.d.) translated by F. Maitland from *Poincare's Science et Methode*, (Paris: Flammarion, 1908).
Polanyi, Michael, *Personal Knowledge*, (University of Chicago Press, 1958).
Popper, Karl R., *The Logic of Scientific Discovery*, (New York: Harper Torchbooks, Harper & Row, Publisher, 1968).
Popper, K. R., *Conjectures and Refutations*, (New York: Basic Books, 1963).
Quine, W. V., *Pursuit of Truth*, (Cambridge, MA: Harvard University Press, 1990).
Ravetz, Jerome R., *Scientific Knowledge and its Social Problems*, (Oxford University Press, 1979).
Robbins, Lionel, *The Evolution of Modern Economics Theory*, (London: MacMillan, 1970).
Samuelson, Paul A., *Foundations of Economic Analysis*, (Harvard Economic Studies, Volume 80, 1947, New York: Atheneum 1974).
Samuelson, Paul A., *Problem of the American Economy, The Stamp Memorial Lecture 1961*, (London: The Athlone Press, 1962).
Samuelson, Paul A., "An Exact Consumption-Loan Model of Interest with or without the Social Contrivance of Money," *The Journal of Political Economy*, Volume LXVI, No. 6, (December 1958), 467–482.
Samuelson, Paul A., *Collected Scientific Papers of Paul A. Samuelson*, edited by Joseph E. Stiglitz, (Cambridge, MA: The MIT Press, Volume 1 and 2, 1966).
Samuelson, Paul A., "Collected Scientific Papers of Paul A. Samuelson," edited by Robert C. Merton, (Cambridge, MA: The MIT Press, Volume 3, 1972).
Samuelson, Paul A., *The Collected Scientific Papers of Paul A. Samuelson*, edited by H. Nagatani and K. Crowley, Volume 4, (Cambridge, MA: MIT Press, 1978).
Samuelson, Paul A., *Collected Scientific Papers of Paul A. Samuelson*, edited by Kate Crowley, (Cambridge, MA: The MIT Press, Volume 5, 1986).
Samuelson, Paul A., "My Life Philosophy: Policy Credos and Working Ways," in Michael Szenberg, ed., *Eminent Economists, Their Life Philosophies*, (Cambridge University Press, 1993).
Samuelson, Paul A., "Foreword," in Michael Szenberg, ed., *Passion and Craft, Economists at Work*, (Ann Arbor, MI: University of Michigan Press, 1999).
Sraffa, P., *Production of Commodities by Means of Commodities*, (Cambridge University Press, 1960).
Szenberg, Michael, Aron A. Gottesman and Lall Ramrattan, *Paul Samuelson on Being an Economist* with a Foreword by Joseph E. Stiglitz, (New York: Jorge Pinto Books, Inc., 2005).
von Mises, Ludwig, *Epistemological Problems of Economics*, (New York: D. Van Nostrand Company, Inc., 1960).
Walker, Donald W., *William Jaffe's Essays on Walras*, (Cambridge University Press, 1983).

Part I

Analysis of Samuelson's Specific Contributions

1

Overlapping Generations

Robert M. Solow

A little over 20 years ago, Cary Brown and I edited a book with the title *Paul Samuelson and Modern Economic Theory* (1983). Kenneth Arrow, Robert C. Merton, and I are the only carryovers from that book to this. My contribution to the first volume was a chapter on the Modern Theory of Capital. Before the book was sent to the printer, but after it was no longer possible to make any real changes, I realized that Samuelson's invention in 1958 of the overlapping-generations model had fallen through the cracks. It was not included in my chapter, nor did the authors of other plausibly appropriate chapters take account of it. Already in 1983, and even more so now, a much elaborated overlapping-generations (OLG) model was and is one of the standard vehicles for studying questions of intertemporal equilibrium. It occupies all of chapter 3 of the Blanchard–Fischer *Lectures on Macroeconomics* (1989) and recurs throughout that excellent compendium of "What Every Graduate Student Should Know". So I will use this opportunity to sketch its origin in Samuelson's work.

The basic article is "An Exact Consumption-Loan Model of Interest with or without the Social Contrivance of Money" (1958). In fact, though Samuelson did not know this, Maurice Allais had already formulated a fairly straightforward overlapping-generations model in an appendix to his *Économie et Intérêt* (1947). Samuelson's use of the model, however, is quite different from that of Allais. In any case the subsequent literature had its source in Samuelson's paper, not Allais's appendix with its misfortune to be written in French. The scope of the model has broadened considerably during the 50 years since Samuelson's paper. (An excellent modern survey is the article by John Geanakoplos in the *Palgrave Dictionary*.)

For his particular purposes, Samuelson outlines a model in which identical agents are born, live for three periods, and then disappear. Most OLG models get along with two-period lives; allowing for more than three gets laborious, though numerical computation is always possible even with many-period lives. Samuelson's project of a pure consumption-loan model *with perishable goods* needs three periods. (The perishability assumption is a way of ruling out any determination of interest rates via the productivity of investment.) People work in the first two periods of their lives, and produce one unit of perishable output each time; everyone retires and produces nothing in period three. Suppose I am in my middle period, looking to make provision for my old age in period three, when I will have no earned income. I must lend part of my current income to someone who will be able to pay me back, with interest, next period. Older people obviously won't do; they will not be around when I am retired. Nor can I deal with my contemporaries who are in exactly my position. So I will have to contract with younger people who will have earnings next period. With two-period lives, there would be no such people; with three or more, there are.

The inhabitants have identical well-behaved utility functions over three-period-long consumption sequences, with no presumptions about time preference. Let R_t, R_{t+1}, . . . be the successive discount factors, effectively the price of a unit of good at $t + 1$ ($t + 2$) in terms of the same good at t ($t + 1$), etc. Thus $R = (1 + i)^{-1}$. It is elementary to deduce the demand functions $C_k(R_t,R_{t+1})$ ($k = 1,2,3$), with the usual properties, for a person new-born at t; with incomes of 1,1,0, the budget constraint is $C_1 + R_tC_2 + R_tR_{t+1}C_3 = 1 + 1R_t$. It is then trivial to change notation to the savings functions $S_k(R_t, R_{t+1})$.

Suppose B_t people are born at t, so at time t the population consists of B_t first-period people, B_{t-1} second-period people and B_{t-2} third-period (retired) people. Since there is no possibility of investment, the goods-market-clearing equilibrium condition is that

$$B_tS_1(R_t,R_{t+1})+B_{t-1}S_2(R_{t-1},R_t)+B_{t-2}S_3(R_{t-2},R_{t-1})=0$$

In principle there are infinitely many such equations, one for each t, to determine the infinite sequence of discount factors or interest rates. Even starting at t, with R_{t-1} and R_{t-2} predetermined, so to speak, we still have R_t and R_{t+1} as unknowns; adding the next equation introduces the next unknown.

If the population is stationary ($B_t = B$ for every t), it is easily seen that one solution is $R_t = 1$, that is, a zero interest rate in every period, because then the sequence of equilibrium conditions reduces to the sequence of budget constraints, which are always satisfied. There can, however, be other solutions. This possibility of multiple equilibria enriches or plagues the long history of OLG models, depending on your point of view. Here it is already. I will say a little more about this property later.

There is a quick and, at least at first, rather surprising generalization of this result: Samuelson calls it the "biological theory of interest." Let the number of births (and therefore the population) grow geometrically through all time: $B_t = (1 + g)B_{t-1}$. Then one can look for a solution in which R is constant. There is one such, $R = (1 + g)^{-1}$, or $i = g$: so one possible equilibrium interest rate is the population growth rate itself.

Samuelson finds this result odd. He goes on to ask what was, at least for him, a characteristic question. This is a competitive equilibrium with no externalities: what is it "trying" to optimize? What planner's problem is "the market" solving? The answer emerges straightforwardly. If you imagine this economy being run always by an immortal dynastic family, with no beginning and no end, playing no favorites, the natural objective would be to maximize the lifetime utility ($U(C_1,C_2,C_3)$) shared by every member of the family throughout—doubly—infinite time.

Indeed it is easy to see that the steady-state equilibrium corresponding to the biological rate of interest has just this property. There is a fly in this particular ointment, however. Samuelson shows that if the economy starts anywhere outside the biological equilibrium, even nearby, and evolves by equating supply and demand period by period, it will not move toward the biological steady-state equilibrium. This sort of instability is another endemic characteristic of OLG models, as the later literature documents in many different contexts.

Abba Lerner would have none of this, by the way. In a comment on the 1958 article—to which Samuelson replied politely but firmly—Lerner argued that the welfare problem should be formulated differently. Take the stationary case for simplicity. In any period t there are three (or $3N$) people alive, one (or N) at each age. One of them is retired, so total consumption available is two. A benevolent planner would distribute the consumption to equalize marginal utility for each living person. Under the sort of strong symmetric, time-neutral assumptions of the Samuelson article, each person would get exactly 2/3 units of the good to consume. When the population is growing geometrically, the calculation is only slightly more complicated. In any case, the period by period social optimum as defined by Lerner is not the dynastic optimum previously defined and described. Samuelson was not about to deny Lerner the right to define social welfare according to his lights; but he was not inclined to abandon his own definition.

One could pursue this line of thought further. Indeed Samuelson surfaced some interesting questions about the doubly infinite nature of time in the model. For instance, what happens if this world will (might) come to an end at some specified time? Obviously some debts will not get settled. That is very like asking about the fate of the first or the last generational cohort in a pay-as-you-go social security scheme. I think it is much more enlightening to observe that these welfare-economic issues that seemed to attract the immediate interest of Samuelson, Lerner, W. J. Meckling, and other commentators turned out not to be the enduring value of the OLG model. The model itself could be fleshed out into a flexible vehicle for intertemporal general equilibrium theory, and proved to be capable of many different applications. (The study of social security systems was one of them.) In 1958, no one foresaw the future scope and power of Samuelson's little invention. It has to be said, however, that Samuelson understood at the very beginning one important implication of the OLG set-up, to which I have already alluded in passing. The determination of equilibrium interest rates is inherently forward-looking, of course; but the OLG model makes it very clear that every time you tack on another time period, and thus another equation, you also pick up another unknown. This is not trivial.

I will conclude by saying a little about the later development of the OLG model. But first it will be useful to pick out one further common characteristic of those models that emerged in the original paper, and in Samuelson's reply to an early comment by Meckling. Again I will stick to the stationary case to avoid notation. I will also take it for granted that in this case we are looking for an equilibrium with a constant interest rate and discount factor. So $S_1(R,R)$, $S_2(R,R)$, $S_3(R,R)$ are the savings functions for first, second, and third-period agents.

Since numbers are the same in all three age groups, and since perishability and non-satiation imply that all income is consumed, equilibrium requires that aggregate net saving vanish at each time. Thus $S_1(R,R) + S_2(R,R) + S_3(R,R) = 0$. And the intertemporal budget constraint for each agent says $S_1(R,R) + RS_2(R,R) + R^2S_3(R,R) = 0$. These two equations imply that $(1\text{-}R)S_1(R,R) = (1 - R)RS_3(R,R)$. We already knew that $R = 1$ satisfies this last equation. But we are alerted to the fact that there may be other (constant) solutions, in particular any R that satisfies $S_1(R,R) = RS_3(R,R)$. (And that is only for constant solutions.) There is no guarantee that other solutions exist, but they may. If they do, clearly S_3 $(= 0-C_3)$ is negative; and so is S_1 $(= 1 - C_1)$, meaning that the middle-aged are lending to the young now, looking for repayment next period. The point is that the ubiquity of multiple equilibria was present and seen to be present at the birth of the OLG model. When the model grew up, multiplicity played an even larger role.

With his usual acute historical sense, Samuelson had invented the pure consumption-loan model to test Böhm-Bawerk's idea that time preference would be needed to produce a positive rate of interest. (It turned out to be wrong.) It was only necessary to introduce production and durable assets to convert the OLG model into a neat, transparent, tractable vehicle for intertemporal general-equilibrium analysis at various levels of aggregation.

The power of the idea was established clearly with Peter Diamond's "National Debt in a Neoclassical Growth Model" (1965). The basic model was equipped with a stock of real capital, and with a paper asset to serve as an alternative way of holding wealth. The OLG set-up became established as one of the workhorse models for macroeconomics. It provided, among other things, a way to escape the temptation induced by use of the Ramsey model to formulate any long-run equilibrium process in a way that guarantees nice properties without further thought. As already indicated, the Blanchard–Fischer text exhibits the wide range of macroeconomic applications that followed after Diamond's work. I feel an urge to mention that the first chapter of Hahn and Solow's universally unread *Critical Essay* (1995) uses an OLG model with money to show that "perfect" nominal wage flexibility, while guaranteeing full employment by definition, is likely to lead to clearly pathological fluctuations in output, induced by necessary variations in the real interest rate.

Earlier on came the discovery by Jean-Michel Grandmont (1985) that a well-posed real competitive OLG model had the capacity to generate continuing fluctuations, indeed a large variety of fluctuating trajectories. These are not the business cycles of the older literature (or of reality), but they exemplify the capacity of the OLG model to uncover unsuspected possibilities in otherwise well-behaved economies.

The last such line of research I want to mention harks back to Samuelson's observation, in his reply to Meckling, that: "To know today's interest rate we have to know tomorrow's interest rate, because that helps determine today's saving on the part of the young. Inductively, then, today's interest rate is determined simultaneously with—and not prior to—*all* subsequent interest rates." A formulation like that points irresistibly to the idea of an equilibrium trajectory as a self-validating prophecy: a consistent pattern of expectations which, if held, will induce just the decisions that will make the expectations come true.

Further work along these lines was soon forthcoming, as for instance with Costas Azariadis's paper "Self-Fulfilling Prophecies" (1981). This path led to the work by David Cass and Karl Shell (1983) and by Roger Farmer (1993), among many others, on what has come to be called "sunspots." A fundamentally irrelevant process (like the waxing and waning of sunspots) might come to serve as a way of coordinating expectations. If everybody believes that sunspots determine economic outcomes in a certain way, is it possible that their resulting actions will confirm—and therefore strengthen—that belief? And if sunspots, why not other irrelevant processes as well? The answer is that many such equilibrium trajectories can exist, in some cases a continuum of them. The deep point here is not to detect or classify or interpret sunspot equilibria. What is really interesting is the demonstration that a fairly plain vanilla intertemporal model can easily fall into self-consistent modes of behavior that bear no relation to "fundamentals." Who would have expected that?

Thus this innocent little device of Samuelson's has been developed into a serious and quite general modeling strategy that uncovers equilibrium possibilities not to be found in standard Walrasian formulations. What is there about the OLG model that does this? Is it the overlapping structure, or the infinity of time, or something else? Apparently it is all of those characteristics together, as Geanakoplos remarks at the end of his compact survey. Probably it is a strategic mistake to worry about the essence of the OLG model. The sensible course is to forget about essences and study how the model behaves.

References

Allais, Maurice. (1947). *Economie et Intérêt*. Paris, Imprimerie Nationale.

Azariadis, Costas. (1981). "Self-fulfilling prophecies," *Journal of Economic Theory*, 25, 380–396.

Blanchard, Olivier and Stanley Fischer. (1989). *Lectures on Macroeconomics*. Cambridge, MA: The MIT Press.

Cass, David and Karl Shell. (1983). "Do Sunspots Matter?" *Journal of Political Economy*, 91, 193–227.

Diamond, Peter. (1965). "National Debt in a Neoclassical Growth Model," *American Economic Review*, 55(5), 1126–1150.

Farmer, Roger. (1993). *The Macroeconomics of Self-Fulfilling Prophecies*. Cambridge, MA: The MIT Press.

Geanakoplos, John. (1987). "The Overlapping Generations Model of General Equilibrium," in J. Eatwell, M. Milgate, P. Newmann (eds.), *The New Palgrave Dictionary of Economics*, Vol. 3. London: The Macmillan Press, pp. 767–779.

Grandmont, Jean-Michel. (1985). "On Endogenous Competitive Business Cycles," *Econometrica*, 53(5), 995–1046.

Hahn, Frank and Robert Solow. (1995). *A Critical Essay on Modern Macroeconomic Theory*. Cambridge, MA: The MIT Press.

Lerner, Abba. (1959). "Consumption-loan interest and money," *Journal of Economic Perspectives*, 67, 512–525.

Meckling, W.H. (1960). "An exact consumption-loan model of interest: a comment," *Journal of Political Economy*, 58(1), 72–75.

Samuelson, P.A. (1966). "An exact consumption-loan model of interest with or without the social contrivance of money," *Journal of Political Economy*, December 66 (1958) 467–482. *The Collected Scientific Papers of Paul A. Samuelson*, Vol. 1, Chap. 21, 219–234. Cambridge, MA: The MIT Press.

——. (1966). "Reply," (Consumption-loan interest and money) *Journal of Political Economy*, 67 (1959) 518–22. *The Collected Scientific Papers of Paul A. Samuelson*, Vol. 1, Chap. 22, 235–239. Cambridge, MA: The MIT Press.

——. (1966). "Infinity, Unanimity and Singularity: A Reply," *The Journal of Political Economy*, 68 (1960) 76–83. *The Collected Scientific Papers of Paul A. Samuelson*, Vol. 1, Chap. 23, 240–247. Cambridge, MA: The MIT Press.

2

Paul Samuelson's Amazing Intergenerational Transfer

Laurence J. Kotlikoff

I am deeply honored to participate in this forum celebrating Paul Samuelson's ongoing contributions to economics. Paul's work has profoundly influenced, irrevocably altered, and dramatically improved economic analysis in virtually all areas of economics. A prime example is the field of generational policy, which focuses on the extent and means by which governments redistribute across generations. Paul's masterpiece—"An Exact Consumption-Loan Model of Interest with and without the Social Contrivance of Money"—is *the* seminal article in this field and permeates virtually all postwar research on the issue. The paper's insights and messages have particular salience today given what many view as the grave demographic/fiscal threat facing the developed world.

Like all of Paul's writings, this paper is a literary gem with copious references to our intellectual forefathers. Bentham, Mills, Engels, Myrdal, Kant, Robertson, Böhm-Bawerk, Harrod, Fisher, Landry, Hobbes, Rousseau, and others make an appearance. But the paper's real appeal is the theoretical vistas it provides. Here in one fell swoop we learn that competitive economies can be Pareto inefficient (dynamically inefficient), that altruism can promote survival, that constitutions and social norms can have economic determinants, that dynamic economies can have an infinite number of equilibria, that biology can determine interest and inflation rates, that financial markets can be highly volatile, if not unstable, that monetary and fiscal policy can be isomorphic, that fiscal policy can be

I thank Herakles Polemarcharkis and Karl Shell for extensive and extremely valuable comments.

endogenous, that the same economic policy can be labeled a zillion different ways, and that there is an economic limit to expropriating the young.

The paper and Paul's *Journal of Political Economy* subsequent exchange (Samuelson, 1960) with W. H. Meckling (1960) provide a winding road through this splendid garden of issues and ideas. Just when you think you've come to the end, there's another twist presenting an even more striking view. Paul clearly delights in story telling, knows how to keep his reader in suspense, and waits until the last minute to pull his paper oblongs out of the hat.

A simple rendition of Paul's story takes place on a very hot island with very tall cocoa trees, which only the young can climb. At the top of the trees grow the only source of sustenance—Hershey chocolate bars.[1] The young climb the trees, harvest the bars, and eat them immediately for they won't keep in the heat. The earth-bound elderly grovel for chocolate, but to no avail. Their elevated kids see no quo for their quid, have no *Up* in their *Uc*, and experience no qualm in watching their parents starve.

This unfortunate state of competition continues year after year until some enterprising generation of oldsters offers to swap chocolate for pink sea shells that have washed up on shore. The young could not care less about sea shells, but they make the swap in order to have shells with which to swap when old.

Voila! The economy moves from brutish to blissful. People no longer starve when old, everyone is better off, and the young and old celebrate the economy's Pareto improvement by washing each other with melted chocolate.

Now what determines the price level—the rate at which shells swap for chocolate? The answer is expectations. The price today depends on what people think it will be tomorrow. But what it will be tomorrow depends on what tomorrow's people think it will be the day after, and so on. Nothing in the economic environment pins down these expectations, so nothing limits the number of paths the price level and, thus, the economy can take. In particular, nothing says the price level will change in line with population growth or, if this does occur, when such a steady state will arise. Moreover, since the public's expectations of future prices determine the course of chocolate transfers, such transfers, which might be termed fiscal policy, are endogenous.

Since the change in the price level determines the rate at which one can swap consumption today for consumption tomorrow, the dynamics of the price level are also those of the implicit interest rate. When prices move in line with population growth, the interest rate equals the population growth rate (the biological rate). But when they do not, the interest rate can go its merry way, including fluctuating wildly. So our little chocolate paradise can have lots of what some would describe as "financial instability" along any given equilibrium path or, indeed, across paths, if the economy jumps equilibria.[2]

Regardless of what path the economy takes—what equilibrium prevails—birds (nonedible ones) perched in the cocoa trees will take notice. They will no longer hear the moans of starving geezers or watch the young pelt the old with candy wrappers. But while the birds will all agree about the amount of chocolate being passed from the young to the old each period, they will vehemently disagree as to the policy in place. Some birds will claim that monetary policy is at work and that the shells are money. Others will see a pay-as-you-go social security system in which the chocolate handed over when young constitutes a tax and the shells simply represent bookkeeping for one's future claim to chocolate social security benefits. Yet others will claim the shells are bonds that are purchased when young and sold when old. And there will even be some birds who will claim that the shells are irrelevant—just a shell game, if you will—and that the chocolate eaters must have drawn up a constitution forcing each generation of young to make transfers to the old.

After the birds spend several centuries arguing and forming societies called the Monetarists, the Socialists, the Keynesians, and the Strict Constructionists, a young bird named Paul points out that the argument is not about economics, but about language. This stops the fight for a full nanosecond, after which it proceeds apace.

Like this island, our society contains a lot of bird brains, many located in Washington, who constantly mistake linguistics for economics. They would do well to read Paul's article.

We economists, in contrast, have read and reread Paul's article and incorporated it fully into our teaching and research. In this respect, Paul's paper is the gift that keeps on giving—not a chocolate bar, but a cocoa tree! This is plain to see in Edmund Phelp's (1961, 1965) work on the golden rule and dynamic efficiency, Peter Diamond's (1965) analysis of debt in an OLG model, Martin Feldstein's (1974) work on pay-as-you-go social security, Robert Barro's (1974) work on Ricardian Equivalence, Karl Shell's (1971, 1977) work on the economics of infinity and sunspots, David Cass and Karl Shell's (1983, 1989) work on sunspots, Costas Azariadis (1981) and Roger Farmer's (1993) work on sunspots, Yves Balasko and Karl Shell's (1980, 1981a,b) detailed investigation of the OG model, Glenn Loury's (1981) work on intra-family human capital transfers, Jean-Michel Grandmont's

(1985) work on "temporary equilibrium," Richard Benveniste and David Cass' (1986) work on optimal stationary equilibria, the work of Andy Abel *et al.* (1989) on dynamic efficiency under uncertainty, Michael Woodford's (1990) work on the convergence of rational expectations equilibrium under adaptive learning, the recent work by Rochon and Polemarchakis (2005) distinguishing money and debt in OLG models, and in the work of literally thousands of others. Indeed, since 1988 alone Paul's paper has been cited 638 times in published articles and books!

For my part, I encountered Paul's paper in several courses in graduate school and was immediately intrigued by the issues it raised, although I was not able to clearly sort them out in my mind or fully grasp the lessons being taught. (I am still doing that.) But Paul's article, its offshoots, and the strong influence of my thesis advisor, Marty Feldstein, got me completely hooked on generational economics.

Let me connect my own research in this field to Paul's paper. I do so not to put my work on the same plane. It is in a much lower dimensional manifold. I do so to suggest the reach of Paul's intellectual transfer.

One of the key issues raised by Paul's paper is the role of intergenerational altruism in society. In considering the possibility that kids might let their parents starve, Paul was inviting economists to find out if that was really the case. And, by extension, he was inviting us to study whether parents would let their kids starve.

Starvation is, of course, an extreme outcome that arises only in unusual circumstances. So we need to test altruism in our everyday world in which both parents and kids have access to their own chocolate. The simple way to test intergenerational altruism is to see whether parents and kids share resources when it comes to consumption. Consumption sharing means that the consumption levels of those doing the sharing should move together. If parents get more (less) income, both their consumption and that of their kids should rise (fall). If kids get more (less) income, the same thing should happen. Stated differently, the ratio of the kids' consumption to that of the parents should be independent of the ratio of the kids' resources to that of the parents. Moreover, a dollar taken from a child and given to a parent should lead to a dollar increase in the parent's transfer to the child. Finally, when altruism is operational, other family decisions, like living together, should depend on the sum, not the division, of resources.

Over the years I and a variety of coauthors have conducted a number of studies to test these propositions using cross section, cohort, and time series data.[3] We have even tested altruism within extended families in which parents are actively making transfers to their children. The tests have all strongly rejected intergenerational altruism. Thus, Paul's assumption of selfish behavior is, regrettably, on the mark. In particular, when it comes to consumption, there is no evidence that cohorts share resources very much, that extended family members share resources very much, or that nuclear families share resources very much. And there is no evidence that parents whose incomes rise substantially compensate their kids whose incomes fall. This last finding holds even for parents who are actively making transfers to their children!

Paul's paper also raises questions about the range of social compacts that can be sustained and the manner of their enforcement. In Kotlikoff, Persson, and Swensson (1988) my coauthors and I pointed out that the old can sell the young more than simple covenants to support the elderly. They can also sell the young other economic laws, including a law prohibiting capital levies. Such a law can prevent second best taxation from degenerating into third best taxation due to the time inconsistency problem noted by Fischer (1980). The young can make their payment in the form of tax contributions to finance public goods for the old or transfer payments to the old.

Kotlikoff, Persson, and Swensson (1988) also explore ways of enforcing the sale of social contracts. In particular, we showed that if setting up new social contracts involves transactions costs, it will be easier to sustain existing social contracts. The first generation that sets up such a contract is forced to pay the setup costs, but has an offsetting advantage in not having to pay for the law. Subsequent generations find it cheaper to buy the law and then resell it (effectively rent the law) than incurring the setup costs from scratch. Our paper also showed that laws could be sold (laws are assets) even in the absence of transactions costs if generations adopt strategies under which they only purchase laws that have never been broken.

A third research area that intersects with Paul's paper and Diamond's (1965) own diamond involves trying to understand how interest and wage rates evolve in dynamic general equilibrium. My work with Alan Auerbach and others in this area adds capital accumulation, variable labor supply, demographics, multiple periods, and a variety of fiscal policies to Paul's framework.[4] These additions plus the assumption of CES production and CES intertemporal preferences admit unique and dynamically efficient equilibria.

My graduate student, Javier Hamann (1992), showed that adding money to this model as well as nominal government liabilities permits one to calculate a unique path for the price level. Here we see the price level endogenously determining real fiscal policy, just as in Paul's paper, Sargent and Wallace's examination of monetarist arithmetic, and Woodford's (1994) fiscal theory of the price level. The fact that nicely behaved, dynamically efficient, neoclassical models can have unique equilibria is reassuring given Paul's concern, raised in response to Meckling (Meckling, 1960; Samuelson, 1960), that "a perpetual competitive system seems to be an indeterminate one." But, as Nakajima and Polemarcharkis' (2005) work suggests, indeterminacy may yet rear its ugly head if the monetary-fiscal authorities adjust real fiscal policy in response to changes in prices and interest rates, where such changes are governed by rational, but otherwise freely determined expectations.

A fourth connection between my work and Paul's paper involves generational accounting. The impetus for generational accounting derives from Paul's insight that the same policy can be "run" in different ways. But since the math makes no distinction between one way and the other, any one way can be called the other. So Paul's point is really that a given policy can be labeled different ways; that is, whether we call a policy one thing or another is a matter of language, not economics.

This labeling problem is not specific to Paul's model, as shown in Kotlikoff (2003) and Green and Kotlikoff (2006). The problem is generic to any neoclassical model with rational agents. This fact calls into question essentially all conventional analysis of fiscal affairs given that such analysis is predicated on deficit accounting. Paul's point, writ large, is that governments are free to choose fiscal labels so as to report any time-path of deficits or surpluses independent of the actual policy they are running. We could well call this Samuelson's Relativity Theory. It shows that each observer's reference point (his/her choice of labels) alters the perception of economic policy, as conventionally measured, but not the reality of what the policy actually is or what it is doing to the economy.[5]

Generational accounting, when properly conducted, does not suffer from this labeling problem. Its assessment of the fiscal burden facing future generations is the same regardless of the government's nomenclature. So are its measures of changes in the fiscal burdens facing current and generations arising from policy changes. This is not surprising since generational accounting is trying to answer an economic question rather than engage in mindless measurement.

Given the nature of the fiscal/demographic problems facing the developed world, we no longer have the luxury of relying on inherently uninformative indicators of nations' fiscal conditions. Generational accounting, while far from perfect, is, at this point, a necessity, not an option. In the case of the United States, generational accounting indicates that if current adults do not step up to the plate, young and future generations will face lifetime net tax rates that are twice those of current adults. Attempting to foist such a burden on the next generation is not only immoral; it is also economically infeasible. There is a limit to fiscal child abuse, and the United States and other developed countries are, in my view, rapidly approaching that limit. Corroborating evidence on this score comes from Gokhale and Smetters's (2005) measure of the fiscal gap, which is closely related to the measure of the collective fiscal burden facing future generations discussed in Auerbach, Kotlikoff, and Gokhale (1991).[6] The fiscal gap, which is also a label-free measure, compares the present value of all projected future US government expenditures, including official debt service, with the present value of all projected future government receipts. Gokhale and Smetters's estimate of the fiscal gap for 2005 is $65.9 trillion or 8.5 percent of the present value of GDP. To put this figure in perspective, note that 2004 federal personal and corporate income taxes totaled 8.6 percent of 2004 GDP.

What alternative policies could be taken to eliminate the US fiscal gap? One is to immediately and permanently double person and corporate income taxes.[7] A second option is to immediately and permanently cut all Social Security and Medicare benefits by two thirds. A third alternative is to cut federal discretionary spending immediately and permanently; but even eliminating all such spending would leave us significantly short of the needed $65.9 trillion.

The Gokhale and Smetters's estimates are updates of the fiscal gap accounting they did while working at the US Treasury under former Treasury Secretary Paul O'Neill.[8] Their analysis relies exclusively on government projections or extensions of such projections. These projections are quite optimistic with respect to future demographics and growth in Medicare and Medicaid spending per beneficiary.

Notwithstanding the magnitude of the fiscal gap and the downward bias in its measurement, some prominent economists[9] see the short- and medium-term projected deficits as manageable and assume the long run will take care of itself. This, to be kind, is misguided. Paul's relativity theory tells us that we can choose labels to arrive at whatever deficit, tax, and transfer projections we want. Hence, there is no legitimate way to consider the short-term apart from the long-term. Only the infinite horizon measures calculated in the generational accounting and fiscal gap analyses are label-free and, thus, well defined.[10]

The fiscal/demographic optimists might well respond that the government's real borrowing rate is low relative to the economy's growth rate and that, given this fact, taking from the young and giving to the old could continue to work well for decades, if not centuries. These modern-day Ponzis should re-read the Abel *et al.* (1989) study, which shows that comparing the government's borrowing rate and the economy's growth rate is not appropriate in a setting in which both growth rates and rates of return to capital are uncertain. They should also think about how Paul's model works if the government finds itself taking ever more chocolate from the young in order to satisfy promises made to the old. At some point, the young run out of chocolate to hand over. At that point, it is the young, not the old, who are starving.

Kotlikoff and Burns (2004) raise the alarm about excessive transfers from the young to the old. In particular, we suggest that the US economy could go critical once financial markets recognize the implications of the magnitude of the fiscal gap for US money creation and inflation. But what if there is no financial meltdown to awaken the country to the limits to fiscal child abuse? How will these limits be reached?

As mentioned, in Paul's model the limit hits when all the chocolate is taken from the young and handed to the old. If we add capital to Paul's model, the limit is reached when the young are using all of their after-tax savings to purchase government bonds and, thus, are unable to accumulate physical capital. At this point, the game is over since production requires capital as well as labor. From a general equilibrium perspective, things would get pretty dicey well before this limit was hit. The reason is that wages depend on capital, so every period the capital stock falls, wages fall as well, which reduces what the young have to save.

This simple model suggests that we need to look at net national saving to understand if we are eating up our capital stock or would be doing so were foreigners to stop investing in the United States. In this regard, last year's net national saving rate is quite telling. It was only 2.2 percent of national income! With the exception of 2003's 2.1 percent rate, this is the lowest US rate of net national saving in 45 years. By way of comparison, note that the US net national saving rate averaged 13.0 percent in the 1960s, 10.3 percent in the 1970s, 7.6 percent in the 1980s, 5.6 percent in the 1990s, and 3.8 percent since 2000.

The decline in the rate of net national saving in the United States reflects the ever growing rate of household consumption. Government (federal, state, and local) consumption as a share of national income was 17.6 percent in 2004, which is lower than the average rate observed in each of the last four decades. For example, the government consumption rate was 19.5 percent in the 1970s. In contrast, the ratio of household consumption to the difference between national income and government consumption—what I call the household consumption rate—is now at a postwar high of 97.3 percent. This rate averaged 84.0 percent in the 1960s, 87.2 percent in the 1970s, 90.6 percent in the 1980s, 93.1 percent in the 1990s, and 95.5 since 2000.

As shown in Gokhale, Kotlikoff, and Sabelhaus (1996), the dramatic increase in the household consumption rate can be traced to higher levels of consumption of the elderly. My extrapolation from that study is that the per capita consumption of middle-aged retirees relative to that of middle-aged workers has doubled since 1960. The reason is simple. The government is taking ever more chocolate from young and, implicitly, future generations and giving it to the old, increasingly in the form of medical goods and services.

The huge US current account deficit is, of course, reflective of our country's low saving rate. Last year foreigners invested 3 dollars in the United States for every dollar Americans invested here![11]

While it may be hard to believe, the ever rising transfers to the elderly could shortly lead the US net national saving rate to go negative. At this point, we'll be eating up our national wealth.[12] Ignoring government assets (could we really sell the White House?) and assets held by nonprofits, my guestimate of current national wealth is $35 trillion. Were the United States saving rate to hit, say, −5 percent, and who is to say it will not given the trend and the pending retirement of the baby boomers, we would be eating up close to $2 trillion a year of national wealth. At that rate we would have only 15 or so years before the country was out of wealth and also out of income from that wealth. At that point we would have only our wages to finance our consumption. And US labor income is significantly less than US consumption. So we would, indeed, reach a limit to our intergenerational profligacy. Consumption would have to fall. In Herb Stein's words, "Something that can't go on has to stop." The problem with Stein's aphorism is that it fails to clarify that when things that cannot go on finally stop, they may stop at a very bad place and stay there forever. The bottom line here is that Paul's model identifies not just how intergenerational transfers can help the old, but also how they can hurt the young. As we all continue to study, learn from, and build upon his absolutely brilliant analysis, we, unfortunately, need to keep this concern front and center.

Notes

1. Karl Shell appears to be the first to use the chocolate metaphor for the good in Paul's model.
2. Paul's concern (Samuelson, 1960), raised in response to Meckling (1960), that "a perpetual competitive system seems to be an indeterminate one" depends, as most recently shown by Rochon and Polemarchakis (2005), on whether the economy in question is dynamically efficient.
3. See Kotlikoff (2001).
4. See, for example, Auerbach and Kotlikoff (1987).
5. The term "relativity theory" seems apt since this situation is akin to Einstein's revelation that different observers of the same physical reality will describe it differently depending on their relative speed.
6. The fiscal gap is the present value net tax burden on future generations that is calculated in Auerbach, Kotlikoff, and Gokhale (1991) less the present value of net taxes future generations would pay were they to face the same lifetime net tax rates as current generations.
7. This abstracts from tax evasion and tax distortions as well as "Laffer curve" effects.
8. Gokhale and Smetters (2003) is, in fact, the Treasury study commissioned by Treasury Secretary Paul O'Neill. It was published through the American Enterprise Institute rather than the Treasury because the Treasury censured the study within a few days of O'Neill's being fired.
9. See, for example, Porter (2005).
10. As a public service, the government should present alternative official deficit time series (past and projected) based on alternative labeling conventions. Some of these series would show the deficit soaring; others would show it heading south at exponential rates; still others would place and keep it at zero. Economists yearning to support their theories of how deficits connect to interest rates, saving rates, or other economic variables would surely find a series to meet their needs. Politicians dying for a balanced budget could die in peace. Others who crave red or black ink would shout for joy. And the public would finally see that the deficit has no clothes.
11. In 2004, the US rate of net domestic investment (measured relative to national income) was 8.7 percent. The US net national saving rate was 2.2 percent. The 6.5 percent difference represents the current account deficit as a share of US national income.
12. For example, over the past four years Medicare benefits per beneficiary grew sixteen times faster than real wages per worker.

References

Abel, Andrew B., N. Gregory Mankiw, Lawrence H. Summers, and Richard J. Zeckhauser. (1989). "Assessing dynamic efficiency: theory and evidence," *The Review of Economic Studies*, 56(1), 1–19.

Auerbech, Alan J. and Laurence J. Kotlikoff, *Dynamic Fiscal Policy*, Cambridge, England: Cambridge University Press, 1987.

Auerbach, Alan J., Jagadeesh Gokhale, and Laurence J. Kotlikoff. (1991). "Generational accounting: a meaningful alternative to deficit accounting," in David Bradford (ed), *Tax Policy and the Economy*, Vol. 5, Cambridge, MA: MIT Press, 55–110.

Azariadis, Costas. (1981). "Self-fulfilling prophecies," *Journal of Economic Theory*, 380–396.

Balasko, Yves and Karl Shell. (1980). "The overlapping-generations model, I: The case of pure exchange without money," *Journal of Economic Theory*, 23(3), 281–306.

—— and ——. (1989a and b) "The overlapping-generations model, II: The case of pure exchange with money", *Journal of Economic Theory*, 24(1), 112–142. See also "Erratum," *Journal of Economic Theory*, 25(3), 471.

Barro, Robert J. (1974). "Are government bonds net wealth?," *The Journal of Political Economy*, 82(6), 1095–1117.

Benveniste, Lawrence M. and David Cass. (1986). "On the existence of optimal stationary equilibria with a fixed supply of fiat money: I. The case of a single consumer," *The Journal of Political Economy*, 94(2), 402–417.

Cass, David and Karl Shell. (1983). "Do sunspots matter?" *Journal of Political Economy*, 91(2), April 1983, 193–227.

—— and ——. (1989). "Economic complexity: chaos, sunspots, bubbles, and non-linearity," William A. Barnett, John Geweke, and Karl Shell (eds), *Proceedings of the Fourth International Symposium in Economic Theory and Econometrics*, Cambridge, England: Cambridge University Press.

Diamond, Peter A. (1965). "National debt in a neoclassical growth model," *The American Economic Review*, 55(5), 1126–11250.

Farmer, Roger. (1993). *The Macroeconomics of Self-Fulfilling Prophecies*. Cambridge, MA: MIT Press.

Feldstein, Martin. (1974). "Social security, induced retirement, and aggregate capital accumulation," *The Journal of Political Economy*, 82(5), 905–926.

Fischer, Stanley. (1980). "Dynamic inconsistency, cooperation and the benevolent dissembling government," *Journal of Economic Dynamics and Control*, 2, 93–107.

Hamann, Alfronso Javier. (1992). *A Quantitative Assessment of the Effects of Inflationary Finance in an Overlapping Generations Model*, Ph.D. dissertation, Boston University.

Gokhale, Jagadeesh and Kent Smetters. (2003). *Fiscal and Generational Imbalances: New Budget Measures for New Budget Priorities*. Washington, D.C.: AEI Press.

Gokhale, Jagadeesh, Laurence J. Kotlikoff, and John Sabelhaus, "Understanding the Postwar Decline in United States Saving: A Cohort Analysis," *The Brookings Papers on Economic Activity*, No. 1, 1996, 315–407.

—— and ——. (January 2005). "Measuring social security's financial problems," NBER working paper 11060.

Grandmont, Jean-Michel. (1985). *Money and Value*. Cambridge, England: Cambridge University Press.

Green, Jerry and Laurence J. Kotlikoff. "On the General Relativity of Fiscal Language," forthcoming *Key Issues* in Public Finance, Alan J. Auerbach and Daniel Shapiro, eds. New York, NY: New York University Press, 2006.

Kotlikoff, Laurence J. (2001). *Essays on Saving, Bequests, Altruism, and Life Cycle Planning*. Cambridge. MA: MIT Press.

——. 2003. *Generational Policy*. Cambridge, MA: MIT Press.

—— and Scott Burns. (2004). *The Coming Generational Storm*. Cambridge, MA: MIT Press.

——., Thorsten Persson, and Lars E. O. Svensson. (1988). "Social contracts as assets: a possible solution to the time consistency problem," *The American Economic Review*, 78(4), 662–677.

Loury, Glenn. (1981). "Intergenerational transfers and the distribution of earnings," *Econometrica*, 49(4), 843–867.

Meckling, W. H. (1960), "An exact consumption-loan model of interest: a comment," *The Journal of Political Economy*, 68(1), 72–76.

Nakajima, Tomoyuki and Herkales Polemarcharkis. (2005). "Money and prices under uncertainty," *Review of Economic Studies*, 72, 233–246.

Phelps, Edmund S. (1961). "The golden rule of accumulation: a fable for growthmen," *American Economic Review*, 51, 638–43.

——. (1965). "Second essay on the golden rule of accumulation," *American Economic Review*, 55, 793–814.

Porter, Eduardo. (2005). "Maybe we're not robbing the cradle," *The New York Times*, Sunday, April 10, Section 4, 1, 3.

Rochon, Cleine and Herakles M. Polemarchakis. (2005). "Debt, liquidity, and dynamics," forthcoming *Economic Theory* 2006.

Samuelson, Paul A. (1958). "An exact consumption-loan model of interest with or without the social contrivance of money," *The Journal of Political Economy*, 66(6), 467–482.

——. (1960), "Infinity, unanimity, and singularity: a reply," *The Journal of Political Economy*, 68(1), 76–83.

Sargent, Thomas and Neil Wallace. (1981). "Some unpleasant monetarist arithmetic," *Federal Reserve Bank of Minneapolis Quarterly Report*.

Shell, Karl. (1971). "Notes on the economics of infinity," *Journal of Political Economy*, 99(5), 1002–11.

——. (1977). "Monnaie et Allocation Intertemporelle," Malinvaud Lecture, Centre National de la Recherche Scientifique, November (http://www.karlshell.com/pdfs/monnaie.pdf).

Woodford, Michael. (1990). "Learning to believe in sunspots," *Econometrica*, 58, 277–307.

——. (1994). "Monetary policy and price level determinancy in a cash-in-advance economy," *Economic Theory*, 4, 345–380.

3

Social Security, the Government Budget, and National Savings

Peter Diamond

3.1 Introduction

Paul Samuelson has had an enormous impact on the public economics of the twentieth century. In models with heterogeneity in the population, Pareto improvements are not possible from policies that are restricted to even vaguely resemble realism. Thus, the Bergson–Samuelson social welfare function plays a key role in the evaluation of alternative policies. Since this key contribution was discussed by Kenneth Arrow in the 1983 Festschrift for Paul (Brown and Solow, 1983), I will merely say that I foresee no diminution in the importance of this contribution in the twenty-first century.[1] Similarly, the formulation of public goods by Paul was discussed by Richard Musgrave in the same volume and I foresee no diminution in its importance either.[2] Alas, the use of fiscal policy as part of the stabilization of an economy has moved out of contemporary public economics (and apparently macroeconomics as well). Thus his writings, celebrated by Tobin in the Festschrift, must await a revival in this key topic for a future impact.[3] As explained in the introduction to the 1983 Festschrift, Paul's development of the overlapping generations (OLG) model and applications to social security fell between the cracks of chapter assignments for that volume. Thus it is fitting that I provide an example of the use of that extraordinarily fruitful model in analysis of a social security question for this volume.[4] This list of Paul's direct contributions to public economics

I am grateful to Henry Aaron, Jeff Liebman, Peter Orszag, Jim Poterba, and members of the MIT macro lunch for comments, to Tal Regev and Maisy Wong for research assistance, and to the National Science Foundation for financial support under grant SES-0239380.

leaves out Paul's enormous impact through his writings on both individual choice and equilibrium, which have affected all of economic theory, but that would take me astray.

But first, I want to say a few words about how twenty-first century public economics may differ from that of the twentieth, and how that might affect the Samuelsonian legacy. When I look at the recent research trends that I expect to continue, two developments stand out. One is rapid growth of interest in behavioral economics, while the other is the use of computers for calculations of far more complex examples, both deterministic and stochastic, than could have been contemplated before. Computerized examples rely on theory in the same way that simpler examples do. And while some bottom up interactive simulations might make little use of the economic theory that Paul has helped to build, overwhelmingly, to date, the calculations and simulations have relied on the same basic theory. I do not expect that to change.

There are two complementary developments in theoretical behavioral economics. One is the development of new models of individual choice that rely heavily on empirical input from psychology. The second is the development of equilibrium models that make use of simplified models of behavior that are informed by both empirical findings on behavior and the first strand of new individual behavioral modeling. Thus these models are not consistent with the standard model. In Social Security, such modeling has gone on for a considerable time. In particular there are a number of analyses employing the OLG model while assuming nonstandard behavior in savings (and sometimes in labor supply as well). These still rely on the Samuelsonian OLG model as before—changing the model of individual choice does not remove the legacy. This model is an example of such modeling, offered as a tribute to Paul.

3.2 Social Security

In the 1983 Social Security reform, Congress chose to build a substantial trust fund, with principal and interest both to be used for later benefits. That is, Congress chose payroll tax rates higher than pay-as-you-go levels while the baby-boomers were in the labor force in order to have payroll tax rates lower than pay-as-you-go while the baby-boomers were retired. The impact on national capital of these higher payroll taxes, with the implied trust fund buildup, has been controversial. The impact depends on the response of the rest of the government budget as well as the responses of individuals to these government actions.[5]

In the absence of an empirically supported, widely accepted connection between Social Security and non-Social Security budgets, research has naturally considered the implications of alternative ways of modeling this connection. In particular, Elmendorf and Liebman (2000) analyzed the impact of Social Security savings on national savings under different assumptions as to the response of the rest of the budget to a Social Security surplus. Implicitly, they assumed a representative taxpayer and so did not distinguish between a payroll tax increase and an income tax cut that might be induced by the payroll tax increase. Yet the distribution of payroll and income tax burdens by income level are very different and propensities to save by income level are also very different. The top quintile in earners in 1995 paid 71 percent of the individual income tax and 37 percent of the Social Security payroll tax.[6]

The 1983 legislation can be viewed as a commitment to finance the additional debt in the Trust Fund out of future income taxes insofar as it resulted in offsetting expenditure increases or tax decreases. That is, pre-funding through the payroll tax should be seen as a commitment to workers, whether the government and the country save more overall or not. If tax changes are proportional to taxes and if income tax changes fully offset payroll tax changes (a balanced unified budget on the margin), then the legislation could be viewed in part (roughly one-third say, reflecting the differences in shares of the two taxes paid by low earners) as a transfer from current payroll tax payers to current income tax payers with an exactly offsetting (in present discounted value terms) future transfer from income tax payers to payroll tax payers. I believe that very little of the trust fund buildup of the 1980s and early 1990s resulted in offsetting budgetary changes.[7] Since this belief is not held by all analysts, it is helpful to consider the model with a parametric level of offset.

This note contributes to evaluating the impact of the 1983 reform on national savings by considering a one-period rise in the payroll tax to permanently increase the trust fund, with the increased interest income used to finance a decrease in all future payroll tax rates. Since future social security budgets are balanced, it is assumed that the income tax rate decreases to partially offset the social security surplus in the first period and thereafter the income tax rate rises by enough to pay the increase in the interest owing on the national debt. That is, after the initial period it is assumed that both the Social Security budget and the unified budget are always balanced. The impact of these government actions on national capital is solved for the end of the initial period and for the asymptotic steady state (reached after all those alive in the initial period have died since the production technology is assumed to be linear). Capital is larger at the end of the initial period. Whether it is higher or lower in the asymptotic steady state depends on the fraction of the payroll tax revenue change that is offset by the income tax. A simple calculation suggests that the break-even point for long-run capital is with an 80 percent offset. In a setting of a temporary trust fund buildup, eventually the only effects are those of the income tax increase, thereby lowering national capital, before the model eventually returns to the same long-run capital as would have happened without the temporary trust fund buildup.[8]

These effects are derived in a two-types model (as in Diamond and Geanakoplos, 2003), where one group, called workers, does no savings while the other group, called savers, are standard life-cycle optimizers.[9] For convenience the savers are assumed to plan constant consumption as they would with a discount rate equal to the interest rate. Reflecting the empirical observation that those with higher earnings have higher propensities to save (Dynan, Skinner, and Zeldes, 2004; Saez, 2002), and the patterns of payroll and income tax liabilities by earnings level, the model assumes that workers pay only payroll taxes and savers pay only income taxes. Thus the model should be interpreted in terms of the differences between the two types of taxes at the margin in response to a payroll tax excess over the level needed for pay-as-you-go.

The logic behind the effects in the initial period in both settings is clear. While the initial payroll tax increase comes fully out of worker consumption, the initial income tax cut is partially saved. This savings comes from a forward-looking spreading of a one-period income increase over consumption in all the remaining periods of life and from the assumed awareness that future income tax rates will be increased. While solved in a specific model, this result would follow more generally when payroll taxpayers have a lower propensity to save out of payroll taxes than income taxpayers do out of the income tax, as is plausible.

The model structure is presented in Section 3.3. Analysis of a permanent trust fund buildup is in Section 3.4, with concluding remarks in Section 3.5.

3.3 Model Structure

There is great diversity in earnings, savings propensities, and in the ratios of payroll to income taxes paid. The starting place for this model is the diversity in savings. Assume two-types, so that in each cohort there are n "workers" who do no saving whatsoever and N "savers" who are standard life-cycle savers. We use lower-case letters to refer to workers and upper-case letters to refer to savers. For notational simplicity, assume no population growth. Given the positive correlation between savings propensities and earnings (Dynan, Skinner, and Zeldes, 2000; Saez, 2002), the ratio of payroll taxes to income taxes is higher for workers than savers. For simplicity, we model this by assuming that the workers pay no income taxes at all—a simplification which calls for interpreting the model relative to tax differences. While most savers are also covered by Social Security, for notational simplicity we assume that they are not. Again, this calls for interpretation in terms of the difference between types of taxes paid.

The workers rely on social security for retirement consumption, while the savers do their own retirement savings. In recognition of the tax advantages of retirement savings, we model the income tax as falling only on the earnings of savers. We also assume that labor is inelastically supplied—with work for L periods (length of career) and retirement for $D-L$. We assume that careers are longer than retirements, $L > D-L$. We do not consider differences in career length or life expectancy between the two types.

For simplicity, assume a linear technology, with each worker earning w per period, each saver earning w per period, and capital earning a gross return $R(=1+r > 1)$.[10] With constant payroll taxes, t, each worker would consume $w(1-t)$ while working and a social security benefit of b while retired. For simplicity, assume that savers equalize the consumption each period over their entire lives or their remaining lives when there is a policy change. This would follow from the standard model if the savers have additive lifetime utility functions with the same period utility functions in each period and a utility discount rate that equals the interest rate. With savers choosing the same level of consumption, C, in each of the D periods of life, the present discounted value (PDV) of period consumption for a saver newly entering the labor force is equal to the PDV of L periods of net-of-tax earnings, $W(1-T)$. With unanticipated changes in income taxes, T, we will have to pay attention to the timing of tax changes.

The social security system is partially funded, with a fund of size F. With equally sized cohorts, the Social Security budget constraint if the fund is held constant is

$$n(D-L)\,b = nLtw + rF \tag{3.1}$$

That is, benefits of b are paid to each of the $n(D-L)$ retirees alive in each period. Financing comes from payroll tax revenues and the interest on the trust fund.

For simplicity, we assume no government expenditures other than interest on the outstanding public debt, denoted G. If the debt is constant, per period non-Social Security budget balance implies

$$NLTW = rG \tag{3.2}$$

That is, the interest on the total debt outstanding is paid from the income tax on the earnings of the NL savers in the labor force in each period. Thus the income tax on savers finances the non-Social Security budget while the payroll tax on workers finances the Social Security budget. The public debt held by the savers is $G-F$, the rest of their savings being in physical capital.

3.4 Permanent Fund Increase

Assume that the government increases the payroll tax rate by Δt for one period, using the revenue to permanently increase the trust fund, with the additional interest earnings used to lower the payroll tax rate thereafter. Assume that the government decreases the income tax in the initial period by an amount chosen to offset the fraction α ($0 \leq \alpha \leq 1$) of the additional payroll tax revenue, with no changes in either public consumption or government investment.

$$\alpha nLw\Delta t = -NLW\Delta T \tag{3.3}$$

We assume unified budget balance in all later periods. That is, we are assuming that the deviations from budget balance for the non-Social Security budget are $-\alpha$ times the deviations in the Social Security budget. The analysis would be different if the non-Social Security budget responded to the social security payroll tax revenue less benefit payments, thereby ignoring the interest on the trust fund. Initially this policy change decreases the debt held by the public by $(1-\alpha)$ times the increase in the trust fund. That is, G increases by α times the increase in F. The trust fund increases in the initial period by $nLw\Delta t$. Thereafter, neither the trust fund nor the debt held by the public make further changes.

With benefits and cohort size unchanged, the payroll tax rate can be reduced because of the interest on the increased revenue from the initial tax increase. Thus, the payroll tax rate after the initial period, t', satisfies

$$t' = t - r\Delta t \tag{3.4}$$

Similarly, the income tax rate thereafter, T', is increased to pay the increase in interest from the increase in the public debt

$$T' = T - r\Delta T = T + \alpha r \frac{nw}{NW} \Delta t \tag{3.5}$$

That is, there is an intertemporal trade between payroll taxpayers and income taxpayers, which is balanced in PDV. This also involves changes in the timing of tax payments by each agent and redistribution across cohorts of each type.

The central question is what happens to the time shape of national capital.

3.4.1 *National Savings in the Initial Period*

To analyze the impact of the changes in payroll and income taxes on national savings in the initial period, we can examine the changes in consumption of workers and savers. In the period of the initial tax change, the aggregate consumption of workers falls by their tax increase: $nLw\Delta t$. In all later periods, the aggregate consumption of workers is higher by $rnLw\Delta t$. This is equal to the return on the increase in the trust fund.[11] Thus, if the trust fund increase were fully an increase in national savings, there would be no impact on national savings after the initial period as the increase in consumption by workers would match the increase in national income. That is, national capital would increase in the initial period and remain at the higher level thereafter. This would be the case in this model if the government did not alter the income tax ($\alpha = 0$). But we have assumed that the income tax may change, so we must examine the response of savers to the income tax changes, which is more complicated.

The change in income tax in the initial period for a saver who is still working is $W\Delta T$, equal to $-\alpha nw\Delta t/N$. Thereafter there is a tax change of $-rW\Delta T$, equal to $\alpha rnw\Delta t/N$ in each of the remaining $L-z-1$ periods until retirement for a saver of age z in the initial period. In PDV terms, the tax change for an age z saver is $(\alpha nw\Delta t/N)(-1+r\sum_{s=z+1}^{L} R^{z-s})$. With a discount rate equal to the interest rate, each saver preserves equal consumption in each remaining period of life. With an unexpected change in taxes starting at age z, the change in consumption each remaining period of life that preserves equality of consumption for the rest of life is

$$\Delta C_z \sum_{s=z}^{D} R^{z-s} = (\alpha nw\Delta t/N)\left(1 - r \sum_{s=z+1}^{D} R^{z-s}\right) \tag{3.6}$$

The change in consumption in the initial period is less than the tax cut for two reasons—anticipation of future tax increases and the spreading of consumption over the rest of life.

Summing over working savers, we get an initial consumption increase for savers of

$$\Delta C = N\sum_{z=1}^{L}\Delta C_z = \alpha nw\Delta t\sum_{z=1}^{L}\frac{1-r\sum_{s=z+1}^{L}R^{z-s}}{\sum_{s=z}^{D}R^{z-s}} \tag{3.7}$$

The change in national savings, ΔNS, in the initial period is equal to minus the change in aggregate consumption:

$$\Delta NS = nw\Delta t\left(L-\alpha\sum_{z=1}^{L}\frac{1-r\sum_{s=z+1}^{L}R^{z-s}}{\sum_{s=z}^{D}R^{z-s}}\right)$$

$$= nw\Delta t\sum_{z=1}^{L}\left(1-\frac{\alpha}{\sum_{s=z}^{D}R^{z-s}}+\alpha r\frac{\sum_{s=z+1}^{L}R^{z-s}}{\sum_{s=z}^{D}R^{z-s}}\right)>0 \tag{3.8}$$

If savers were to consume all of their income tax cut in the initial period and the tax cut balanced the unified budget ($\alpha = 1$), there would be no increase in national savings. But they do not consume all of the income tax cut. They save part of their initial tax cut to finance later consumption and part of it to finance higher tax payments in their remaining working years. Thus national savings increase in the initial period even if $\alpha = 1$. Insofar as α is less than one, there is a further increase in savings in the initial period.

3.4.2 *National Capital in the Steady State*

In later years the pattern changes. Once the savers who received the initial tax cut have all died off, all savers have the same net earnings and so the same consumption and we are in a steady state. To examine the impact on steady-state capital, we can consider the impact on consumption since in a steady state with no growth, aggregate consumption equals aggregate output. With a linear technology, the change in output is equal to the interest rate times the change in capital. For convenience we now switch from discrete time to continuous time.

In aggregate, workers have consumption which is higher by the amount of their tax decrease: $rnLw\Delta t$. For savers we need to consider lifetime planning, which determines the constant level of consumption that they choose. We need to calculate how their consumption changes in response to an income tax rate increase of $\alpha rnLw\Delta t/NW$.

The lifetime budget constraint for a saver is

$$C'\int_0^D e^{-rs}ds = W(1-T')\int_0^L e^{-rs}ds \tag{3.9}$$

or

$$C' = W(1-T')\frac{1-e^{-rL}}{1-e^{-rD}} \tag{3.10}$$

The change in aggregate consumption by savers is $ND\Delta C'(=-W\Delta T'((1-e^{-rL})/(1-e^{-rD})))$, which equals $-D((1-e^{-rL})/(1-e^{-rD}))\alpha rnw\Delta t$.

Adding the two pieces, aggregate consumption changes by $rnLw\Delta t - D((1-e^{-rL})/(1-e^{-rD}))\alpha rnw\Delta t$, which equals $rnw\Delta t(L-\alpha D((1-e^{-rL})/(1-e^{-rD})))$. Thus aggregate capital changes by $nw\Delta t(\mathrm{L}-\alpha D((1-e^{-rL})/(1-e^{-rD})))$.

Note that if D were equal to L and α equal to 1, this expression would be zero. Moreover, the expression $D/(1-e^{-rD})$ is increasing in D, implying that the expression is everywhere negative for $\alpha = 1$ and $D > L$. Thus if $\alpha = 1$, capital is decreased in the steady state. The result follows from the same logic as above, run in reverse. Workers have lower taxes, all of which flows into higher consumption. Savers have higher taxes, but the induced consumption decrease is spread over their entire lives. With positive interest, there is a smaller consumption decrease for savers than the increase in consumption of workers.

Thus national capital increases in the steady state if $\alpha = 0$ and decreases in the steady state if $\alpha = 1$. For intermediate values of α we get an increase or decrease depending on whether α is below or above a critical value, denoted α^*. To find this critical value, we set the change in aggregate capital to zero:

$$\alpha^* = \frac{L(1-e^{-rD})}{D(1-e^{-rL})} \tag{3.11}$$

For example, with $L = 40$, $D = 60$, and $r = 0.03$, we have $\alpha^* = 0.8$. That is, long-run capital is increased if the income tax cut uses up no more than 80 percent of the revenue raised by the payroll tax increase.

3.5 Concluding Remarks

The distributions of income and social security taxes are very different. Assuming proportional cuts in income taxes in response to a surplus generated by the payroll tax, there are winners and losers from the two tax changes. Also, there are future winners and losers insofar as current tax changes result in future tax changes. It was convenient to model the economy with savers paying only the income tax and workers paying only the payroll tax. In order to interpret the results, we need to consider the net change in taxes for each group that comes about from the policy change. We have no simple way of distinguishing savers from workers, but approximating this by assuming that top quintile of individuals in terms of family income are savers and the rest are workers, roughly one-third of the payroll tax change can be modeled as above (see footnote 7).[12] For the other two-thirds, an offsetting income tax change results in no net effect.

In the formal model, legislated decisions about income taxes and expenditures are influenced by the deficit but not the level of debt. This simplification is missing an effect that is plausible (at least for high levels of debt) and has been found by Bohn (1998). While the debt level influences the deficit level through interest expenditures, it is plausible that there is also a direct influence. (Also missing in the model is any effect of debt levels on government interest rates.)

Given my view that very little of the Social Security surplus showed up in changes in the rest of the budget during the 1980s and 1990s, I think that most of the surplus has represented an increase in national savings. It is not clear what impact the surplus has had on the Bush tax cuts—the first was sold as not touching the Social Security surplus and the second happened despite touching the surplus. Taking a view that the political process was more responsive to this change in the unified budget balance than I believe to be the case, one still has a short run increase in savings, while in different years after the baby-boomers retire and the accumulated trust fund is used to help finance their benefits, there are increases and then decreases in capital.

The development of the OLG model and its application to analyzing social security represents an achievement of Paul Samuelson that will influence at least the next century.

Notes

1. Arrow wrote: "The analysis of concepts that lie so close to the roots of the social essence of humanity can never be definitive, but certainly the formulation of Bergson and Samuelson profoundly affected the direction of all future thinking, at least by economists." Page 15.
2. Musgrave wrote: "Never have three pages had so great an impact on the theory of public finance." Page 141.
3. Tobin wrote: "In this appreciation of Paul Samuelson as macroeconomist I shall concentrate on his contributions to the methodology and substance of macro-model building and to the positive and normative theory of stabilization, with emphasis on fiscal policy. This was Samuelson's own emphasis in his first twenty-five years, both in his pathbreaking early papers on multiplier statics and dynamics and in his crystallization of the neoclassical synthesis after the second world war." Page 191.
4. Samuelson's role in the revival and extension of Ramsey pricing was not so central, but that topic will last as long as there are linear taxes. And his analysis of tax deductibility of economic depreciation (1964) while a big help in my analysis of adjusting income taxes for inflation (1975), has not generated much response that I am aware of. And his introduction of the LeChatelier principle into economics (1947) helped my optimal tax paper with Mirrlees.
5. I ignore any possible impact on employer-provided pensions.
6. In 1995, the individuals and families in the top quintile of people in cash income have incomes above $71,510 (CBO, 1998). These are estimated to pay 71 percent of the individual income tax and 41 percent of social insurance taxes (Table 5). (They also pay 66 percent of the corporate income tax.) Social insurance taxes include the uncapped Medicare tax, and perhaps the unemployment insurance tax, as well as the capped Social Security tax. Ignoring unemployment insurance and using SSA data (2002) to convert the percentage of total payroll taxes into the percentage of Social Security payroll taxes (since almost all of Medicare taxes due to earnings above the Social Security taxable maximum of $61,200 are paid by the top quintile in cash incomes, we calculate as if all of it were), we estimate that those in the top quintile pay 37 percent of the relevant payroll tax. Thus approximately one-third of exactly offsetting income and payroll tax changes would be a redistribution between the top quintile and the other four quintiles.
7. For an interpretation of the historic record, see Diamond and Orszag (2004, pp. 47–54).
8. A longer working paper version of this paper includes examination of a temporary trust fund buildup, to follow more closely the plan for addressing the retirement of the baby-boomers.
9. Two-types models can have very different results than representative agent models. For example, see Diamond and Geanakoplos (2003) on diversifying Social Security assets and Saez (2000) on taxing interest income. The contrast

between types is stark and overstates the differences between them—many people doing little saving may have a small response to a tax change rather than zero and many people doing considerable savings may not be so responsive to future taxes as is assumed in the model.

10. Without this linearity assumption we would need to track the changes in wages and interest rates and their impact on taxes and savings.
11. The lack of growth of the labor force simplifies the calculation.
12. This assumes that the income tax change is proportional to average taxes.

References

Arrow, Kenneth. (1983). "Contributions to Welfare Economics," in E. Cary Brown and Robert M. Solow (eds), *Paul Samuelson and Modern Economic Theory*. New York: McGraw Hill. pp. 15–30.

Bohn, Henning. (1998). "The behavior of US Public Debt and Deficits?" unpublished.

Brown, E. Cary, and Robert M. Solow (eds) (1983). *Paul Samuelson and Modern Economic Theory*. New York: McGraw Hill.

Congressional Budget Office. (May 1998). "Estimates of federal tax liabilities for individuals and families by income category and family type for 1995 and 1999."

Diamond, Peter. "Inflation and the Comprehensive Tax Base," *Journal of Public Economics*, 4, 227–244, 1975; Correction 16, 129, 1981.

——. and John Geanakoplos. (2003). "Social security investment in equities," *American Economic Review*, 93(4), 1047–1074.

——. and James Mirrlees. "Optimal Taxation and the Le Chatelier Principle," unpublished.

——. and Peter R. Orszag. (2004). *Saving Social Security: A Balanced Approach*. Washington, D.C.: Brookings Institution Press.

Dynan, Karen E., Jonathan Skinner, and Stephen P. Zeldes. (2004). "Do the rich save more?" *Journal of Political Economy*, 112(2), 397–444.

Elmendorf, Douglas W. and Jeffrey B. Liebman. (2000). "Reform and National Saving in an Era of Budget Surpluses," *Brookings Papers on Economic Activity*, 2, 1–71.

Musgrave, Richard. (1983). "Public goods," in E. Cary Brown and Robert M. Solow (eds), *Paul Samuelson and Modern Economic Theory*. New York: McGraw Hill. pp. 139–156.

Saez, Emmanuel. (2002). "The desirability of commodity taxation under non-linear income taxation and heterogeneous tastes," *Journal of Public Economics*, 83, 217–230.

Samuelson, Paul. (1947). *Foundations of Economic Analysis*. Cambridge: Harvard University Press.

——. (1964). "Tax deductibility of economic depreciation to insure invariant valuations," *Journal of Political Economy*, 72(6), 604–606.

4

Prospective Shifts, Speculative Swings: "Macro" for the Twenty-First Century in the Tradition Championed by Paul Samuelson

Edmund S. Phelps

The markets have predicted nine of the last five recessions.

Paul A. Samuelson

In recent decades many of the best minds in macroeconomics have been dedicated to the development of dynamic, recursive models portraying the market economy as a stationary stochastic process in rational-expectations equilibrium. Prototype models include Lucas (1972) and Lucas and Prescott (1971, 1974). Such is the influence of these powerful models that central bankers boast that their monetary policies incorporate the considerations highlighted by these models. I myself, in close or loose collaboration with Columbia colleagues, injected staggered wages and staggered markups into just such models.[1] The pride and enthusiasm the innovators and developers take in this project is understandable. I for one place some heuristic value in these models for some purposes, so I have no intention to dismiss them. Yet some of us dissent from those who say that with the perfection of these models the task of macroeconomics is becoming fully achieved. Paul Samuelson's is a long dissenting voice, as I will document below.

Models I built in the 1960s introduced "expectations" about the current or incipient general wage level as a determinant of current or incipient employment or, if it could not jump, its rate of change.[2] The models implied that the unemployment rate would never stay far from some medium-term "natural rate" determined by nonmonetary mechanisms and forces, since wage expectations begin adjusting to a large and long-lived error. In the back of my mind, the demand increase under study was caused by some discrete and idiosyncratic event of a permanent nature; for example, the demand for money was shifted down by some innovation in banking that initially was not widely understood. After the event and its impacts, wage-level expectations (and thus the wage level itself) did not react by enough immediately to drive the true "expected value" of employment to its natural level since there was no knowledge of the event's permanence.[3] There was no "class" of disturbances in which the event could be placed about which there was statistical knowledge.[4]

The rational-expectations revolution utterly transformed these expectational models. Abstracting from imperfect knowledge about the economy's structure and the structure's shifts, it took the expectational setup but equated expectations of wages (and prices) to expected values. "Macro" became the study of the vibrations (to use Robert Hall's coinage) of a statistical equilibrium induced by stochastic "shocks" of known statistical properties and of a stationary sort. The idiosyncratic forces that in 1960s thinking were behind large demand changes were replaced by a random disturbance term that is the sum of myriad small and independent forces. But the loss of historical concreteness is not the main cost of the revolution. If it were it might well be regarded as offset by the benefit of the findings generated.[5]

There are two difficulties with rational expectations. One is that, even on favorable terrain, rational expectations lack microfoundations. The meaning of rational expectations goes far beyond correct expectations in a still, tranquil setting: it means correct expectations in every state of the economy that turns up. So an economy's ability to acquire rational expectations must be demonstrated. Unfortunately, there seem to be obstacles to actors' convergence to a model's rational-expectations solution in stationary stochastic settings.[6]

The trouble with rational expectations that this chapter addresses is that they cannot be applied to the expectations that are at the core of enterprise economies: the fresh visions and fears that entrepreneurs and financiers have about the evolving future—novel forces in the future and factors affecting the future consequences of innovative actions in the present. (The visions and fears of future entrepreneurs and financiers are also absent.) The attractiveness of the dynamic recursive RE—of restricting attention to objective and observable forces, which rational might imaginably apply to—led the model builders to turn their backs to a whole category of forces to which rational expectations would not appear to apply.[7] This shortcoming deprives recursive dynamic models from giving any meaningful explanation of the big swings of economic history.

Excluding expectations about the future has operated to reorient macroeconomics 180 degrees from what it had been over most of the twentieth century. From Spiethoff and Cassel to Schumpeter, Knight, and Keynes and on to Samuelson, the major figures in macroeconomics all thought that the big business swings were triggered by new expectations by entrepreneurs about the future profits to be earned from new investments. This orientation had been inspired by studies of the German School connecting surges in investment activity to commercial prospects opened up by technological and navigational discoveries.

Paul Samuelson almost single-handedly synthesized and transmitted to the next generation this macroeconomics tradition in all its breadth. The first tenet of these figures from Spiethoff onward was a lesson that Samuelson never tired of emphasizing—the centrality of the future. The importance of the future was driven home for me when I was a young student, as it doubtless was for many other readers, by Samuelson (1948) with one of those lyrical images he so often summoned up in making a major point: "An outside observer would be struck with the fact that . . . almost everyone is doing work of a preparatory nature, with final consumption a distant goal." (Samuelson, 1958, p. 46.) If expectations about the future drive the directions of economic activity, which was Samuelson's context, it is hardly surprising that they also drive the level of activity, as Cassel and Keynes argued in their different models, the one nonmonetary, the other monetary.[8]

The next tenet of this macroeconomics tradition that Samuelson passed down is that future developments are subject to radical uncertainty, which was basic to the thinking of Knight and Keynes. Samuelson as an undergraduate at the University of Chicago had the opportunity to learn about Knightian uncertainty from Knight himself. In a meditation on the problem of inference in a changing world (1963), Samuelson does not presuppose that the current structure of equations describing the system is a known structure; it is unknown and the problem of the economic actors is to decide how much weight to give new evidence in revising their guesses or estimates of the structure.

Samuelson added that, as he saw it, the probabiltity distributions of the basic forces driving the economy are nonstationary, contrary to the rational expectations models. Of course, the presence of nonstationarity, such as random walk behavior, must further limit the possibilities of forecasting and further widen the errors from using the past to forecast the future.

Owing to this complex of factors, Samuelson concluded, market expectations about whole *classes* of prices and earnings, namely, asset prices in the future and thus asset prices in the present and earnings in the future, cannot be supposed to predicted by some model's rational expectations, since they are not predictable. Although Samuelson was a pioneer of rational expectations theory and appreciated the rational calculation that went into the relative price of, say, Oracle shares relative to the price of SAP shares or IBM shares, he did not regard the broad market indexes of share prices as an outcome of rational expectations (Samuelson, 1998). Samuelson's famous quip that "the markets have predicted nine of the last five recessions" could be interpreted to mean simply that the stock market is a sideshow without consequences for investment and employment activity. But it can just as well be interpreted to mean primarily that markets are skittish and take fright more often than they would under rational expectations, if such foresight were possible.

Thus Samuelson for decades virtually stood alone preserving and illuminating the perspective that the rational-expectations movement excluded.

The consequences of this exclusion have been striking. Real business cycle theory has not illuminated the US boom in the late 1920s, the record-length Great Depression in the United States in the 1930s, the gathering slump in the United States in the 1970s, Europe's deep slump in the 1980s, the still high unemployment on the Continent, and the investment boom in several economies in the late 1990s.[9] In contrast, models oriented to prospects of future parameter shifts have been able to make some sense of the 1920s boom in share prices, investment and employment in the United States, the huge swelling of unemployment in Europe and Japan from the mid-1970s well into the 1980s, and the great investment boom in the second half of the 1990s in several economies.

Some recent papers of mine are all about a category of influences on economic activity that might be called *future prospects*.[10] In this view, at any moment there may occur a *new* future prospect—either a qualitatively new development or a purely quantitative change in some future prospect. This concept is not exactly the "animal spirits" in Keynes (1936). A "prospect" will refer to *expectations* of some *future event*, or *state*, and "prospects" will refer to the set of such future events or states. In general, a prospect has an influence—the more so the less uncertain it is—on the willingness of existing firms and start-up firms to invest and the willingness of investment bankers and the stock market to finance them; thus a prospect or a change in its uncertainty may lift or depress business "spirits." (Possibly Keynes thought such "spirits" depended on so many prospective future events and states that it would be unworkable to hope to solve for spirits as a function of prospects.) Neither does attention to future prospects mean a return to the "optimism" and "pessimism" dwelled on by A. C. Pigou (1927, Chap. VII). His thesis was that the response of investments to a class of future prospects exceeded what "rational" calculation would suggest ("errors in optimism"). The recent papers I cited analyze the effects of future prospects that it is "rational" for investments of various kinds to respond to.

Part I below takes up three future events and shows that, in the model used, the prospect of each has an impact through the capital market channel on the course of economic activity. In each case I point to *topical* or *historical* evidence bearing out such an impact on economic activity. Part II looks at share prices as a proxy for the shadow values of the business assets to get a sense of the *statistical* importance of future prospects in general—of speculation about the future—relative to the importance of unexpected developments actually observed, that is, shocks. Part III concludes that considering future prospects helps us to understand the big swings noted above. It also suggests that uncertainty about future prospects strengthens the modernist views that wage and price levels are not correctly forecast.

Let me remark here that much of the analysis below is devoted to the benchmark case in which, when the new expectations about the future arrive, the economy's participants are supposed to work out the correct-expectations path to that new future—as if they possessed rational expectations over the rest of the future. In that respect the analysis resembles rational-expectations methodology. But in other respects it is different. The new expectations are not a regime—one of many regimes that are already incorporated into some grand model and have known probabilities of switching on and switching off. In general, the new expectations refer to a future that has never been imagined before. The picture is one of an open system of ever richer possibilities rather than the closed system of rational-expectations equilibrium.

4.1 Future "Debt Bombs," Productivity Surges and Wars

In the category of future prospects perhaps the oldest topic among economists is the prospect—for simplicity, the newly arisen prospect—of a delayed-fuse "debt bomb," as I have dubbed it—a "time bomb" of exploding public debt, such as the present enactment of a tax cut to become effective at a future date and with a sunset provision soon thereafter. (Thus there is some small interval over which there is a big government deficit.) Another topic in this category is the sudden expectation of a future step-increase in productivity at some specific date. A third topic, which I bring up here, is the expectation of the start of a war or of the end of a war. Maybe a terrorist attack would be a more modern interpretation. In all these cases I will discuss—very informally—some piece of historical evidence.

I will *not* allow for differences of opinion about the size or the timing of the prospective events; where a probability is introduced, it is a subjective probability held by all. This restriction may block dynamics of interest in some cases.[11] Yet it does sometimes happen that a conventional view is virtually universal.

4.1.1 Future "Debt Bombs" and Pension Overhang

The literature on the present expectation of a future fiscal shock goes back quite far. In the 1980s Keynesian treatments were offered by Olivier Blanchard (1981) and William Branson (1986). They obtain the proposition that enactment of an explosion of transfer payments or of temporary tax cuts in the neighborhood of some future date $t1$ may be a depressant for real asset prices at that time and, if so, the public's grasp of that prospect will have repercussions for the level of real asset prices in the present. However, the proposition undoubtedly antedates Keynesian modeling. And since many "future shocks" are several years off, few readers can be satisfied with an argument resting on the money wage/price stickiness of a Keynesian model.[12] A few years ago, however, Hian Teck Hoon and Phelps (2001) extended a structuralist model of the closed economy model, this one with a customer market, to show that the sudden prospect of a temporary future tax cut or temporary future transfer payment, if built at once into the expectations of firms, causes immediately—thus, ahead of the event—an anticipatory drop in the shadow price they attach to a unit of the business asset—with contractionary consequences for employment.

It will be easier to argue such a proposition from a structuralist model that is less rich, namely, the *turnover-training model* (Hoon and Phelps, 1992). Take the closed economy case. The increase in the public debt around some future date $t1$ can be seen to have two contemporary effects: first, to rebalance the budget after the splash of debt issues, it will then be necessary to service the increased debt by an increase in tax rates: either tax rates on *wage income*, which will have deleterious effects on employees' quit rates and thus raise business costs, or on business income, which will directly reduce after-tax profits; second, it will force an elevation of real interest rates at that time, provided we exclude the Ricardo–Ramsey–Barro case where government debt is not net wealth. Both of these impacts will cause the shadow price of the business asset—the shadow price of an extra job-ready employee—to be lower at that time and beyond than it otherwise would have been, evaluated at the original, or reference, level of employment. By a standard inductive argument it follows that the shadow price at the present moment *t*0 is also depressed below what it was; in fact, we do not need such an inductive argument, since the integral giving the present shadow price involves increased interest rates after *t*1 and decreased gross profits (or quasi-rents) after *t*1, so the impact on the value of the integral from *t*0 is unambiguously negative.

A beautiful observation by Hian Teck is that the short-term real interest rate will actually drop at *t*0, since consumption will jump up and thereupon be steadily falling, thus possibly causing the long real rate of interest required by savers to decrease at first before rising toward its elevated future level. Hence, the argument of skeptics that the specter of bulging future deficits cannot be contractionary, otherwise we would observe an elevation of real interest rates, is unsatisfactory because, theoretically, the contractionary effect does not imply and does not require any such elevation of interest rates—only a drop in the shadow value attached to the business asset.

In the small *open-economy* version of the turnover-training model, in which output is sold at unchanging terms in the world product market, the public debt's net wealth impact on *future real interest rates* will not be operative, since domestic interest rates are given by overseas real interest rates, which the country is too small to affect. Yet the increase in public debt at *t*1, most clearly if it results from a tax cut on wage incomes, has the effect of making workers richer (at the expense of future generations of tax payers). And this extra net wealth may increase employment costs by worsening employees' quit rates, shirking and unreliability.[13]

Some cross-section evidence. There is evidence of the empirical significance of such future fiscal prospects for the present level of economic activity. Investors in many countries have come to recognize a huge looming overhang of pension liabilities in relation to present projections of GDP and tax revenues, owing either to the government's having overestimated the growth of tax revenue when they were setting benefit levels or to having shrunk from raising tax rates by the amount that was necessary for intertemporal budget balance in view of the bulge of baby boomers soon to retire. Allison Schrager, a doctoral candidate at Columbia, has regressed the average price-dividend ratio (and soon the price-earnings ratio) on the projected pension benefits to GDP ratio alongside standard explanatory variables for a cross-section of OECD economies. The results show a statistically significant coefficient of the right (negative) sign on the pension variable. If right, the result means that prospect of delayed increases in public debt and of paper wealth from pension entitlements do indeed impact the capital market, just as the theory implies. There is also ample evidence that a decrease of share prices has, in turn, contractionary consequences for the level of economic activity as measured by unemployment and participation rates.

4.1.2 Future Productivity Surges

To analyze the sudden expectation of a future step-increase, or lift, to productivity, we can revert to the turnover-training model, which is so convenient. A simple analysis is provided in two recent papers (Fitoussi *et al.*, 2000; Phelps and Zoega, 2001).[14] The basic proposition there is illustrated by a phase diagram. Here I have simplified the model further by replacing the premise of rising marginal hiring costs with the premise of constant hiring costs. As a result the locus of points at which the stock of employees is constant at a firm is horizontal. (If employment is increased, the quit rate is increased as a result, with the consequence that there must be an equal increase in the hire rate; but since the derivative of the hire rate with respect to the shadow price of the employee is infinite in the constant-costs case, no increase in the shadow price is required to maintain a steady state at the increased employment level.) The phase diagram in Figure 4.1 shows that the shadow price jumps up, causing employment to grow until *t*1, at which point the path of the system must have just reached the new saddle path; from that point, the system follows the new saddle path, proceeding toward the new rest point. The equations of the dynamic system are in the aforementioned papers.

To gain the essential insight, we need only consider an integral expression giving the value of the shadow price at the present time, *t*0. The step-increase in the prospective future rents on the business asset—the employees—unambiguously increases the value of the integral, evaluated at the initial employment path. And, again, any such increase in the shadow price of the employee, unaccompanied by any increase in the opportunity cost of training additional employees, unambiguously stimulates a sharp increase in hiring, which pulls up employment.

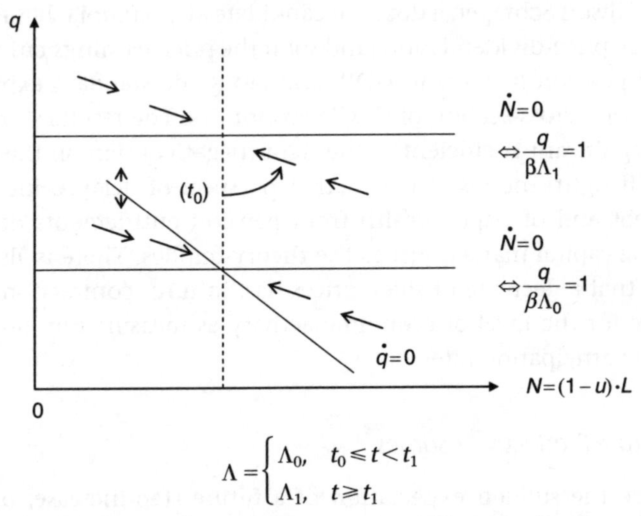

$$\Lambda = \begin{cases} \Lambda_0, & t_0 \leqslant t < t_1 \\ \Lambda_1, & t \geqslant t_1 \end{cases}$$

Figure 4.1 Anticipatory effects of the prospect and the realization of a future step-increase of total factor productivity

Some historical evidence. How can we adduce evidence that the investment boom of the late 1990s in the US economy and several others did rest, at least to an important degree, on newfound expectations of a lift to productivity on the horizon? And, similarly, how can we test the thought that the great investment boom of the 1920s was likewise driven by expectations of rapid productivity growth over the future? Perhaps we can never obtain strong enough evidence to satisfy all skeptics. However, for me at any rate, it is important circumstantial evidence supporting that interpretation of the 1990s boom that productivity growth has in fact been startlingly rapid in the four years beginning in 2000 and appears to be slowing down only very gradually. With productivity growth so rapid in those years, it is easy for me to believe that many managers in industry had information in the second half of the 1990s leading them to expect a very substantial lift to productivity and hence to investment returns in the next several years.

Now consider the 1920s boom. The parallels of that boom with the 1990s boom have led several of us to dig out the Kendrick data on productivity growth in that bygone era. I was stunned to see in Commerce Department's *Long Term Economic Growth 1860–1965* that productivity lifted off like a rocket during the 1930s.[15] Alex Field's calculation in a paper a few months later showed that growth rates of total factor productivity were unprecedented between 1929 and 1941.

I alluded to the productivity gains in the 1930s and, to date, in the 2000s in a couple of pieces in the financial press where I argued that Alan Greenspan was mistaken to think that the recent spate of productivity gains translates into high employment: if the productivity gains were already anticipated in the mid- and late 1990s and were precisely the inspiration for the wave of new investments at that time, then the realization of these gains will not occasion another wave of investment; the realized gains are "how booms end, not how they begin."[16] Employment as a ratio to active-age population in this decade too is still a bit subdued, though it has recovered most of the lost ground by now. The question, now resolved, was only whether other forces may stall that march back to full normalcy, as happened in 1937–38 when the clouds of war derailed the recovery, leaving employment depressed for the rest of the decade.

4.1.3 War Prospects

The essence of my thesis is as follows. At the present time, the value, to be denoted $q(0)$, that a firm's manager would put on having an additional functioning employee is a probability mixture of the value of that employee in the scenario in which war breaks out, weighted by the subjective probability of war, π, and the value in the scenario in which war does not break out, weighted by the probability the war does not break out, $1 - \pi$. The war scenario gives a lower value, since the manager anticipates that there will be an increased tax burden on the firm's profits or sales or both in the event of the war. The conclusion that can be deduced is that any *small increase* in the subjective probability of war *lowers* the value of the probability mixture—the so called "expected value" of the two integrals (the one the no-war integral, the other the war integral). The argument for that conclusion involves the point that the firm's reactions in the event of war do not have to be factored into the result, since small adjustments by the firm in its hiring rate will not have a first-order effect on the value of the integral, the hiring rates having been in the neighborhood of their q-maximizing levels to begin with.

Another proposition that is obvious at least to economists is that, with the passage of time, the date at which the war is feared to break out draws *nearer*—unless $t1$ is pushed back one day (or more!) for every day that goes by after $t0$. So the present discounted value of having an extra employee, which means discounting back to the current time t, not to the initial time, $t0$, is *falling*, since the *losses from the war* in the event it occurs are getting nearer, hence *discounted less heavily*.

Once a war has broken out, the passage of time is the firm's friend: The date at which the war is hoped to *end* draws nearer unless that date, *t*2, say, is pushed back one day or more for every day that the war goes on after *t*1. Here the *gains* from the war's end are being discounted less heavily as the end of the war nears.

Some evidence. If I am not mistaken, then, this analysis leads to the proposition that the prospect of war ahead causes a drop in the shadow prices put on business assets. In almost any theory, there will be, in reflection of that drop, a sympathetic drop in share prices too. And if, during a war, the prospective time left to go before the war's end keeps shrinking as expected or even faster than expected, these shadow prices—and share prices too—will tend to be recovering. Is this what happens, at least in normal cases? Certainly the evidence in the years leading up to the Second World War bear out this story. Painting with a broad brush, I would say, going largely by my recollection of the data, that share prices fell and fixed investment expenditures as a share of GDP fell in the United States from 1937 to 1941. The same was true, I remember from a look at the data years ago, in the Netherlands over the late 1930s. Then, during the war years 1942–45, the stock market in the United States was strongly rising—in a recovery mode.

I would add that the real prices of shares did not recover fully to their lofty levels of 1936 and 1937 for quite some time—not until the last years of the 1960s, if I remember correctly. I would say by way of explanation—entirely in the spirit of my thesis that future prospects are important—that the cloud of the cold war came over the US economy by 1948, blocking any chance of a full recovery. With the Korean War of the early 1950s this tension broke out into open conflict.

4.1.4 Drawing Conclusions

If these future prospects and possibly others not treated here are empirically important, we can conclude that real-life economies with an active commercial character are almost *never* "vibrating" up and down their saddle path. They are almost always *off* their saddle path. Somewhat surprisingly, the trajectory of shadow value of the employee in the above model jumps off the saddle path in spite of the simplifying postulate of constant (rather than increasing) marginal hiring costs.

The pressing question now is whether changes in future prospects are pronounced enough from one year to the next or from one decade or era to the next to generate a generally important—and typically fluctuating—discrepancy from the saddle path. I would like in the second part of this chapter to tackle that question.

4.2 Evidence of the Mutability of Future Prospects

A long-time theme of mine regarding fluctuations is that most of the national economies of the past few centuries are *mutable*—especially the more capitalist economies and those highly interdependent with the capitalist world.[17] I mean that a capitalist economy is always changing qualitatively and often lastingly. So the description of a theoretical economy given by a stochastic steady-state model does not really fit this sort of economy. Maybe some macrostatistics will pass some tests for stationarity but, if so, that may indicate only that it takes a few decades for an economy to transform itself; it doesn't mean that we can use a model estimated on nineteenth century data to obtain the best possible prediction of, say, the rate of technical progress or the long-term natural unemployment rate. Although some of these "parameters" appear to be trendless, they also appear to be capable of shifting perceptibly from one half-century to another. Some theorists speak of regime change or model change, but why not admit that the regime is always evolving, sometimes abruptly, and the model with it? I have to add that I am not exactly sure what it means to speak of the best possible, or true, prediction or the expected value of these things: using what model?

As Part I showed, the shadow value of the business asset is capable of jumping off the saddle path; in fact, the shadow value may never be on the saddle path for a single day of its life except to pass through to the other side on some occasions. (This is true even though I posited constant costs of hiring.) But how much do these shadow prices move in fact? And do their movements, such as they are, match up with shifts (surges) and swings in investment activities of the various kinds—hiring, customer chasing (advertising, cutting markups), plant and office construction, etc.?

4.2.1 Inferential Movements in the Shadow Values

Hian Teck Hoon came across a paper by Casey Mulligan (2002) that examines the part played by public finance distortion in the swings in the American labor supply over the period 1889–1996. For his neoclassical model Mulligan adopts the neoclassical model of labor-leisure choice, with its condition, $\text{MRS}(C, \overline{L} - L) = v^h$, where the MRS function gives the marginal rate of substitution (MRS) between consumption and work, or "marginal value of time" in terms of the final good, and is increasing in current consumption C and in hours worked L, hence decreasing in leisure; the right-hand side variable, ν^h, is the after-tax hourly wage rate. The latter is related to the firms' demand wage ν^f and to the proportional tax rate τ on after-tax wage income by $\nu^h \equiv (1 + \tau)^{-1}\nu^f$. Invoking pure competition, he equates ν^f to the marginal product of labor, MPL. The result is $(C, \bar{L} - L) = (1 + \tau)^{-1}$ MPL. The implication is that an increase of τ, in decreasing the right-hand side, operates to decrease hours, given consumption and the value of MPL. Mulligan argues from his empirical exercise that marginal tax rates are well correlated with labor–leisure distortions at low frequencies, but they cannot explain the distortions during the Great Depression, the Second World War and the 1980s: the decade-to-decade fluctuations in consumption, wages, and labor supply do not jibe very well with this competitive equilibrium model.

From the perspective of my structuralist models, the difficulty with this competitive-equilibrium theory—adopted wholesale by the real-business-cycle school in the 1980s—is that it lacks business assets and the possibility of corresponding fluctuations in the shadow values attaching to those assets; as a result, the model is hopelessly myopic. Hian Teck, viewing the matter accordingly, reasoned that to understand the depth of the downturn in the 1930s it might be of crucial help to introduce such shadow prices. From customer market theory, Hian Teck derived a contrasting employment equation: In the Phelps-Winter model, a firm generally profits from the sluggishness of information, for it can "mark up" its price above marginal cost without at once losing all its customers; this transient monopoly power gives value to its current stock of customers. Let m denote the markup $(P - \mathrm{MC})/P$, where P is price and MC is marginal cost. Then it is straightforward to deduce that $1 + m \equiv \Psi$, where the function Ψ makes m inversely related to $\tilde{q}$, the shadow price that firms attach to a customer when taken as a *ratio* to how much output a customer has to be supplied. (That ratio is fully analogous to Tobin's Q ratio.) In this model, the labor-market relation becomes $\mathrm{MRS}(C, \bar{L} - L) = (1 + \tau)^{-1} [\Psi(\tilde{q})]^{-1}$ MPL. If we substitute for MPL the parameter $\wedge$ and, in the closed economy case, substitute $\wedge L$ for C in MRS, then L is fully determined. An increase of $\tilde{q}$ pulls up the right-hand side (i.e. it increases the ν^h that firms are willing to offer); since $\mathrm{MRS}(\wedge L, \bar{L} - L)$ is doubly increasing in L, that induces an increase in hours supplied. Thus the *markup* wedge between net pay and labor's marginal value productivity joins the *tax* wedge as a potential factor in the determination of the equilibrium (i.e. correct-expectations) path of employment, here average hours. Sometimes both are needed in an analysis since they move in opposite directions, so the one helps to escape from the other.

My point here, after that lengthy exposition, is that we can *infer* what the 1930s shadow price of customers must have dropped to from the 1920s by solving for the $\tilde{q}$ ratio that solves the equation, given the data and given our "knowledge" of the functions appearing in the equations. We can do that for each decade of the past century, thus obtaining a century of inferred $\tilde{q}$ ratios attaching to the business asset we call the customer.

To do the same with the turnover-training model we can use the equation giving the incentive wage as a function of the unemployment rate and the shadow price of the functioning employee to solve for the shadow price that delivers the correct wage rate, taking account of tax rates. Thus we could calculate decadal levels of the shadow value of the employee.

Since these shadow values of the various business assets have a lot of work to do to reconcile the equation with the observed employment levels in the 1930s, the Second World War years (1941–45) and the 1980s, one can presume that the required shadow values will exhibit quite a lot of fluctuation from decade to decade. This is one piece of circumstantial evidence for believing that future prospects are important. It suggests that, over the past century, the world real interest rate, trend growth rates of national productivity and tax rates have not shown enough variation to be able by themselves to push the shadow values enough to explain the huge swings of the 1930s, the war years, and the 1980s.

4.2.2 What do Share Price Time Series Say?

To obtain another somewhat indirect view of the movements of the shadow prices of business assets, we might do well to examine the time series of stock-price indexes, such as the Standard and Poor 500 index (and its predecessors).

We would like to find evidence that would help to establish (or to dis-establish, as you like) the proposition that share prices are driven by subject understandings of future prospects to an important degree, not just by unexpected developments in the situation and performance of the economy. How to do that? To do that we need to distinguish the actual change of the share price level from the change that was previously expected; then we have to decompose this into the component attributable to surprises in observable things and the component presumably reflecting unanticipated revisions, based possibly on reappraisals of existing information or surprising new information, of the economy's future prospects. The dichotomy is between the unexpected changes in observed levels of present variables and the unexpected changes in the forecast future.

To this end, let R*x* denote the logarithmic rate of change of any variable *x*; and let *F* (*y*) denote the expected, or forecast, value of any variable *y*. In this notation, the familiar Fisher equation applied to the expected proportionate rate of change of the real share price is

$$F(R(p)) = [F(r) - d/p] \tag{4.1}$$

where *p* denotes the real share-price level, *r* is the short-term real rate of interest and *d*/*p* is the dividend per share as a ratio to price per share (hereafter, the dividend-price ratio). The utility of this equation lies in its implication that the right-hand side can serve as a proxy for what is not directly measurable, namely the expected algebraic real capital gain.

If we subtract the *actual* R(*p*) from both sides, add to and subtract from the right-hand side the current growth rate of real earnings per share, *R*(*e*), and multiply both sides by minus one we get

$$R(p) - F(R(p)) = d/p + R(e) - F(r) + [R(p) - R(e)]. \tag{4.2}$$

This equation is reminiscent of the thesis of John Bogle (2000) that there were in the history of the US stock market a *few* decades in which the dividend yield plus the growth rate of real earnings per share, $d/p + R(e)$, thus the rate of return that would have been earned on stocks if the price-earnings ratio had not changed—neglecting F(*r*), the right-side of (4.2) if the bracketed expression were zero—was less than the rate of return from the rise of the price-earnings ratio, $R(p) - R(e)$. The 1950s were one such decade, Bogle observes. But there were not many.[18]

For our purposes we want to look not at the returns to shares but rather at the real *price* of shares as a ratio to, say, GDP per share, since that can serve as a crude proxy for the shadow price of the business asset as a ratio to the asset's productivity and this cousin of the "Tobin Q ratio" is a key determinant of the current investment expenditure on the asset. If for the sake of exploration we take that ratio to be proxied satisfactorily by the price-earnings ratio, that approach can be investigated by going back to equation (4.1) and rewriting it to derive

$$R(p) - R(e) = [F(r) - d/p - R(e)] + R(p) - F(R(p)). \qquad (4.3)$$

This equation decomposes the *growth rate* of the price-earnings ratio into two components, the explained part and the unexplained part—the latter being the unexplained portion of the growth rate of share prices. The former component, in square brackets, is the *expected* growth rate of real share prices, as stated in (4.1), *net* of the growth rate of real earnings per share. That component is in a sense the *explicable* portion, or—better perhaps—the *determinable* portion, of the growth rate of the price-earnings ratio, since the expected growth rate of share prices is theoretically given by the observed excess of interest rate over observed dividend yield. The lower is the ratio of dividend to price or the higher the expected real interest rate, the higher the expected growth rate of the real share is implied to be. The second component is just the residual portion of the growth rate of real share prices, which is given by the last two terms. (Capital gains on shares based on the *nearing* of unchanging expected future events are theoretically reflected in the first two terms. Unexpected growth in *earnings*, other things equal, also cause unexpected growth in the share price but not unexpected growth of the price-earnings ratio.) This residual component is, in the same sense, the *inexplicable*, or *undeterminable*, part of the growth rate of the price-earnings ratio. As should be clear, the framework here portrays this latter component as driven by *changes* in *future prospects*. It could therefore also be dubbed the *speculative* component of the change in the price-earnings ratio. This part of the change in the price-earning ratio the outsider-modeler and outsider-analyst would have no clue about, especially if future prospects are multidimensional, even infinite-dimensional.

The attached Figure 4.2 plots separately the two components, using 5-year backward growth rates and representing the expected real interest rate by the actual real rate, over the period 1920–2000. It is clear that the residual, which I interpret as speculative, is large, especially in some epochs, for example, the early part of the gathering boom in the second half of the 1990s. That suggests that changes in the future prospect, though heretofore neglected, are indeed a powerful cyclic force driving employment swings.

I would remark that the theory sketched here offers no theoretical reason to believe that the *speculative*, or undeterminable, component, which is the excess of the *actual* over the *expected* growth rate of real share

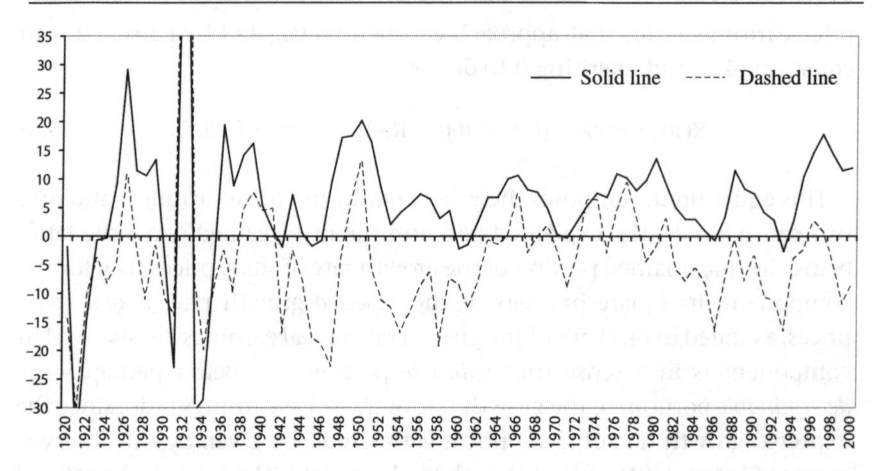

Figure 4.2 The 5-year growth rate of the average price-earnings ratio of standard and poor 500 stocks (solid line) and the part explained by the excess of the real interest rate over the expected growth rate of the average share price net of the average growth rate of earnings per share (dashed line), yearly, 1920–2000.

prices, is the *more* powerful influence on the actual growth rate of the price-earnings ratio and thus of the improvement ahead in business activity. (Theoretically the ups and downs of real interest rates and of the underlying determinants of dividends per share could be the more important force.) It does appear, though, that the episodes of rapid expansion—the last half of the 1920s, the years 1934–37, the early 1950s and the latter half of the 1990s—were more strongly associated with a rise of the *speculative* component (i.e. the difference between the total, charted by the solid line, and the determinate part, charted by the dashed line) than with the determinate component. However, this question is not crucial. It is enough to show that the speculative component is an important driver of the price-earnings ratio, thus of Tobin's Q, and hence investment activity and "natural" employment.

4.3 Concluding Remarks

My thesis here is that macroeconomics will flourish in the twenty-first century—it will capture the causes and mechanisms of the big swings in growth and in economic activity—only if it returns to the grand tradition championed by Samuelson. That means, to begin with, the introduction of future prospects into our macro models. Investment, growth, and the (current) natural level of employment are *conditional* on expectations about the future. Incorporating that into our thinking is crucial for our theory of how the economy works, the economic history we write, and the policy advice we give.

At the level of theory, the level of activity is *always* being driven—up or down—by the prospects for the future *in the minds* of entrepreneurs, financiers and holders of stocks. The logic of these propositions is straightforward. In the structuralist models I have been using, firms' rates of investment in employees, customers, plant, and office space are a key force determining the course of economic activity, as measured by employment and unemployment. And future prospects are a driver of these investment decisions. In the models here, which abstract from nontradeable physical capital, Tobin's Q is driven by the *expected* future productivity developments, by *expected* future fiscal burdens (and expected future immigration helping to deal with them), and *expectations* about peace in the future; "shocks" affecting *actual* productivity, foreign labor and perhaps actual peace may make little difference and are, in any case, a different story.

The revival of the grand tradition also means the recognition in our models of Knightian uncertainty and the complications that follow from it. Fellner had the idea that uncertainty operates to scale down the probabilities that decision makers attach to the contingencies they know about in recognition of what they know they do not know. Where there is uncertainty there is also the possibility of speculative gyrations. Frydman and Goldberg (2003) have delved into the mechanism of overshooting so common in stock markets and foreign exchange markets.

To conclude: Until macroeconomics opens up to the study of economies driven by new conceptions, new visions, new fears—mostly about the future—and comes to grips with the attending uncertainty our macroeconomic models will not fit very well the world we live in. There will always tend to be individuals willing to step out of the tightly closed models and fashion special-purpose models with which to address current questions about the future. These efforts will go better, though, if a range of future prospects become a normal part of standard models. The big opportunity for progress in macroeconomics now appears to be in that direction.

Notes

1. See Phelps and Taylor (1977), Phelps (1978), Taylor (1979), and Calvo (1983).
2. Phelps (1968, 1969, 1970).

3. As I saw later, such equilibrium expectations would also have required participants to understand that the inferences drawn by others were the same as their own (Phelps, 1983; Woodford, 2003).
4. It was not dreamt of in my philosophy that every event, once the news was out, could be classified as being of one or another type, each of which had a known probability of terminating.
5. In any model-theoretic analysis of a macro question, the *equilibrium* case is an indispensable benchmark, even if nonequilibrium effects seriously alter the equilibrium ones.
6. See Frydman (1982) and Frydman and Phelps (1983).
7. The reason, I suspect, was that while it proved attractive to impute known statistical properties to a visible force that is already upon the economy, it would have put in question the plausibility of the whole rational-expectations project to impute known statistical properties to the entire panoply of uncertain future prospects that entrepreneurs and speculators entertain or invent.
8. My book *Structural Slumps* presents models forging a link between expectations of the future, which influence the expectational shadow value per unit placed on each business asset and the path of the natural unemployment rate. Samuelson in his ninetieth birthday dinner speech recalls studying Gustav Cassel in his first economics course at the University of Chicago.
9. Eclectics who tried to apply these models were driven to supplement them with generally underdeveloped arguments about oil prices in the 1970s, exchange rates in the 1980s, and productivity growth in the 1990s. But without attention to shifts in the climate of future expectations, they were unable to get very far.
10. Fitoussi *et al.* (2000); Phelps and Zoega (2001); Hoon and Phelps (2001, 2004)
11. See Phelps (1983). Roman Frydman and Michael Goldberg in some of their works have modeled an economy containing "bulls" and "bears."
12. It would be bizarre to apply Keynesian analysis to the pension benefit explosion centered around 2015. Furthermore, as I showed in a talk given in the 1980s at Queens University, Kingston, even when the future prospect is only several years away, if the economy can be projected to reach its medium-run natural rate in a prior year, the present expectation of fiscal stimulus *after* that year cannot cause a recession below the natural level *before* that year.
13. There is another open-economy model in the structuralist family, one based on customer markets at home and abroad (Hoon and Phelps, 2004). Thanks to these customer markets and the non-Ricardian property that public debt is net wealth, the future step-increase of public debt causes domestic real interest rates to be elevated at that time, which crowds out overseas or domestic customers. As a result, customers are worth less in the present, which, if recognized, immediately prompts firms to raise markups and decrease employment. Hian Teck has proved that, on certain conditions, the real exchange rate abruptly *depreciates* at $t0$, then gradually recovers to its long-run purchasing-power-parity level.

14. The ink had hardly dried on the manuscript for the April 2000 Brookings Panel on Economic Activity meeting at Brookings, where the idea was first presented, when another paper emerged, that by Beaudry and Portier (2001), having the same theme. See also the related paper by Steffen Reichold (2002).
15. Phelps (2003b). See also Field (2003) and Phelps (2004b).
16. Phelps (2003a, 2004a). These and two other essays are combined in Phelps (2004b).
17. In *Webster's*: **mutable** adj. 1 prone to change 2 capable of or liable to mutation (from the Latin *mutare* to change).
18. If doing these calculations over again I would prefer earnings per share to dividends per share.

References

Beaudry, Paul and Franck Portier. (2001). "An Exploration into Pigou's Theory of Cycles," CEPR Discussion Paper 2996, October.

Blanchard, Olivier J. (1981). "Output, the Stock Market and Interest Rates," *American Economic Review*, 71.

Bogle, John C. (2000). *Common Sense on Mutual Funds: New Imperatives for the Intelligent Investor*, New York, John Wiky and Sons, Inc.

Branson, William, A. Fraga, and R. Johnson (1986). "Expected Fiscal Policy and the Recession of 1982," in M.H. Peston and R.E. Quandt (eds.), *Prices, Competition and Equilibrium*. Totowa, NJ: Barnes and Noble.

Calvo, Guillermo A. (1983). "Staggered prices in a utility-maximizing framework," *Journal of Monetary Economics*, 12, 383–398.

Field, Alexander J. (2203). "The most technologically progressive decade of the century," *American Economic Review*, 93, 1399–1413.

Fitoussi, Jean-Paul, David Jestaz, Edmund Phelps, and Gylfi Zoega. (2000). "Roots of the recent recovery," *Brookings Papers on Economic Activity*, 2000-I.

Frydman, Roman and Michael D. Goldberg. (2003). "Imperfect-knowledge expectations, uncertainty-adjusted interest rate parity and exchange Rate Dynamics," in P. Aghion, R. Frydman, J. E. Stiglitz, and M. Woodford (eds.), *Knowledge, Information and Expectations in Modern Macroeconomics: in Honor of Edmund S. Phelps*. Princeton, NJ: Princeton University Press.

Frydman, Roman and Edmund Phelps, eds. (1983). *Individual Forecasting and Aggregate Outcomes*. Cambridge: Cambridge University Press.

Hoon, Hian Teck, and Edmund S. Phelps. (1992). "Macroeconomic shocks in a dynamized model of the natural rate of unemployment," *American Economic Review*, 82, 889–900.

—— and ——. (2001). "Tax Cuts, Employment and Asset Prices: a Real Intertemporal Model," Columbia Economics Working Paper, October. Revised July 2002.

Hoon, Hian Teck and Edmund S. Phelps. (2004). "A Structuralist Model of the Small Open Economy in the Short, Medium and Long Run," ms., Singapore Mgmt. Univ., May.

Keynes, John Maynard. (1936). *The General Theory of Employment Interest and Money*. London: Macmillan and Co.

Kydland, Finn and Edward C. Prescott. (1982). "Time to build and aggregate fluctuations," *Econometrica*, 50, 1345–1370.

Lucas, Jr, Robert E. (1972). "Expectations and the Neutrality of Money," *Journal of Economic Theory*, 4, 103–124.

—— and Edward C. Prescott. (1971). "Investment under uncertainty," *Econometrica*, 39, 659–681.

—— and ——. (1974). "Equilibrium search and unemployment," *Journal of Economic Theory*, 7, 188–209.

Mulligan, Casey. (2002). "A century of labor-leisure distortions," National Bureau of Economic Research, Working Paper 8774.

Phelps, Edmund S. (1968). "Money-wage dynamics and labor-market equilibrium," *Journal of Political Economy, 76* Part II, August, 678–711.

——. (1978). "Disinflation without recession," *Weltwirtschaftliches Archiv*, 100, December.

——. (1969). "The emerging microeconomics in employment and inflation theory," *American Economic Review Papers and Proceedings*, May.

—— *et al.* (1970). *Microeconomic Foundations of Employment and Inflation Theory*. New York: W. W. Norton and Co.

——. (1983). "The trouble with rational expectations," in R. Frydman and E. S. Phelps (eds.), *Individual Forecasting and Aggregate Outcomes: 'Rational Expectations' Examined*. Cambridge: Cambridge University Press.

——. (1994). *Structural Slumps: The Modern Equilibrium Theory of Unemployment, Interest and Assets*. Cambridge, MA: Harvard University Press.

——, and Gylfi Zoega. (2001). "Structural booms: productivity expectations and asset valuations," *Economic Policy*, 32, April.

——. (2003a). "False hopes for the economy—and false fears," *Wall Street Journal*, June 3.

——. (2003b). Interview with Dino Pesole, *Il Sole/24 Ore*, Rome.

——. (2004a). "Crash, bang, wallop," *Wall Street Journal*, January 5.

——. (2004b). "The boom and the slump: A causal account of the 1990s/2000s and the 1920s/1930s," *Journal of Policy Reform*, 7, 3–19.

Pigou, Alfred Cecil. (1927). *Industrial Fluctuations*, 2nd ed. London: Macmillan and Co. 1929.

Reichold, Steffen (2002). "'New economy' and 'productivity slowdown': Can learning about rare regime shifts explain aggregate stock market behavior?" Columbia University, Department of Economics, PhD thesis, May.

Samuelson, Paul A. (1948). *Economics: An Introductory Analysis*, 4th edn., New York: McGraw-Hill, 1958, Chapter 3.

——. (1963). "The weight of evidence," mimeo., M.I.T., unpublished.

——. (1998). "Micro efficiency and macro inefficiency in the stock market," *Federal Reserve Bank of Boston Bulletin*.

Taylor, John B. (1979). "Staggered wage setting in a macro model," *American Economic Review*, 69, 108–113.

Woodford, Michael (2003). "Imperfect common knowledge and the effects of monetary policy," in P. Aghion, R. Frydman, J. Stiglitz, and M. Woodford (eds.), *Knowledge, Information and Expectations in Modern Macroeconomics*. Princeton, NJ: Princeton University Press.

5

Paul Samuelson and Global Public Goods

A commemorative essay for Paul Samuelson

William D. Nordhaus

It is both easy and hard to write an essay commemorating Paul Samuelson's contributions to economics. Easy, because he has created so much of modern economics that you could write on virtually anything—stabilization policy, economic growth, international trade, welfare economics, or just about any topic that caught your fancy. Hard, because, like Buridan's ass, you could easily procrastinate forever in deciding which of the many treasures of his ideas to draw from.

In the end, I chose to draw from Paul's writings on public goods. In two and one-half pages, he reshaped the way economists and political philosophers think about the distinction between private goods and public goods.[1] Once those concepts are learned, we can never again forget why the allocational questions for bread are fundamentally different from those of lighthouses. I will focus on an important example of this topic, and one that poses particularly thorny practical issues, which is the case of global public goods. A brief intellectual history of the concepts is appended.

What great blessings or scourges have befallen humanity? Consider issues as disparate as greenhouse warming and ozone depletion, the Internet and William Shakespeare, terrorism and money laundering, the discovery of antibiotics and nuclear proliferation. Each is an example of a complex system whose effects are global and resist the control of individuals and even the most powerful governments. These are examples of *global public goods*, which are goods whose impacts are indivisibly spread around the entire globe. These are not new phenomena. However, they are becoming more important in today's world, because of rapid technological change and of the astounding decline in transportation and communication costs.

What makes global public goods different from other economic issues, however, is that there is no workable mechanism for resolving these issues efficiently and effectively. If a terrible storm destroys a significant fraction of America's corn crop, the reaction of prices and farmers will help equilibrate needs and availabilities. If scientists discover the lethal character of lead in the air and soil, the government is likely, eventually and often haltingly, to undertake to raise the necessary resources and regulations to reduce lead in gasoline and paint. But if problems arise for global public goods, such as global warming or nuclear proliferation, there is no market or government mechanism that contains both political means and appropriate incentives to implement an efficient outcome. Markets can work wonders, but they routinely fail to solve the problems caused by global public goods.

This chapter examines four facets of global public goods. I begin with a discussion of the nature of global public goods. I then discuss the stock nature of many global public goods and the consequent involvement of the time dimension. I next discuss why global public goods pose such a difficult decision problem. Finally, I describe how the production technologies may affect the production of global public goods.

5.1 The Character of Global Public Goods

Most of economic life involves voluntary exchange of private goods, like bread or blue jeans. These are commodities consumed by one person and which directly benefit no one else. However, many activities involve spillovers among producers or consumers. A polar case of an externality is a *public good*. Public goods are commodities for which the cost of extending the service to an additional person is zero and for which it is impossible or expensive to exclude individuals from enjoying.

In other words, public goods have the two key properties of nonrivalry and nonexcludability. Nonrivalry denotes that the consumption of the public good by one person does not reduce the quantity available for consumption by another person. Take global positioning systems as an example. These are used for hiking, missile guidance, and determining the distance of a golf ball from a hole. These are public goods because people who find their location are not reducing the value of signals for others. The second feature of a pure public good is nonexcludability. This means that no person can be excluded from benefiting from or being affected by the public good (or can only be excluded at a very high exclusion cost). In the case of smallpox eradication, once smallpox was eradicated, no person could be excluded from the benefits.

The important point about public goods, which was carefully analyzed in Samuelson's 1954 article, is that private markets generally do not guarantee efficient production. In this respect, then, production of public goods such as GPS signals differs from production of bread. Efficient production of public goods requires collective action to overcome the inability of private firms to capture the benefits of a cure for malaria. The inefficiencies are the greatest for global public goods, whose benefits are spread most widely across space and time.

In reality, there are many shades of privateness and publicness; there are "pure" public goods and "impure" public goods. Consumption of bread probably has some public-good qualities from fertilizer use, emissions from the transportation system, and garbage. Similarly, a few public goods are really pure because most public goods have some privateness at different points of space or time. Global public goods are not qualitatively different from other public goods. They are the only ones where the effects spill widely around the world and for a long time to come.

5.2 Stock Externalities and the Time Dimension in Global Public Goods

One of the distinguishing features of most global public goods is that they are generally "stock externalities." This term means that their impact depends upon a stock of a capital-like variable that accumulates over time. For example, the impacts might be functions of pollution concentrations or knowledge, which are augmented by flows of emissions or learning, and which depreciate according to some process such as precipitation or obsolescence.

The stock character is particularly important when depreciation rates are low, as with Plutonium-239, which has a half-life of 24,000 years. In global warming, the impact of greenhouse gases depends upon the concentrations of greenhouse gases in the atmosphere rather than on the current flow of emissions, and the most important gas, carbon dioxide, has an atmospheric residence time with a half-life in the order of a century. Most important global public goods involve some kind of stock—stocks of pollution, piles of radioactive wastes, stocks of knowledge, biological or genetic stocks, reputational stocks in the case of monetary systems, and institutional stocks in the cases of market and democratic systems. Being stock externalities gives global public goods special characteristics. By their nature, stocks accumulate, often very slowly, so that it may be difficult to recognize the symptoms of the associated ailment until it is too late to cure. Moreover, because stocks accumulate slowly, and some depreciate very slowly, stock externalities often have long-lasting consequences and are irreversible or near-irreversible. For example, once the stock of a species has disappeared, it is gone forever (or until science fiction becomes science reality) as a viable biological system. Because of the long time lags, the impacts may fall far in the future, which lends enormous uncertainties to the problem. Our actions today will affect the climate many decades in the future, but who knows where, when, how, or how much? These features of stock public goods make analysis and policy-making more difficult than with transient or flow public goods.

The stock character of global public goods also adds a time dimension to the dilemmas involved in public goods. The nature of the spillover depends upon the depreciation rate of the stock. If the depreciation rate is high, then most of the impacts will occur quickly (as would be the case with flow pollutants). However, when the depreciation rate is low (as in global warming or many radioactive wastes) or even negative (as might be the case of knowledge), then the impacts will occur over many generations as well as many nations, and presumably even for nations that have no current legal existence. Just as children and the unborn cannot vote, so unborn nations cannot represent their interests under international law.

Just as global public goods involve externalities over space, in the case of stock public goods they involve externalities over time. While markets are linked over time through capital markets, there is no similar linkage over time for stock global public goods. No market today accurately reflects the impact of global warming on the possible deterioration of air quality or cross-country skiing a century from now. Appropriate decisions must weigh the intergenerational benefits across time just as in conventional public goods they must weigh the benefits across space. It seems likely that, for stock global public goods with low depreciation rates, we will shortchange unborn generations, and even unborn nations, because their interests will be discounted by under-representation and too-high market or decisional discount rates.

5.3 Global Public Goods, Federalism, and the Westphalian Dilemma

While global public goods raise no new analytical issues, they do encounter a unique political hurdle, which is the Westphalian dilemma. Whenever we encounter a social, economic, or political problem, one of the first questions concerns the level at which the problem should be addressed. We expect households to deal with children's homework assignments and taking out the trash; we expect local or regional governments to organize schools and collect the trash; we expect national governments to defend their borders and manage their currencies.

For the case of global public goods, there exists today no workable market or governmental mechanism that is appropriate for the problems. There is no mechanism by which global citizens can make binding collective decisions to slow global warming, to cure overfishing, to efficiently combat AIDS, to form a world army to combat dangerous tyrants, or to rein in dangerous nuclear technologies.

The decision-making difficulties of global public goods raise what might be called the Westphalian dilemma. National governments have the actual power and legal authority to establish laws and institutions within their territories; this includes the right to internalize externalities within their boundaries and provide for national public goods. Under the governing mechanisms of individual countries, whether they are acts of democratic legislatures or despotic decrees, they can take steps to raise taxes or armies and command their citizens to clean their air and water.

By contrast, under international law as it has evolved in the West and then the world, there is no legal mechanism by which disinterested majorities, or supermajorities short of unanimities, can coerce reluctant free-riding countries into mechanisms that provide for global public goods. Participants of the Treaty of Westphalia recognized in 1648 the *Staatensystem*, or system of sovereign states, each of which was a political sovereign with power to govern its territory. As the system of sovereign states evolved, it led to the current system of international law under which international obligations may be imposed on a sovereign state only with its consent.

Because nations, particularly the United States, are deeply attached to their sovereignty, the Westphalian system leads to severe problems for global public goods. The requirement for unanimity is in reality a recipe for inaction. Particularly where there are strong asymmetries in the costs and benefits (as is the case for nuclear non-proliferation or global warming), the requirement of reaching unanimity means that it is extremely difficult to reach universal and binding international agreements. One answer to the political vacuum is to create international institutions, such as the Intergovernmental Panel on Climate Change or the International Maritime Organization. Such organizations generally work by unanimity, have few provisions that are binding on recalcitrant countries, and in any case apply only to countries which have agreed to participate. Even for life and death issues such as nuclear weapons, if a state like North Korea declines to participate in the Non-Proliferation Treaty, there is no provision for forcing its agreement.

To the extent that global public goods may become more important in the decades ahead, one of our major challenges is to devise mechanisms that overcome the bias toward the status quo and the voluntary nature of current international law in life-threatening issues. To someone who is an outsider to international law, the Westphalian system seems an increasingly dangerous vestige of a different world. Just as economists recognize that consumer sovereignty does not apply to children, criminals, and lunatics, international law must come to grips with the fact that national sovereignty cannot deal with critical global public goods.

5.4 The Production Technology for Global Public Goods

Most discussions of public goods focus on the nonrivalry and nonexcludability in their *use*. A neglected feature is the nature of the technology for *production* of public goods, that is, the technology underlying the production of the indivisible benefits. Most analyses of public goods such as global warming, deforestation, or information tend to view the production of public goods as an "additive" technology, akin to pouring water in a vat or adding houses in the suburbs. In fact, the production technologies of public goods vary considerably, and the kinds of policies or institutions that are necessary for efficient provision of public goods will also differ according to the technology.

5.4.1 Three Production Technologies

Three interesting examples of production technologies for public goods provide quite different outcomes.[2]

1. *Additive technologies*. The conventional case, stemming from the original Samuelson 1954 model, comes where the production of the public good is simply the sum of the contributions of the different producers.

This is exemplified by global warming, where total emissions are equal to the sum of the emissions of different parties. In this case, it makes no difference whether ten units are produced by one country or by ten countries.

2. *Best-shot technologies*. Quite a different situation comes when the outcome is the result of the maximum of the individual contributions. For example, if ten missiles are fired at an incoming warhead, then the success of the effort will be largely determined by the missile that comes closest to the target. Another important example is technological change: If ten researchers are trying to find a cure for malaria, the payoff will generally come from the best outcome.

3. *Weakest-link technologies*. Many cases exhibit a technology where the overall production is only as good as the weakest link in the chain. For example, when different communities are building a dike, the success in holding back the waters will depend upon the minimum strength or height of the different parts. Similar outcomes sometimes occur in protecting the spread among countries of infectious diseases like SARS, combating illegal drugs, or preventing money laundering. Perhaps the most frightening example is nuclear proliferation, where countries or groups can buy or steal nuclear materials and designs from countries with the weakest security protection.

5.4.2 Efficient Provision

We introduce the different cases because they have different implications for efficient provision and for the equilibrium outcome. (This discussion relies on the analysis referred to earlier by Hirshleifer.) In the additive case, efficient provision requires the familiar rule that everyone contribute to the point where private marginal cost equals social marginal benefit.

While the equilibrium condition is unchanged, the outcomes for the other cases are different and even strange. Efficient production for the weakest-link technology would require that all parties contribute equally. Efficient dike building requires that each section have equal height and strength (ignoring water pressure, water flows, and other similar factors). If a virulent influenza or SARS-like illness began to spread, good public health protocols in our highly linked world require that all countries are vigilant in tracking and treating the disease. Similarly, efficient prevention of nuclear proliferation requires stringent minimum standards for all countries possessing the relevant technologies.

The best-shot technology is the opposite of the weakest-link technology. It requires that production be concentrated in the low-cost or most efficient producer. Ignoring uncertainty, production should follow the rule that private marginal cost of production of the low-cost producer should equal social marginal benefit, while production of all other higher-cost producers should be zero. In climate-change policy, this rule would definitely not be appropriate for emissions reductions. However, in other aspects of global warming, specialization might be appropriate. For example, we would expect that the research and development on low-carbon fuels should be concentrated in the most efficient research environments. Similarly, if it were thought that geoengineering approaches to climate change (such as shooting smart particles into the stratosphere) were appropriate, it would be natural that the high-technology countries would undertake this task.

5.4.3 Noncooperative Provision

Similarly, we can inquire into the equilibrium production of global public goods for different production technologies. It is sensible for global public goods, given the Westphalian dilemma, to examine an equilibrium in which different parties (nations) behave in a noncooperative fashion. The additive case would provoke the standard syndrome of free riding and underprovision of the public good, with small and poor countries underproviding more than large and rich countries.

In the weakest-link case, by contrast, we see strong incentives for parties to cooperate and provide for the common defense. Since I will be inundated if I do not keep up my share of the dike, there is little incentive (or possibility) for free riding. Weakest-link technologies, then, are ones where the noncooperative outcome most closely approaches the efficient outcome as long as countries have similar tastes and incomes. With weakest-link technologies, coordination and technological cooperation may be sufficient to produce reasonably efficient outcomes.

The best-shot case poses serious problems. In the case of a single superpower, that country will naturally be the low-cost provider and is likely to end up being the single provider. The equilibrium outcome is likely to be the most inefficient of all three cases. This result occurs because the low-cost provider still equates marginal private cost with marginal private benefit, but other providers drop out and produce nothing. Thus, in the cases of providing security guarantees, GPS systems, or combating international security threats, the United States is clearly the dominant provider, with more than half of defense and intelligence spending. It is likely to remain the sole provider of the public good (if this term is aptly applied here) as long as it remains so dominant.

However, as long as the US decisions adopt a noncooperative strategy, provision of global public goods will be highly inefficient. Particularly when the benefits of action are widely dispersed or perceived as insignificant by the United States (as is apparently the case for technological development of low-carbon fuels to slow climate change or developing effective treatment against African AIDS or malaria), it is likely that there will be serious underinvestment in the global public good.

It is tempting to divide views of global issues into those who see the world largely in terms of the additive technology and those who view events through the lens of the non-linear technologies. Those who see the world in terms of additive public goods would tend to emphasize policies requiring cooperative efforts by all or most nations. There is, in that view, no substitute for finding cooperative Coase-type solutions in which bargaining leads to efficient outcomes. By contrast, those whose worldview is largely shaped by conflict and military doctrines may view the world more as one in which unilateral or imposed solutions are necessary. Action in the best-shot world requires but a single actor, whose role is to govern benevolently while taking into account the aggregate of impacts across all nations. Alas, it is but a small step from the benevolent actor to the nationalistic actor, one who acts unilaterally and concentrates on the benefits to the dominant country, perhaps with a bow to the interests of friends and coalitions of the coerced.

5.5 Conclusion

In this chapter, I have reviewed the fascinating problem involved in managing global public goods. All public goods pose severe challenges, but global public goods are even more daunting, and stock global public goods are the polar case of affecting vast numbers of people for long periods of time. The structure of international law and political power raises enormous obstacles to obtaining the unanimous or near-unanimous consent of sovereign nations to take collective international action. Problems of global public goods will also differ depending upon the production process underlying the public good. The peril of using the incorrect mental model of global public goods is that a proposed solution will lead to little improvement over the status quo. Solving the problems involved in global public goods is an open and fascinating economic question with major consequences for our world.

These thoughts recall for me a time when I was a graduate student at MIT and we were having a bad day in one of Paul's classes on advanced capital theory. His questions—perhaps on E. v. Böhm-Bawerk or I. Fisher—were eliciting no sensible answers. Eventually, he looked out at us and remarked to the effect that we were the returns on his human capital, but he was not sure that he was earning a supernormal return. Fortunately, the returns on his human capital are the ultimate global public good. To paraphrase Jefferson, Paul does not diminish the light of his wisdom and generosity when he passes that light to his students and colleagues; rather it glows larger than ever.

5.6 Historical Notes on Public Goods

The germinal article on public goods is Paul Samuelson (1954), "The pure theory of public expenditure," *The Review of Economics and Statistics*, 36(4), 387–389. He originally called these "collective consumption goods." The first use of the term "public good" in this context in the JSTOR archives of economies journals (at www.jstor.org) appears to be in Paul A. Samuelson (1955), "Diagrammatic exposition of a theory of public expenditure," *The Review of Economics and Statistics*, 37(4), 350–356.

Samuelson referred to earlier writings on the theory of public expenditure of Emil Sax, Knut Wicksell, Erik Lindahl, and Richard Musgrave. Early writers, such as Musgrave, generally used the term "social goods." An early definition of what we today mean as public goods (using the term "social goods") appears in Howard R. Bowen (1943), "The interpretation of voting in the allocation of economic resources," *The Quarterly Journal of Economics*, 58(1), 27–48. The notion of public goods is implicit in the discussion in Richard Musgrave (1939), "The voluntary exchange theory of public economy," *The Quarterly Journal of Economics*, 53(2), 213–237. One of the most influential analyses was in Richard Musgrave (1959), *The Theory of Public Finance*, New York, McGraw-Hill.

The notion of global public goods appeared sometime in the early 1990s in the context of global environmental issues. These were analyzed in my work on global warming, particularly William Nordhaus (1994), *Managing the Global Commons: The Economics of Change*, Cambridge, MA, MIT Press. An excellent early study surveying the area is Todd Sandler (1997), *Global Challenges: An Approach to Environmental, Political, and Economic Problems,*

Cambridge, U.K., Cambridge University Press. Many of the issues discussed here were presented in a lecture I delivered, "Global Public Goods and the Problem of Global Warming," Annual Lecture of The Institut d'Economie Industrielle (IDEI), Toulouse, France, June 14, 1999. The United Nations has a web page devoted to global public goods at www.undp.org/globalpublicgoods/.

Notes

1. Paul Samuelson. (1954). "The pure theory of public expenditure," *The Review of Economics and Statistics*, 36(4), 387–389.
2. This discussion draws upon Jack Hirshleifer in "From weakest-link to best-shot: the voluntary provision of public goods," *Public Choice*, 41, 371–386, 1983.

6

Revealed Preference

Hal R. Varian

6.1 Introduction

In January 2005 I conducted a search of JSTOR business and economics journals for the phrase "revealed preference" and found 997 articles. A search of Google scholar returned 3,600 works that contained the same phrase. Surely, revealed preference must count as one of the most influential ideas in economics. At the time of its introduction, it was a major contribution to the pure theory of consumer behavior, and the basic idea has been applied in a number of other areas of economics.

In this chapter I will briefly describe the history of revealed preference, starting with descriptions of the concept in Samuelson's papers. These papers subsequently stimulated a substantial amount of work devoted to refinements and extension of Samuelson's ideas. These theoretical works, in turn, led to a literature on the use of revealed preference analysis for empirical work that is still growing rapidly.

6.2 The Pure Theory of Revealed Preference

Samuelson (1938) contains the first description of the concept he later called "revealed preference." The initial terminology was "selected over."[1] In this paper, Samuelson stated what has since become known as the "Weak Axiom of Revealed Preference" by saying "if an individual selects batch one over batch two, he does not at the same time select two over one." Let us state Samuelson's definitions a bit more formally.

Definition 6.1 (Revealed Preference) *Given some vectors of prices and chosen bundles (p^t, x^t) for $t = 1, \ldots, T$, we say x^t is directly revealed preferred to a bundle x (written $x^t R_D x$) if $p^t x^t \geq p^t x$. We say x^t is revealed preferred to x (written $x^t Rx$) if there is some sequence r, s, t, . . . , u, v such that $p^r x^r \geq p^r x^s$, $p^s x^s \geq p^s x^t, \ldots, p^u x^u \geq p^u x$. In this case, we say the relation R is the transitive closure of the relation R_D.*

Definition 6.2 (Weak Axiom of Revealed Preference) *If $x^t R^D x^s$ then it is not the case that $x^s R^D x^t$. Algebraically, $p^t x^t \geq p^t x^s$ implies $p^s x^s < p^s x^t$.*

Subsequently, building on the work of Little (1949), Samuelson (1948) sketched out an argument describing how one could use the revealed preference relation to construct a set of indifference curves. This proof was for two goods only, and was primarily graphical. Samuelson recognized that a general proof for multiple goods was necessary, and left this as an open question.

Houthakker (1950) provided the missing proof for the general case. As Samuelson (1950) put it, "He has given us the long-sought test for integrability that can be formed in finite index-number terms, without need to estimate partial derivatives."

Houthakker's contribution was to recognize that one needed to extend the "direct" revealed preference relation to what he called the "indirect" revealed preference relation or, for simplicity, what we call the "revealed preference" relation. Houthakker's condition can be stated as:

Definition 6.3 (Strong Axiom of Revealed Preference (SARP)) *If $x^t R_x{}^s$ then it is not the case that $x^s Rx^t$. Algebraically, SARP says $x^t Rx^s$ implies $p^s x^s < p^s x^t$.*

Afriat (1965) later offered a formal argument that the Strong Axiom and the Weak Axiom were equivalent in two dimensions, providing a rigorous, algebraic foundation for Samuelson's earlier graphical exposition.

Samuelson (1953), stimulated by Hicks (1939), summed up all of consumer theory in what he called the *Fundamental Theorem of Consumption Theory*. "Any good (simple or composite) that is known always to increase in demand when money income alone rises must definitely shrink in demand when its price alone rises." In this paper he lays out a graphical and algebraic description of the Slutsky equation and the restrictions imposed by consumer optimization. Yokoyama (1968) elegantly combined Samuelson's verbal and algebraic treatments of the Slutsky equation and made the connection between the Samuelson and the Hicks approaches explicit.

By 1953, the basic theory of consumer behavior in terms of revealed preference was pretty much in place, though it was not completely rigorous.

Subsequent contributors, such as Newman (1960), Uzawa (1960), and Stigum (1973) added increasing rigor to Houthakker and Samuelson's arguments.

During the same period Richter (1966) recognized that one could dispense with the traditional integrability approach using differential equations and base revealed preference on pure set-theoretic arguments involving the completion of partial orders.

This period culminated in the publication of Chipman *et al.* (1971), which contained a series of chapters that would seem to be the last word on revealed preference. Several years later Sondermann (1982), following Richter (1966)'s analysis, provided a one-paragraph proof of the basic revealed preference result, albeit a proof that used relatively sophisticated mathematics.

6.3 Afriat's Approach

Most of the theoretical work described above starts with a demand function: a complete description of what would be chosen at any possible budget. Afriat (1967) offered quite a different approach to revealed preference theory. He started with a *finite* set of observed prices and choices and asked how to actually construct a utility function that would be consistent with these choices.[2]

The standard approach showed, in principle, how to construct preferences consistent with choices, but the actual preferences were described as limits or as a solution to some set of partial differential equations.

Afriat's approach, by contrast, was truly constructive, offering an explicit algorithm to calculate a utility function consistent with the finite amount of data, whereas the other arguments were just existence proofs. This makes Afriat's approach much more suitable as a basis for empirical analysis. Afriat's approach was so novel that most researchers at the time did not recognize its value. In addition, Afriat's exposition was not entirely transparent. Several years later Diewert (1973) offered a somewhat clearer exposition of Afriat's main results.

6.4 From Theory to Data

During the late 1970s and early 1980s there was considerable interest in estimating aggregate consumer demand functions. Christensen *et al.*

(1975) and Deaton (1983) are two notable examples. In reading this work, it occurred to me that it could be helpful to use revealed preference as a pre-test for this econometric analysis.

After all, the Strong Axiom of Revealed Preference was a necessary and sufficient condition for data to be consistent with utility maximization. If the data satisfied SARP, there would be some utility function consistent with the observations. If the data violated SARP, no such utility function would exist. So why not test those inequalities directly?

I dug into the literature a bit and discovered that Koo (1963) had already thought of doing this, albeit with a somewhat different motivation. However, as Dobell (1965) pointed out, his analysis was not quite correct so there was still something left to be done.

Furthermore I recognized the received theory, using WARP and SARP, was not well-suited for empirical work, since it was built around the assumption of single-valued demand functions. In 1977, during a visit to Berkeley, Andreu Mas-Collel pointed me to Diewert (1973)'s exposition of Afriat's analysis, which seemed to me to be a more promising basis for empirical applications.

Diewert (1973) in turn led to Afriat (1967). I corresponded with Afriat during this period, and he was kind enough to send me a package of his writing on the subject. In his monograph, Afriat (1987) offered the clearest exposition of his work in this area, though, as I discovered, it was not quite explicit enough to be programmed into a computer.

I worked on reformulating Afriat's argument in a way that would be directly amenable to computer analysis. While doing this, I recognized that Afriat's condition of "cyclical consistency" was basically equivalent to Strong Axiom. Of course, in retrospect this had to be true since both cyclical consistency and SARP were necessary and sufficient conditions for utility maximization. Even though the proof was quite straightforward, this was a big help to my understanding since it pulled together the quite different approaches of Afriat and Houthakker.

During 1978–79 I worked on writing a program for empirical revealed preference analysis. The code was written in FORTRAN77 and ran on the University of Michigan MTS operating system on an IBM mainframe. This made it rather unportable, but then again this was before the days of personal computers, so everything was unportable. During 1980–81 I was on leave at Nuffeld College, Oxford and became more and more intrigued by the empirical applications of revealed preference. As I saw it, the main empirical questions could be formulated in the following way.

Given a set of observations of prices and chosen bundles, (p^t, x^t) for $t = 1, \ldots, T$, we can ask four basic questions.

Consistency. When is the observed behavior consistent with utility maximization?

Form. When is the observed behavior consistent with maximizing a utility function of particular form?

Recoverability. How can we recover the set of utility functions that are consistent with a given set of choices?

Forecasting. How can we forecast what demand will be at some new budget?

In the rest of the chapter I will review some of the literature concerned with pursuing answers to these four basic questions.

6.5 Consistency

Consistency is, of course, the central focus of the early work on revealed preference. As we have seen, several authors contributed to its solution, including Samuelson, Houthakker, Afriat, and others. The most convenient result for empirical work, as I suggested above, comes from Afriat's approach.

Definition 4 (Generalized Axiom of Revealed Preference) *The data* (p^t, x^t) *satisfy the Generalized Axiom of Revealed Preference (GARP) if* $x^t R_x{}^s$ *implies* $p^s x^s \leq p^s x^t$.

GARP, as mentioned above, is equivalent to what Afriat called "cyclical consistency." That the only difference between GARP and SARP is that the strong inequality in SARP becomes a weak inequality in GARP. This allows for multivalued demand functions and "flat" indifference curves, which turns out to be important in empirical work.

Now we can state the main result.

Theorem 1 (Afriat's Theorem) Given some choice data (p^t, x^t) *for* $t = 1, \ldots, T$, the following conditions are equivalent.

1. There exists a nonsatiated utility function *u(x)* that rationalizes the data in the sense that for all *t*, $u(x^t) \geq u(x)$ for all *x* such that $p^t x^t \geq p^t x$.
2. The data satisfy GARP.
3. There is a positive solution (u^t, λ^t) to the set of linear inequalities $u^t \leq u^s + \lambda^s p^s (x^t - x^s)$ for all *s*, *t*.
4. There exists a nonsatiated, continuous, monotone, and concave utility function $u(x)$ that rationalizes the data.

This theorem offers two equivalent, testable conditions for the data to be consistent with utility maximization. The first is GARP, which, as we have seen, is a small generalization of Houthakker's SARP. The second condition is whether there is a positive solution to a certain set of linear inequalities. This can easily be checked by linear programming methods. However, from the viewpoint of computational efficiency it is much easier just to check GARP. The only issue is to figure out how to compute the revealed preference relation in an efficient way.

Let us define a matrix m that summarizes the direct revealed preference relation. In this matrix the (s, t) entry is given by $m_{st} = 1$ if $p^t x^t \geq p^t x^s$ and $m_{st} = 0$ otherwise. In order to test GARP, all that is necessary is to compute the transitive closure of the relation summarized by this matrix. What algorithms are appropriate?

Dobell (1965) recognized that this could be accomplished simply by taking the Tth power of the $T \times T$ binary matrix that summarizes the direct revealed preference relation. However, it turned out the computer scientists had a much more efficient algorithm. Warshall (1962) had shown a few years earlier how to use dynamic programming to compute the transitive closure in just T^3 steps.

Combining the work of Afriat and Warshall effectively solved the problem of finding a computationally efficient method of testing data for consistency with utility maximization. One could simply construct the matrix summarizing the direct relation, compute the transitive closure, and then check GARP.

6.5.1 Empirical Analysis

Several authors have tested revealed preference conditions on different sorts of data. The 'best' data, in some sense, is experimental data involving individual subjects since one can vary prices in such a setting and so test choice behavior over a wide range of environments.

Battalio *et al.* (1973) was, I believe, the first paper to look at individual human subjects. The subjects were patients in a mental institution who were offered payments for good behavior. Cox (1989) later examined the same data and extended the analysis in several ways.

Kagel *et al.* (1995) summarizes several studies examining animal behavior. Harbaugh *et al.* (2001) examined choice behavior by children, and Andreoni and Miller (2002) looked at public goods experiments to test for rational behavior in this context.

Individual household consumption data is the next best set of data to examine in the context of consumer choice theory. I believe that Koo (1963) was the first paper to look at household data. See also the subsequent exchange between Dobell (1965) and Koo (1965). Later studies using household budgets include Manser and McDonald (1988) and Famulari (1995). Dowrick and Quiggin (1994, 1997) look at international aggregate data.

Finally, we have time series data on aggregate consumption. I used these methods described above to test revealed preference in Varian (1982a). To my surprise, the aggregate consumption data easily satisfied the revealed preference conditions. I soon realized that this was for a trivial reason: the change in expenditure from year to year were large relative to the changes in relative prices. Hence budget sets rarely intercepted in ways that would generate a GARP violation (or so it seemed).

Bronars (1985) offered a novel contribution by investigating the power of the GARP test. Power, of course, can only be measured against a specific alternative hypothesis, and Bronars chose the Becker (1962) hypothesis of random choice on the budget set. He found that Becker's random choice model violated GARP about 67 percent of the time. Contrary to my original impression, there were apparently enough budget intersections in aggregate time series to give GARP some bite.

GARP was even more powerful on per capita data. Of course, another interpretation of these findings is that Becker's random choice model is not a very appealing alternative hypothesis. But, for all the criticism directed at the classical theory of consumer behavior, there seem to be few alternative hypotheses other than Becker's that can be applied using the same sorts of nine data used for revealed preference analysis.

6.5.2 Goodness of Fit

It is of interest to consider ways to relax the revealed preference tests so that one might say "these data are almost consistent with GARP." Afriat (1967) defines a "partial efficiency" measure which can be used to measure how well a given set of data satisfies utility maximization.

Definition 5 (Efficiency levels) *We say that x^t is directly revealed preferred to x at efficiency level e if $ep^t x^t \geq p^t x$.*

We define the transitive closure of this relation as in the usual way. If $e = 1$ this is the standard direct revealed preference relation. If $e = 0$ nothing is directly revealed preferred to anything else, so GARP is vacuously satisfied. Hence there is some critical level e^* where the data just satisfy GARP.

It is easy to find the critical level e^* by doing a binary search. Varian (1990) suggests defining e^t separately for each observation and then finding those e^t that are as close as possible to 1 (in some norm). I interpret these e^t as a "minimal perturbation." They can be interpreted as error terms and thus be used to give a statistical interpretation to the goodness-of-fit measure.

Whitney and Swofford (1987) suggest using the number of violations as a fit measure, while Famulari (1995) uses a measure which is roughly the fraction of violations that occur divided by the fraction that could have occurred. Houtman and Maks (1985) propose computing the maximal subset of the data that is consistent with revealed preference. These measures are reviewed and compared in Gross (1995) who also offers his own suggestions.

6.6 Form

The issue of testing for various sorts of separability had been considered by Afriat in unpublished work and independently examined by Diewert and Parkan (1985). The Diewert–Parkan work extended the linear inequalities described in Afriat's Theorem. They showed that if an appropriate set of linear inequalities had positive solutions, then the data satisfied the appropriate form restriction.

To get the flavor of this analysis, suppose that some observed data (p^t, x^t) were generated by a differentiable concave utility function $u(x)$. Differentiability and concavity imply that

$$u(x^t) \leq u(x^s) + Du(x^t)(x^s - x^t) \quad \text{for all } s,t$$

The first-order conditions for utility maximization imply

$$Du(x^t) = \lambda^s p^t \quad \text{for all } t$$

Putting these together, we find that a necessary condition for the data to be consistent with utility maximization is that there is a set of positive numbers (u^t, λ^t), which can be interpreted as utility levels and marginal utilities of income that satisfy the linear inequalities

$$u^t \leq u^s + \lambda^s (p^s x^t - p^t x^t) \quad \text{for all } s, t$$

Furthermore, the existence of a solution to this set of inequalities is a sufficient condition as well. This can be proved by defining a utility function as the lower envelope of a set of hyperplanes defined as follows:

$$u(x) = \min_{s} u^s + \lambda^s p^s (x - x^s)$$

Afriat (1967) had used a similar construction but went further and showed that cyclical consistency (i.e. GARP) was a necessary and sufficient condition for a solution to this set of linear inequalities to exist. Thus the computationally demanding task of verifying that a positive solution to a set of T^2 linear inequalities could be replaced by a much simpler calculation: checking GARP. Suppose now that the data were generated by a homothetic utility function. Then it is well known that the indirect utility function can be represented as a multiplicatively separable function of price and income: $v(p)m$. This means that the marginal utility of income is simply $v(p)$, which also equals the utility level at income 1.

If we normalize the observed prices so that expenditure equals 1 at each observation, we can write the above inequalities as

$$u^t \leqslant u^s + u^s (1 - p^s x^t) \quad \text{for all } s, t$$

We have shown that the existence of a positive solution to these inequalities is a necessary condition for the maximization of a homothetic utility function. This can also be shown to be sufficient.

One immediately asks: is there an easier-to-check combinatorial condition that is equivalent to the existence of a solution for these inequalities? Varian (1982b) found such a condition. Simultaneously, Afriat (1981) published essentially the same test.

To get some intuition, consider Figure 6.1. The data (p^1, x^1) and (p^2, x^2) are consistent with revealed preference. However, if the underlying preferences are homothetic, then x^3 would be demanded at the budget set p^3 creating a violation of revealed preference.

In general, the necessary and sufficient condition for an observed set of choices to be consistent with homotheticity is given by HARP:

Definition 6 (Homothetic Axiom of Revealed Preference) *A set of data (p^t, x^t) for $t = 1, \ldots, T$, satisfy the Homothetic Axiom of Revealed preference (HARP) if for every sequence r,s,t, . . . ,u,v*

$$\frac{p^r x^s}{p^r x^r} \frac{p^s x^t}{p^s x^s} \cdots \frac{p^u x^v}{p^u x^u} \geq 1.$$

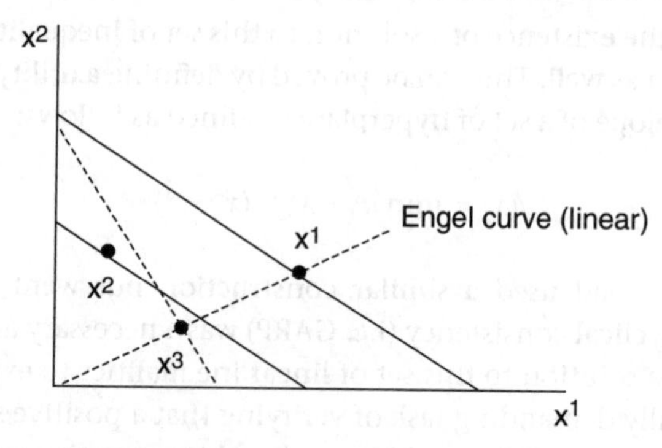

Figure 6.1 GARP with homothetic preference

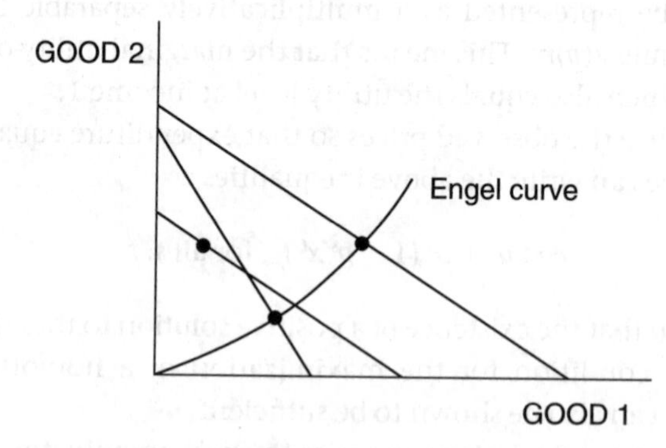

Figure 6.2 GARP with arbitrary Engel curve

It turns out that there is an easy computation to check whether or not this condition is satisfied that uses methods that are basically the same as those in Warshall's algorithm.

Using similar methods, Browning (1984) came up with a nice test for life-cycle consumption models which rests on the constancy of the marginal utility of income in this framework.

Subsequently Blundell *et al.* (2003) recognized that the logic used in the homotheticity tests could be extended to a much more general setting.

Suppose one had estimates of Engel curves from other data. Then these Engel curves could be used to construct a set of data that could be subjected to revealed preference tests. The logic is the same as that described in Figure 6.1, but uses an estimated Engel curve rather than the linear Engel curve implied by homotheticity. See Figure 6.2 for a simple example.

The Blundell–Browning–Crawford approach is very useful for empirical work since cross-sectional household data can be used to estimate Engel curves, either parametrically or nonparametrically. See Blundell (2005) for further developments in this area.

Other restrictions on functional form, such as various forms of separability, have been examined by Varian (1982a). Tests for expected utility maximization and related models are described in Green and Srivastava (1986), Osbandi and Green (1991), Varian (1983, 1988), and Bar-Shira (1992).

6.7 Forecasting

Suppose we are given a finite set of observed budgets and choices (p^t, x^t) for $t = 1, \ldots, T$ that are consistent with GARP and a new price p^0 and expenditure y^0. What are the possible bundles x^0 that could be demanded at (p^0, x^0)?

Clearly all that is necessary is to describe the set of x^0 for which the (expanded) data set (p^t, x^t) *for* $t = 0, \ldots, T$ satisfy GARP. Varian (1982a) calls this the set of supporting bundles. Figure 6.3 shows the geometry.

In an analogous way, one can choose a new bundle y^0 and ask for the set of prices at which this bundle could be demanded. This is the set of supporting prices. Formally,

$$S(x^0) = \{p^0 : (p^t, x^t) \text{ satisfy GARP for } t=0, \ldots, \text{T}\}$$

Of course, one could also ask about demanded bundles or prices that are consistent with utility functions with various restrictions imposed such as homotheticity, separability, specific forms for Engel curves, and so on.

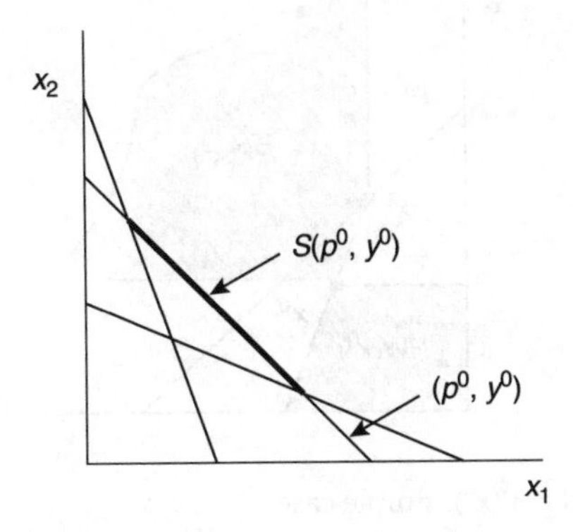

Figure 6.3 Supporting bundles

6.8 Recoverability

As we have seen, Afriat's methods can be used to construct a utility function that is consistent with finite set of observed choices that satisfy GARP. However, this is only one utility function. Typically there will be many such functions. Is there a way to describe the entire set of utility functions (or preferences) consistent with some data?

Varian (1982a) posed the question in the following way. Suppose we are given a finite set of data (p^t, x^t) *for* $t = 2, \ldots, T$ that satisfies GARP and two new bundles x^0 and x^1. Consider the set of prices at which x^0 could be demanded, that is, the supporting set of prices. If every such supporting set makes x^0 revealed preferred to x^1 then we conclude that all preferences consistent with the data must have x^0 preferred to x^1.

Given any x^0, it is possible to define the sets of x's that are revealed preferred to x^0 $(RP(x^0))$ and set of x's that are revealed worse than x^0 $(RW(x^0))$. A very simple example is shown in Figure 6.4. The possible set of supporting prices for x0 must lie in the shaded cone so every such set of prices imply that x^0 is revealed preferred to the points in $RW(x^0)$. Similarly, the points in the convex hull of the bundles revealed preferred to x^0 must themselves be preferred to x^0 for any concave utility function that rationalizes the data.

Of course Figure 6.4 uses only one observation. As we get more observations on demand, we will get tighter bounds on $RP(x^0)$ and $RW(x^0)$, as shown in Figure 6.5. Another approach, also suggested by Varian (1982a) is to try to compute bounds on *specific* utility functions. A very convenient

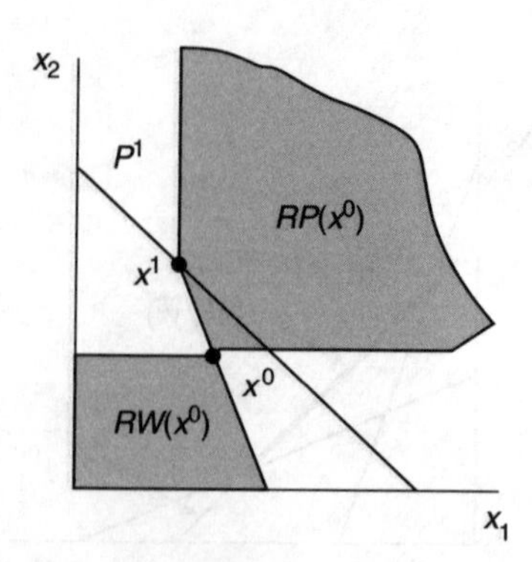

Figure 6.4 $RP(x^0)$ and $RW(x^0)$: simple case

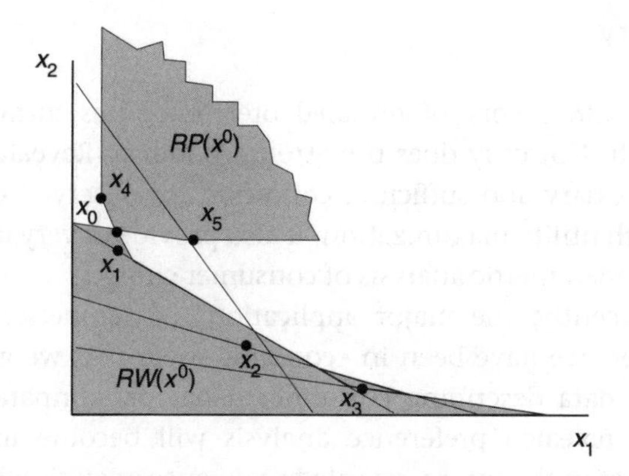

Figure 6.5 $RP(x^0)$ and $RW(x^0)$: a more complex case

choice in this case is what Samuelson (1974) calls the *money metric utility function*. First define the expenditure function

$$e(p,u) = \min pz \text{ such that } u(z) \geqslant u.$$

It is not hard to see that under minimal regularity conditions $e(p,u)$ will be a strictly increasing function of u. Now define

$$m(p,x) = e(p, u(x)).$$

For fixed p, $m(p,x)$ is a strictly increasing function of utility, so it is itself a utility function that represents the same preferences. Varian (1982a) suggested that given a finite set of data $(p^t x^t)$ one could define an upper bound to the money metric utility by using

$$m^+(p, x) = \min pz^t \text{ such that } x^t Rx.$$

Subsequently, Knoblauch (1992) showed that this bound was in fact tight: there were preferences that rationalized the observed choices that had $m^+(p,x)$ as their money metric utility function. Varian (1982a) defined a lower bound to Samuelson's money metric utility function and showed that it was tight.

Of course, using restrictions on utility form such as HARP allow for tighter bounds. There are several papers on the implications of such restrictions in the theory and measurement of index numbers, including Afriat (1981), Afriat (1981), Diewert and Parkan (1985), Dowrick and Quiggin (1994, 1997), and Manser and McDonald (1988).

6.9 Summary

Samuelson's 1938 theory of revealed preference has turned out to be amazingly rich. Not only does the Strong Axiom of Revealed Preference provide a necessary and sufficient condition for observed choices to be consistent with utility maximization, it also provides a very useful tool for empirical, nonparametric analysis of consumer choices.

Up until recently, the major applications of Samuelson's theory of revealed preference have been in economic theory. As we get larger and richer sets of data describing consumer behavior, nonparametric techniques using revealed preference analysis will become more feasible. I anticipate that in the future, revealed preference analysis will make a significant contribution to empirical economics as well.

Notes

1. As Richter (1966) has pointed out, "selected over" has the advantage over "revealed preference" in that it avoids confusion about circular definition of "preference." Unfortunately, the original terminology did not catch on.
2. I once asked Samuelson whether he thought of revealed preference theory in terms of a finite or infinite set of choices. His answer, as I recall, was: "I thought of having a finite set of observations . . . but I always could get more if I needed them!"

References

Afriat, S. N. (1965). "The equivalence in two dimensions of the strong and weak axioms of revealed preference," *Metroeconomica*, 17, 24–28.

——. (1967). "The construction of a utility function from expenditure data," *International Economic Review*, 8, 67–77.

——. (1981). "On the constructibility of consistent price indices between several periods simultaneously," in Angus Deaton (ed.), *Essays in Theory and Measurement of Demand: in Honour of Sir Richard Stone*. Cambridge, England: Cambridge University Press.

——. (1987). *Logic of Choice and Economic Theory*. Oxford: Clarendon Press.

Andreoni, James and John Miller. (2002). "Giving according to GARP: An experimental test of the consistency of preferences for altruism," *Econometrica*, 70(2), 737–753.

Bar-Shira, Ziv. (1992). "Nonparametric test of the expected utility hypothesis," *American Journal of Agricultural Economics*, 74(3), 523–533.

Battalio, Raymond C., John H. Kagel, Robin C. Winkler, Edwin B. Fisher, Robert L. Basmann, and Leonard Krasner. (1873). "A test of consumer demand theory using observations of individual consumer purchases," *Western Economic Journal*, 11(4), 411–428.

Becker, Gary. (1962). "Irrational behavior and economic theory," *Journal of Political Economy*, 70, 1–13.

Blundell, Richard. (2005). "How revealing is revealed preference?" *European Economic Journal*, 3, 211–235.

——, Martin Browning, and I. Crawford. (2003). "Nonparametric Engel curves and revealed preference," *Econometrica*, 71(1), 205–240.

Bronars, Stephen. (1985). "The power of nonparametric tests," *Econometrica*, 55(3), 693–698.

Browning, Martin. (1984). "A non-parametric test of the life-cycle rational expectations hypothesis," *International Economic Review*, 30, 979–992.

Chipman, J. S., L. Hurwicz, M. K. Richter, and H. F. Sonnenschein. (1971). *Preferences, Utility and Demand*. New York: Harcourt Brace Janovich.

Christensen, Dale, Lars Jorgensen, and Lawrence Lau. (1975). "Transcendental logarithmic utility functions," *American Economic Review*, 65, 367–383.

Cox, James C. (1989). On testing the utility hypothesis, Technical report, University of Arizona.

Deaton, Angus. (1983). "Demand analysis," in Z. Griliches and M. Intrilligator (eds), *Handbook of Econometrics*. Greenwich, CT: JAI Press.

Diewert, Erwin and Celick Parkan. (1985). "Tests for consistency of consumer data and nonparametric index numbers," *Journal of Econometrics*, 30, 127–147.

Diewert, W. E. (1973). "Afriat and revealed preference theory," *The Review of Economic Studies*, 40(3), 419–425.

Dobell, A. R. (1965). "A comment on A. Y. C. Koo's an empirical test of revealed preference theory," *Econometrica*, 33(2), 451–455.

Dowrick, Steve and John Quiggin. (1994). "International comparisons of living standards and tastes: A revealed-preference analysis," *The American Economic Review*, 84(1), 332–341.

—— and ——. (1997). "True measures of GDP and convergence," *The American Economic Review*, 87(1), 41–64.

Famulari, M. (1995). "A household-based, nonparametric test of demand theory," *Review of Economics and Statistics*, 77, 372–383.

Green, Richard, and Sanjay Srivastava. (1986). "Expected utility maximization and demand behavior," *Journal of Economic Theory*, 38(2), 313–323.

Gross, John. (1995). "Testing data for consistency with revealed preference," *The Review of Economics and Statistics*, 77(4), 701–710.

Harbaugh, William T., Kate Krause, and Timoth R. Berry. (2001). "GARP for kids: on the development of rational choice theory," *American Economic Review*, 91(5), 1539–1545.

Hicks, J. R. (1939). *Value and Capital*. Oxford, England: Oxford University Press.

Houthakker, H. S. (1950). "Revealed preference and the utility function," *Economica*, 17(66), 159–174.

Houtman, M. and J. A. Maks. (1985). "Determining all maximial data subsets consistent with revealed preference," *Kwantitatieve Methoden*, 19, 89–104.

Kagel, John H., Raymond C. Battalio, and Leonard Green. (1995). *Choice Theory: An Experimental Analysis of Animal Behavior.* Cambridge, England: Cambridge University Press.

Knoblauch, Vicki. (1992). "A tight upper bound on the money metric utility function," *The American Economic Review*, 82(3), 660–663.

Koo, Anthony Y. C. (1963). "An empirical test of revealed preference theory," *Econometrica*, 31(4), 646–664.

——. (1965). "A comment on A. Y. C. Koo's An empirical test of revealed preference theory: Reply," *Econometrica*, 33(2), 456–458.

Little, I. M. D. (1949). "A reformulation of the theory of consumers' behavior," *Oxford Economic Papers*, 1, 90–99.

Manser, Marilyn and R. McDonald. (1988). "An analysis of substitution bias in measuring inflation, 1959–85," *Econometrica*, 56, 909–930.

Newman, Peter. (1960). "Complete ordering and revealed preference," *Economica*, 27, 65–77.

Osbandi, Kent and Edward J. Green. (1991). "A revealed preference theory for ex-pected utility," *The Review of Economic Studies*, 58(4), 677–695.

Richter, Marcel K. (1966). "Revealed preference theory," *Econometrica*, 34(3), 635–645.

Samuelson, Paul A. (1938). "A note on the pure theory of consumer's behavior," *Economica*, 5(17), 61–71.

——. (1948). "Consumption theory in terms of revealed preference," *Economica*, 15(60), 243–253.

——. (1950). "The problem of integrability in utility theory," *Economica*, 17(68), 355–385.

——. (1953). "Consumption theorems in terms of overcompensation rather than indifference comparisons," *Economics*, 20(77), 1–9.

——. (1974). "Complementarity: an essay on the 40th anniversary of the Hicks-Allen revolution in demand theory," *Journal of Economic Literature*, 12(4), 1255–1289.

Sondermann, Dieter. (1982). "Revealed preference: An elementary treatment," *Econometrica*, 50(3), 777–780.

Stigum, Bernt P. (1973). "Revealed preference—A proof of Houthakker's theorem," *Econometrica: Journal of the Econometric Society*, 41(3), 411–423.

Uzawa, H.(1960) "Preference and rational choice in the theory of consumption," in K. J. Arrow, S. Karlin, and P. Suppes (eds), *Mathematical Models in Social Science.* Stanford, CA: Stanford University Press.

Varian, Hal R. (1982a). "The nonparametric approach to demand analysis," *Econometrica*, 50(4), 945–972.

——. (1982b). "Nonparametric test of models of consumer behavior," *Review of Economic Studies*, 50, 99–110.

——. (1983). "Nonparametric tests of models of investor behavior," *Journal of Financial and Quantitative Analysis*, 18(3), 269–278.

——. (1988). "Estimating risk aversion from Arrow-Debreu portfolio choice," *Econometrica*, 56(4), 973–979.

——. (1990). "Goodness-of-fit in optimizing models," *Journal of Econometrics*, 46, 125–140.

Warshall, S. (1962). "A theorem on Boolean matrices," *Journal of the Association of Computing Machinery*, 9, 11–12.

Whitney, Gerald A. and Swofford, James L. (1987). "Nonparametric tests of utility maximization and weak separability for consumption, leisure and money," *The Review of Economic Statistics*, 69(3), 458–464.

Yokoyama, T. (1968). "A logical foundation of the theory of consumer's demand," in P. Newman (ed.), *Readings in Mathematical Economics*. Baltimore: Johns Hopkins Press.

7

Samuelson's "Dr. Jekyll and Mrs. Jekyll" Problem: A Difficulty in the Concept of the Consumer

Robert A. Pollak

In 1956 Samuelson posed what he memorably called the "Dr Jekyll and Mrs Jekyll" problem. Observing that most individuals live in families, Samuelson asked: "...how can we expect family demand functions observed in the market place to obey the consistency axioms of revealed preference or any other regularity conditions?" (Samuelson, 1956, p. 9). Samuelson went on to establish the conditions under which family demand functions obey the revealed preference axioms, but he clearly thought that these conditions were unlikely to be satisfied.

In the 50 years since Samuelson posed the Dr Jekyll and Mrs Jekyll problem, the economics of the family has sharpened our understanding of family decision-making. In this chapter I begin by describing Samuelson's formulation of the Dr Jekyll and Mrs Jekyll problem. I then discuss the implications of developments in the economics of the family for our understanding of family demand functions.

Recent work is transforming the neoclassical theory of consumer's behavior by incorporating insights from the economics of the family. Unlike the neoclassical theory of consumer's behavior, which focuses on the demand functions for goods and supply functions for labor, the economics of the family uses the tools of economics to analyze a wide range of nonmarket behaviors, including marriage, divorce, and fertility.[1] More relevant for demand analysis, the economics of the family analyzes the

I am grateful to Joanne Spitz for editorial assistance and to the John D. and Catherine T. MacArthur Foundation for their support. The usual disclaimer applies.

allocation of goods and time within the family. This analysis has implications for the family's market behavior, that is, for the demand functions for goods and supply functions for labor.

The neoclassical theory of consumer's behavior begins with "economic agents" who have preferences and face constraints. To operationalize this theory requires specifying the empirical counterparts of economic agents. Economists have traditionally identified these agents with individuals, and for this reason Samuelson (1956, p. 8) insists that it is properly called the theory of "consumer's" behavior, not the theory of "consumers'" behavior. But, as Samuelson points out, once we recognize that most individuals live in families, the identification of economic agents with individuals poses theoretical difficulties.[2] The theoretical difficulty Samuelson exposed, which he felicitously called the Dr Jekyll and Mrs Jekyll problem, arises in using the theory of consumer's behavior to provide a foundation for demand analysis. Samuelson began by assuming that each spouse has a utility function. This assumption marked a radical departure from the standard assumption of a household or family utility function. Samuelson then asked: "... how can we expect family demand functions observed in the market place to obey the consistency axioms of revealed preference or any other regularity conditions?" (p. 9).[3]

Samuelson posed the Dr Jekyll and Mrs Jekyll problem in a throw-away section in his classic 1956 paper, "Social Indifference Curves." The paper is concerned primarily with international trade and, more specifically, the conditions under which the demand functions of a country can be treated as if they were the demand functions of an individual. Samuelson saw that aggregating the demands of the individuals in a family into the family's demand functions is formally analogous to aggregating the demands of the individuals in a country into the country's demand functions. He showed that the consistency axioms would be satisfied if the spouses somehow agreed on a family Bergson–Samuelson welfare function that specified how alternative distributions of utility are evaluated and, hence, how to trade off the utility of one spouse against the utility of the other. If the spouses could agree to maximize a family welfare function subject to a family budget constraint, then the family's demand functions would be indistinguishable from the demand functions of a utility-maximizing individual. More precisely, if the family welfare function and the spouses' utility functions are well-behaved, then the demand functions that solve this constrained maximization problem depend only on prices and family income, and exhibit all the standard properties of neoclassical demand functions. I call any model in which a family Bergson–Samuelson welfare function is defined over the spouses' utilities a "consensus model."

Samuelson did not purport to explain how spouses might achieve a consensus regarding a family welfare function or, once achieved, how that consensus might be maintained. Indeed, he is openly skeptical, pointing out that constructing a family welfare function for spouses requires solving the two-person version of the problem that Arrow (1950) investigated in the context of aggregating individuals' preferences into a social welfare function. Arrow's paper, "A Difficulty in the Concept of Social Welfare," began by stating a set of appealing and apparently weak axioms. His celebrated "impossibility" theorem asserts that the preferences of individuals can be aggregated into group preferences in a way that satisfies these axioms if and only if one member of the group is a dictator.

Samuelson, however, was not interested in constructing family welfare functions but in establishing the conditions under which a family's demand functions are indistinguishable from the demand functions of a neoclassical consumer. Nerlove (1974) describes Samuelson's resolution to the Dr Jekyll and Mrs Jekyll problem as the "Samuelson finesse," and I suspect that Samuelson would not object to this description. Samuelson did not claim that the assumption of a consensus family welfare function was plausible, nor did he investigate the properties of family demand functions in the absence of a family welfare function.

Although Samuelson posed the Dr Jekyll and Mrs Jekyll problem, Becker was responsible for putting the family on the research agenda of the economic profession. Becker (1974, 1981) began by proposing a model of family interaction—the "altruist model." Becker's altruist model provides an alternative to, or at least an alternative interpretation of, Samuelson's consensus family welfare function. Unlike Samuelson, who was skeptical of the consensus assumption, Becker was a vigorous advocate of the altruist model.

Becker introduced the altruist model in the context of a family consisting of a group of purely selfish but rational "kids" and one altruistic "parent" whose utility function incorporates the utility functions of the kids. Unlike Samuelson, for whom the paradigmatic family is a married couple, for Becker the paradigmatic family is an altruistic father and his children. Becker's assumption of interdependent preferences departs from the usual neoclassical assumption that each individual is concerned only with his or her own consumption. Samuelson (1956, pp. 9–10) anticipated the need for such a departure: "Where the family is concerned the phenomenon of altruism inevitably raises its head: if we can speak at all of the indifference curves of any one member, we must admit that his tastes and marginal rates of substitution are contaminated by the goods that other members consume." Indeed, Samuelson's verbal formulation is compatible with a much more general specification than Becker's highly restrictive definition of altruism.[4]

Becker's Rotten Kid Theorem and Samuelson's consensus model reach virtually identical conclusions about the properties of family demand functions. The Rotten Kid Theorem asserts that the presence of a parent with altruistic preferences who makes positive transfers to each of the selfish kids will induce the kids to act so as to maximize the altruist's utility function subject to the family's resource constraints. Hence, Becker's analysis implies that the altruist's utility function is the family welfare function. The benevolence of the altruist is reflected in the weight he gives to his own consumption relative to the well-being of other family members. In Pollak (1988) I call Becker's altruist the "husband-father-dictator-patriarch." Although Becker's altruist is not a dictator in the technical sense in which social choice theorists use that term, the altruist model comes uncomfortably close to implying that one member of the family is a dictator.

Although Becker introduced the altruist model in the context of parents and children, he reinterprets it in terms of husbands and wives. The reinterpretation casts the husband in the role of the altruistic parent and the wife as the selfish kid; the husband's utility function can then be equated with Samuelson's consensus family welfare function. Becker's altruist model, like Samuelson's consensus model, implies that the family's demand functions for goods and its supply functions for labor are indistinguishable from those of a neoclassical consumer. Samuelson's consensus model does not purport to derive the family's welfare function or relate it to the spouses' utility functions or bargaining power. In contrast, Becker's altruist model purports to derive the family's welfare function and claims that it coincides with the altruist's utility function. The power of the altruist arises not from assumptions about the altruist's preferences but from assumptions about the structure of the implicitly specified bargaining game. The bargaining game underlying Becker's model is best interpreted as a one-shot noncooperative game in which the altruist moves first and confronts the other family members with take-it-or-leave-it offers. Without this take-it-or-leave-it structure proposed by Pollak (1985) or some alternative special conditions, the conclusion of the altruist model fails to hold. The take-it-or-leave-it structure of the altruist game is essentially that of an "ultimatum game."

Both Samuelson's consensus model and Becker's altruist model imply that families act as if they are maximizing family utility functions subject to family budget constraints. Models with this property are called "unitary models."[5] Unitary models provide a rationale for treating families as economic agents and thus are simple, powerful mechanisms for generating demand and supply functions with familiar properties for use in applied economics. Only serious deficiencies could justify replacing unitary models with more complicated alternatives. Although unitary models remain the dominant theoretical framework for analyzing labor supply and goods demand, in recent years they have come under a barrage of methodological, theoretical, and empirical criticisms.

Much of the criticism of treating families as economic agents is a byproduct of the study of marriage and divorce. Models of marriage and divorce require a theoretical framework in which individuals compare their expected utility or well-being inside marriage with their expected utility or well-being outside marriage. The need to recognize the individual utilities of spouses implies the inadequacy of simply postulating that families are economic agents. Approaches that postulate household preferences directly, however, have limitations that go beyond their inadequacy for studying marriage and divorce. In virtually all bargaining models the possibility and anticipated consequences of divorce constrain equilibrium allocations within marriage.[6] For example, when unilateral divorce is possible, individual rationality implies that if the spouses remain together, then the equilibrium allocation in the marriage must be better (or, more precisely, at least as good) for each spouse as divorce. Models that ignore individuals and begin by postulating that families are economic agents cannot be used to study marriage, divorce, or allocation within marriage.

At the level of methodology or "meta-theory," Chiappori (1992, p. 440) argues that economics is committed to "methodological individualism" and that this commitment is inconsistent with simply postulating that the household is an economic agent. In response it might be argued that neither Samuelson's consensus model nor Becker's altruist model postulate household preference directly, but derive them from more primitive assumptions. Alternatively, it might be argued that methodological individualism is better treated as a research strategy than a sacred principle: for some purposes economists can usefully treat households and firms as fundamental units of analysis, just as biologists, for some purposes, treat plants and animals rather than genes or molecules as fundamental units. Finally, it might be argued that unitary models such as Samuelson's consensus model that begin with the utility functions of individuals are consistent with the tenets of methodological individualism and thus immune to Chiappori's methodological critique. In response to this, Chiappori could assert that methodological individualism requires not only utility functions for individuals but also an economic model relating individuals' preferences to family behavior.

The development of bargaining or game theoretic alternatives to the consensus model and the altruist model has changed the theoretical landscape. Proponents of bargaining models do not claim that Samuelson's consensus model or Becker's altruist model are formally incorrect—everyone recognizes that there could be worlds in which families behave as these models predict. The claim is that game theoretic bargaining models are equally consistent with the modeling conventions of economics and, hence, that theory does not favor the consensus model or the altruist model over bargaining models—even though some bargaining models are inconsistent with the unitary model.

Bargaining models from cooperative game theory dominate family economics.[7] A typical bargaining model of marriage begins by assuming, with Samuelson, that each spouse has a utility function that depends only on his or her own consumption. If the spouses fail to reach agreement, both husband and wife receive the utilities associated with a default outcome. The utilities associated with the default outcome are usually described as the "threat point." In some models the threat point is interpreted as divorce, in others as a noncooperative equilibrium within the marriage.

The Nash bargaining model provides the leading solution concept in cooperative bargaining models of marriage. The Nash bargaining solution is the allocation that maximizes the product of the gains to cooperation, measured in utility, subject to the constraint that the spouses' joint income equal joint expenditure. More precisely, the Nash product function is given by: $N = (U^h - T^h)\,(U^w - T^w)$, where U^h and U^w denote the utilities of the husband and wife. Nash (1950) shows that a set of four axioms—including Pareto efficiency, which ensures that the solution lies on rather than inside the utility possibility frontier—uniquely characterizes the Nash bargaining solution.[8]

The utilities received by husband and wife in the Nash bargaining solution depend upon the threat point; the higher a spouse's utility at the threat point, the higher the utility that spouse will receive in the Nash bargaining solution. This dependence is the critical empirical implication of Nash bargaining models: family demands depend not only on prices and total family resources, but also on the threat point. Thus, the precise empirical implications of the Nash bargaining model depend on whether the threat point corresponds to divorce, as in the divorce threat models of Manser and Brown (1980) and McElroy and Horney (1981), or to a noncooperative outcome within the marriage, as in the separate spheres model of Lundberg and Pollak (1993).[9] In both the divorce threat and separate spheres models, Nash bargaining may imply violations of income pooling.

Income pooling implies a restriction on family demand behavior that is simple to explain and apparently simple to test: if family members pool their incomes and allocate the total to maximize a single objective function, then only total family income will affect family demand behavior. That is, the fraction of income received or controlled by one family member does not influence those demands, conditional on total family income. A large number of recent empirical studies have rejected income pooling, finding instead that the fraction of earned or unearned income received by the husband or the wife significantly affects demand patterns when total family income or expenditure is held constant. Rejections of family income pooling have been most influential in undermining economists' attachment to the unitary approach.

With 20/20 hindsight, I am tempted to say that resource pooling is obviously the crucial empirical issue. But it was not obvious to Manser and Brown, to McElroy and Horney, nor to me when, as editor of the *International Economic Review*, I accepted their papers for publication. The earliest attempts to investigate the compatibility of bargaining models with the unitary model focused on whether the Slutsky matrix corresponding to the family's demand functions was symmetric and negative semi-definite. The focus on the Slutsky conditions was understandable given the influence of Samuelson's formulation of consumer's demand theory in *Foundations of Economic Analysis*. In the 1980s, revealed preference tests were the only alternative to Slutsky conditions as a test of whether demand functions could be derived by maximizing a family utility function subject to a family budget constraint.[10] Pooling, like intrafamily allocation, had yet to be discovered.

The ideal test of the pooling hypothesis would be based on an experiment in which some husbands and some wives were randomly selected to receive income transfers. A less-than-ideal test could be based on a "natural experiment" in which some husbands or some wives received exogenous income transfers. Lundberg, Pollak, and Wales (1997) examine the effects of such a natural experiment—a policy change in the United Kingdom that transferred a substantial child allowance from husbands to wives in the late 1970s. They find strong evidence that a shift toward relatively greater expenditures on women's clothing and children's clothing followed this policy change, and they interpret this as a rejection of the income pooling hypothesis. These empirical results provide convincing evidence against unitary models. Using the same natural experiment, Ward-Batts (2000) provides further evidence. Ward-Batts used disaggregated data that distinguished between cigarettes and "other tobacco"—that is, pipe tobacco and cigars—which she characterized as "men's tobacco." Ward-Batts found that the policy change was followed by a substantial and significant decrease in expenditure on men's tobacco, providing further evidence that control over resources affects household expenditure patterns and allocation within households.

The "collective model" proposed in Chiappori (1988, 1992) characterizes intrafamily allocation by a single-valued, Pareto-efficient "sharing rule" that is assumed to satisfy certain regularity conditions. Both Chiappori's collective model and Samuelson's consensus model are defined by requiring that the solutions to a particular problem exhibit certain properties, but neither examines the conditions under which solutions will exhibit the required properties. Chiappori's sharing rule can be regarded as the reduced form of an unspecified bargaining game. As such, it can provide a convenient mechanism for bracketing some problems in order to focus on others. If we accept the Coasian view that bargaining leads to Pareto-efficient outcomes and if we assume that the Pareto-efficient equilibrium is unique, then we are close to Chiappori's single-valued, Pareto-efficient sharing rule.

The assumption that family behavior can be characterized by a Pareto-efficient sharing rule, although it has important advantages, has three significant limitations. First, because the collective model does not specify a particular bargaining model or class of bargaining models, it offers no guidance for choosing which variables to include in the sharing rule as determinants of bargaining power. Second, as Lundberg and Pollak (2003) argue, unless family members can make binding agreements, the assumption that bargaining outcomes are efficient is implausible when the family must take major decisions that affect future bargaining power. The efficiency of family decisions needs to be investigated, not assumed. Third, both cooperative and noncooperative bargaining models can yield multiple equilibria.

When Samuelson posed the Dr Jekyll and Mrs Jekyll problem in 1956, he recognized that his consensus model did not provide a satisfactory resolution. Fifty years later, economists are still grappling with the difficulty in the concept of the consumer that Samuelson exposed. In the intervening years, the economics of the family emerged as an established field with its own North-Holland Handbook. Where Samuelson focused on the family's demand functions for goods and supply functions for labor, the economics of the family now takes as its domain a wide spectrum of family behaviors: household production, the allocation of time and goods within the family, marriage, divorce, fertility, investment in children's human capital, and care of disabled family members.

Samuelson recognized that the unitary model, which provides a rationale for treating families as economic agents, is valid only under highly restrictive conditions. Samuelson's consensus model provides one such set of conditions and Becker's altruist model provides another. The development of cooperative and noncooperative bargaining models of the family has demoted unitary models by clarifying the assumptions—about the rules of the game or its outcome—under which the unitary model is valid. Theorists may debate the plausibility of alternative models, but the unitary model has been mortally wounded by empirical evidence that married couples do not pool their resources. I believe the demise of the unitary model would not have surprised Samuelson.

Notes

1. Samuelson appears to have been hostile to Becker's economic approach to the family, or at least to its application to the study of fertility. Praising Easterlin's relative income hypothesis, Samuelson (1976) goes on to criticize Becker and T. W. Schultz: "Thus, the Easterlin hypothesis can explain fertility waves not unlike those actually experienced in the United States during the last 40 years [footnote omitted]. The Easterlin theory is all the more valuable for its scarcity among economic theories, standing out in welcome relief from the rather sterile verbalizations by which economists have tended to describe fertility decisions in terms of the jargon of indifference curves, thereby tending to intimidate non-economists who have not mis-spent their youth in mastering the intricacies of modern utility theory." To make clear the targets of his criticism, Samuelson followed this sentence with a footnote citing an article by Leibenstein "for a survey of economists' theories of fertility, including that of the Chicago School theorists, Gary Becker and T. W. Schultz..."
2. It also poses empirical difficulties because consumption data are almost always collected for households or "consumer units," rather than for individuals.
3. In this chapter I treat the term "family" as synonymous with "household." I also treat utility functions and preference orderings—preferences, for short—as equivalent.
4. In Pollak (2003) I argue that much of Becker's analysis rests on a special case of interdependent preferences that he calls "altruistic" and I call "deferential."

5. Sometimes they are called "common preference models."
6. In divorce threat bargaining models, the anticipated utilities of the spouses in the event of divorce determine allocation within marriage.
7. Lundberg and Pollak (2005) survey cooperative and noncooperative bargaining models of the family.
8. The standard Nash axioms are Pareto efficiency, invariance to linear transformation of individuals' von Neumann–Morgenstern utility functions, symmetry (i.e. interchanging the labels on the players has no effect on the solution), and a contraction consistency condition.
9. Woolley (1988) appears to have been first to use a noncooperative Cournot-Nash equilibrium within marriage as the threat point in a bargaining model.
10. Samuelson, of course, invented revealed preference, but that is a story for another chapter.

References

Arrow, Kenneth J., "A Difficulty in the Concept of Social Welfare," *Journal of Political Economy*, Vol. 58, No. 4 (August 1950), 328–346.

Becker, Gary, "A Theory of Social Interactions," *Journal of Political Economy*, Vol. 82, No. 6 (December 1974), 1063–1094.

Becker, Gary S., (1991). *Treatise on the Family*, Cambridge: Harvard University Press, original edition, 1981.

Chiappori, Pierre-André, "Rational Household Labor Supply," *Econometrica*, Vol. 56, No. 1 (January 1988), 63–89.

Chiappori, Pierre-André, "Collective Labor Supply and Welfare," *Journal of Political Economy*, Vol. 100, No. 3 (June 1992), 437–467.

Lundberg, Shelly and Robert A. Pollak, "Separate Spheres Bargaining and the Marriage Market," *Journal of Political Economy*, Vol. 101, No. 6 (December 1993), 988–1010.

Lundberg, Shelly and Robert A. Pollak, "Efficiency in Marriage," *Review of Economics of the Household*, Vol. 1, No. 3 (September 2003), 153–168.

Lundberg, Shelly and Robert A. Pollak, "Bargaining in Families," Working Paper.

Lundberg, Shelly, Robert A. Pollak, and Terence J. Wales, "Do Husbands and Wives Pool Their Resources? Evidence from the U.K. Child Benefit," *Journal of Human Resources*, Vol. 32, No. 3 (Summer 1997), 463–480.

Manser, Marilyn and Murray Brown, "Marriage and Household Decision-Making: A Bargaining Analysis," *International Economic Review*, Vol. 21, No. 1 (February 1980), 31–44.

McElroy, Marjorie B. and Mary J. Horney, "Nash-Bargained Household Decisions: Toward a Generalization of the Theory of Demand," *International Economic Review*, Vol. 22, No. 2 (June 1981), 333–349.

Nash, John F., "The Bargaining Problem," *Econometrica*, Vol. 18, No. 1 (April 1950), 155–162.

Nerlove, Mark, "Household and Economy: Toward a New Theory of Population and Economic Growth," *Journal of Political Economy*, Vol. 83, No. 2, Part II, (March/April 1974), S200–S218.

Pollak, Robert A., "A Transaction Cost Approach to Families and Households," *Journal of Economic Literature*, Vol. 23, No. 2 (June 1985), 581–608.

Pollak, Robert A., "Tied Transfers and Paternalistic Preferences," *American Economic Review*, Vol. 78, No. 2 (May 1988), 240–244.

Pollak, Robert A., "Gary Becker's Contributions to Family and Household Economics," *Review of Economics of the Household*, Vol. 1, No. 1–2 (January–April 2003), 111–141.

Samuelson, Paul A., (1947) *Foundations of Economic Analysis*, Cambridge: Harvard University Press.

Samuelson, Paul A., "Social Indifference Curves," *Quarterly Journal of Economics*, Vol. 70, No. 1 (February 1956), 1–22.

Samuelson, Paul, "An Economist's Non-Linear Model of Self-Generated Fertility Waves," *Population Studies*, Vol. XXX, No. 2 (July 1976), 243–247.

Ward-Batts, Jennifer, "Out of the Wallet and into the Purse: Using Micro Data to Test Income Pooling," working paper, 2005, Clarement McKenna College.

Woolley, Frances, "A Non-cooperative Model of Family Decision Making," manuscript, 1988, London: London School of Economics.

8

Paul Samuelson on Karl Marx: Were the Sacrificed Games of Tennis Worth It?

G. C. Harcourt

> ...around 1955 I volunteered mentally...to investigate whether [Marxian economics] was truly as lacking in merit as seems to be thought the case. (Mark Twain: Wagner is not as bad as he sounds)...colleagues and friends thought it strange of me to waste good tennis time on so irrelevant a subject.
>
> (Samuelson, 1997a, p. 190)

8.1 Introduction and motivation

In his ninth decade Paul Samuelson said in an address to the Bank of Italy on October 2, 1997, in which he compared the difference experiences of present-day American and European economies:

> I lay stress on two main factors, both new and neither one predicted...by any economists writing in the 1980s.
>
> One. In America we now operate... the Ruthless Economy.
>
> Two. In America we now have A Cowed Labor Force...two features...interrelated...[yet]...somewhat distinguishable (Samuelson, 1997b, pp. 6–7).

When I read this, I thought: "Karl, that you should have lived to see this hour." So, when I was asked by Michael Szenberg to contribute to the volume in honor of Paul's 90th birthday, I thought it would be interesting and certainly appropriate to sketch Samuelson's views on Marx as an economist, and any changes in them, over Samuelson's working lifetime (to date, of course).[1] As well as rereading some of his papers on Marx,

I went through the references to Marx and topics related to him cited in the indexes of the various editions of Paul's famous introductory textbook (since the 14th edition of 1992, Samuelson and Nordhaus) in order to trace both the waxing and waning over time of the space given to Marx, to see whether and, if so, how his views have changed. Because, with Prue Kerr (see Harcourt and Kerr, 1996; 2001), I have tried to explain to business people and managers what *we* think the essence of Marx's legacy is, I have taken our evaluations as the backdrop against which to assess agreement and disagreement with Samuelson's interpretations and evaluations. I hope he will find the chapter topic acceptable, not least because his contribution (Samuelson, 1997a), to volume I of the Festschriften for me was on Marx.

8.2 Overview of Samuelson's views on Marx

Starting with the introductory text, Marx certainly receives mentions from the first edition (1948) on, but discussions of him and topics related to him—for example, Friedrich Engels, the labor theory of value (LTV), simple and expanded reproduction in the context of modern (now dubbed "old") growth theory, the iron law of wages, and so on—really took off in the late 1960s and the 1970s: whole sections were devoted to the contributions of Marx, the economist. Furthermore, running through other chapters and discussions of other topics are references to, for example, Marx's predictions about history, the nature of technical progress, and the role of the reserve army of labor. There are also sections discussing the economic principles of ideal socialist states vis-à-vis those of pure competitive capitalist economies and the like. In the ninth edition (1973) there is introduced for the first time an eight-page appendix on the rudiments of Marxian economics (pp. 858–866).

Overall, Marx does not get that bad a press from Samuelson, either as told to beginning students or in his various papers[2]: it is true that in his 1961 Presidential Address to the American Economic Association, Samuelson damned Marx with faint praise—"From the viewpoint of pure economic theory, Karl Marx can be regarded as a minor post-Ricardian" (Samuelson, 1962, p. 12; 1966b, p. 1510)—but he quickly backed off—a little—from this in later evalu-ations, for example, his article in the *American Economic Review* celebrating the centenary of the publication of volume I of *Das Kapital*. While "only the Good Fairies should be invited [to] such a birthday party . . . , a great scholar deserves the compliment of being judged seriously" (Samuelson, 1967; 1972a, p. 268). In the latest editions of the introductory textbook, while the number of references to Marx are much reduced, they are still not *that* unfavorable. Indeed, they are more favorable in the Samuelson and Nordhaus editions than in the latest "Australian Samuelson" (Samuelson *et al.*, 1992), some of whose authors are unrepentant cold war warriors!

As is to be expected, Samuelson comes to his evaluation of Marx as an economic theorist par excellence. In an autobiographical essay published in 1972, Samuelson records that he felt he "was made for economics." "To a person of analytical ability, the world of economics was his oyster in 1935 . . . a terrain strewn with beautiful theorems begging to be picked up and arranged in unified order" (Samuelson, 1972b, p. 161). The same enthusiastic approach characterizes his writings on Marx. While he is careful never to put Marx down because Marx did not have access to the same technical and mathematical tools that Samuelson had, he nevertheless emphasizes what he sees as lack of basic logic in many of Marx's arguments, especially in relation to the labor theory of value. Samuelson takes his most severe stance in his well-known 1971 *Journal of Economic Literature* survey of the literature relating to the Marxian transformation problem. Marx argued that the pattern of labor values of commodities in the sphere of production and the pattern of competitive prices of production in the sphere of distribution and exchange are integral to each other, but that labor values are dominant in a logical sense because of the essential nature of the capitalist mode of production. It was necessary therefore to explain the nature of the deviations of one pattern from the other.

In the survey, Samuelson gives a virtuoso performance in his technical discussion of the issues. He provides wonderful diagrams for teaching and the profession alike; he likens labor values of commodities to the outcome of mark-ups akin to value added taxes on the stages of their production, and prices of production to the outcome of mark-ups akin to turnover taxes, making clear the nature of the inevitable divergences of the relative prices of production from the labor values Marx claimed underlay them.

Samuelson will have none of this. He argues that the essential solution to the transformation problem is contained in an eraser (a rubber to Australians and Limeys) with which to erase (rub out) the value scheme and, making a new start, replace it with the prices of production scheme—"the 'transformation algorithm' is. . . : 'Contemplate two alternative and discordant systems. Write down one. Now transform by taking an eraser and rubbing it out. Then fill in the other one. *Voilà!* You have completed your transformation algorithm'" (1971; 1972a, p. 277).

8.3 The transformation problem

Generations of students introduced to economics through Samuelson's textbook are told that the LTV is a theory of prices, the proposition that commodities exchange in proportion to the labor directly and indirectly embodied in them, and that as Smith knew—Ricardo too (but he did not want to)—once we leave Smith's "early and rude state of society," these labor values are both inaccurate and unnecessary in an explanation of the pattern of the relative (long-period) prices that a competitive situation will tend to establish. Moreover, labor is not alone the source of value and therefore price (a meaningless distinction to modern readers but not to the classical political economists (see Cohen and Harcourt (2003)) once land and capital goods come into the story. Then, we need a general equilibrium system in order to determine *simultaneously* both prices of commodities and payments for the services of the factors involved in producing commodities, so that labor values as defined by Marx are both misleading and unnecessary.

No one has ever established, though many have tried, that Marx himself solved the transformation problem in an agreeable way, and Engels behaved badly in not paying up to those who anticipated or even improved upon Marx's proposed solution after he and Marx had issued just such a challenge. Nevertheless, it is wrong to give the impression that Marx thought the LTV was a literal theory of the pattern of prices of production—we know (and Samuelson makes this explicit) that he had written volume III of *Capital* before the publication of volume I in which, probably understandably but nevertheless wrongly, the price system is identified with a simple LTV. What Marx claimed—this is well documented by, for example, William Baumol, Maurice Dobb, and Ronald Meek, as Samuelson acknowledges—was that he could predict the deviations of the prices of production around the underlying labor values once we considered more complicated models of the pure competitive capitalist mode of production in which organic compositions of capital differed as between industries even though rates of exploitation tended to be the same.

Prue Kerr's and my interpretation of Marx's method of analysis and of the LTV is as follows. Marx came to political economy from philosophy; he was crucially influenced by the philosophical views of Hegel and the principle of dialectical change. The use of the dialectic led him always to look for internal contradictions both in systems of thought and in the working out of social processes. His organizing concept when he came to political economy was the notion of *Surplus*—how it was created, extracted, distributed, and used in different societies. Marx looked at human history as succeeding epochs of different ways of surplus creation, and so on; he was determined to find by analysis of the power patterns of each the seeds of both their achievements and their internal contradictions and eventual destruction and transformation as, through the endogenous processes thus discovered, one form gave way to the next. The jewel in his crown was his analysis of capitalism.

Marx's method of analysis may be likened to an onion. At the central core underlying the overlapping outer layers of skin is the pure, most abstract yet fundamental model of the mode of production (Marx's phrase) being analyzed. All fossils from the past, all embryos of what is to come, are abstracted. The system is revealed in its purest form. Yet, the aim is to show that the fundamental characteristics and relationships thus revealed are robust—that they survive intact the complications provided by adding back (in analysis) the inner and outer layers of skin of the onion, that they still remain the ultimate determinants of what is observed on the surface. Thus, if we may illustrate from the transition from volume I to volume III of *Capital*, though there is little explicit mention in volume I of the (near) surface phenomenon of prices of production of volume III, the links from the underlying labor values of volume I are always at the forefront of Marx's intention—not in the mainstream sense of providing a theory of relative prices (the mainstream interpretation of what the LTV is about) but in making explicit the link as a necessary part of the story of production, distribution, and accumulation in capitalism.

Let us now see what we understand by the dreaded term LTV. As we said, the principal task Marx set himself was to explain the creation and so on of the surplus in capitalism. Naturally he linked this in capitalism with an explanation of the origin of profits and the determination of the system-wide rate of profits. He identified in previous modes the role of classes in each, one dominant, one subservient, with reference to the creation of wealth and so social and economic power, and the connection of their relationship to the creation and so on of the surplus by a process of explicit exploitation of one class by another. For example, in feudalism, the process was obvious: its institutions and laws ensured that the lords of the manor could physically extract from the serfs part of the annual product, either by making the serfs work for set periods on the lords' lands or because the serfs were tenants, requiring them to "hand over" part of the product of the land which their labor had brought forth.

When we get to pure *competitive* capitalism, such a process seems impossible. For one aspect of capitalism, purified in modern theory to become price-taking behavior by all agents with prices set by the impersonal forces of the market, in classical and in Marx's times more robustly specified as wide diffusion of power amongst *individual* capitalists and *individual* wage-earners, seems to make it impossible for individual capitalists to coerce free wage-earners into doing what they do not wish to do. They could always leave one and work for another, just as any one capitalist and his or her capitals could leave or enter any activity—hence the *tendency* for rates of profits to be equalized in all activities and the need to explain what determines the origin and size of the systemic rate of profits to which their individual values tended. Moreover, each free wage-laborer was paid a definite money wage for all the hours he or she worked. Under these conditions, how could exploitation occur or a surplus arise, and where *did* profits come from?

Marx answered this by distinguishing between necessary and surplus labor time associated with the class relations of capitalist society. Capitalists *as a class* (subset into industrial, commercial, and finance capital) had a monopoly of the means of production and finance. Workers *as a class*, having only their labor power to sell, had to do as they were told in the workplace. As property-less, landless but free wage-laborers, whose creation was the by-product of feudalism giving way to capitalism, they had but one choice—*either* to work under the conditions established by the capitalist class *or* to withdraw from the system entirely, and starve. Therefore the working day could conceptually be split into two parts: the hours needed with the existing stock of capital goods, methods, and conditions of production to produce wage goods (necessary labor) and the rest (surplus labor) which was the source of surplus value in the sphere of production, and of profits in the sphere of distribution and exchange. Marx adopted the classical idea, especially Ricardo's, that all commodities had an embodied labor value to explain how labor services, a commodity saleable just like any other in capitalism, would tend to sell at a price determined by its value. But human labor had the unique property that it would create more value—produce more commodities—than was needed for its own reproduction and this was embodied in the commodities corresponding to this surplus labor time.

A subsidiary part of the story was that the actual operations of capitalism resulted in the waxing and waning of the reserve army of labor (RAL)—a much more suitable euphemism for the unemployed than the modern description of the same phenomenon as flexible labor markets—causing actual wages to tend toward (or fluctuate around?) their natural values (a purely classical story). But the main story was that while the surface phenomenon seemingly reflected fairness and efficiency—people being paid fully for what they did and all the hours they worked—this masked the underlying exploitation process arising from the situation of class monopoly. In the sphere of production there was a tendency to equality in the length of the working day (week, year) and intensity of work too. In the sphere of distribution and exchange, abstracting from actual (market) prices, there was a tendency for the prices of production to be such that a uniform rate of profits was created (the first great empirical generalization of classical political economy) and for the profit components of the prices of production to be such as to constitute uniform rates of return on total capitals, similarly measured, in all activities.

Many, including Samuelson, have come to see the "transformation problem" as a sterile exercise and debate. Yet viewed in this way I think it makes sense, both in explaining a fundamental characteristic of capitalism and in illustrating the power of Marx's method and approach. In order to show that anything classical political economy could do Marx could do as well and better, it was necessary to reconcile the pure theory of the origin of profits in the capitalist mode of production with the other major "finding" of political economy—the tendency to a uniform rate of profits in all activities—and also to "explain" what determines the size of the system-wide rate of profits. (Piero Sraffa, who had a deep knowledge of and admiration for Marx's work, always spoke of the rate of profits, indicating that it *was* the system-wide concept which needed to be explained within the classical and Marxist system. As Luigi Pasinetti said of his own modern variant of the theory of the rate of profits, "It is macro-economic because it could not be otherwise" (Pasinetti, 1974, p. 118)).

The various conundrums arise because, while competition would ensure a uniform rate of exploitation (s/v, where s = surplus labor and v = necessary labor) in all industries because, as we have seen, free wage-laborers can always move from one occupation to another, there is nothing obvious or even not obvious in the forces of competition and their impact on technical progress to ensure that the corresponding organic compositions of capital (c/v) (with some license, the capital-labor ratios) should also tend to equality. But since a well-known Marxist result is that $r = s/v/(1 + c/v)$, when all variables are measured in terms of abstract socially necessary labor time, *if* the LTV meant that commodities exchanged in proportion to their embodied labor mounts, there would not be a tendency, not even a long-run one, to equality of rates of profit (so measured) in all activities.

Therefore it became necessary to explain the deviations of the prices of production with their uniform profit components around the underlying labor values, at the same time requiring the explanation to embrace the magnitudes of surplus value *et al.* in the sphere of production.

This step is what the various proposed "solutions" of the transformation problem were meant to establish—Sraffa's is the most satisfying as Ronald Meek pointed out in his 1961 review article of *Production of Commodities* (Meek, 1961; 1967). Baumol in his comment (Baumol, 1974a) in 1974 on Samuelson's *Journal of Economic Literature* survey (in which he was only concerned to establish what Marx really said, not that he was necessarily correct) set out a parable which I believe is consistent with our interpretation.[3] Baumol (1974a, p. 153) wrote:

> My contention is that Marx['s] interest in the transformation problem analysis as a sequel to his value theory was not a matter of pricing. [He] sought to describe how *non* wage incomes are *produced* and then how this aggregate is redistributed... first... substantive issue to Marx and the one he discusses in volume I, while the latter is the surface manifestation known to all bourgeois economists and which Marx only deigns to consider in volume III.
>
> The substance of Marx's analysis can be summarised in a simple parable... the economy is described as an aggregation of industries each of which contributes to a storehouse containing total surplus value... Each industry's contribution is proportionate to the quantity of labor it uses... how society's surplus value is *produced*.
>
> The distribution of surplus value from the... storehouse takes place via the competitive process which assigns to each industry for profit... an amount... proportionate to its capital investment... the heart of the transformation process—the conversion of surplus value into profit... takes from each according to its workforce and returns to each according to its total investment (emphasis in original).

"Values," adds Baumol, "are not approximations to prices nor a necessary step in their calculation... one is a surface manifestation—the latter... intended to reveal an underlying reality" (p.55). (Baumol (1974b) and Samuelson (1974a) subsequently had an exchange over Baumol's comment. Samuelson, in effect, restated his original position and Baumol thought Samuelson's reply was to an article he never wrote.)

I would also argue that Piero Sraffa's solution of the transformation problem (Sraffa, 1960), the nature of which is brought out beautifully in Ronald Meek's illuminating review article of Sraffa's classic (Meek, 1961; 1967), arises because Sraffa's analysis is set in a context that accepts Marx's general approach, even though he is critical of specific incoherence and his analysis is also directed at unfinished business. Meek showed the striking similarity between Marx's, ultimately unsatisfactory, concept of the average industry and Sraffa's precise account of the Standard system, Standard commodity and the relationship $r = R(1 - w)$, where r = rate of profits, R = the maximum rate of profits in the Standard system (and actual economy) and w = share of wages in the Standard national income. "What both economists are trying to show... is that the average rate of profits, *and therefore the deviations of price ratios from embodied labour ratios*, are governed by the ratio of direct to indirect labour in the industry whose conditions of production represents a sort of 'average' of those prevailing in the economy as a whole" (Meek, 1961; 1967, pp. 176–178, emphasis added).

Furthermore I would submit that, in general terms, Samuelson's (1997a) address in Rome draws on the idea that it is the creation of the potential surplus in the sphere of production via the activities of the business class, now with international as well as national aims, that provides the backdrop to the realization (or not) of profits and accumulation in the sphere of distribution and exchange. The person who has set this out extremely clearly is Donald Harris in his 1975 *American Economic Review* article and 1978 book. Joan Robinson, who was contemptuous of the LTV—she used to say in effect that she could not see why the LTV is needed to explain that chaps who owned the means of production and had access to finance could push around chaps who did not—nevertheless was at one with Harris on this interpretation. Samuelson also seems to be at one with Marx in recognizing the internal contradictions in the operation of capitalism, whereby in the attempt through harsh monetary policy to create a larger potential surplus, the impact on Keynesian "animal spirits" maybe such as to prevent the potential surplus becoming an actual surplus.[4] Witness the disappointing rates of accumulation in many economies in recent years, relatively to those of the years of the Long Boom (or Golden Age of capitalism).

8.4 Samuelson on Marx: Accumulation and growth

One of the headings in the 1960s and 1970s editions of *Economics*, for example, the eighth edition (1970, p. 718), at first sight may tend to cause raised eyebrows. Samuelson refers to "Ricardo–Marx–Solow models of capitalist accumulation"! But on further reflection, Samuelson has made an incisive point here (marred only by his omission of Trevor Swan's name from the list), as Bob Rowthorn, for one, has often argued. For if we ignore the adjectives involved, there *is* a family resemblance between, for example, the narrative that James Meade told in his neoclassical theory of growth (Meade, 1961)—itself explicitly based on Swan's work, especially on the feedback between relative factor prices, choice of technique, and induced technical change—and the narratives that we find in volumes II and III of *Capital*. All these authors were striving toward what we now call a theory of endogenous technical change to which, of course, Samuelson has also made important contributions.

From some of his earliest postwar writings, Samuelson has always been keen to test whether classical and Marxian conjectures are confirmed when the latest technical advances, for example, linear programming, are used to specify their ideas in models. Thus, we have here his papers in the 1950s on Marx and Ricardo (Samuelson, 1957, 1959a, 1959b, 1960, all reprinted in Samuelson, 1966a, Part IV), and later in his textbooks, on schemes of simple and expanded reproduction in Marx. Samuelson sees these classical and Marxian contributions as early forerunners of modern (now "old") growth theory associated with Harrod (1939, 1948) and with Solow and Swan's responses to the puzzles thrown up by Harrod's contributions: that is to say, the analysis of steady states and their stability, especially the stability of the warranted rate of growth, g_w, itself, and the possibilities of g_w finding its way to the natural rate of growth, g_n, if initially their values are not equal.

But perhaps this is a misreading of what Marx principally had in mind. Claudio Sardoni (1981) has pointed out that Marx was asking the question: what conditions have to be satisfied in order that aggregate demand and its components match aggregate supply and *its* components, period by period, and that this did not necessarily imply advance in a steady state at a constant rate of growth. Marx did the analysis in terms of his three departmental schema, which Samuelson reproduces in his discussions. Marx asked in effect what conditions will ensure that each department either directly (i.e. from within itself) or indirectly can find markets for its output. The point is that by establishing the very special conditions involved, Marx illustrated how unlikely it was that a competitive capitalist economy, with each individual capitalist doing his/her own thing concerning production, employment, and accumulation, would lead to an uncoordinated collective outcome that satisfied the conditions for balance of both totals and compositions.

The next question then was what would the nonfulfilment lead to as far as systemic behavior was concerned? Marx thought it would create cycles and even crises. Joan Robinson once pointed out that Harrod had rediscovered this insight when he set out what were the consequences of the nonattainment of the warranted rate of growth, that is, of the actual rate of growth not immediately (and thus not ever) coinciding with the warranted rate.

8.5 Marx and Samuelson's method and approach

Samuelson's Italian address reflects, I think, a central characteristic of Marx's procedure. As pointed out above (see pp. 130–132), Marx divided history into distinct periods classified by the specific way the surplus was created and so on. Allied with this insight was the view that each period has a dominant class, the nature of whose dominance determined the nature of surplus creation. Nothing in Marx's account of surplus creation in capitalism is inconsistent with the view, shared by Samuelson in many of his comments in his textbook and essays, that capitalism was an extraordinarily dynamic mode of production which through accumulation and innovation raises productivity and at least potential standards of living over time.

Those scholars who were more favorable to Marx in general, for example, Dobb, Meek, Sraffa, took this narrative for granted when they contributed their formal analysis of the characteristics of the two spheres of operation in capitalism. So too does Samuelson now, or so I interpret him as doing; but in his earlier discussions at least he seems not to have accepted the prior narrative. Partly, this may be due to Samuelson's comparative advantage in presenting technical analysis, the establishing of pleasing lemmas and theorems; partly, it may be due to his being adverse to "the late Prof. Wildon Carr's admirable motto... 'It is better to be vaguely right than precisely wrong.' "[5]

Samuelson and Marx have some, perhaps many, things in common in their methodology and general approach. Both always steeped themselves in what had gone before, provided an internal critique, and then built their own often innovative but also synthetic contributions on the basis of their absorption of the writings of their predecessors. Samuelson is very careful to name predecessors of ideas, both in his textbook and in his articles, before he uses his powerful technical skills to see whether conjectures or less rigorous (in his terms) arguments of predecessors go through. Usually this proves to be most illuminating and helpful, especially in teaching, by extracting in a simple precise way the essence of some conventional doctrines. Though it runs the risk sometimes, as

Keynes said of Russell, Wittgenstein, and Ramsey's "gradual perfection of the treatment [of logic]," to run the risk of reducing it to "mere dry bones" (Keynes, *CW*, Vol. X, 1972, p. 338); dry bones into which, moreover, life may not be breathed. That is to say, while the systems formed may be self-consistent, they are too far removed from the reality from which they started to serve to provide illuminations.

8.6 Increasing misery and skilled labour

Samuelson used his method and approach to criticize the "doctrine of increasing misery" (Meek, 1967, p. 113) of Marx, whereby both the rate of profits tends to fall over time and the situation of the wage-earners to worsen, as one prediction too many. I suppose a riposte could be that if accumulation too were falling as a result so that unemployment was rising, both tendencies could be present. But this is not a convincing response, especially when we take, as we must in this context, long-term advances in technical progress into account. We must agree therefore with Samuelson's contention that Marx was wrong and so must be content with being "just another genius" as Meek (1967, p. 128) told us many years ago.[6]

Samuelson lists in many places as one of his criticisms of the LTV the incoherence introduced by the presence of skilled labor, in that a way of measuring its amounts in a common unit of socially necessary labor cannot be found or, at least, not in a manner that is independent of the wage structure which it ought to be one of the tasks of economic theory to explain. There are perhaps two comebacks. First, in order to make the point at a high level of abstraction that surplus labor and value are both the source of profits and vital determinants of their size, assuming homogeneous labor may be a legitimate simplification. Second, Rowthorn (1988) has set out an ingenious way of getting over the problem of reduction of skilled to unskilled labor. He follows a suggestion of Hilferding. This involves tracing back and adding together the amounts of socially necessary labor needed to produce skilled labor. Rowthorn provides an elegant formal exposition using simultaneous equations, which no doubt would warm Samuelson's heart. It, moreover, allows technical advances to be incorporated and so "the reduction of skilled to unskilled labour can be performed quite independently of the level of wages and the analysis avoids Böhm-Bawerk's charge of circularity" (Rowthorn, 1980, p. 233).

8.7 Conclusion

To conclude: Samuelson in his Italian Address has, to some extent anyway, accepted Marx's desire to explain in simple pure (or ideal) models the various processes at work in capitalism then and now. He has also accepted some of the ingredients of Marx's own explanations while not jettisoning his own use of more mainstream ingredients.

I hope that I have not done Paul Samuelson any gross injustice in this evaluation. If I have, no doubt he will respond by emulating Marx (but, I am sure, much more politely) in the manner in which Samuelson at the end of his essay celebrating the Centenary of the publication of volume I of *Capital* describes Marx's own likely response:

> But this is a birthday party and I [PAS] approach the boundaries of good taste. Let me conclude by wishing that, like Tom Sawyer attending his own funeral, Karl Marx could be present at his own centennial. When the 'the Moor' rose to speak, how we would all pay for our presumptuousness! (Samuelson, 1967; 1972a, p. 275).

Notes

1. May I say how honored and delighted I feel to have been asked to contribute to the volume? Though we do not agree on some issues, I have always admired Paul and his work. I have especially appreciated the graciousness he has always shown to me, despite—or perhaps because—of our differences over the years: the graciousness he also showed my mentor, Joan Robinson, despite *their* many intellectual battles over the years. He is a role model and an inspiration to our profession.
2. I must admit, though, that after having done my homework, I looked again at Paul's essay (1997a), "Isolating sources of sterility in Marx's theoretical paradigms," only to read that "at the end of the day I never could find analytical pearls to cast before orthodox economist swine... *Capital's* volume 2 tableaux of reproduction and balanced exponential growth [is]... Karl Marx's sole contribution to economic theory" (p. 190)—and then only in a (very) special case!
3. Indeed, in my case—I cannot speak for Prue—I was very much influenced by Baumol's comment and parable, as well as by many discussions with and the writings of my three former research students, Prue Kerr, Allen Oakley, and Claudio Sardoni on these and related matters.
4. Samuelson surely would also appreciate Tommy Balogh's quip that "Monetarism is the incomes policy of Karl Marx" (Balogh, 1982, p. 177).

5. This was quoted by Gerald Shove in his evaluation of Marshall's *Principles* 50 years on from their publication. Shove thought it "might well have been Marshall's" as well (see Shove, 1942, p. 323).
6. In fairness to Marx it may be said that all the major classical political economists thought there would be a long-run tendency for the rate of profits to fall, though they differed fundamentally in their explanations why.

References

Arestis, Philip, Gabriel Palma, and Malcolm Sawyer (eds.) (1997). *Capital Controversy, Post-Keynesion Economics and the History of Economics. Essays in honour of Geoff Harcourt*. Vol. 1. London: Routledge.

Balogh, Thomas. (1982). *The Irrelevance of Conventional Economics*. London: Weidenfeld and Nicholson.

Baumol, William J. (1974a). "The transformation of values. What Marx "really" meant (An interpretation)," *Journal of Economic Literature*, XII, pp. 51–61.

——. (1974b). "Comment," *Journal of Economic Literature*, XII, pp. 74–75.

Cohen, Avi J. and G. C. Harcourt (2003). "Whatever happened to the Cambridge Capital Theory Controversies?" *Journal of Economic Perspectives*, 17, pp. 199–214.

Harcourt, G. C. (2001). *50 Years a Keynesian and Other Essays*. London: Palgrave.

——. and Prue Kerr. (1996). "Marx, Karl Heinrich (1818–83)," in Warner (ed.), (1996), pp. 4355–4362. Reprinted in Harcourt (2001), *50 Years a Keynesian and Other Essays*. London: Palgrave, pp. 157–168.

Harris, Donald J. (1975). "The theory of economic growth: A critique and reformulation," *American Economic Review, Papers and Proceedings*, 65, 329–337.

——. (1978). *Capital Accumulation and Income Distribution*. Stanford, CA: Stanford University Press.

Holten, Gerald. (ed.). (1972). *The Twentieth-Century Sciences*. New York: Norton and company incorporated.

Keynes, J. M. (1972). *CW*, Vol. X, London: Macmillan.

Meade, J. E. (1961). *A Neo Classical Theory of Economic Growth*. London: Allen and Unwin. Rev. new 2nd edn. 1964.

Meek, Ronald L. (1967). *Economics and Ideology and Other Essays. Studies in the Development of Economic Thought*. London: Chapman & Hall Ltd.

Pasinetti, Luigi L. (1974). *Growth and Income Distribution. Essays in Economic Theory*. Cambridge: Cambridge University Press.

Rowthorn, Bob. (1980). *Capitalism, Conflict and Inflation. Essays in Political Economy*. London: Lawrence and Wishart.

Samuelson, Paul A. *Economics: An Introductory Analysis* (1948–2004). New York, Toronto, London: McGraw-Hill Book Coy., 18 editions, from 1992 on (14th edition), co-authored with William D. Nordhaus.

——. (1966a). *The Collected Scientific Papers of Paul A. Samuelson*, Vol. I. (edited by Joseph E. Stiglitz), Cambridge, MA and London: The MIT Press.

——. (1966b). *The Collected Scientific Papers of Paul A. Samuelson*, Vol. II. (edited by Joseph E. Stiglitz), Cambridge, MA and London: The MIT Press.

——. (1971). "Understanding the Marxian motion of exploitation: A summary of the so-called transformation problem between Marxian values and competitive prices", *Journal of Economic Literature*, IX, pp. 399–431.

——. (1972a). *The Collected Scientific Papers of Paul A. Samuelson*, Vol. III. (edited by Robert C. Merton), Cambridge, MA and London: The MIT Press. (In the text the original dates of publication of papers by Samuelson are given but the page references, where relevant, i.e., collected, are to the three volumes of *Collected Scientific Papers*.)

——. (1972b). "Economics in a Golden Age: A personal memoir," in Holton (ed.), (1972), *The Twentieth-Century Sciences*. New York: Norton and company incorporated. pp. 155–170.

——. (1974a). "Insight and detour in the theory of exploitation," *Journal of Economic Literature*, XII, pp. 62–70.

——. (1997a). "Isolating sources of sterility in Marx's theoretical paradigms," in Arestis, Palma and Sawyer (eds), *Capital Controversy, Post-Keynesion Economics and the History of Economics. Essays in honour of Geoff Harcourt.* Vol. 1. London: Routledge, pp. 187–198.

——. (1997b). "Wherein do the European and American models differ?" Address delivered at the Bank of Italy, October 2, 1997, Number 320, mimeo.

——. William D. Nordhaus, Sue Richardson, Graham Scott, and Robert Wallace. (1992). *Economics. Third Australian Edition*, 2 volumes. Sydney, New York: McGraw-Hill Book Company.

Sardoni, C. (1981). "Multi-sectoral models of balanced growth and the Marxian schemes of expanded reproduction," *Australian Economic Papers*, 20, pp. 383–397.

Shove, G. F. (1942). "The place of Marshall's *Principles* in the development of economic theory," *Economic Journal*, 52, pp. 294–329.

Sraffa, Piero. (1960). *Production of Commodities by Means of Commodities. Prelude to a Critique of Economic Theory*. Cambridge: Cambridge University Press.

Warner, Malcolm. (ed.) (1996). *International Encyclopaedia of Business and Management*. London: Routledge.

9

Paul Samuelson and the Stability of General Equilibrium

Franklin M. Fisher

The study of the stability of general equilibrium is not a popular indoor sport among present-day economists. Yet, the lack of a fully satisfactory stability analysis is a gaping hole in microeconomic theory. In particular, the First and Second Welfare Theorems on which so much policy depends are theorems about the efficiency properties of general equilibrium. If general equilibrium is not satisfactorily stable, then the usefulness of those theorems is in question. Further, to assume that the economy is always at or near equilibrium is to beg the question of why that is so, and to fail to notice that relative prices do change in fact.

In short, economists' concentration on equilibrium analysis seems grounded only in elegant convenience rather than in soundly based proof. It looks at economies only after the Invisible Hand has ceased its activity and ignores the way in which such activity operates. The Rational Expectations school of thought is the prime example of this error, but it is far from the only one.

Despite the fact that stability theory has yet to reach a satisfactory conclusion, it remains my hope that the twenty-first century will see more attention paid to this area and considerable progress made. If that turns out to be the case, it will have been Paul Samuelson who long ago set the subject on the right path, even while, at the same time, introducing a then necessary construct whose dismantling appears now to be a crucial step.[1]

The pre dawn of stability theory occurred with the publication of John Hicks's *Value and Capital* (Hicks, 1939). In the appendix to that influential volume, Hicks set forth a set of conditions that he regarded as important (perhaps even necessary and sufficient) for the stability of prices in a general equilibrium system of multiple markets. He began with the proposition that stability in a single market depended on excess demand being a decreasing function of the price of the commodity there traded, and then added conditions to ensure that this property would be preserved even when other markets and prices were permitted to adjust in reaction to a non-equilibrium price in the first one.

But however interesting the Hicks Conditions might be,[2] Samuelson pointed out that their relation to stability of anything was questionable (Samuelson, 1941; see also Samuelson, 1947, chap IX, especially pp. 269–270). Indeed, more importantly, he pointed out that the study of stability necessarily requires consideration of dynamics and hence of a process that unfolds over time. This observation and his suggestion of how such a process should be modeled were the foundation of the stability literature.

Samuelson suggested that one should model the behavior of prices in disequilibrium according to the following equation (somewhat generalized and updated):

$$\dot{p}_i = F^i(Z^i(p)) \quad \text{when } p_i = 0 \text{ and } Z^i(p) < 0 \text{, in which case } \dot{p}_i = 0.$$

Here, p_i denotes the price of the ith commodity, p is the price vector, $Z^i(p)$ is the excess demand for the ith commodity, and $F^i(\bullet)$ is a continuous, sign preserving function. This means that each price moves in the direction indicated by the excess demand for the corresponding commodity—up when demand exceeds supply and down when supply exceeds demand. (The second part of (9.1) is a later addition, designed to take account of the fact that prices cannot be negative.)

Samuelson went on to point out that, for local movements, this could be represented as a linear differential equation, and, following that, the literature went on to consider whether the Hicks Conditions were either necessary or sufficient for the local stability of the process of price adjustment being modeled. It was shown (Metzler, 1945) that this could be analyzed under the assumption that all commodities are gross substitutes, and eventually shown (Hahn, 1958; Negishi, 1958) that the gross substitutes assumption implied the Hicks Conditions and hence local stability. It was then shown (Arrow and Hurwicz, 1958) that the gross substitutes assumption itself implies global stability.[3]

Where Equation (9.1) is the only equation of motion, only prices adjust, no disequilibrium trade takes place, and the process is known as "*tâtonnement.*" It is not generally stable. But Samuelson's reasonable-appearing suggestion survived into the far more fruitful non-*tâtonnement* literature, where trade does take place out of equilibrium and thought has been given as to *how* it takes place.

The problem with (9.1), however, is that, appealing as it is, we have no good reason for believing in it. This can be described as follows:

We are dealing with a competitive economy, in which all participants take prices as given. But, as Arrow, among others, aptly remarked, if everyone takes prices as given, how do prices ever change?[4]

Indeed, the same problem exists even when dealing with a single competitive market in isolation. The explanation commonly given in elementary classes is that, if demand exceeds supply, unsatisfied buyers offer higher prices, and that, if supply exceeds demand, unsatisfied sellers offer lower ones. At some level, this is doubtless correct, but it lacks rigor.

The common fiction in the general equilibrium literature is that this is the job of an "auctioneer" who compares demand and supply and behaves according to (9.1). But such auctioneers generally do not exist.

This problem is symptomatic of a larger one. Economic theory provides a truly elegant explanation of the behavior of the individual maximizing agent in a competitive economy and of how all plans can be consistent in general competitive equilibrium. But it is practically silent on how agents behave when their planned actions do *not* turn out to be feasible. Yet the question of out-of-equilibrium behavior is central to any examination of dynamics and stability. Ironically, Samuelson pointed out that the modeling of disequilibrium behavior over time was essential, but also suggested an adjustment equation that has little or nothing to do with such behavior.

In some ways, this may have been fortunate, however. With the methods known at the time, analysis of stability with individuals setting prices might have been even more frustratingly difficult than it turned out to be in the late twentieth century. At that time, I was able to show that price-setting depended on each seller's (to make it simple) perception of its monopoly power. Unfortunately, even if one can prove stability this means that convergence of the system to a *Walrasian, competitive* equilibrium will only happen if such perceived monopoly power asymptotically lessens to zero (Fisher, 1983, chapter 6). Interestingly, this is related to liquidity problems and to the liquidity trap of Keynes' *General Theory*.

But it also turns out that the stability proof involved depends on a strong assumption about individual perceptions generally—an assumption that new favorable opportunities do not arise as sudden surprises in the course of the adjustment process. I believe that assumption to be probably inevitable when dealing with a process that depends on individual behavior and expectations, but that does not make the result very appealing.

Still, if progress is to be made, economists cannot refrain from considering such issues. One cannot understand the workings of the Invisible Hand by examining only situations where the Hand has already done its work. Paul Samuelson may have been the first to truly understand this.

Notes

1. For a general review of the subject and a detailed analysis of its importance and problems, see Fisher (1983), especially chapter 2.
2. It is now known that they ensure uniqueness of general equilibrium and follow from the assumption that all goods are gross substitutes—hence also ensuring global stability of the *tâtonnement* process.
3. Much later, McFadden (1968) showed that the Hicks Conditions could be interpreted in terms of relative speeds of adjustment in a model in which they imply global stability without the Gross Substitutes assumption.
4. I have been unable to track down the exact reference.

References

Arrow, K. J. and L. Hurwicz (1958). "On the stability of the competitive Equlibrium, I," *Econometrica*, 26, 522–552.

Fisher, F. M. (1983). *Disequilibrium Foundations of Equilibrium Economics*. Cambridge (UK): Cambridge University Press.

Hahn, F. H. (1958). "Gross substitutes and the stability of general equilibrium," *Econometrica*, 26, 169–170.

Hicks, J. R. (1939). *Value and Capital*. New York: Oxford University Press (Clarendon Press).

McFadden, D. (1968). "On Hicksian stability," in J. N. Wolfe (ed.), *Value, Capital, and Growth. Papers in Honour of Sir John Hicks*. Edinburgh: Edinburgh University Press.

Metzler, L. (1945). "The stability of multiple markets: The Hicks conditions," *Econometrica*, 13, 277–292.

Negishi, T. (1958). "A note on the stability of an economy where all goods are gross substitutes," *Econometrica*, 26, 445–447.

Samuelson, P. A. (1941). "The stability of equilibrium," *Econometrica*, 9, 97–120.

——. (1947). *Foundations of Economic Analysis*. Cambridge, MA: Harvard University Press.

10

Paul Samuelson and Piero Sraffa—Two Prodigious Minds at the Opposite Poles

Luigi L. Pasinetti

10.1 Introduction

This chapter is concerned with two giants in the history of economic thought, who stand at the opposite poles. Paul Samuelson is one of the main architects—perhaps *the* main architect, and in any case the leading symbol—of what nowadays is known as neoclassical economics—that is, dominant economics. Piero Sraffa has been the most acute critical mind of Marginal, and hence neoclassical, economics and the leading promoter of a resumption of that classical economic analysis, which—born at the eve of the Industrial Revolution—was (as he claims) "nipped in the bud," and unduly submerged by an over-flowing of (Marginal) economic theory. If the mark of a great leader is the recognition he or she obtains by the leader of the opposite camp, we must admit that Paul Samuelson never spared enthusiastic appreciations of the greatness of Piero Sraffa. "Did any scholar have so great impact on economic science as Piero Sraffa did in so few writings? One doubts it. [...] Piero Sraffa was much respected and much loved. With each passing year, economists perceive new grounds for admiring his genius" (Samuelson, 1987, p. 460).

Yet, while Samuelson, with his articles—hundreds of them—and with his successful textbook—the most successful textbook ever written in

I am very grateful to GianPaolo Mariutti for research assistance. I am also thankful to Enrico Bellino and Angelo Reati for comments and discussions. Financial support from Università Cattolica S.C., Milano is gratefully acknowledged. (Research project D.3.2.)

economics—has become the undisputed icon of mainstream economics, in the United States and throughout the world, Sraffa remains almost an unknown soldier, above all, in Samuelson's homeland. Sraffa never wrote any textbook, even less did he write popular articles in influential magazines or newspapers. He was always reluctant to publish anything, and the very few times he did publish, he even eschewed—unlike his mentor, John Maynard Keynes—any attempt to actively promote the diffusion of his publications. Nevertheless, the influence of Sraffa on shaping the course of economics science in the twentieth century is unquestionable. He was the mind behind "the imperfect competition revolution" of the 1920s and behind the famous *Economic Journal* discussion on "returns to scale" in the 1930s. His *Works and Correspondence of David Ricardo* (Sraffa, 1951–72) has made him the most celebrated critical Editor in economics ever. He was the inspirer of the debate on capital theory of the 1950s and 1960s. And just when almost nobody expected anything from him anymore, he published his masterpiece—an amazingly compact 99-page book, with an apparently innocent title, *Production of Commodities by means of Commodities* (Sraffa, 1960, *PCmC* from now on).

Samuelson acknowledged Sraffa's achievements with no hesitation. In a commemoration article, "A genius with few works," published in Italian at the time of Sraffa's death, Samuelson (1983) remarked that each single page Sraffa published has left a mark in the economic literature. Samuelson has even gone to the point of calling the two decades that followed the Second World War, "the age of Leontief and Sraffa" (Samuelson, 1971). Yet, three years later, the same *Journal* offered its readers another article—"The Age of Leontief and Who?"—in which its author, Levine (1974), showed surprise, claiming that the work of Sraffa "does not appear to have penetrated very deeply into the consciousness of the economics profession in North America, nor... into that of the United Kingdom" (Levine, 1974, p. 872).

All this makes any parallel between Samuelson and Sraffa even more intriguing. The keen interest that Samuelson showed in Sraffa's contributions is puzzling, as much as genuine. Samuelson was one of the few economists to read the proofs of *PCmC*. They were sent to him by the Cambridge University Press—as he tells us—with the question: "Shall we bring out a separate American publication?" And his reply was an "enthusiastic affirmation" (Samuelson, 2000a, p. 113). Ever since, he never ceased writing and conjecturing on Sraffa's arguments and findings. So much so that Samuelson has devoted to Sraffa's *PCmC* a number of pages that are more than double the length of Sraffa's book itself. Where does this unusual interest originate from? And why does Samuelson remain one of the few US economists who continues to be keenly concerned with the Cambridge Italian economist? The present chapter makes an attempt at peeping into this sort of mystery.

10.2 Different Styles and Reciprocal Fascination

As far as sheer personalities are concerned, we could not imagine a wider gap between Samuelson and Sraffa. Paul Samuelson's extrovert temperament and great communicative disposition are well known. A delightful occasion such as the present celebration could never have been imagined to happen in the case of Sraffa. Again, on sheer ground of research organization, the central place that Samuelson has always held in the economics Department of M.I.T., his participation to innumerable meetings, congresses, conferences, at home and abroad, stand out as diametrically opposite to the unobtrusive, almost hidden role, to the solitary life, of Piero Sraffa, as a near anonymous Fellow of a Cambridge college. At the same time, Sraffa's contacts with, and remarkable influence on, outstanding intellectuals of his generation (think of Wittgenstein, of several notable Cambridge mathematicians and economists of his time) are well known and widely acknowledged, even if they took place in lonely conversations, restricted encounters in college rooms, or in the college backs, or in esoteric places, such as mountains, seaside secluded places, or accidental spots. All this being said, the reciprocal intellectual fascination and attraction of Paul Samuelson and Piero Sraffa are an undeniable fact, even if they lived far away from each other. (Piero did not even ever visit the United States.) Perhaps, the longest time they happened to be together was confined to the few days of the Corfù Conference on the *Theory of Capital* (1958), a very rare (perhaps unique) occasion in which Austin Robinson succeeded in convincing Piero (thanks to the sheer beauty of the chosen island) to attend one of his numerously organized International Economic Association Conferences. One can have some ideas of the problems they may have been talking about in their exchanges from the (published) minutes of the Conference. An amusing impression of what may have gone on between the two can also be glimpsed from the correspondence (rather restricted, but not insignificant) that followed those encounters.[1] Reading the jokes that the two were improvising in their exchanges is exhilarating delight. But of course it is to their works that one must look to find the source of their intellectual attraction and reciprocal fascination.

Samuelson is one of "the last generalists economists"—as he defined himself.[2] His interests ranged over so varied and numerous fields as to make it impossible even to list them synthetically here. But there is one major work—his masterpiece, *Foundations of Economic Analysis* (1947)—that, besides having established his fame all over the world, is at the very basis of his scientific contributions. This work, more than any other, shaped the direction of modern economic analysis and brought infant Walrasian economics to its mature neoclassical shape. Sraffa, on his part, by distilling his words in his rare publications and by leaving us an enormous heap of unpublished notes, has equally proved to aim at fundamental results, though on a strikingly different route. He is the (so far unsurpassed) champion of a reconstruction of classical economics, and the major critic of the (marginal economics) theories that have spread since the end of the nineteenth century. His masterpiece, *PCmC*, is, as Samuelson's *Foundations*, of equally foundational character. It is not therefore so surprising that it should have attracted Samuelson's attention since the beginning.

10.3 Alternative "Foundations"

"Comparison is a death knell to sibling harmony." It may be wise to proceed with caution. *Foundations of Economic Analysis* (Samuelson, 1947) and *Production of Commodities by means of Commodities* (Sraffa, 1960) are two books that tackle economic theory at its foundations; but they do so by proceeding on two quite different tracks.

Samuelson has, in a sense, chosen an easier route. His foundational contribution is covering, and crowning, an enormous number of works carried out over decades, since the 1870s, by hundreds of economists. His genius has led him to discover that all these works are carrying out the same basic conceptual process, and are applying it over and over again to a whole variety of economic problems. He has thus been able to single out a central (*mathematical*) principle—maximization under constraints—that allows him to insert all those works into a grand general theoretical frame. In this way, his scheme, ambitiously and—from the result he has achieved, we must say—successfully pursues the aim of absorbing all specific economic theories in order ideally to unify them, under the same comprehensive over-all (neoclassical) umbrella.

The route which Sraffa decides to take is a much thornier one. He goes back, so to speak, to where modern economics began (under the strong impact—we must remember—of a major historical event, the Industrial Revolution). He goes back to classical economics, which, when it was started and developed, got enmeshed into no few analytical problems (left unsolved). Sraffa is convinced that he must, first of all, eliminate all ambiguities and definitely solve those analytical problems in an unassailable way. This task constrains him to a preliminary stage, which, to be successful, must be placed on absolutely solid bases, even if it must be left open in many directions. He feels this so strongly as to append an apparently disconcerting subtitle—*Prelude to a critique of economic theory*—to the title of his book. If taken literally, this would confine his investigation to a *destructive* stage, which—we must acknowledge—he accomplishes rather successfully. But of course this cannot be the whole thing; and he says so. Of course, one should then proceed beyond the *Prelude to the critique*. And even this cannot be enough. We are reasonably entitled to ask: When and in which way will the *constructive* phase set in? And to what extent? And in which way will it be able to absorb, and thus include, into its ideally more general framework whatever acceptable contributions may already have been achieved elsewhere?

The Levine (1974) quotation mentioned above shows the "normal" way to react to questions of this type. Levine simply records the lack of interest from the (American and U.K.) profession. But this is not Samuelson's reaction! He responds in an exceptionally perceptive and concerned way. This is the intriguing point.

There must be a clue (or clues). I can immediately see at least a methodological one. Under the full title of his *Foundations*, in the front page of his book, Samuelson appends, as epigraph, a proposition by J. Willard Gibbs: "Mathematics is a language," which sounds as a sort of *manifesto*. No doubt, Sraffa's book is perfectly in line with this declaration of intents. It even goes beyond it; and in two ways. First, by pursuing the conviction that absolutely water-tight, coherent, logic is even more important than strict mathematics itself, as he always argued (with some vindication) with his mathematician colleagues in Cambridge. Second, by claiming that even strict, logically consistent, mathematical language may not be enough.

But at this point I am risking to begin to walk on a ground "where angels fear to tread." For the limited purposes of this chapter, I shall limit myself to briefly consider two historical instances in which, between the two prodigious minds we are considering, there was a clash. Confronting disagreements may sometimes turn out to be more helpful in improving understanding than considering common views.

10.4 The Re-switching of Techniques Debate

The first example I shall consider is the one in which there was a clash to begin with, which was then followed by a meeting of the minds, in spite of differences in interests and methods. This is the case of the well-known debate that took place in the 1960s, on the phenomenon of the *re-switching of techniques*.

For brevity's sake, I shall condense the essential points in five steps:

1. A preliminary stage, in which Joan Robinson (1953–54) broke on the scene with a vehement critique of the use of the concept of an aggregate "quantity capital" in the theory of economic growth. Almost by chance, she came across a *curiosum* in capital theory, which she could not herself clearly explain (but the point became clear later on). Robert Solow (1955–56) and Trevor Swan (1956) replied to the critique by strenuously defending the concept of a neoclassical production function. Both sides of the debate remained adamant on their positions, without succeeding in gaining conviction from the other side.

2. The publication of Piero Sraffa's slim book, *PCmC* (1960), where—in a very concise seven-page chapter XII, "Switch in methods of production"—Sraffa showed that the same method of production can become the most profitable one, as against many other alternatives, at different, separate, levels of the *w/r* (wage-rate/rate-of-profit) distribution curve, thus contradicting the neoclassical basic contention of a monotonic inverse relationship between capital and its "price" (the rate of profit);

3. Samuelson's *RES* (1962) article, where he constructed a *surrogate production function*, that is generated when there is a succession of linear *w/r* alternative relations. Such *surrogate* function mimics—it was hoped for the general case; this was the conjecture—all the relevant features connected with a full, "well-behaved", neoclassical production function;

4. A *QJE* article by David Levhari (1965), in which the author, at that time a graduate student at MIT, developed Samuelson's conjecture into a full *non-switching theorem*. The claim was that a succession of techniques, each of which yielding a polynomial (not a linear!) *w/r* relation, could cross each other only once in the positive quadrant. This theorem, if true, would have falsified Sraffa's result and would have given full generality to Samuelson's claim of a "well-behaved" production function;

5. A paper presented by Pasinetti at the Rome 1st Congress of the *Econometric Society* (1965), in which the Levhari–Samuelson nonswitching

theorem was proved to contain a logical flaw, with the devastating implication (for neoclassical economics) that, in general, the *w/r* relations of any two techniques may intersect each other more than once in the relevant quadrant. Other disproofs of the same theorem followed in a *QJE Symposium* (Samuelson, 1966a).

To Samuelson's merit we must record that his response astonished the world of professional economists. He immediately admitted that "the non-switching theorem is false" (Levhari-Samuelson, 1966), and went on to draw the implied logical consequences. In his concluding words,

> Pathology illuminates healthy physiology... re-switching is a logical possibility in any technology, indecomposable or decomposable... There often turns out to be no unambiguous way of characterising different processes as more "capital-intensive", more "mechanized", more "roundabout"... Such... labelling is shown, in the case of re-switching, to lead to inconsistent ranking between pairs of unchanged technologies, depending upon which interest rate happens to prevail in the market". (Samuelson, 1966b, pp. 582–83.)

This provided in fact the basic conclusion of the debate. A vast literature followed, in the 1960s and 1970s, which did refine, or try to minimize (or try to extend), the results stated above. But the logic (and Samuelson's conclusion) of the whole debate had made the point clear. Samuelson and Sraffa, though with different visions, and moving from different premises, had been confronted with an important theoretical issue. When it became possible to state the problem in clear, logical terms, they reached the same analytical conclusions, though with inevitably different nuances, accentuation of details, or shades of emphasis.

10.5 The "Standard Commodity" Case

There is another notable case in which the two minds came to a clash. In this case, alas, they never succeeded in meeting, and remained wide apart from each other, in spite of the fact that the subject itself entailed advanced mathematical analysis, which by itself would have made one expect it to be a helpful feature in closing up the differences.

The case concerns one of the most cherished of Sraffa's brain children—what he called the *Standard commodity*, an entirely novel and original concept that he had coined.

Let me explain briefly the problem at stake in the simplest of all cases—the case of circulating capital only—which is sufficient for our purposes.

I shall be using what appears to me Sraffa's point of view, and a terminology as close as I can imagine to his own.

As we all know, the Sraffa price system contains two degrees of freedom, which can be closed by fixing, from outside, the price of any particular (single or composite) commodity as the *numeraire,* and the rate of profit at any point between zero and its technical maximum, R (which is yielded by the relation $R = \lambda_m^{-1} - 1$, where, λ_m is the maximum eigenvalue of the technical coefficient matrix). When we fix r from outside,[3] we in fact fix the distribution of income between the wage rate (w) and the rate of profit (r). The set of all such possible income distributions is in general expressed by a rather complex relation between w and r (a ratio of polynomials of degrees depending on the rank of the technical coefficient matrix).

Let us review this set of possibilities. Consider first the two extreme cases in which $r = 0$ or $r = R$, respectively. When $r = 0$, all prices (let us call them by vector $p(l)$) turn out to be proportional to the (direct and indirect) quantities of labor embodied in each commodity. We may say that prices, in this ($r = 0$) extreme case, embody a *pure labor theory of value.* Profits play no role in them. When $r = R$ (and thus $w = 0$), all prices (let us call them by vector p^*) turn out to be proportional to the current values of the capital goods. If we want to follow the same logic, we should say that, in this second ($r = R$) extreme case, prices embody a *pure capital theory of value.* Wages, and hence labor, play no role in determining them. Consider now all the other cases, in which $0 < r < R$. Prices will be determined *both* by wages on (direct and indirect) labor inputs *and* by profits on the value of capital goods inputs, and will vary in a very complicated (polynomial) way as r is hypothetically increased from the one extreme (zero) to the other extreme (R).

If we continue to use Sraffa's approach, we might at this point realize that Ricardo had discovered a very peculiar technical case in which the *pure labor* prices of the first extreme happen to coincide with the *pure capital* prices of the second extreme, which implies that they also coincide with the labor *cum* capital prices of all intermediate cases. This case (in our modern terms) is the very particular case in which the labor coefficients happen to coincide with the left-hand-side eigenvector of the technical coefficient matrix. The economic meaning of this case is that all production processes require the same proportion of labor to capital (in Marxian terms they happen to have the same "organic composition" of capital). In this peculiar technical case, the w/r relation, which in general is a ratio of complicated high degree polynomials, reduces to the, by now well-known, linear relation:

$$r = R(1 - w). \qquad (10.1)$$

Relation (10.1) allows us to talk of the distribution of income between wages and profits in physical terms, and thus *independently of prices*. If 3/4 of the net output goes to labor, 1/4 goes to profits, and vice versa; and so on for any other complementary fractions of the net output.

It should be stressed that, in classical-like economic reasoning, the relevance of (10.1) derives—not from its linearity, but from the fact that it is independent of the system of prices. The left-hand-side eigenvector of the coefficient matrix ensures that all prices remain *invariant* in the whole range of the income distribution alternatives, from $r = 0$ to $r = R$.

What has Sraffa discovered? He has discovered that there exists a dual, symmetrical, case to the Ricardo case, which shares the same analytical properties. The right-hand-side eigenvector of the technical coefficient matrix defines a very particular composition of output—let us call it by vector y^*—which is precisely the one that Samuelson calls the von Neumann output composition, and which Sraffa's calls the *Standard commodity*. This particular commodity, if adopted as the *numeraire* of the price system (and we are always entitled to do this, since the choice of the *numeraire* is arbitrary), yields exactly the same linear relation (10.1) between w and r. Again it is important to repeat that the relevance of (10.1) is due not to its linearity, but to the fact that it is independent of prices—it makes all prices disappear from the w/r relation.[4] To underline this remarkable property, I shall mention that, if we were to change Sraffa's assumption on the timing of wage payment and suppose that wages are paid at the beginning (instead of being paid, at the end) of the production period, the w/r relation would be transformed from a line to a hyperbola,[5] but its basic property would persist: the w/r relation (no longer a line, but a hyperbola) would continue to remain entirely independent of prices.

Sraffa rightly points out that there is no need that wages should actually be paid with the physical quantities constituting the Standard commodity. The only requirement that is needed is that the Standard commodity is chosen as the *numeraire* of the price system. By the same token, there would be no need to pay wages, let us say, with "gold," if gold were to be chosen as the *numeraire*, since the choice of the *numeraire* is arbitrary. Sraffa goes on to propose to choose the Standard commodity as the *numeraire* of the price system. We would be able to take advantage of all its unique properties, among which is the one of yielding a w/r relation entirely independent of prices.

This is an extraordinarily beautiful analytical result. An added remarkable circumstance is that Sraffa reached it without using vector and matrix algebra and even without knowing the Perron–Frobenius theorems on nonnegative matrices; yet with an impeccable logical reasoning that has astonished mathematicians—as I have had the opportunity of realizing, for instance, through my personal contacts with Carlo Felice Manara.

Why hasn't such an analytically beautiful result impressed Paul Samuelson? It may well have at first; but further reflection must have led him to a quite different stance.

10.6 Samuelson's Difficulties with Sraffa's Cherished Brainchild

It took some time, at least to my knowledge, before Paul Samuelson explicity reacted to Sraffa's concept of Standard commodity. Apparently there was a sort of uneasiness on his part at first, which was then turned into open hostility. The singling out of the reasons for this attitude is the most intriguing puzzle that prompted the present investigation.

Samuelson's first open criticism of the Standard commodity is to be found in "Sraffian Economics" (Samuelson, 1987), published in the *New Palgrave Dictionary* four years after Sraffa's death.[6]

Samuelson opens his criticism with what appears to me a key proposition:

> for reasons not easy to understand, Sraffa thought that [(10.1)]'s truth somehow provided Ricardo with a defence of his labour theory of value. (p. 456).

I see three relevant points in this sentence:

(1) Samuelson acknowledges that there is something in Sraffa that he finds "not easy to understand";

(2) He does not attempt in the least to refute Sraffa's analytical achievement. Relation (10.1), yielded by using the Standard commodity as the *numeraire*, is "true."

(3) He attributes to Sraffa the intention of using the Standard commodity for a defense of Ricardo's labor theory of value.

Let me start with point (2). Samuelson acknowledges the analytical correctness of Sraffa's Standard commodity construction. But then, in his article, he proceeds to reject it outright on the ground that it is "useless." This claim is made even stronger and more emphatic in his later writings. "Uselessness," "irrelevance," "futility" of the Standard commodity are all terms that are repeatedly used, even in the titles of his articles' sections (see Samuelson, 1990, 2000b,c). This is an unusually severe verdict from Samuelson, especially if one thinks that he could not have corresponded with, and thus elicited any a reaction from, Sraffa. I find it disconcerting.

The objections that Samuelson gives to substantiate his claim are *not* of an analytical nature. They are all focused on what he calls the "restrictiveness" of Sraffa's concepts. He gives a long list—by mentioning, among others, aspects concerning the joint product cases, the nonproduced factors of production, the composition of market quantities deriving from intertemporal preferences, the availability of many techniques of production, etc. These objections do not point out anything analytically "wrong" in Sraffa's arguments. They all essentially concern—not just the (mathematically well-defined) concept of Standard commodity but—the whole of Sraffa's way of doing economics. It is significant that, to conclude the list, Samuelson should return to Ricardo:

> The purported defence of Ricardo's absolute standard has collapsed (Samuelson, 1987, p. 456)

So, we must infer that what Samuelson is really concerned with is Ricardo's labor theory of value—the above point (3). This is puzzling.

I myself have not been able to find in *PCmC* any place where Sraffa defends Ricardo's labor theory of value. Yet the clue to the puzzle must precisely be here. By carefully considering the use of the very term "labor theory of value," as used by Samuelson, one realizes that it does not fit into what Sraffa is doing with his *w/r* relation in terms of the Standard commodity.

It seems that Samuelson has in his mind the same *w/r* relation, but referred to Ricardo's particular case of homogeneous proportion of capital to labor in all production sectors. If this were so, it would not apply to Sraffa's case. The *w/r* relation yielded by the use of the Standard commodity as the *numeraire* has for Sraffa the crucial property of being independent of the price system. No more. It has nothing to do with the labor theory of value, except at the single, extreme, point $r = 0$. At all other points, in Sraffa's analysis, prices contain *both* wage *and* profit components, in varying proportions. Significantly, at the other extreme point, $r = R$, they contain only *profits* components, and thus they embody, as we have seen, a *pure capital* theory of value! If we were to persist in thinking in terms of a labor theory, we would fall into the same contradiction, which I had the occasion of attributing to both Ricardo and Marx, when I suggested that it was presumably such contradiction that induced them to adopt the obviously unrealistic assumption of a homogeneous technical composition of labor and capital in all sectors, since this assumption is the only one that can save them from that contradiction.[7]

Has Samuelson by any chance fallen into the same trap, from a symmetrical, dual, point of view? Since vector price p^*, associated with the net product composition y^*, which defines both von Neumann output composition and Sraffa's Standard commodity, embodies a *pure capital* theory of value, then—by extending Samuelson terminology to Sraffa's results—we should (incorrectly) say that the whole w/r relation, expressed in terms of the Standard commodity, is representing a generalized version of the *pure capital* theory of value! This seems unconceivable.

We are here putting our fingers on some terminological paradoxes that stand to indicate that the two minds cannot meet because they are following conceptions, and lines of thought, each of which does not fit into the other. They do not seem to talk the same language. Curiously enough, it is Samuelson (not Sraffa) that, in this case, has abandoned the mathematical language. If this is so, a clash (or rather a lack of understanding) is inevitable.

An explanation of this curious way in which the two opposite views are clashing seems to be revealed by the concluding sentence which Paul Samuelson states at the end of his arguments:

> MORAL. The Walrasian paradigms are in general unavoidable in the most unrestricted von Neumann paradigm (Samuelson, 1987, pp. 456–457) [which one must presume should also include the Sraffa paradigm]

But are they? At this point, one must go right back to point (1) at the beginning of the section. There is something in Sraffa which Samuelson finds "not easy to understand." This may well be so. But if the clash, in this case, is revealed to concern two incommensurably different "paradigms," two different ways of conceiving economics as a whole, what else could we expect?

10.7 Two Different Foundational Conceptions of Economics

Thomas Kuhn (1962, 2000), who invented the concept of "paradigm," in order to explain the discontinuous way in which sciences evolve (through *breaks* from one "paradigm" to another), relates many instances of lack of communication that have taken place when scientists have been trying to talk to each other across different paradigms. (The process may turn out to be even more complex, and not so linear in time, in the social sciences.) Just to mention one of them (which may be helpful for our purposes), let me recall the episode, in chemistry, that Kuhn describes, concerning

Joseph Priestley and Antoine Laurent Lavoisier. Through their experiments, they observed the appearance of the same new gas (oxygen) and yet, by moving within entirely different paradigms, they gave entirely different explanations—the one in terms of common air with less than the usual quantity of phlogiston, the other in terms of a gas of a distinctly new discovered species. Perhaps Priestly might even be entitled to claim priority in the discovery, and yet—immersed as he was in the prevailing phlogiston-based paradigm—was never able to accept the idea of the existence of the new gas—a total breakdown of possibility of communication. I have no intention to suggest, by quoting this episode, who could be prefigured by whom in our case. The only point I want to stress is the inherent lack of communication across paradigms.

In presenting his further developments, in *The Road since Structure* (2000), Kuhn has elaborated the problem further. When scientific arguments are based on different foundational conceptions, they face both methodological incommensurability (because each scientist takes the fundamentals of his/her paradigm for granted) and a semantic incommensurability, that terribly complicates the efforts of understanding each other. The methodological incommensurability has the effect, within each paradigm, to marginalize or even disregard the significance of the contradictions between theory and reality. The semantic incommensurability is even trickier, as it may lead scientists, moving within radically different paradigms, to use the very same words and phrases with entirely different meanings.

It does not require much effort to realize that what has been described in Sections 10.4–10.6 could be explained quite beautifully in Kuhn's terms. The basic results of the capital controversy have been accepted because they have been kept within an unambiguous logical–mathematical framework, and Samuelson must be given credit for achieving this. It must be admitted, at the same time, that ever since, all efforts on the neoclassical side have been in the direction of minimizing the results which Samuelson had acknowledged, so as to shift these results out of the protected belt of the neoclassical theoretical core. In practice, in today's mainstream economics textbooks, that controversy is simply not mentioned, and the underlying problems are simply ignored.

The misunderstandings on concepts and language that have emerged from the Standard commodity clash are more serious and at the same time more significant. They concern directly the two very different conceptual foundations of economics as they are intended by Samuelson (1947) and Sraffa (1960) respectively.

Two quotations may suffice, I hope, to explain clearly enough how far apart Samuelson and Sraffa stand in this respect. The first quotation comes from one of the most recent comments of Samuelson's. The other comes from early notes retrieved in the *Sraffa Papers*.

Here is Samuelson's:

> I strongly believe on the evidence, that Smith, Ricardo and J.S. Mill used essentially *the same logical paradigm* as did Walras and Arrow and Debreu [...]. Until missing papers surface in the Sraffa files with *new* devastating critiques of "marginalism," or until living Sraffians produce such new critiques not yet to be found in the literature, there will seem no need to qualify the first two sentences of this paragraph. [italics in original] (Samuelson, 2000b, p. 140)

Samuelson is (with justification) proud of the generalizations he carried out in his *Foundations*. The basic principle that he had proposed (expressed in the mathematical language of maximization under constraints) is here hinted at in bold terms, as a powerful all-inclusive unifying algorithm. Unlike what the early Marginalists had thought[8] Samuelson is stoutly—and no doubt justifiably—sure of his achievements. His *Foundations* are for him strong enough, as to be susceptible to bear extensions backward in the history of economic thought, so as to absorb classical (including Ricardian) economics, and at the same time as susceptible to support extensions forward, so as to absorb even the consequences of the "Keynesian Revolution" of the 1930s.

Quite sensibly, Samuelson can claim that the *onus* of a disproof falls on his opponents. Let Sraffians produce arguments, or even unpublished papers, if they can; let them come out into the open and state their case. From his strong, lofty standpoint, almost from a pinnacle-like altitude, Paul Samuelson is challengingly ready to stand back and listen, and only then, if necessary, to react. To many of his colleagues it appears almost unbelievable that he should consider (widely unknown) Sraffa as a possible challenger. That he should do so and take the challenge seriously is—to me—only a sign of his prodigious mind.

But let me come to the second excerpt, which I want to quote. It comes indeed from Sraffa's unpublished papers.[9] It dates back to the late 1920s, or at most to the very early 1930s, at a time when Sraffa had begun to consider resignation from his Cambridge lectureship (from which he then actually did resign), out of disillusionment with the then current state of economic theory:

> It is terrific to contemplate the abysmal gulf of incomprehension that has opened itself between us and the classical economists. Only one century separates us from

them: [then the following sentence, here reproduced in italics, is added as a footnote] *I say a century; but even 1/2 a century after, in 1870, they did not understand it. And during the preceding century an obscure process of "disunderstanding" had been going on.* How can we imagine to understand the Greeks and the Romans? [then the following sentence, again here reproduced in italics, is added as a footnote] *Or rather, the extraordinary thing is that we do understand, since we find them perfect: Roman law and Greek philosophy*. The classical economists said things which were perfectly true, even according to our standards of truth: they expressed them very clearly, in terse and unambiguous language, as is proved by the fact that they perfectly understood each other. We don't understand a word of what they said: has their language been lost? Obviously not, as the English of Adam Smith is what people talk today in this country. What has happened then?

This was written, as we may now realize, three decades before Kuhn (1962) could have given us some clues in justifying Sraffa's troubling reflections.

10.8 Perspectives for Economic Theory in the Twenty-First Century

The twenty-first century has opened with the legacy of a "Samuelsonian economics" at the apex of its success. "Sraffian economics" is striving for survival in the economics dictionaries. The former dominates the valleys of many social sciences—not only economics. The latter is a niche territory fighting for existence in—not even all—University economics departments and in some learned journals.

In the last fifty years, the Samuelson way of doing economics has become orthodoxy. If nowadays one finds the term "Samuelsonian economics" unusual, this is only because, by and large, it has become a synonym of mainstream economics. Yet we know how attentive and perceptive (no matter how critical) Samuelson has been to the claims of alternatives.

Sraffian economics started less than fifty years ago, with a *prelude to a critique* of orthodoxy. On the critical front it has left a mark, as Samuelson has acknowledged. But Sraffa seems to have offered us—not only a critique, but also a *seed* of a theory that revives the classical method and looks at the history of economic thought in terms of discontinuity. Admittedly, Sraffa's theory—as we have it at present—is far from being a complete theory. In *Production of Commodities by means of Commodities* many blocks are missing or are just sketched out or hinted at. (Samuelson has called it a "one leg theory," owing to its avoidance of the demand side aspects.) But the laid foundations have proven solid.

Our investigation has, I think, unveiled something more. Why has Samuelson been so interested in Sraffa? I think a better answer can be given at the end of this chapter than one could have imagined at the beginning. Samuelson's stated desire "of formulating a general theory of economic theories" (Samuelson, 1947 [1983, p. xxvi]) would seem to imply the absorption and inclusion also of Sraffa. But what has been reviewed above gives us several reasons to say that, despite Samuelson's skills, this attempt has not succeeded in the past and may prove impossible even in the future. "Samuelsonian economics" and "Sraffian economics" are running, as we have seen, on two different tracks. They start from different roots and look at the world from two different perspectives. "Samuelsonian economics" seems to me the latest ring in the chain of evolution of what elsewhere (Pasinetti, 1986) I had the opportunity of calling an "exchange paradigm." Sraffian economics belongs to what I called a "production paradigm." The reference point of the former is a world of pure markets. The reference point of the latter is, more fundamentally, a world of pure production.

What can the future of these two paradigms be? Events will of course tell. But my conviction is that Sraffa's theory has future contributions in reserve. The economies in which we live at present are "production economies" and they are likely to remain production economies, at a global level, for some time to come. The Classical School made its mark just after the First Industrial Revolution. We seem to be under the effects, on a larger scale, of a more acute expression of the same revolution, with consequences not dissimilar from, and in fact deeper than, those of two centuries ago. This may offer an opportunity—an open window we may say—for an originally framed resumption and revival of concepts typical of classical economics. True, the course of economic history will not be sufficient by itself to induce forsaking "Samuelsonian economics," but it might well teach us to use it in a different way. To supercede a theory, one necessarily needs an alternative theory. The one proposed by Sraffa, though solid on its bases, does not yet show all the legs necessary to run on its own. The crucial question therefore is to see to what extent *Production of Commodities by means of Commodities* may be armed with those parts it is still lacking. The economic profession should not be disappointed if a new paradigm, openly alternative to the present mainstream one, is allowed to be built and to be developed. I am sure Paul Samuelson would be the last economist not to accept the proposition that, also for economic theory, healthy competition is bound to be superior to a situation of monopoly.

Notes

1. A dozen of letters or so may be found in the *Sraffa Papers* in the Wren Library of Trinity College Cambridge and in the manuscripts Library of the Mattioli Foundation in Milan.
2. Quoted in the biographical presentation of his Nobel Prize lecture (Samuelson, 1970a, 1970b).
3. An alternative procedure would of course be to fix the wage rate, instead of the rate of profit, from outside. I leave this alternative aside to keep near Sraffa's arguments.
4. An interesting and elegant way of showing how all prices cancel out in, and disappear from, the *w/r* relation, when the Standard commodity is used as the *numeraire*, has recently been presented by Bellino (2004).
5. I may refer for convenience to Pasinetti (1977), pp. 78–80.
6. There are hints that Samuelson (perhaps provisionally) tried ways to deal with the problem much earlier, but in seminars (see Burmeister, 1968, 1984).
7. See Pasinetti (1977), pp. 78–80.
8. Let me recall that, at the dawn of Marginal economics (in the 1870s), the early Marginalists, with William Jevons (1871) in the fore-front, stressed the deep break between Marginalism and the earlier (especially Ricardian) economics. Samuelson clearly thinks that, with his method, he has overcome this split.
9. I have had already the opportunity of reproducing this excerpt in Pasinetti (2003), p. 153. I renew my thanks to Sraffa's literary executor (Pierangelo Garegmani) for allowing me to reproduce it here.

References

Bellino, Enrico. (2004). "On Sraffa's standard commodity," *Cambridge Journal of Economics*, 28(1), 121–132.

Burmeister, Edwin. (1968). "On a theorem of Sraffa," *Economica*, New Series, 35, 83–87.

——. (1984). "Sraffa, labor theories of value, and the economics of real wage rate determination," *Journal of Political Economy*, 92, 508–526.

Jevons, W. Stanley. (1871). *The Theory of Political Economy* (2nd edn, 1879), London: Macmillan.

Kuhn, Thomas (1962). *The Structure of Scientific Revolutions* (2nd edn, 1970). Chicago, IL: University of Chicago Press.

——, James Conant, and John Haugeland (eds.) (2000). *The Road since Structure: Philosophical Essays, 1970–1993*. Chicago, IL: University of Chicago Press.

Levhari, David (1965). "A nonsubstitution theorem and switching of techniques," *The Quarterly Journal of Economics*, 79, 98–105.

Levhari, David and Paul A. Samuelson (1966). "The nonswitching theorem is false," *The Quarterly Journal of Economics*, 80(4), 518–519.

Levine, A. Lawrence. (1974). "This age of Leontief ... and who? An interpretation," *Journal of Economic Literature*, 12(3), 872–881.

Pasinetti, Luigi L. (1965). "Changes in the rate of profit and degree of mechanization: A controversial issue in capital theory," paper presented at the 1st World Congress of the Econometric Society, Rome, September 9–14, 1965, pp.13, unpublished.

——. (1966). "Changes in the Rate of Profit and Switching of Techniques," *The Quarterly Journal of Economics*, 80(4), 503–517.

——. (1977). *Lectures on the Theory of Production*. London: The Macmillan Press Ltd.

——. (1986). "Theory of value—a source of alternative paradigms in economic analysis," in Mauro Baranzini and Roberto Scazzieri (eds), *Foundations of Economics—Structure of Inquiry and Economic Theory*. Basil Blackwell: Oxford, pp. 409–431.

——. (2003). "Continuity and change in Sraffa's thought—an archival excursus," in Terenzio Cozzi and Roberto Marchionatti (eds), *Piero Sraffa's Political Economy*. London and New York: Routledge.

Robinson, Joan (1953–4). "The production function and the theory of capital," *The Review of Economic Studies*, 21(2), 81–106.

Samuelson, Paul A. (1947, 1983, 2nd ed.), *Foundations of Economic Analysis*, Cambridge, MA: Harvard University Press.

——. (1962). "Parable and realism in capital theory: The surrogate production function," *Review of Economics Studies*, 29(3), 193–206.

——. (1948). "Economics—an introductional analysis," New York: McGraw-Hill Book Co.

——. ed. (1966a). "Paradoxes in capital theory: a symposium," (with contributions by: Luigi Pasinetti, David Levhari–Paul Samuelson, Michio Morischima, Michael Bruno–Edwin Burmeister–Etyan Sheshinski, P. Garegnani, Paul Samuelson). *The Quarterly Journal of Economics*, 80(4), 503–583.

——. (1966b). "A summing up," *The Quarterly Journal of Economics*, November, 80(4), 568–583.

——. (1970a). "Paul A. Samuelson," A biography, presented for the Prize in Economic Sciences in Memory of Alfred Nobel, reproduced in Lindbeck, Assar (ed.) (1992) *Nobel Lectures, Economic Sciences 1969–1980*. London: World Scientific Publishing Co.

——. (1970b). "Maximum principles in analytical economics," Nobel Lecture, reproduced in *American Economic Review*, 62(3), 249–262.

——. (1971) "Understanding the Marxian notion of exploitation: a summary of the so-called transformation problem between Marxian values and competitive prices," *Journal of Economic Literature*, 9(2), 399–431 .

——. (1975). "Steady state and transient relations: a reply on reswitching," *The Quarterly Journal of Economics*, 89(1), 40–47.

——. (1978). "Interest rate equalization and nonequalization by trade in Leontief-Sraffa models," *Journal of International Economics*, 8(1), 21–27.

——. (1983). "Un genio con poche opere" [*A genius with few works*], *Corriere della Sera*, September, 6, 1983.

Samuelson, Paul A. (1987). "Sraffian economics," in J. Eatwell, M. Milgate, and P. Newmann,(eds), *The New Palgrave: a Dictionary of Economics*. London: Macmillian, pp. 452–461.

——. (1990). "Revisionist findings on Sraffa," in *Essays on Piero Sraffa*, K. R. Bharadwaj, and B. Schefold (eds), pp. 263–279, London:Unwin Hyman; re-printed in *Critical Essays on Piero Sraffa's Legacy in Economics*, H. D. Kurz (ed.), pp. 25–45, Cambridge, Cambridge University Press, 2000.

——. (1991). "Sraffa's other leg," *Economic Journal*, 101: (406), pp. 570–575.

——. (1999). "The special thing I learned from Sraffa," in *Value, distribution and capital: Essays in honour of Pierangelo Garegnani*, G. Mongiovi, and F. Petri (eds), London and New York: Routledge, pp. 230–237.

——. (2000a). "Revisionist findings on Sraffa: reply," in *Critical Essays on Piero Sraffa's Legacy in Economics*, H. D. Kurz (ed), pp. 87–108, Cambridge: Cambridge University Press.

——. (2000b). "Sraffa's hits and misses," in H. D. Kurz (ed), *Critical Essays on Piero Sraffa's Legacy in Economics*, pp. 111–152, Cambridge University Press, Cambridge.

——. (2000c). "Sraffa's hits and misses: reactions to Kurz-Salvadori's comments," in *Critical Essays on Piero Sraffa's Legacy in Economics*, H. D. Kurz (ed), pp. 163–180, Cambridge: Cambridge University Press.

——. (2001a). "A modern post-mortem on Böhm's capital theory: its vital normative flow shared by Pre-Sraffian mainstream capital theory", *Journal of the History of Economic Thought*, 23 (3), 301–317.

——. (2001b). "A Ricardo-Sraffa paradigm comparing gains from trade in inputs and finished goods," *Journal of Economic Literature*, 39 (4), 1204–1214.

Solow, Robert M. (1955–6). " The production function and the theory of capital", *The Review of Economic Studies*, 23 (2), 101–108.

Sraffa, Piero (ed.) (1951–72). *The Works and Correspondence of David Ricardo*, 9 vols, Cambridge: Cambridge University Press.

Sraffa, Piero (1960). *Production of Commodities by Means of Commodities- Prelude to a Critique of Economic Theory*, Cambridge: Cambridge University Press.

Swan, Trevor W. (1956). "Economic growth and capital accumulation," *The Economic Record*, Vol. XXII, pp. 334–361.

11

Paul Samuelson as a "Keynesian" Economist

L.R. Klein

11.1 The Meaning of a Keynesian Economist

To brand or label someone as a Keynesian economist or to define a school of thought or a branch of economic analysis as Keynesian is not very constructive, from my point of view. There are groupings such as New or Neo Keynesian, Liberal, Progressive, or various adjectives connected to the thinking of John Maynard Keynes, who was, in my opinion, the most significant economist of the first half of the twentieth century. Paul Anthony Samuelson is unquestionably my choice as the most significant economist of the second half of the twentieth century. Since Keynes died prior to 1950 and Samuelson began his professional career before 1950, the split between the two half century periods is not precise; perhaps prewar and postwar (Second World War) would be a better designation.

In the course of this essay, I am going to come to the concept of the *Neoclassical Keynesian Synthesis*, which I believe provides a more accurate designation for the role and influence of Paul Samuelson. Though I have found in practice that many economists look upon this longer classification as clumsy and not sufficiently decisive, I believe that it is much more inclusive of Paul Samuelson's achievements in the economics profession.

There is also an important distinction to be made between economic analysis and economic policy (also known as political economy, applied economics, or just plain *politics*). Media writers, in particular, are very liberal in treating Keynesian economics (or economists) as advocating (advocates of) public spending to promote production and jobs. This way of looking at Keynesian economics was, at the beginning of use of the concept, known as depression economics or, more broadly, economics of state intervention. The latter concept would cover anti-inflation policy as well as anti-recession policy.

11.2 The Origins of Keynesian Economics

The economic turbulence of the period after the First World War laid the foundation for new thinking about how to bring afflicted countries out of the grip of the Great Depression that followed the crises in financial markets after the 1929 Crash. There were two seemingly unrelated developments. One dealt with the rising tide of mathematics and, more generally, quantitative economics, particularly in the form of econometrics, which was meant to unify economic theory, mathematical methods of analysis (mathematical economics), and statistical methods of analysis of economic information (econometrics). These developments occurred mainly in North America and Europe, including of course the United Kingdom and Ireland as well as continental Europe.

Somewhat later than the mathematical developments, Keynesian economics grew out of the informal groupings inspired by Keynes in Cambridge, England. This became known as Keynes's *Circus*, and culminated in the publication of the *General Theory of Interest, Employment and Money* in 1936.

In the United States, at Harvard University in Cambridge, Massachusetts, there was a study group that included Paul Samuelson, other advanced students of economics, and some members of Harvard's faculty. The American group members were analyzing the deep meaning and potential importance of the ideas emanating from the Circus, and some visiting participants from the group in England, notably a Canadian economist, Robert Bryce, who prepared a set of notes about the discussions that were taking place in Cambridge, England.

A remarkable feature of the activities of these two study groups is how much detail of the thinking of the Circus group in England was known to the Harvard group. When I went to Cambridge, England for a short visit in summer, 1948, I met Richard Kahn, Joan Robinson, Piero Sraffa and other participants from the Circus, all of whom marveled at the precise detail that Paul Samuelson knew about their thinking in the decade of the 1930s, while the *General Theory* was being formulated. They said to me that Paul had the discussions in Cambridge, England, just right, without being there in person.

As an undergraduate student in California between 1938 and 1942, I had only one significant exposure to Keynesian economics. That was in the

1940–41 academic year when Wassily Leontief visited for an evening seminar. I was struck by the amount of time he devoted to Keynesian economics in his presentation dealing with contemporary economic issues. He was surely influenced by the Harvard discussion, although he would not be considered as a Keynesian economist, for their mode of analysis was too aggregative.

11.3 Paul Samuelson, an Architect of Modern Mathematical Economics

From my perspective, the development of Keynesian economics is closely related to the parallel development of mathematical methods in economics, both theoretical and statistical. In fact, my going to MIT for their new graduate program in economics, introduced in the academic year 1941–42, was motivated by an interest in the general issue of formulating economic analysis in mathematical terms. On browsing through some issues of *Econometrica* I was genuinely stimulated by some recent articles of Paul Samuelson. They did not deal with Keynesian economics, but with subjects that eventually appeared in *Foundations of Economic Analysis*. In terms of the present essay this material fits well with the case for classifying Paul Samuelson as an exponent of the *Neoclassical Keynesian Synthesis*. My first substantive experience with Paul ties together his work in general economic analysis and Keynesian economics.

The economics program at MIT was only one year old, when I arrived, and there were approximately ten students for the 1942–43 academic year. Each student was assigned to a faculty member for research guidance, and I had the extremely good fortune to be assigned to Professor Samuelson. He immediately suggested a small research investigation concerning the statistical estimation of savings and investment functions for the United States, in particular, because he was dissatisfied with the methodology used in a recently published piece in the *American Economic Review* by Mordecai Ezekiel. His insight into the econometrics of that paper as a contribution to Keynesian economic analysis was very perceptive. His reasoning was as follows: In early econometric studies of supply and demand functions in economics, generally, but in agriculture, in particular, because Dr Ezekiel was a statistician in the US Department of Agriculture, Paul presumably knew the *identification* issues from his contact with Henry Schultz at the University of Chicago.

The typical or classical problem in the early days of econometrics had been to identify, separately, estimates of demand and/or supply functions

$$q_t = S(p_t) + e_t$$

$$q_t = D(p_t) + u_t$$

where S denotes a supply function, while D denotes a demand function, on the basis of regressions between q_t (quantity at time t) and p_t (price at time t). Random errors are denoted by e_t and u_t. There is not enough information given here to distinguish the estimated supply function, especially in linear form, from the estimated demand function, also in linear form, without there being what econometricians now call *identifying* restrictions on the two equations. This problem is well understood now but was not clearly and generally formulated in published econometric theory at that time.

Mordecai Ezekiel considered the macroeconomic relation, in Keynesian theory, between savings and investments as

$$S_t = S(Y_t, \Delta Y_t, t) + e_t$$

$$I_t = I(Y_t, \Delta Y_t, t) + u_t$$

$$S_t = I_t$$

The identification issues with respect to this problem are practically the same as those for the agricultura1 supply-demand relationships being examined by agricultural economists.

Dr Ezekiel argued that by disaggregating I_t into many subcategories, the aggregate saving and investment functions could be identified. I was assigned the research task of determining whether Dr Ezekiel had satisfactorily dealt with the same problem that the agricultural statisticians had to confront. They had the vagaries of nature (climate, pestilence, use of fertilizer, use of insecticide, etc.) to put in the supply functions as additional variables or to cause large variances of supply function error (e_t) and obtain identification that way, by information on relative error variances. Dr Ezekiel estimated a single relationship between savings and income, but a four-fold decomposition of investment into different types with separate effects coming from ΔY_t and t in each case. Thus by disaggregation of investment he hoped to be able to estimate an investment function from the sum of separate subinvestment equations. Paul Samuelson could see this approach as a possible violation of identification principles. Over the years of subsequent savings studies, trend and income dynamics have also been used in savings functions. Econometricians later pointed out that disaggregation, as in the case of Dr Ezekiel's specification of investment was not, by itself, a satisfactory route for achieving identification. Paul Samuelson's original insight was that "the savings-investment cross" from Keynesian economics posed the same identification problem as "the supply-demand cross" from agricultural economics.

11.4 Keynes the Investor and Samuelson the Investor

There have been many stories about Keynes's judgment and foresight in amassing wealth, during his lifetime. Some of the stories focus on Keynes's failures in speculation; others feature his insight into the value of art, in particular, that associated with well-known painters, often of ballet scenes. It is undoubtedly the case that Keynes *earned* and *lost* in his speculative investments, but he died a wealthy person, with a country estate, the founding of an art theater in Cambridge and the strong institutional portfolio following his sage investment advice to King's College.

In his famous textbook, *Economics*, Paul Samuelson has this to say about Keynes's ability as an investor: "He was also an economist who knew how to make money, both for himself and for King's College Cambridge." In spite of some point of disagreement by biographers with Keynes's early speculation and comments on investment methodology, there is no doubt that Paul Samuelson appreciated the end result.

It is evident that the royalties from the publication of so many editions of *Economics*, coupled with the explicit admiration for Keynes as an investor, may have influenced Paul Samuelson to follow Keynes's footsteps. Paul Samuelson, however, respects the insight and techniques of modern mathematics and econometrics of investment, as well as the sage investment strategy of Warren Buffet and his devotion to Graham's principles of investing that seem to be far removed from some of the speculative ventures of Keynes. Roy Harrod notes in his biographical volume on Keynes that the greatest contribution to Keynes's very significant portfolio at the time of his death came from investment in American utilities during the Great Depression. This fact suggests that Keynes was a very wise value-investor who recognized fine bargains at times when the financial markets were in a great slump. It suggests that Keynes was, in fact, a very astute investor for the medium to long run. There can be no doubt that Paul Samuelson emulated this aspect of Keynes's life. After having served on the Finance Committee of the National Academy of Sciences for almost three decades with Paul, I can fully attest to his investment insight, not by the methodology of Keynes, but by the successful attention to investment principles. In many aspects, the above quotation from *Economics* about Keynes as an investor would be eminently suitable for Paul A. Samuelson's biographer.

11.5 Antecedents and Cranks in the Keynesian Spirit

Keynes refers explicitly to Gesell, Malthus, and Hobson in the *General Theory*. These are all early thinkers who had some ideas about problems with the prevailing economic system and either particular policies for making it perform better, or warnings about approaches of the economy to conditions of basic conflicts or incompatibilities.

For example, Malthus feared that population growth would overtake the world's ability to provide sustenance. In more than two centuries, Malthusian warnings have not been heeded, nor has widespread world hunger appeared, although there have been some special, but limited, examples.

Paul Samuelson, at times, has shown some interest in the writings of people who anticipated some aspect of a Keynesian system of thought, without bringing the issues to the point of self-contained systems that would be able to encounter an episode as serious as that of the Great Depression, which clearly brought Keynesian thinking to the fore.

There are, however, two important academic economists who played very important roles in the founding of the Econometric Society or figured in early meetings of the Society in Europe. They are well recognized in other facets of Paul Samuelson's view of economics in the time of the rising Keynesian tide, but they do not figure significantly in his analysis of Keynesian economics, as do Gesell, Malthus, Foster and Catchings, and Hobson. My recollections of Professor Samuelson's classroom macroeconomics, or suggestions in the role of dissertation supervisor, is that one should look for grains of truth in their writings.

There are, however, deeper analytical reasons for mentioning the work of Frisch and Kalecki in the context of anticipating Keynes. The two cases are quite different. Ragnar Frisch was a key figure in the formation of the Econometric Society, at the time when Keynes was developing the *General Theory*, but also during this period Frisch was making policy suggestions to the Norwegian public on reasons for the unusual economic collapse and on ways of emerging toward recovery. On the occasion of the 100th anniversary of Frisch's birth in 1895, there was a series of lectures and discussions about his work, and at a dinner (hosted by Trygve Haavelmo),

I was asked to address the audience. I took up the subject of Frisch's policy advice, to a Norwegian radio audience in 1932, in which he explained to the public the need to encourage consumer spending, completely in the Keynesian fashion. The significant point about these lectures is that they spelled out clearly the macroeconomic reasoning of the "paradox of thrift," namely if the society tries to save (not spend) more, they are likely to end up by saving less. This paradox can be illustrated simply by analysis of the savings-investment cross, which of course Paul Samuelson knows so well. The only issue is that Frisch did not take his message in English, beyond the scope of Scandinavian listeners.

Kalecki's case is more complex, but in a short period of time he, by himself, developed a small macro model that was capable of generating cycles and covering the same ground as the early Keynesian models. His system consisted of a consumption equation, an investment-orders equation, and a velocity-interest rate equation. With slight variations, these are practically the same as the Hicks and Lange representations of the Keynesian system. The works of Frisch and Kalecki were developed independently of the discussions in the Keynesian Circus, but they arose in the same time period and when both econometricians were prominent in the early years of the Econometric Society, while Paul Samuelson was framing his own version of the Neoclassical Keynesian synthesis.

11.6 The Existence of An Unemployment Equilibrium

A major theoretical inquiry of the new Keynesian doctrines being discussed in the two Cambridges was whether the system being proposed by Keynes could have an equilibrium position at less-than-full-employment. This is one of the first analytical problems of macroeconomic analysis that I took up when I started work on my dissertation, *The Keynesian Revolution*. The debate with Mordecai Ezekiel on identification, in connection with the savings-investment cross was mainly an issue of identification, as that subject was then being refined by Trygve Haavelmo and, later, econometricians at the Cowles Commission.

As I was speaking, from time to time, with Professor Samuelson about a fresh topic for my dissertation, he suggested that I consider a thesis on "The Keynesian Revolution." When he suggested that, I found a close fit with my own interests and immediately took it up since it was a subject that had a great appeal to me. Early in my thesis research, I was asked to make a seminar presentation before an economic study group at Harvard.

I chose the Keynesian model that was shaping in my thinking and ran into a dispute at the Harvard session whether one would need to specify an unusual nonlinear labor supply function or an inhomogeneous function in which labor supply depended on the nominal wage rate rather than the real wage rate, in order to have unemployment in equilibrium.

On the morning-after, Professor Samuelson inquired about the course of discussion at the seminar. When I told him about the issues of labor supply specification, he immediately suggested that maybe the long-run equilibrium point of the final system, reduced, after substitution, into two equations depending on two variables would have a logical intersection point only in an invalid quadrant—one where the real wage or some other positive variable would have to be negative. He then said it would be impossible to get the economy to that point, but in the process of trying to do so, there would be unstable deflationary movements with wages being competitively bid downward. In terms of the IS–LM diagram, the curves would be shifted through a search for an equilibrium solution that exists only in a quadrant that permits negative interest rates. In *The Keynesian Revolution*, this situation was depicted graphically as shown in Figure 11.1.

Later, in continuing discussions at the Cowles Commission, among Don Patinkin, Trygve Haavelmo, and myself, Trygve suggested that the Keynesian model be specified as one that always had a valid solution, in which negative wages or interest rates would not be present, as long as the system was in motion, in a dynamic sense, but when one imposed equilibrium conditions which included full employment a solution would not exist. Personally, I find that explanation attractive. There is yet another approach to this problem, through the Pigou effect. Pigou introduced another variable, the real stock of cash balances, in the savings equation,

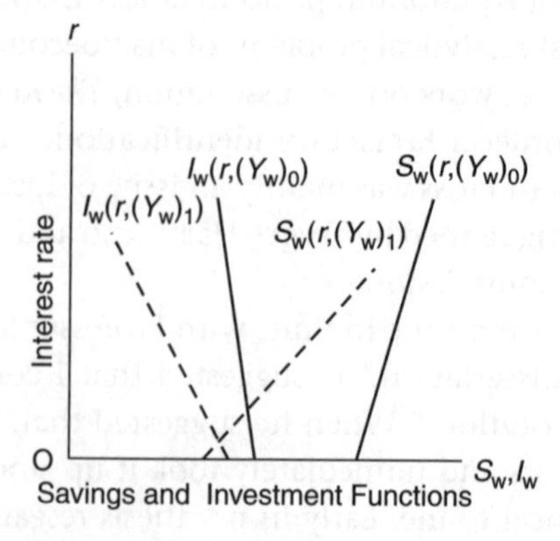

Figure 11.1 Saving and Investment functions

essentially as an indicator of real wealth, in addition to real income. In such a modification of the Keynesian system, flexible wage bargaining—as long as employment is not full—would expand the value of real wealth with falling wage rates until full-employment equilibrium is found.

The Pigou effect, putting real cash balances in the saving or consumption function became an important policy issue immediately after the Second World War because households in the United States had accumulated large reserves of government bonds, a popular type being Series E, purchased in units costing $18.75 and maturing in ten years at $25.00 to yield 2.9 percent. Paul Samuelson remarked on many occasions that US workers could be nicely rewarded for being patriotic in financial support of the war effort, receiving a very secure investment at 2.9 percent interest. For many people, the process was made easy, through payroll deduction plans.

There were limited goods to purchase with the savings; so the war ended with many households in possession of a significant stock of liquid assets, by adding the values of Series E bonds to ordinary cash balances. An immediate question arose, would American consumers draw upon their liquid assets for spending on goods that were not available during the war? Statistical correlations with both disposable personal income and liquid assets (as enlarged cash balances) could motivate consumer spending beyond the amounts that were being estimated by conventional Keynesian consumption functions. The answer was not clear, especially because Series E bonds did not have a long history in a statistical sample. Most calculations indicated existence of some positive effect, but not with a high degree of statistical significance. There undoubtedly was some positive effect, and I can recall inconclusive discussions with Professor Samuelson about the importance of Pigou's article soon after it was published, but before peace settlements and demobilization had begun.

11.7 Keynesian Policy

In 1944, I went to meetings of the Econometric Society which were just being reconvened after postponement during the war. I was asked to present a paper dealing with my discussion of the approach by Mordecai Ezekiel on the savings-investment cross and my dissertation work on *The Keynesian Revolution*. I was deeply interested in the program listing of a paper entitled "Will There Be Business Cycles after the War?" Unfortunately that paper was cancelled, but Jacob Marschak, after inquiring about professor Samuelson and his latest professional activities, said to me, "What this country needs is a new Tinbergen model to forecast the performance of the American economy after the War." This remark excited me, and I was more than pleased to consider his offer of my coming to the Cowles Commission to take up this task.

These events have relevance for another side of Paul Samuelson's views as a "Keynesian" economist. Keynes was both an academic economist and a popular economist who contributed often to the media, one source being the *New Statesman*. In 1944, when the issues surrounding the end of the war were being intensively discussed, Paul Samuelson contributed two articles to the *New Republic* in the United States.

11.8 Unemployment Ahead

I. A Warning to the Washington Expert
 September 11, 1944, pp. 297–99

II. The Coming Economic Crisis
 September 18, 1944, pp. 333–35

The predominant view at the Econometric Society meetings was that the United States would face the problem of a weak civilian economy after the war. Very elementary Keynesian models, emphasizing the consumption function, were presented at the professional meetings. In Europe some economists, particularly in Sweden, suggested a new orientation to the East instead of the West because they feared that the United States would not have a robust economy after the stimulus for production on a war footing was taken away.

In the *New Republic*, Paul Samuelson did not make such a judgment. He was much more cautious about the uncertainty of the pessimistic forecasts. He concluded "the government under any party will have to take extensive action in the years ahead." The emphasis was on his graph of the enormous ratios of federal government war expenditure to nonwar expenditures, and his reaction was to remark on "the startlingly large proportion of the former."

How did things work out after 1945? There was no large increase in unemployment. During that year, after our preliminary calculations with the first version of the Tinbergen-type model at the Cowles Commission (on request from the Committee for Economic Development), my position was completely changed to one of no immediate serious recession. In office after office in Washington, economic analysts, such as those anonymously

referred to in Paul Samuelson's *New Republic* articles, responded to the calculations from the Cowles Commission, "Just wait until mid 1946; there will be 6 million unemployed." A better response would have been about 2 million (Table 11.1).
As the military sector expanded, employment became "overfull," but the reconversion was gradual.

This brings me to Paul Samuelson's view of Jan Tinbergen, whose 100th anniversary of birth was memorialized two years ago in Rotterdam, and for which Paul Samuelson sent a fond statement of admiration and achievement. In the first place, Tinbergen received unfortunate review commentary from Keynes for the work at the League of Nations in constructing an econometric model of the United States during the interwar period. Tinbergen told me a few years earlier that he genuinely admired Keynes and was simply trying to find empirical support for the abstract model of the *General Theory*. Professor E. B. Wilson, a distinguished professor at Harvard and MIT, who was admired by Paul Samuelson, told me and other MIT students who attended Wilson's lectures at Harvard in 1942, that Keynes should be regarded in the role of "the theoretical physicist," while Tinbergen filled the role of "the experimental physicist." A careful examination of Tinbergen's US model reveals that he made two improvements over the conventional Keynesian consumption function: (1) He paid explicit attention to the distribution of incomes. (2) He generalized the Pigou effect by allowing for the influence of wealth in the form of equities. He introduced the rate of change of stock market prices in an equation for the rate of change of consumption. In a sense he led Keynesian scholars in one step toward generalizing the Pigou effect to a broader wealth effect. A combination of wealth and government spending for demobilized military (the GI Bill—investing in human capital) and support for Europe, Korea, and Japan turned the end of the Second World War into an immediate gain,

Table 11.1 Forces to be Demobilized and Unemployment

	Armed forces (million)	Unemployment (million)
1942	4.0	2.7
1943	8.9	1.1
1944	11.4	0.7
1945	11.6	1.0
1946	3.8	2.3
1947	1.7	2.4
1948	1.5	2.3

Source: Statistical Abstract of the United States

plus a longer sustained gain for the US economy. Also the new technological spin-offs of the military research (radar, jet engines, large, high speed computers, etc.) paved the way for technical change, which is not at all incompatible with Keynesian economics, but not emphasized. Once an explicit production function is introduced, with allowance for ample technical change, the system can go far toward enhancing Keynesian analysis of aggregate demand with aggregate supply and emphasizing the Neoclassical Keynesian Synthesis.

11.9 The Early Postwar Period

A leading expositor and analyst of Keynesian economics in the United States was the Harvard economist, Alvin H Hansen, and his large coterie of students and colleagues contributed to a Festschrift entitled *Income, Employment, and Public Policy, Essays in Honor of Alvin H Hansen*. (W W Norton Inc., 1948). A leading contributor was his student, Paul Samuelson. In an article in the volume on "The Simple Mathematics of Income Determination" one can readily see the deep meaning of describing Paul Samuelson as a Keynesian economist. He wrote that the heart of income determination was the simple equation that stated: for a given level of investment I, the simple equation $Y = C(Y) + I$, which Paul Samuelson described as "the nucleus of the Keynesian reasoning." He compared this simple equation, which is basic to the Keynesian system, with $D(p) = S(p)$, the "equating of supply and demand to determine market price." For me, it is a clear reminder of his concern over Mordecai Ezekiel's analysis of estimation of savings and investment equations as functions of income, to determine Y_i.

The chapter in the volume honoring Hansen deals very much with such things as various multiplier concepts and formulas, the balanced-budget theorem, to show how stimulus for an underperforming economy can be realized even though deficit spending is not involved. In addition, Paul Samuelson's leaning was toward fiscal policy of public spending instead of tax reduction for moving a weak economy toward stronger performance. As for international trade, he wrote that this component of total production and demand "will be implicitly rather than explicitly in the income system." In the present globalized world economy, conditions have changed so much that full explicit treatment of international trade is of top priority in many or most economies.

If this chapter in honor of Alvin Hansen shows clearly the Keynesian side of Paul Samuelson's macro policy analysis, one can find other clear expressions of neoclassical reasoning, especially in his admiration for the work of Keynes's student, at an earlier time than the Circus discussions, Frank Ramsey. While Paul Samuelson thought highly of Keynes, he simultaneously was keen on the neoclassical reasoning of medium-to-long-term growth studied by Ramsey. On the occasion of the World Congress of the Econometric Society in Cambridge, England in 1970, Paul gave a lecture, billed as an examination of the work of an important Cambridge economist. There was a guessing game taking place about who was this person. It turned out to be Frank Ramsey. He was a student of Keynes, but not for Keynesian economic analysis as we know it today (or even then).

References

Ezekiel, Mordecai (1942). "Statistical investigations of saving, consumption and investment," *American Economic Review* 32, 22–49, March 272–307.
Harrod, Roy F. (1951). *The Life of John Maynard Keynes*. New York: Harcourt Brace.
Keynes, John Maynard (1936). *The General Theory of Interest, Employment, and Money*. New York: Harcourt Brace.
——. (1939). "Professor Tinbergen's method," *Economic Journal*, 49, 558–568.
Klein, Lawrence R. (1947). *The Keynesian Revolution*. New York: Macmillan.
——. (1951). "The life of John Maynard Keynes," *The Journal of Political Economy*, LIX, 443–451.
Pigou, A.C. (1943). "The classical stationary state," *Economic Journal*, LIII. 343–351.
Samuelson, Paul A. (1944). "A warning to the Washington Expert," *New Republic*, 297–299.
——. (1944). "The coming economic crisis," *New Republic*, 333–335.
——. (1947). *Foundations of Economic Analysis*. Cambridge: Harvard University Press.
——. (1948). "The simple mathematics of income determination," in *Income Employment, and Public Policy, Essays in Honor of Alvin H Hansen*, NY, W.W. Norton, pp. 24–36.
——. (1948). *Economics*, New York: McGraw-Hill, p. 253.

12

Samuelson and the Keynes/Post Keynesian Revolution

Paul Davidson

For most students who studied economics in any American university during the last half of the twentieth century, Paul A. Samuelson was thought to be a direct disciple of Keynes and his revolutionary general theory analysis. Samuelson is usually considered the founder of the American Keynesian school which he labeled neoclassical synthesis Keynesianism because of the classical microeconomic theory that Samuelson believed was the foundation of Keynes's macro analysis. As we will explain, Samuelson's neoclassical synthesis brand of "Keynesianism" was not analytically compatible with the theoretical framework laid out by Keynes in *The General Theory of Employment Interest and Money* (1936).

Explaining the differences between Samuelson's version of Keynesianism and Keynes's *General Theory* is the essence of this chapter. Given Samuelson's dominance of the American macroeconomic scene after the Second World War, the analytical different foundation of Samuelson's Keynesianism vis-a-vis Keynes's *General Theory* aborted Keynes's truly revolutionary analysis from being adopted as mainstream macro economics. Consequently in the 1970s academic literature, the Monetarists easily defeated the Samuelson's neoclassical synthesis Keynesianism on the grounds of logical inconsistency between its microfoundations and its macroeconomic analysis and policy prescriptions. The effect was to change the domestic and international choice of policies deemed socially acceptable to prevent unemployment, to promote economic development, and even the method to finance government social security systems away from prescriptions founded on Keynes's *General Theory* and to the age-old laissez-faire policies promoted by classical theory that had dominated nineteenth and early twentieth century thought.

As a result of the Monetarist victory over Samuelson's neoclassical Keynesianism in the 1970s, New Keynesian theory was developed to replace Samuelson's Keynesianism. Just as Friedman's Monetarism had conquered Samuelson's brand of Keynesianism, New Classical theory easily made a mockery of the New Keynesians approach which relied on the rigidity of wages and prices to achieve Keynesian-like results. New Classicists argued that price and wage rigidity was associated with government interference in the competitive market place. The result was to lead policy makers to dance to the Panglossian siren song that "all is for the best in the best of all possible worlds provided we let well enough alone" by encouraging adoption of policies of liberalizing all markets.

Accordingly, as we entered the twenty-first century, only the Post Keynesians remain to carry-on in Keynes's analytical footsteps and develop Keynes's theory and policy prescriptions for a 21st century real world of economic globalization.

12.1 The Coming of Keynesianism to America

In their wonderful book *The Coming of Keynesianism to America*, Colander and Landreth (1996, p. 23) credit Paul Samuelson with saving the textbook pedagogical basis of the Keynesian Revolution from destruction by the anti-communist spirit (McCarthyism) that ravaged America in the years immediately following the Second World War.

Lori Tarshis, a Canadian who had been a student attending Keynes's lectures at Cambridge during the early 1930s had, in 1947, written an introductory textbook that incorporated Tarshis's lecture notes interpretation of Keynes's *General Theory*. Colander and Landreth note that despite the initial popularity of the Tarshis textbook, its sales declined rapidly as it was attacked, by trustees of and donors to American colleges and universities, as preaching an economic heresy. The frenzy about Tarshis's textbook reached a pinnacle when William Buckley, in his book *God and Man at Yale* (1951), attacked the Tarshis analysis as communist inspired.

In August 1986 Colander and Landreth (hereafter C–L) interviewed Paul Samuelson, (C–L, 1996, pp. 145–178) about his becoming an economist and a "Keynesian". Samuelson indicated that he recognized the "virulence of the attack on Tarshis" and so he wrote his textbook "carefully and lawyer like" (C–L, 1996, p. 172). The term "neoclassical synthesis Keynesianism" did not appear in the first edition of Samuelson's textbook, *Economics An Introductory Analysis* (1948), which was published after the attack on

Tarshis's text. This neoclassical synthesis terminology, however, does appear prominently in the later editions of Samuelson's textbook. From hindsight it would appear that Samuelson's assertion that his brand of Keynesian macroeconomics is synthesized with (and based on) traditional neoclassical microeconomic assumptions made the Samuelson version of Keynesianism less open to attacks of bringing economic heresy into University courses on economics compared to Tarshis's Keynesian analysis.

Unlike Tarshis's analysis which was based on separate aggregate supply and demand functions, the analytical foundation of Samuelson's Keynesianism was imbedded in Samuelson's 45 degree Keynesian cross. Samuelson derived this cross analysis from a single equation aggregate demand function. This mathematical derivation in conjunction with the claimed synthesis of neoclassical theory made it more difficult to attack the Samuelson version of textbook Keynesianism as politically motivated. Thus for several generations of economists educated after the Second World War, Samuelson's name was synonymous with Keynesian theory as various editions of Samuelson's neoclassical Keynesian textbook was a best seller for almost a half century. Even those younger economists who broke with the old neoclassical synthesis Keynesianism and developed their own branch of New Keynesianism based their analytical approach on the Samuelson's *Foundation of Economic Analysis* (1947) and its classical microeconomic foundations.

From an historical perspective it appears to me that Samuelson may have saved the textbook pedagogical basis of the Keynesian Revolution from McCarthyism destruction simply by ignoring the axiomatic foundation of Keynes's analytic revolution.

12.2 How did Samuelson Learn Keynes's Theory?

In his 1986 interview Samuelson indicated that in the period before the Second World War, "my friends who were not economists regarded me as very conservative" (C–L, 1996, p. 154). Samuelson graduated the University of Chicago in June 1935 and, as he explained to Colander and Landreth, were it not for the Social Science Research Council fellowship that he received upon graduation, he would have done his graduate studies at the University of Chicago (C–L, 1996, pp. 154–155). Consequently, it was the visible hand of a fellowship offer that placed Samuelson at Harvard when Keynes's *General Theory* was published in 1936. What information about Keynes's *General Theory* was Samuelson exposed to at Harvard?

Robert Bryce, a Canadian, had attended the same Keynes Cambridge lectures as Tarshis between 1932 and 1935. In a 1987 interview with Colander and Landreth (1996, pp. 39–48) Bryce indicated that in the spring of 1935 he (Bryce) spent his weeks at the London School of Economics and Cambridge. At LSE Bryce used his Cambridge lecture notes to write an essay on Keynes's revolutionary ideas—without having read *The General Theory*—for the people at the LSE. This essay so impressed Hayek that Hayek let Bryce have four consecutive weeks of Hayek's seminar to explain Keynes's ideas as Bryce had written them out in this essay. Bryce's lectures were a huge success at the LSE (C–L, 1996, p. 43).

In the fall of 1935 Bryce went to Harvard and stayed for two years. During that time, an informal group met during the evenings to discuss Keynes's book. Bryce, using the same pre-General Theory essay that he had used as the basis for his talks at the LSE, presented to this group what he believed was Keynes's *General Theory* analysis—although he still had not read the *General Theory*. As Bryce put it "In most of the first academic year (1935–36) I was the only one who was familiar enough with it [Keynes' theory] to be willing to argue in defense of it" (C–L, 1996, pp. 45–46). So in 1936 Bryce's essay became the basis of what most economists at Harvard, probably including Samuelson, thought was Keynes's analysis—even though Bryce had not read *the* book when he made his presentations. Even in 1987, Bryce stated that, "anyone who studies that book is going to get very confused. It was . . . a difficult, provocative book" (C–L, 1996, pp. 44–46). The immediate question therefore is: "Did Bryce ever really comprehend the basis of Keynes's analytical framework?" And if he did not, how did that affect how the young Samuelson and others at Harvard in 1936 learn about Keynes's analytical framework.

Bryce's presentations at the LSE and Harvard were supposed to make Keynes's ideas readily understandable—something that Bryce believed Keynes could not do in his *General Theory* book. Bryce indicated that in his first year at Harvard "I felt like the only expert on Keynes's work around" (C–L, 1996, p. 45).

Samuelson has indicated that his first knowledge of Keynes's *General Theory* was gained from Bryce (C–L, 1996, p. 158). Moreover, even after reading the *General Theory* in 1936, Samuelson perhaps reflecting Bryce's view of the difficulty of understanding Keynes's book, found the *General Theory* analysis "unpalatable" and not comprehensible (C–L, 1996, p. 159). Samuelson finally indicated that "The way I finally convinced myself was to just stop worrying about it [about understanding Keynes's analysis]. I asked myself: why do I refuse a paradigm that enables me to understand the Roosevelt upturn from 1933 till 1937? . . . I was content to assume that there was enough rigidity in relative prices and wages to make the Keynesian alternative to Walras operative" (C–L, 1996, pp. 159–160).

Keynes's biographer, Lord Skidelsky (1992, p. 512) recognized the problem with this Samuelson interpretation of Keynes when he wrote "the validity of Keynes's 'general theory' rests on his assertion that the classical theory . . . is, as he put it in his lectures, 'nonsense.' If it [Walrasian classical theory] were true, the classical 'special case' would, in fact, be the 'general theory'[1] and Keynes's aggregative analysis not formally wrong, but empty, redundant. It is worth noting, at this point, that mainstream economists after the Second World War treated Keynes's theory as a 'special case' of the classical [Walrasian] theory, applicable to conditions where money wages and interest were 'sticky'. Thus his theory was robbed of its theoretical bite."[2]

Apparently Samuelson never tried to comprehend Keynes's analytical foundation and framework. For in 1986 Samuelson was still claiming that "we [Keynesians] always assumed that the Keynesian underemployment equilibrium floated on a substructure of administered prices and imperfect competition" (C–L, 1996, p. 160). When pushed by Colander and Landreth as to whether this requirement of rigidity was ever formalized in his work, Samuelson's response was "There was no need to" (C–L, 1996, p. 161).

Yet, specifically in chapter 19 of *The General Theory* and even more directly in his published response to Dunlop and Tarshis, Keynes (1939b) had already responded in the negative to this question of whether his analysis of underemployment equilibrium required imperfect competition, administered prices, and/or rigid wages. Dunlop and Tarshis had argued that the purely competitive model (i.e. the Walrasian model) was not empirically justified, therefore it was monopolistic price and wage fixities that was the basis of Keynes's unemployment equilibrium. Keynes's reply was simply: "I complain a little that I in particular should be criticised for conceding a little to the other view" (Keynes, 1973b, p. 411). In chapters 17–19 of his *General Theory*, Keynes explicitly demonstrated that even if perfectly flexible money wages and prices existed ("conceding a little to the other side"), there was no automatic mechanism that could restore the full employment level of effective demand. In other words, Keynes's general theory could show that, as a matter of logic, less than full employment equilibrium could exist in a purely competitive economy with freely flexible wages and prices.

Obviously, Samuelson, who became the premier American Keynesian of his time, had either not read, or not comprehended, (1) Keynes's response to Dunlop and Tarshis or even (2) chapter 19 in *The General Theory* which was entitled "Changes in Money Wages." In chapter 19 Keynes explicitly indicates that the theory of unemployment equilibrium did not require "a rigidity" in money wages (Keynes, 1936a, p. 257). As Keynes put it:

For the classical theory has been so accustomed to rest the supposedly self-adjusting character of the economic system on the assumed fluidity of money wages; and, when there is rigidity, to lay on this rigidity the blame of maladjustment . . . My difference from this theory is primarily a difference of analysis (Keynes, 1936a, p. 257).

Keynes (1936a, p. 259) indicated that to assume that rigidity was *the* cause of the existence of an unemployment equilibrium lay in accepting the argument that the micro-demand functions "can only be constructed on some fixed assumption as to the nature of the demand and supply schedules of other industries and as to the amount of aggregate effective demand. It is invalid, therefore to transfer the argument to industry as a whole unless we also transfer the argument that the aggregate effective demand is fixed. Yet, this assumption reduces the argument to an *ignoratio elenchi*."

An ignoratio elenchi is a fallacy in logic of offering a proof irrelevant to the proposition in question. Unfortunately Samuelson invoked the same classical ignoratio elenchi when he argued that Keynes's general theory was simply a Walrasian general equilibrium system where, if there is an exogenous decline in effective demand, rigid wages and prices created a temporary disequilibrium that prevented full employment from being restored in the short-run.[3]

As Keynes went on to explain, "whilst no one would wish to deny the proposition that a reduction in money wages *accompanied by the same aggregate effective demand as before* will be associated with an increase in employment, the precise question at issue is whether the reduction in money wages will or will not be accompanied by the same aggregate effective demand as before measured in term of money, or, at any rate, by an aggregate effective demand which is not reduced in full proportion to the reduction in money-wages" (Keynes, 1936a, pp. 259–260). Keynes then spent the rest of chapter 19 explaining why and how a general theory analysis must look at the relationship between changes in money wages and/or prices and changes in aggregate effective demand—an analysis that, by assumption, is not relevant to either a Walrasian system or Samuelson's neoclassical synthesis Keynesianism.

At the same time that Samuelson became a Keynesian by convincing himself not to worry about Keynes's actual analytical framework, Tarshis had obtained a position at Tufts University, a mere half-hour of travel from Harvard. Tarshis would often met with the group at Harvard, including Bryce, who were discussing Keynes. Tarshis notes that "Paul Samuelson was not in the Keynesian group. He was busy working on his own thing. That he became a Keynesian was laughable" (C–L, 1996, p. 64).

Yet, Paul Samuelson has called himself a "Keynesian" and even a "Post-Keynesian" in several editions of his famous textbook. Nevertheless, as we will explain in section 12.4 infra, Samuelson's theoretical neoclassical synthesis axiomatic foundations is logically not the general theory spelled out by Keynes.

12.3 The Axiomatic Differences between Samuelson's Neoclassical Keynesianism and Keynes/ Post Keynesian Theory

At the same time that Samuelson was developing his neoclassical synthesis Keynesianism, he was working on his masterful *Foundations of Economic Analysis* (1947). In his *Foundations*, Samuelson asserts explicitly (or implicitly) certain specific classical axioms are the basis of both classical micro theory and his neoclassical Keynesian macroeconomic analysis. For example, Samuelson noted that "in a purely competitive world it would be foolish to hold money as a store of value as long as other assets had a positive yield" (Samuelson, 1947, pp. 122–124). This statement means that (1) any real producible capital goods that produce a positive yield are a gross substitute for money and (2) money is neutral. Thus as he was promoting his pedagogical brand of Keynesianism in his textbook Samuelson was arguing that the gross substitution axiom and the neutral money axiom are the foundations upon which all economic analysis including neoclassical synthesis Keynesianism must be built. (We shall indicate infra that Keynes specifically rejected these two classical axioms as a foundation for his *General Theory*.)

Furthermore, in an article published in 1969, Samuelson argued that the "ergodic hypothesis [axiom]" is a necessary foundation if economics is to be a hard science (Samuelson, 1969, p. 184). (As explained in section 12.4 infra, Keynes also rejected this ergodic axiom.) What is this ergodic hypothesis?

If one conceives of the economy as a stochastic (probability) process, then the future outcome of any current decision is determined via a probability distribution. Logically speaking, to make statistically reliable forecasts about future economic events, the decision maker should obtain and analyze sample data from the future. Since that is impossible, the assumption of an ergodic stochastic process permits the analyst to assert that samples drawn from past and current data are equivalent to drawing a sample from the future. In other words, the ergodic axiom implies that the outcome at any future date is the statistical shadow of past and current market data.

A realization of a stochastic process is a sample value of a multidimensional variable over a period of time, that is, a single time series of recorded outcomes. A stochastic process provides a universe of such time series. *Time statistics* refers to statistical averages (e.g. the mean, the standard deviation, etc.) calculated from a singular realization over an indefinite time space. *Space statistics*, on the other hand, refers to statistical averages calculated at a fixed point of time observation and are formed over the universe of realizations (i.e. space statistics are calculated from cross-sectional data).

If the stochastic process is ergodic, then for an infinite realization the time statistics and the space statistics will coincide. For finite realizations of ergodic processes, time and space statistics coincide except for random errors, that is, they tend to converge (with the probability of unity) as the number of observations increase. Consequently, if the ergodic axiom is applicable, statistics calculated from either past time series or cross-sectional data are statistically reliable estimates of the space statistics that will occur at any future date.

The ergodic axiom therefore assures that the outcome associated with any future date can be reliably predicted by a statistical analysis of already existing data. The future is therefore never uncertain—it can always be reliably predicted by a sufficient statistical analysis of already existing data. Future outcomes, in an ergodic system, are probabilistically risky but reliably predictable. (In a nonstochastic deterministic orthodox economic model, the classical ordering axiom plays the same role as the ergodic axiom of classical stochastic models.[4])

In an ergodic world, in the long run, the future is predetermined and cannot be changed by anything human beings or governments do. It follows that any government market regulation or interference into normal competitive market (assumed ergodic) processes, may, in the short run, prevent the system from achieving the full employment level assured by the axioms of a classical Walrasian system. In an ergodic system where the future can be reliably predicted so that future positive yields of real assets can be known with actuarial certainty, and where the gross substitution axiom underlies all demand curves, then as long as prices are flexible, money must be neutral and the system automatically adjusts to a full employment general equilibrium. If, on the other hand, prices are sticky in the short run, then it will take a longer time for the gross substitution theorem to work its way through the system but, at least in the long run, a full employment general equilibrium is still assured. In Keynes's general theory analysis, a full employment equilibrium is not assured in either the short run or the long run.

Samuelson (C–L, 1996, p. 163) has stated that in his view Keynes's analysis is a "very slow adjusting disequilibrium" system where the "full Walrasian equilibrium was not realized" in the short run because prices and wages do not adjust rapidly enough to an exogenous shock. Nevertheless, the economic system would, if left alone, achieve full employment in the long run.

In contrast, on the very first text page of *The General Theory*, Keynes (1936a, p. 3) explained "that the postulates of the classical [Walrasian] theory are applicable to a special case only and not to the general case . . . Moreover the characteristics of the special case assumed by the classical theory happen not to be those of the economics society in which we actually live, with the result that its teaching is misleading and disastrous if we attempt to apply it to the facts of experience."

In the preface to the German language edition of *The General Theory* (1936b, p. ix) Keynes specifically noted "This is one of the reasons which justify my calling my theory a *general* (emphasis in the original) theory. Since it is based on *fewer restrictive assumptions* ('weniger enge Voraussetzunger stutz') than the orthodox theory, it is also more easily adopted to a large area of different circumstances" (Second emphasis added). In other words, Keynes argued that what made his analytical system more general than the classical (or more recent Walrasian general equilibrium) analysis is that Keynes's general theory requires a smaller common axiomatic base (fewer restrictive axioms) than any other alternative theory. Alternative theories then are special cases that impose additional restrictive axioms to the common axiomatic foundation of the general theory. The onus is therefore, on those who add the restrictive axioms to the general theory to justify these additional axioms. Those theorists who invoke only the general theory axiomatic base are not required, in logic, to prove a general negative, that is, they are not required to prove the additional restrictive axioms are unnecessary.

12.4 Samuelson's Keynesian Axioms that Keynes and the Post Keynesians Overthrow in their General Theory Revolution

Keynes was primarily a monetary theorist. The words money, currency, and monetary appear in the titles of most of his major volumes in economics.

Post Keynesian monetary theory evolves from Keynes's revolutionary approach to analyzing money-using economy where money was never neutral even if a hypothetical pure competitive market conditions including instantaneously flexible wages and prices exist. Keynes (1936a, p. 26) argued that even if such a purely competitive market existed it would not automatically achieve a full employment general equilibrium in a money-using economy.

Keynes compared those economists whose theoretical logic was grounded on the classical special case additional restrictive axioms to Euclidean geometers living in a non-Euclidean world

> who discovering that in experience straight lines apparently parallel often meet, rebuke the lines for not keeping straight—as the only remedy for the unfortunate collisions which are taking place. Yet, in truth, there is no remedy except to throw over the axiom of parallels and to work out a non-Euclidean geometry. Something similar is required today in economics. (Keynes, 1936a, p. 16)

To throw over an axiom is to reject what the faithful believe are "universal truths." The Keynesian revolution in economic theory required economists to "throw over" three restrictive classical axioms from its theoretical foundation. Post Keynesian monetary theory has followed Keynes's fewer restrictive axiom analytical framework. In light of Keynes's analogy to geometry, Post Keynesian monetary theory might be called non-Euclidean economics.

The classical axioms that Keynes threw out in his revolutionary general analysis were (1) *the neutrality of money axiom*, (2) *the gross substitution axiom*, and (3) *the axiom of an ergodic economic world*.

In 1935 Keynes explicitly noted that in his analytic framework money matters in both the long and short run, that is, money is never neutral. Money affects real decision making. In 1935 Keynes wrote:

> the theory which I desiderate would deal . . . with an economy in which money plays a part of its own and affects motives and decisions, and is, in short, one of the operative factors in the situation, so that the course of events cannot be predicted either in the long period or in the short, without a knowledge of the behavior of money between the first state and the last. And it is this which we mean when we speak of a monetary economy. (Keynes, 1935, pp. 408–409).

As Keynes's developed his theory of liquidity preference he recognized that his theory of involuntary unemployment required specifying "The Essential Properties of Interest and Money" (1936a, ch. 17) that differentiated his results from classical theory. These "essential properties" assured that money and all other liquid assets are never neutral. These essential properties (Keynes, 1936a, pp. 230–231) are:

(1) the elasticity of production of all liquid assets including money is zero or negligible, and
(2) the elasticity of substitution between liquid assets (including money) and reproducible goods is zero or negligible.

A zero elasticity of production means that money does not grow on trees and consequently workers can not be hired to harvest money trees when the demand for money increases. Or as Keynes wrote: "money . . . cannot be readily reproduced;-labour cannot be turned on at will by entrepreneurs to produce money in increasing quantities as its price rises" (Keynes, 1936a, p. 230). In other words, when the demand for money (liquidity) increases, private sector entrepreneurs cannot hire labor to produce more money to meet this increase in demand for a nonreproducible (by the private sector) good.

In classical theory, on the other hand, money is a reproducible commodity. In many neoclassical textbook models as well as in the Walrasian system, peanuts or some other reproducible product of industry is the money commodity or *numeraire*. Peanuts may not grow on trees, but they do grow on the roots of bushes. The supply of peanuts can easily be augmented by the hiring of additional workers by private sector entrepreneurs.

The zero elasticity of substitution assures that portion of income that is not spent on by the products of industry for consumption purposes, that is, savings, will find, in Hahn's (1977, p. 31) terminology, "resting places" in the demand for nonproducibles. Some 40 years after Keynes, Hahn rediscovered Keynes's point that a stable involuntary unemployment equilibrium could exist *even in a Walrasian system with flexible wages and prices* whenever there are "resting places for savings in other than reproducible assets" (Hahn, 1977, p. 31).

Hahn rigorously demonstrated what was logically intuitive to Keynes. Hahn (1977, p. 37) showed that the view that with "flexible money wages there would be no unemployment has no convincing argument to recommend it. . . . Even in a pure tatonnement in traditional models convergence to [a general] equilibrium cannot be generally proved" if savings were held in the form of nonproducibles. Hahn (1977, p. 39) argued that "any non-reproducible asset allows for a choice between employment inducing and non-employment inducing demand." Accordingly, the existence of a demand for money and other liquid nonreproducible assets (that are *not* gross substitutes for the products of the capital goods producing industries) as a store of "savings" means that all income earned by households engaging in the production of goods is not, in the short or long run, necessarily spent on the products of industry. Households who want to store that portion of their income that they do not consume (i.e., that they do not spend on the products of industry) in liquid assets are choosing, in Hahn's words "a non-employment inducing demand" for their savings.

If the gross substitution axiom was universally applicable, however, any new savings that would increase the demand for nonproducibles would increase the price of nonproducibles (whose production supply curve is, by definition, perfectly inelastic). The resulting relative price rise in nonproducibles vis-a-vis producibles would, under the gross substitution axiom, induce savers to increase their demand for reproducible durables as a substitute for nonproducibles in their wealth holdings. Consequently nonproducibles could not be ultimate resting places for savings as they spilled over into a demand for producible goods (cf. Davidson, 1972).

Samuelson's assumption that all demand curves are based on an ubiquitous gross substitution axiom implies that everything is a substitute for everything else. In Samuelson's foundation for economic analysis, therefore, producibles must be good gross substitutes for any existing nonproducible liquid assets (including money) when the latter are used as stores of savings. Accordingly, Samuelson's *Foundation of Economic Analysis* denies the logical possibility of involuntary unemployment[5] as long as all prices are perfectly flexible.

Samuelson's brand of Keynesianism is merely a form of the classical special case analysis that is "misleading and disastrous" (Keynes, 1936a, p. 3) if applied to the real world. In the absence of a restrictive universally applicable axiom of gross substitution, however, income effects (e.g. the Keynesian multiplier) can predominate and can swamp any hypothetical classical substitution effects. Just as in non-Euclidean geometry lines that are apparently parallel often crash into each other, in the Keynes-Post Keynesian non-Euclidean economic world, an increase demand for "savings" even if it raises the relative price of nonproducibles, will not spill over into a demand for producible good and hence when households save a portion of their income they have made a choice for "non-employment inducing demand."

Finally, Keynes argued that only in a money-using entrepreneur economy where the future is uncertain (and therefore could not be reliably predicted) would money (and all other liquid assets) always be nonneutral as they are used as a store of savings. In essence Keynes viewed the economic system as moving through calendar time from an irrevocable past to an uncertain, not statistically predictable, future. This required Keynes to reject the ergodic axiom.

Keynes never used the term "ergodic" since ergodic theory was first developed in 1935 by the Moscow School of Probability and it did not become well known in the West until after the Second World War and Keynes was dead. Nevertheless, Keynes's main criticism of Tinbergen's econometric "method" (Keynes, 1939a, p. 308) was that the economic data "is not homogeneous over time." Nonhomogeneous data over time means that economic time series are nonstationary, and nonstationary is a sufficient (but not a necessary condition) for nonergodic circumstances. Consequently, Keynes, with his emphasis on uncertainty had, in these comments on Tinbergen, specifically rejected what would later be called the ergodic axiom—an assumption that Samuelson has declared is a foundation necessary to make economics a hard science.

In sum, Samuelson theoretical foundations requires three classical axioms that are the equivalent of the axiom of parallels in Euclidean geometry. Clearly then Samuelson's macroeconomics is not applicable to the "non-Euclidean" economics of a money-using entrepreneurial system that Keynes developed in his *General Theory*.

12.5 Liquidity and Contracts

Nevertheless, the question may remain "Does applying Keynes's smaller axiomatic base make any difference in our understanding of the real world in which we live vis-a-vis applying Samuelson's classical axiomatic foundation version of Keynesianism?" The answer is definitely yes because only if we overthrow these three classical axioms that are an essential part of Samuelson's foundations of economic analysis can the concept of liquidity play an important role in our analysis—as it does in our lives.

Important decisions involving production, investment, and consumption activities are often taken in an uncertain (nonergodic) environment. Hiring inputs and buying products using forward contracts in money terms are a human institution developed to efficiently organize time consuming production and exchange processes. Since the abolition of slavery the money-wage contract is the most ubiquitous of these contracts. Unemployment, rather than full employment, is a common laissez-faire outcome in such a market oriented, monetary production economy.

The economy in which we live utilizes money contracts—not real contracts—to seal production and exchange agreements among self-interested individuals. The ubiquitous use of money contracts is an essential element of all real world entrepreneurial economies. Moreover *recontracting without income penalty* (an essential characteristic of the Walrasian system) whenever parties have entered into a contract at a price other than the implicit full employment general equilibrium price *is never permitted under the civil law of contracts*. Why, one might ask Samuelson, do economies continue to organize production and exchange on the basis of money contracts, if such use interferes with the rapid achievement of a socially optimal general Walrasian equilibrium?

The use of money contracts has always presented a dilemma to classical theorists. Logically consistent classical theorists must view the universal use of money contracts by modern economies as irrational, since such agreements fixing payments over time in nominal terms can impede the self-interest optimizing pursuit of real incomes by economic decision makers. Mainstream economists tend to explain the existence of money contracts by using noneconomic reasons such as social customs, invisible handshakes, etc.—societal institutional constraints which limit price signaling and hence limits adjustments for the optimal use of resources in the long run.

For Post Keynesians, on the other hand, *binding* nominal contractual commitments are a sensible method for dealing with true uncertainty regarding future outcomes whenever economic activities span a long duration of calendar time. In organizing production and exchange on a money contractual basis, buyers need not worry about what events happen in the uncertain future as long as they have, or can obtain, enough liquidity to meet these contractual commitments as they come due. Thus liquidity means survival in a money-using contractual entrepreneurial directed market economy. Bankruptcy, on the other hand, occurs when significant contractual monetary obligations cannot be met. Bankruptcy is the equivalent of a walk to the economic gallows.

Keynes's general theory that emphasizes money and liquidity implies that agents who planned to spend in the current period need not have earned income currently, or previously, in order to exercise this demand in an entrepreneur system. All these buying agents need is the liquidity to meet money contractual obligations as they come due. This means that investment spending, which we normally associate with the demand for reproducible fixed and working capital goods, is not constrained by either actual income or inherited endowments. This type of exogenous spending is constrained, in a money-creating banking system, solely by the expected future *monetary* (not real) cash inflow (Keynes, 1936a, ch. 17) upon which banks are willing to make additional loans.

In a world where money is created only if someone increases his/her indebtedness to banks in order to purchase newly produced goods, then real investment spending will be undertaken as long as the purchase of newly produced capital goods are expected to generate a future of cash inflow (net of operating expenses) whose discounted present value equals or exceed the money cash outflow (the supply price currently needed to purchase the capital good).

For any component of aggregate demand not to be constrained by actual income, therefore, agents must have the ability to finance purchases by borrowing from a banking system that can create money. This Post-Keynesian financing mechanism where increases in the nominal quantity of money are used to finance increased demand for producible goods results in increasing employment levels. Money, therefore, cannot be neutral and can be endogenous.

To reject the neutrality axiom does not require assuming that agents suffer from a money illusion. It only means that "money is not neutral" (Keynes, 1935, p. 411) in the sense that money matters in both the short run and the long run, affecting the equilibrium level of employment and real output. If it were not for Samuelson's insistence on neutral money as foundations for all economic theory, economists might recognize that in a money-using entrepreneurial economy that organizes production and exchange with the use of spot and forward money contracts, money is a real phenomenon. The money neutrality axiom must be rejected.

Arrow and Hahn (1971, pp. 356–357) implicitly recognized this necessity of overthrowing the neutral money axiom when they wrote:

> The terms in which contracts are made matter. In particular, if money is the goods in terms of which contracts are made, then the prices of goods in terms of money are of special significance. This is not the case if we consider an economy without a past or future . . . *if a serious monetary theory* comes to be written, the fact that contracts are made in terms of money will be of considerable importance [italics added].

Moreover Arrow and Hahn demonstrate (1971, p. 361) that, if production and exchange contracts are made in terms of money (so that money affects real decisions) in an economy moving along in calendar time with a past and a future, then *all general equilibrium existence theorems are jeopardized*. The existence of money contracts—a characteristic of the world in which we live—implies that there need never exist, in the long run or the short run, any rational expectations equilibrium or general equilibrium market clearing price vector. Samuelson's Walrasian foundation is not a reliable base for real world economies that use money and money contracts to organize economic activities.

12.6 Conclusion

Paul Samuelson saved the term "Keynesian" from being excoriated from post-Second World War textbooks by the McCarthy anti-communist movement at the time. But the cost of such a saving was to sever the meaning of Keynes's theory in mainstream economic theory from its *General Theory* analytical roots that demonstrated that, in a money-using economy, flexible wages and prices and pure competition are neither necessary nor sufficient conditions to assure full employment equilibrium, even in the long run.

Samuelson's view of Keynesianism resulted in aborting Keynes's revolutionary analysis from altering the foundation of mainstream macroeconomics. Consequently what passes as conventional macroeconomic wisdom of mainstream economists at the beginning of the twenty-first century is nothing more than a high-tech and more mathematical version of the nineteenth century classical theory.

In winning the battle against the forces trying to prevent the teaching of suspected communist inspired "Keynesian" economics in our universities, Samuelson ultimately lost the war that Keynes had launched to eliminate the classical theoretical analysis as the basis for real world economic problems of employment, interest, and money. In 1986 Lorie Tarshis recognized this when he noted "I never felt that Keynes was being followed with full adherence or full understanding of what he had written. I still feel that way" (C–L, p. 72).

Mainstream economics—whether espoused by Old Neoclassical Keynesians, New Keynesians, Old Classical, or New Classical theorists, etc[6]—relies on the three classical axioms that Keynes discarded in his general theory attempt to make economics relevant to the real world problems of unemployment and international trade and international payments. As a result these problems still plague much of the real world in the globalized economy of the twenty-first century.

Notes

1. As Weintraub (2002, p. 113) noted, Debreu was a Student of Bourbakian mathematics and Bourbakians believe "good general theory does not search

for the maximum generality but for the right generality". Keynes searched for a "maximum" general theory, that is a theory built on the smallest axiomatic foundation that could be applied to the real world. Debreu's *Theory of Value* (1959) was a "direct analogue of Bourbaki's (analysis) right down to the title . . . .{Debreu] sought to establish the definitive analytic mother-structure from which all further work in economics would depart . . . But this required one very crucial maneuver that was nowhere explicitly stated, namely that the model of Walrasian equilibrium was the root structure [the right level of generality] from which all further work in economics would eventuate" (Weintraub, 2002, p. 121).

2. Mainstream economists called this sticky interest rate argument the "liquidity trap" where at some low, but positive, rate of interest the demand to hold money for speculative reasons was assumed to be perfectly elastic (i.e. horizontal). After the Second World War, econometric investigations could find no empirical evidence of a liquidity trap. Had mainstream economists read *The General Theory*, however, they would have known that on page 202 Keynes specifies the speculative demand for money as a rectangular hyperbola—a mathematical function that never has a perfectly elastic segment. Moreover eyeball empiricism led Keynes (1936a, p. 207) to indicate that he knew of no historical example where the liquidity preference function became "virtually absolute", that is, perfectly elastic. In sum, from both an empirical and theoretical view, Keynes denied the existence of a liquidity trap.
3. The particular proof that Keynes claimed was irrelevant was the classical assertion that a fixed and unchanging downward sloping marginal product curve of labor was the demand curve for labor and so that falling wages must increase employment. In chapter 20 of *The General Theory* Keynes specifically develops an "employment function" that is not the marginal product of labor curve and does not assure that aggregate effective demand is fixed.

   What the marginal productivity of labor curve indicates is that if in response to an expansion of aggregate effective demand, private sector entrepreneurs hire more workers to produce an additional flow of output per period, then in the face of diminishing returns (with no change in the degree of competition), the rise in employment will be associated with a fall in the real wage rate. In other words, the marginal product of labor curve is, for any given the level of effective demand and employment, the real wage determining curve. For a complete analysis of this point see Davidson (1998) or Davidson (2002).
4. True uncertainty occurs whenever an individual cannot specify and/or order a complete set of prospects regarding the future, either because: (1) the decision maker cannot conceive of a complete list of consequences that will occur in the future; or, (2) the decision maker cannot assign probabilities to all consequences because "the evidence is insufficient to establish a probability" so that possible consequences "are not even orderable" (Hicks, 1979, pp.113, 115). In such cases ordering is not possible.

5. To overthrow the axiom of gross substitution in an intertemporal context is truly heretical. It changes the entire perspective as to what is meant by "rational" or "optimal" savings, as to why people save or what they save. It would deny the life-cycle hypothesis. Indeed Danziger *et al.* (1982–83) have shown that the facts regarding consumption spending by the elderly are incompatible with the notion of intertemporal gross substitution of consumption plans which underlie both life cycle models and overlapping generation models currently so popular in mainstream macroeconomic theory.
6. Some economists, for example behavioral theorists, have tried to erect *ad hoc* models suggesting that agents do not always act with the economic rationality of classical theory's decision makers although there is nothing in their analysis that denies the possibility that rational decision making is possible. Unfortunately, such theories have no unifying underlying general theory to explain why such "irrational" behavior exists. Behavioral theorists can not explain why those who undertake non-rational behavior have not been made extinct by a Darwinian struggle with those real world decision makers who take the time to act rationally.

   Had behavioral theorists adopted Keynes's general theory as their basic framework, irrational behavior can be explained as sensible if the economy is a nonergodic system. Or as Hicks (1979, p. vii) succinctly put it, "One must assume that the people in one's models do not know what is going to happen, and know that they do not know just what is going to happen." In conditions of true uncertainty, people often realize they just don't have a clue as to what rational behavior should be.

References

Arrow, K. W. and F. H. Hahn. (1971). *General Competitive Analysis*. San Francisco: Holden-Day.

Buckley, W. F. (1951). *God and Man at Yale*. Chicago: Henry Rigney.

Colander, D. C. and H. Landreth. (1996). *The Coming of Keynesianism To America*. Cheltenham: Elgar.

Danziger, S. J., J. van der Haag, E. Smolensky, and M. Taussig. (1981–82). "The life cycle hypothesis and the consumption behavior of the elderly," *Journal of Post Keynesian Economics*, 5.

Davidson, P. (1972). *Money and The Real World*. London: Macmillan.

——. (1978). *Money and The Real World*. 2nd, ed. London: Macmillan.

——.(1982). *International Money and The Real World*. London: Macmillan.

——.(Winter1982–83), "Rational Expectations: A Fallacious Foundation for Studying Crucial Decision-Making Processes," *Journal of Post Keynesian Economics*, 5, 182–197.

Davidson, P. (1998). "Post Keynesian employment and analysis and the macroeconomics of OECD employment," *The Economic Journal*, 108.

—— (2002), *Financial Markets Money and The Real World*. Cheltenham: Elgar.

Debreu, G. (1959). *The Theory of Value*. New York: John Wiley & Sons.

Hahn, F. A. (1977). "Keynesian Economics and General Equilibrium Theory," in *The Microfoundations of Macroeconomics*, edited by G. C. Harcourt. London: Macmillan.

Hicks, J. R (1979). *Causality in Economics*. New York: Basic Books.

Keynes, J. M. (1935). "A Monetary Theory of Production," in D. Moggridge (ed.), *The Collected Writings of John Maynard Keynes, XIII*, London, Macmillan, 1973a. All references are to reprint.

——. (1936a). *The General Theory of Employment, Interest, and Money*. New York: Harcourt, Brace.

——. (1936b). *The General Theory of Employment, Interest, and Money*, German Language edition, Duncker and Humboldt, Berlin.

——. (1939a). "Professor Tinbergen's Method", *Economic Journal, 49*, reprinted in D. Moggridge (ed.), *The Collected Writings of John Maynard Keynes, XIV*, London, Macmillan, 1973b. All references are to reprint.

——. (1939b). "Relative Movements of Real Wages and Output," *The Economic Journal, 49*, reprinted in *The Collected Writings of John Maynard Keynes, XIV*, edited by D. Moggridge. London, Macmillan, 1973b. All references are to reprint.

——. (1937). "The General Theory," *Quarterly Journal of Economics*, reprinted in D. Moggridge (ed.), *The Collected Writings of John Maynard Keynes, XIV*, London, Macmillan, 1973b. All references are to reprint.

——. (1973a, 1973b). *The Collected Writings of J. M. Keynes*. London: Macmillan, Volume XIII, 1973(a); Volume XIV, 1973(b).

Samuelson, P. A. (1947). *Foundations of Economic Analysis*. Cambridge: Harvard University Press.

——. (1948). *Economics: An Introductory Analysis*. New York: McGraw-Hill.

Skidelsky, R. (1992). *John Maynard Keynes, Volume 2: The Economist as Savior, 1920–1937*. London: Macmillan.

Weintraub, E. R. (2002). *How Economics Became A Mathematical Science*. Durham: Duke University Press.

13

Paul Samuelson and International Trade Theory Over Eight Decades

Avinash Dixit

Paul Samuelson has made seminal contributions to every major field of economics, but I think international trade theory can rightfully claim to be one of his favorite areas of research. He keeps returning to it after detours into other fields, and invariably finds something new and thought-provoking to say.

He started in the 1930s with pathbreaking work on gains from trade. Then, in a series of celebrated articles over a period of more than a decade, he established the two-by-two model, now called the Heckscher–Ohlin–Samuelson model, as the standard tool for thinking about international trade for the following two decades or longer. The 1950s brought what is my personal favorite article (Samuelson, 1953), which elucidated the interaction between the prices of goods and factors in a general equilibrium with trade. It extended much of the earlier analysis beyond the two-by-two case, and gave us new tools, particularly duality and the revenue or GDP function. Samuelson continued the theme of "beyond two-by-two" with the sector-specific factor model, now called the Ricardo–Viner–Samuelson model, in the late 1960s and the early 1970s, and the Dornbusch–Fischer–Samuelson model of trade with a continuum of commodities in the late 1970s; both models now constitute an essential part of the international trade economists' toolkit. His concern about the normative effects of trade continued with new insights on the transfer problem, further contributions to the issues of gains from trade, and critiques of doctrines of unequal exchange. He has continued to examine and develop classical ideas and theories, and to write perceptive and generous assessments of historical and contemporary pioneers of trade theory. And his most recent explorations of Ricardian theories have brought him into the current policy controversies concerning globalization and outsourcing.

The community of international trade economists has recognized and celebrated Samuelson's role in the development of our subject before. Noteworthy among these writings is Ronald Jones' (1983) survey of Samuelson's impact on trade theory. The last twenty years have brought new contributions from Samuelson, and have seen his influence continue in the work of others; therefore a new overview is justified. But there is a second and perhaps more important reason for a new encomium. Old Nordic and Celtic bards told and retold the deeds of heroes; these rituals were an important part of the collective memory or even identity of their people. The tribe of professional economists should likewise continue to sing of our heroes.

Jones' excellent article saves me the need to describe the technical details of Samuelson's contributions to trade theory. Therefore I can concentrate on my chosen role of a bard or balladeer, which is much more fun.

13.1 Trade Theory and Economic Theory

Samuelson has always seen economics as a unified whole, and indeed has always striven to place it in the even larger context of its connections with other sciences in matters of concepts and techniques of analysis. I believe that the explanation of his special love for international trade theory is to be found in the same trait. He saw from the earliest days that trade theory and general equilibrium theory were very closely linked, and that the linkages flowed both ways. The opening sentence of one of his earliest publications (Samuelson, 1938) is: "Historically the development of economic theory owes much to the theory of international trade." He used the Ricardian model of comparative advantage as the starting point of his exposition of linear programming for economists (Samuelson, 1949b). And recently he said (Samuelson, 1995) "If you've got it, flaunt it. Well, we in trade theory do have a lot to display. ... Thus, the first general equilibrium was not by Léon Walras. Sixty-five years earlier it was by John Stuart Mill—and in connection with international equilibrium. ... Stan Ulam[1] ... once challenged me, saying 'Paul, name me one proposition in the social sciences that is both true and non-trivial.' My reply was: 'Ricardo's theory of comparative advantage.' ... Trade theory leads the way."

13.2 Gains from Trade

Samuelson's early articles on the gains from trade (1938, 1939), and a later one (1962b) stimulated by Kemp (1962), laid down the basic comparisons (free trade versus autarky, free trade versus restricted trade, Pareto efficiency versus social optimality) and the techniques (revealed preference inequalities, consumption, and utility possibility frontiers) that have guided thinking on this issue ever since. Most importantly, Samuelson showed that the utility possibility frontier with free trade lies outside the utility possibility frontier with autarky, provided the aggregate quantities of goods available in both situations can be distributed among the country's consumers by the government. Thus, given any allocation under autarky, a move to free trade accompanied by suitable distribution of commodities can achieve a Pareto superior outcome, whereas, given any allocation under free trade, no move to autarky accompanied by any redistribution can be Pareto improving.

The simplicity and generality of this analysis was a shining contrast to the muddled thinking of many earlier writers, who had been mired in doctrinal debates about the nature of costs, and had been misled into believing that the arguments for trade depended in crucial ways on there being only two goods, or on all goods being tradeable, or on factors being in fixed supply, or on factors being perfectly mobile across sectors within a country, or any of a number of other restrictive assumptions often made for convenience of exposition. Alas, misunderstandings about the normative case for trade persist and continue to resurface periodically even in professional writings, not to mention policy debates in the media where the grasp of logic is feeble. Trade economists must be ever vigilant to combat such errors. Nothing illustrates this better than the reaction in the media to Samuelson's latest (2004) foray into trade theory. He set out to make a perfectly valid point—while there are positive gains from trade, various developments in the rest of the world can either increase or decrease the size of these gains. If the rest of the world gets better at producing the goods that we currently export, our terms of trade decline and our gains from trade are smaller than they were before. He must have been particularly delighted in making this point using a Ricardian model with simple numerical calculations, a method that has always been one of his favorites. And it was a useful reminder to some participants in debates about trade policy who sometimes leave the impression that under free trade things always and continuously get even better and better. However, his work was misinterpreted and hijacked by the truly dangerous participants at the other extreme of the same debates, who favor a fortress America shut off from the rest of the trading world. Nothing in Samuelson's paper denied the existence of gains from trade. He compared two situations, call them B and A, respectively before and after the rest of the world improves its productivity in America's export sectors. He showed that in the aggregate, B was better for America than A. But there is no feasible policy to restore B; how can we reverse the productivity gains in the rest of the world short of conquest and suppression? The relevant policy comparison is of A with a third alternative F, fortress America. And all the analysis stemming from Samuelson's own papers of the late 1930s shows that A is better for America as a whole than F. To be sure, A is not as much better than F as is B, but it would be a mistake to respond to the technological shift from B to A by making a policy shift that would take us from A to F. This logic was either beyond grasp of the protectionists or was deliberately ignored by them, and it is taking Samuelson and others much time and effort to correct the error. Eternal vigilance is the price of good economic policy, and perhaps even an 89-year-old has something to learn about the need to anticipate and avoid such distortions and hijackings of one's ideas by the policy community.

What about research following Samuelson's pioneering analyses of gains from trade? In my opinion, two lines of thought merit special mention. First, in constructing his utility possibility frontiers, Samuelson assumed that the aggregate quantities of commodities could be allocated among consumers without any restrictions, as personalized lump-sum transfers in kind. But a more natural way to distribute gains from trade in a market economy would be to transfer purchasing power, and then let each individual buy the goods or services according to his or her own preference. Can this be done, using personalized lump-sum transfers that are balanced within each country? This requires a careful construction and proof of existence of equilibrium; it was done by Grandmont and McFadden (1972). Second, personalized lump-sum transfers have long been known to be unrealistic, and thanks to Hammond (1979), we now know the precise nature of the difficulty. They are not incentive-compatible: each individual has the incentive and the ability to misrepresent private information about his or her preferences and abilities in an attempt to secure a larger transfer receipt. Commodity taxes or subsidies of the Diamond–Mirrlees kind depend only on statistical or aggregate information about demands; therefore any individual who is small in the economy has negligible ability to gain by such misrepresentation. Dixit and Norman (1986), in exchange with

Kemp and Wan (1986), examined when Pareto superior outcomes can be achieved using such instruments. It emerged that if the full set of commodity tax and subsidy instruments is available, and the Diamond–Mirrlees condition for productive efficiency under commodity taxation is met, then any positive aggregate production gains from trade can be distributed in a Pareto-beneficial way. Subsequent research has examined what happens when this fails, for example, Feenstra and Lewis (1991) and Spector (2001).

13.3 Ricardian Models of Trade

Ricardo's ideas and theories have a natural appeal for Samuelson, given his manifold interests in all aspects of economics. First and foremost, as a serious historian of thought, who has the proper combination of respect for, and critical assessment of, the contributions of the giants who laid the foundations of our subject, he recognizes the pivotal importance of the concept of comparative advantage. That did not stop him being critical of other aspects of Ricardo's theories; see his Presidential Address to the American Economic Association (Samuelson, 1962a, p. 9). He gave Ricardo credit for formulating "a rigorously handled general equilibrium model of primitive type,"[2] but recognized many less formal predecessors, including Adam Smith, when it comes to the policy implication favoring freer trade. And in his masterly[3] exegesis of Ricardo's overall theory of production and prices (Samuelson, 1962a, b), he took Ricardo to task for his "flirtations" with a labor theory of value.

I think the most useful lesson from these articles for posterity, though, is his conclusion about how modern economists compare with classical economists:

> [Ricardo] would have made a most excellent modern economist! Despite though the high native ability of the ancients, we have advanced a long way ahead of their discussions. ... In particular, we are more humble. They declared so many things to be necessarily so that we today recognize as not having to be so. This is, in a sense, a step backward. How exciting to be able to assert definitely that invention of a machine cannot do this and must do that! But alas, dull as it may be, the modern theorist must face the facts of life—the infinite multiplicity of patterns that can emerge in actuality. Good, advanced theory must be the antidote for overly-simple, intuitive theory. (Samuelson, 1962b, p. 231)

What we now know as "the" Ricardian model of comparative advantage has logical delights and expository appeal for economic theorists more generally, not just trade theorists. Samuelson (1949b) saw and exploited its potential for explaining many of the intuitions and techniques of linear programming to economists. The same model and the same geometry of linear programming also serve to express in a simple way the concepts of production efficiency in a world economy when goods can cross international boundaries but labor cannot. The standard decentralized implementation of such an efficient production plan in turn establishes the efficiency of free trade in this context. These technical contributions of Samuelson have been so well expounded by Jones (1983) that I have nothing to add (or subtract).

Another expository use of the Ricardian model is its ability to make many of its points using numerical values and arithmetic calculations, without the need to deploy algebra or calculus. Samuelson has used this device on many occasions, including in his most recent article (2004) on the gains from trade.

13.4 Factor Endowment Models of Trade

Samuelson seems to have regarded differences of factor endowments among countries as a better explanation of trade than Ricardian productivity differences. In his first paper on factor price equalization (Samuelson, 1948), he says: "instead of relying upon such crypto explanations as 'Yankee ingenuity' to explain patterns of comparative advantage, Ohlin would attribute America's comparative advantage in food production—a land-intensive industry—to the fact that each unit of American labor has relatively much land to work with."

He gleaned an astonishingly rich harvest from his work on the factor endowment theory of trade. The two-by-two model is now justly called the Heckscher–Ohlin–Samuelson model. This work produced two of the "four theorems of trade theory." With Stolper (1941), he showed how changes in the international prices of goods lead to magnified changes in the domestic prices of factors, and generated unambiguous predictions about the effects of tariffs on the real returns to factors; this came to be called the Stolper–Samuelson effect. In two papers (Samuelson, 1948, 1949a) he found that free trade in goods will lead to complete equalization of the prices of factors even though factors trade in separate country-specific markets. The question was whether the nonlinear equations relating the world prices of outputs to the domestic unit cost functions for all the goods being produced had a unique solution for the domestic input prices.

This analysis of "global univalance," with more general mathematical analysis in an appendix to Samuelson (1953), actually led to some new mathematics—a global inverse function theorem. Mas-Colell (1985) gives a detailed discussion of this.

The 1949 paper contains another argument, which I believe gets much more directly at the economics of the factor price equalization issue. This is the wonderful "angel and recording geographer" device:

> Let us suppose that in the beginning all factors were perfectly mobile, and nationalism had not yet reared its ugly head. ... [T]here would be one world price of food and clothing, one real wage, one real rent, and the world's land and labour would be divided between food and clothing production in a determinate way, with uniform proportions of labour to land being used everywhere in clothing production, and a smaller—but uniform—proportion of labour to land being used in production of food. Now suppose an angel came down from heaven and notified some fraction of all the labour and land units producing clothing that they were to be called Americans, the rest to be called Europeans. ... Obviously, just giving people and areas national labels does not alter anything; it does not change commodity or factor prices or production patterns. ... [W]hat will be the result? Two countries with quite different factor proportions, but with identical real wages and rents and identical modes of commodity production (but with different relative importance of food and clothing industries). ... Both countries must have factor proportions intermediate between the proportions in the two industries. The angel can create a country with proportions not intermediate between the factor intensities of food and clothing. But he cannot do so by following the above-described procedure, which was calculated to leave prices and production unchanged. (Samuelson, 1949a, pp. 194–195)

The question is whether or when incomplete markets suffice to ensure the full efficiency of complete markets. Even though markets for factors of production are not unified across countries, will trade in unified world markets for goods suffice to equate prices of factors across countries? Put this way, the idea is very similar to that of spanning in financial markets (see Ekern and Wilson (1974) for an early statement and Duffie and Huang (1985) for a more general later development). If a full set of markets for Arrow–Debreu securities corresponding to all states of the world exists, then a competitive general equilibrium will be Pareto-efficient (with the usual caveats about satiation and externalities). Now suppose such a direct set of complete markets does not exist, but there are markets for other composite securities, for example, shares in firms whose production decisions generate particular profit patterns across the states of the world so that the shares constitute prepackaged bundles of Arrow–Debreu securities. This alternative set of markets suffices for Pareto-efficiency if the available set of securities spans the space of purchasing powers in all states of the world. Similarly, when countries differ in their factor endowments, full production efficiency is ensured if they can trade the factors directly. But suppose they can only trade prepackaged bundles of these factors, namely those embodied in units of each of the goods. This suffices if the vectors of factors comprising these bundles together span the factor space in a suitable sense. Of course this is an equilibrium concept. In finance one must find the real choices of firms to know the patterns of profits in the available securities and see if they span the full space; in trade one must solve for the factor proportions in the hypothetical equilibrium of an integrated world with international factor mobility and see if these factor bundles suffice for the purpose. One difference between finance and trade is that finance theory usually allows short sales of securities, while production quantities in trade must be inherently nonnegative in each country. Therefore we must incorporate this restriction and refine the concept of spanning to an appropriately nonnegative spanning; in the two-by-two model this requires that the factor proportions in the two countries should not be too different. But the analogy captures well the economic idea that trade in goods is serving as a substitute for trade in factors, and generates a more useful intuition than the mathematics of univalence. This approach to factor price equalization was developed for the competitive factor endowment models by Dixit and Norman (1980, pp. 110–125, 289–291), and was used in many other contexts including foreign direct investment by Helpman and Krugman (1985).

The Stolper–Samuelson and factor price equalization papers did not actually produce the Heckscher–Ohlin theorem, namely the prediction that the pattern of trade will correspond to relative factor abundance, although the idea was implicit there. As Jones (1983, p. 89) says, "it was left to the next generation to explore this 2×2 model in more detail for the effect of differences in factor endowments and growth in endowments on trade and production patterns." That, plus the Rybczynski theorem which arose independently, completed the famous four theorems. Jones' own article (1965) is my favorite exposition of the complete story; there are also important surveys by Bhagwati (1965) and Chipman (1965, 1966).

All this and much more came together in Samuelson (1953). With any number of goods and factors, he established a duality between prices and quantities (more precisely, a reciprocity relationship linking the Stolper–Samuelson and Rybczynski effects), and studied the univalence question with any number of goods and factors. In the process, he developed tools, most notably the revenue or GDP function, that have found numerous uses in trade theory. The subsequent research can be mostly subsumed in the general theme of "beyond 2-by-2."

Some explored questions such as "Under what conditions do the four theorems directly generalize to the case of many goods and factors?" and "Can the many goods and factors model be reduced to the 2-by-2 case by aggregation?" (see Jones and Scheinkman, 1977 and Neary (1985)). Others explored how the general intuition behind some of the four theorems can be adapted to the multidimensional situation, to obtain results involving alignments or correlations between the vectors of factor endowment differences or autarkic price differences and the vector of trade patterns (see Deardorff (1980, 1982) and Dixit and Norman (1980, pp. 94–102)).

Two of the most influential advances beyond two-by-two came from Samuelson himself. Both were special models that combined a richness of structure and the simplicity of tractability, and led to numerous uses. One was the two-by-three model where one factor was mobile across uses within a country, and the other two factors were each specific to the production of one of the two internationally tradeable goods; this was soon labeled the Ricardo–Viner–Samuelson model. Samuelson developed this in an article that launched the new *Journal of International Economics* (1971a). His aim was to provide a structure that combined the interconnections of general equilibrium essential for trade and the simplicity of rising supply curves in partial equilibrium analysis. He succeeded brilliantly, and the model has been much used in this way, but it soon found implications and significance beyond the original purpose. Samuelson himself found (1971c) that with more factors than goods, factor price equalization became an unlikely or exceptional case, and that Ohlin's arguments for partial but incomplete convergence of factor prices across countries could then be rehabilitated. Most importantly, the model was interpreted as the short run when a slow-adjusting factor (capital) was temporarily sector-specific. The resulting view of a process of adjustment that links the totally sector-specific-factor or pure exchange models on the one hand, and the Heckscher–Ohlin–Samuelson model with full intersectoral mobility of factors on the other, enriched our understanding of the dynamics of production (see Mayer, (1974), Mussa (1974) and Neary (1978)). And in a little-known but excellent paper, Mussa (1984) showed that factor specificity or adjustment costs are not by themselves distortions: in dynamics with rational expectations, producers will make socially efficient decisions about relocation of factors.

Samuelson's second foray beyond two-by-two, joint with Dornbush and Fischer (1977, 1980), is equally influential. They went to the limiting case of a continuum of goods, in Ricardian and Heckscher–Ohlin–Samuelson structures of production with one and two inputs. This created a smooth margin for adjustment in response to changes in underlying conditions or policies; therefore these models were more easily amenable to comparative statics methods.

Recently the generalizations of factor endowment models have gone in a new direction. Empirical research in trade as well as industrial organization showed that there is great intra-industry heterogeneity among firms. This opened up the possibility that in a given country and a given industry, some firms are more productive and are successful exporters, whereas other firms are less productive and struggle to compete against imports and against other domestic producers. Theoretical work developing the implications of firm heterogeneity, as well as empirical work testing the resulting models, constitutes a very active research area these days. And the theoretical models continue to use many of the concepts and tools that have their origins in Samuelson's work: integrated equilibrium, unit cost functions, and more. Some examples of this research are Davis and Weinstein (2003), Melitz (2003).

13.5 And Much More

Even within the field of international economics, I have touched upon Samuelson's contributions to only a few, albeit central, subfields and topics. I have left out his work on the transfer problem, for example Samuelson (1952b, 1954, 1971b), because Jones (1983) has treated the developments through the 1970s so well, and perhaps because the less said about some of the subsequent debates on this topic, the better. I have omitted Samuelson's work on the Hume mechanism and balance of payments, because I am only a microeconomist who cannot hope to do justice to the topic. And I have left out his battles with purveyors of doctrines of "unequal exchange" and the like, for example Samuelson (1975, 1976), because this should have been unnecessary; anyone who had understood the Arrow–Debreu theory of intertemporal equilibrium, especially the article of Malinvaud (1961), should never have been confused in the first place and it should not have been necessary to use up so much of Samuelson's valuable time to correct the errors. Finally, the Balassa–Samuelson (Samuelson, 1964, 1994) effect got short shrift because everyone knows it and it did not fit neatly into any of the above sections.

But I do want to mention another aspect of Samuelson's contribution to the profession—his thoughtful, generous, and witty articles about many seniors, contemporaries and, relative youngsters: Ohlin (Samuelson, 2002), Haberler (Samuelson, 1990a), Stolper (Samuelson, 1990b), and Kemp (Samuelson, 1993), to mention just a few. As if his seminal contributions to our stock of ideas and techniques were not enough, he constantly helps us refresh and celebrate our folk memories. It is only fitting, and a small repayment in kind, that we should continue to remember and celebrate his achievements.

Notes

1. A physicist who played a crucial role in the development of the hydrogen bomb.
2. See also his response to Ulam quoted above.
3. I would like to indulge in an opportunity to criticize the modern tendency to say "masterful" (whose primary meaning is "domineering, imperious") instead of "masterly" ("showing the ability or skill of a master, expert"). (The definitions are from Webster's New World Dictionary.)

References

Bhagwati, Jagdish N. (1965). "The pure theory of international trade: a survey," in *Surveys of Economic Theory*, New York: St. Martin's Press, Volume II.

Chipman, John S. (1965, 1966). "A survey of the theory of international trade: parts I–III," *Econometrica* 33 (July), 477–519; 33 (October), 685–760; 34 (January) 18–76.

Davis, Donald R. and David E. Weinstein. (2003). "Why countries trade: insights from firm-level data," *Journal of the Japanese and International Economies*, 17 (Special Issue, December), 432–447.

Deardorff, Alan V. (1980). "The general validity of the law of comparative advantage," *Journal of Political Economy*, 88 (October), 941–957.

——. (1982). "The general validity of the Heckscher-Ohlin theorem," *American Economic Review*, 72 (September), 683–694.

Dixit, Avinash K. and Victor D. Norman. (1980). *Theory of International Trade*. Cambridge, UK: Cambridge University Press.

—— and——. (1986). "Gains from trade without lump-sum compensation," *Journal of International Economics*, 21 (August), 111–122.

Dornbusch, Rudiger, Stanley Fischer, and Paul A. Samuelson. (1977). "Comparative advantage, trade and payments in a Ricardian model with a continuum of goods," *American Economic Review*, 67 (December), 823–839. Reprinted as item

316 in Kate Crowley (ed.), *The Collected Scientific Papers of Paul Samuelson*, Cambridge, MA: MIT Press, Volume IV, 1986.

Dornbusch, Rudiger, Stanley Fischer, and Paul A. Samuelson. (1980). "Heckscher-Ohlin Trade Theory with a Continuum of Goods," *Quarterly Journal of Economics*, 95 (September), 203–224. Reprinted as item 317 in Kate Crowley (ed.), *The Collected Scientific Papers of Paul Samuelson*, Cambridge, MA: MIT Press, Volume IV, 1986.

Duffie, Darrell and Chi-Fu Huang. (1985). "Implementing Arrow-Debreu equilibria by continuous trading of few long-lived securities," *Econometrica*, 53 (November), 1337–1356.

Ekern, Steinar and Robert B. Wilson. (1974). "On the theory of the firm in an economy with incomplete markets." *Bell Journal of Economics*, 5 (Spring), 171–180.

Feenstra, Robert C. and Tracy R. Lewis. (1991). "Distributing the gains from trade with incomplete information," *Economics and Politics*, 3 (March), 21–39.

Grandmont, Jean-Michel and Daniel L. McFadden. (1972). "A technical note on classical gains from trade," *Journal of International Economics*, 2, 109–125.

Hammond, Peter J. (1979). "Straightforward individual incentive compatibility in large economies," *Review of Economic Studies*, 46 (April), 263–282.

Helpman, Elhanan and Paul R. Krugman. (1985). *Market Structure and Foreign Trade*. Cambridge, MA: MIT Press.

Jones, Ronald W. (1965). "The structure of simple general equilibrium models," *Journal of Political Economy*, 73 (December), 557–572.

——. (1983). "International Trade Theory," in E. Cary Brown and Robert M. Solow (eds.), *Paul Samuelson and Modern Economic Theory*, New York: McGraw-Hill, pp. 69–103.

—— and José A. Scheinkman. (1977). "The relevance of the two-sector production model in trade theory," *Journal of Political Economy*, 85 (October), 909–935.

Kemp, Murray C. (1962). "The gain from international trade," *Economic Journal*, 72 (December), 803–819.

—— and Wan, Henry Y., Jr. (1986). "Gains from trade with and without lump-sum compensation," *Journal of International Economics*, 21 (August), 99–110.

Malinvaud, Edmond. (1961). "The analogy between atemporal and intertemporal theories of resource allocation," *Review of Economic Studies*, 28 (June), 143–160.

Mas-Colell, Andreu. (1985). *The Theory of General Economic Equilibrium*. Cambridge, UK: Cambridge University Press.

Mayer, Wolfgang. (1974). "Short-run equilibrium for a small open economy," *Journal of Political Economy*, 82 (September–October), 955–968.

Melitz, Marc J. (2003). "The impact of trade on intra-industry reallocations and aggregate industry productivity," *Econometrica*, 71 (November), 1695–1725.

Mussa, Michael. (1974). "Tariffs and the distribution of income: the importance of factor specificity, substitutability, and intensity in the short and long run," *Journal of Political Economy*, 82 (November–December), 1191–1204.

——. (1984). "The adjustment process and the timing of trade liberalization," Cambridge, MA: National Bureau of Economic Research, Working Paper No. 1458.

Neary, J. Peter. (1978). "Short-run capital specificity and the pure theory of international trade," *Economic Journal*, 88 (September), 488–510.

——. (1985). "Two-by-two international trade theory with many goods and factors," *Econometrica*, 53 (September 1985), 1233–1247.

Samuelson, Paul A. (1938). "Welfare economics and international trade," *American Economic Review*, 28 (June), 261–266. Reprinted as item 60 in Joseph E. Stiglitz (ed.), *The Collected Scientific Papers of Paul Samuelson*, Cambridge, MA: MIT Press, Volume II, 1966.

——. (1939). "The gains from international trade," *Canadian Journal of Economics and Political Science*, 5 (May), 195–205. Reprinted as item 61 in Joseph E. Stiglitz (ed.), *The Collected Scientific Papers of Paul Samuelson*, Cambridge, MA: MIT Press, Volume II, 1966.

——. (1948). "International trade and equalization of factor prices," *Economic Journal*, 58 (June), 163–184. Reprinted as item 67 in Joseph E. Stiglitz (ed.), *The Collected Scientific Papers of Paul Samuelson*, Cambridge, MA: MIT Press, Volume II, 1966.

——. (1949a). "International factor-price equalization once again," *Economic Journal*, 59 (June), 181–197. Reprinted as item 68 in Joseph E. Stiglitz (ed.), *The Collected Scientific Papers of Paul Samuelson*, Cambridge, MA: MIT Press, Volume II, 1966.

——. (1949b). "Market Mechanisms and Maximization," Research Memoranda, Santa Monica. The RAND Corporation. Reprinted as item 33 in Joseph E. Stiglitz (ed.), *The Collected Scientific Papers of Paul Samuelson*, Cambridge, MA: MIT Press, Volume I, 1966.

——. (1952a). "A comment on factor price equalization," *Review of Economic Studies*, 20 (February), 121–122. Reprinted as item 69 in Joseph E. Stiglitz (ed.), *The Collected Scientific Papers of Paul Samuelson*, Cambridge, MA: MIT Press, Volume II, 1966.

——. (1952b). "The transfer problem and transport costs: the terms of trade when impediments are absent," *Economic Journal*, 62 (June), 278–304. Reprinted as item 74 in Joseph E. Stiglitz (ed.), *The Collected Scientific Papers of Paul Samuelson*, Cambridge, MA: MIT Press, Volume II, 1966.

——. (1953). "Prices of factors and goods in general equilibrium," *Review of Economic Studies*, 21, 1–20. Reprinted as item 70 in Joseph E. Stiglitz (ed.), *The Collected Scientific Papers of Paul Samuelson*, Cambridge, MA: MIT Press, Volume II, 1966.

——. (1954). "The transfer problem and transport costs II: analysis of effects of trade impediments," *Economic Journal*, 64 (June), 264–289. Reprinted as item 75 in Joseph E. Stiglitz (ed.), *The Collected Scientific Papers of Paul Samuelson*, Cambridge, MA: MIT Press, Volume II, 1966.

——. (1959a). "A modern treatment of the Ricardian economy I: the pricing of goods and of labor and land services," *Quarterly Journal of Economics*, 73 (February), 1–35. Reprinted as item 31 in Joseph E. Stiglitz (ed.), *The Collected Scientific Papers of Paul Samuelson*, Cambridge, MA: MIT Press, Volume I, 1966.

——. (1959b). "A modern treatment of the Ricardian economy II: capital and interest aspects of the pricing process," *Quarterly Journal of Economics*, 73 (May), 217–231. Reprinted as item 32 in Joseph E. Stiglitz (ed.), *The Collected Scientific Papers of Paul Samuelson,* Cambridge, MA: MIT Press, Volume I, 1966.

——. (1962a). "Economists and the history of ideas," *American Economic Review*, 52 (March), 1–18. Reprinted as item 113 in Joseph E. Stiglitz (ed.), *The Collected Scientific Papers of Paul Samuelson*, Cambridge, MA: MIT Press, Volume II, 1966.

——. (1962b). "The gains from international trade once again," *Economic Journal*, 72 (December), 820–829. Reprinted as item 62 in Joseph E. Stiglitz (ed.), *The Collected Scientific Papers of Paul Samuelson*, Cambridge, MA: MIT Press, Volume II, 1966.

——. (1964). "Theoretical notes on trade problems," *Review of Economics and Statistics*, 46 (May), 145–154. Reprinted as item 65 in Joseph E. Stiglitz (ed.), *The Collected Scientific Papers of Paul Samuelson*, Cambridge, MA: MIT Press, Volume II, 1966.

——. (1971a). "An exact Hume-Ricardo-Marshall Model of international trade," *Journal of International Economics*, 1 (February), 1–18. Reprinted as item 162 in Robert C. Merton (ed.), *The Collected Scientific Papers of Paul Samuelson*, Cambridge, MA: MIT Press, Volume III, 1972.

——. (1971b). "On the trail of conventional beliefs about the transfer problem," in J. Bhagwati et al. (eds), *Trade, Balance of Payments, and Growth: Papers in International Economics in Honor of Charles P. Kindleberger*. Amesterdam: North-Holland. Reprinted as item 163 in Robert C. Merton (ed.), *The Collected Scientific Papers of Paul Samuelson*, Cambridge, MA: MIT Press, Volume III, 1972.

——. (1971c). "Ohlin was right," *Swedish Journal of Economics*, 73 (December), 363–384. Reprinted as item 254 in Hiroaki Nagatani and Kate Crowley (eds), *The Collected Scientific Papers of Paul Samuelson*, Cambridge, MA: MIT Press, Volume IV, 1977.

——. (1975). "Trade pattern reversals in time-phased ricardian systems and intertemporal efficiency," *Journal of International Economics*, 5 (November), 309–363. Reprinted as item 251 in Hiroaki Nagatani and Kate Crowley (eds), *The Collected Scientific Papers of Paul Samuelson*, Cambridge, MA: MIT Press, Volume IV, 1977.

——. (1976). "Illogic of Neo-Marxian doctrine of unequal exchange," in D. A. Belsley et al. (eds), *Inflation, Trade, and Taxes*, Columbus, OH: Ohio State University Press. Reprinted as item 252 in Hiroaki Nagatani and Kate Crowley (eds), *The Collected Scientific Papers of Paul Samuelson*, Cambridge, MA: MIT Press, Volume IV, 1977.

——. (1990a). "Gottfried Haberler as economic sage and trade theory innovator," *Wirtschaftspolitische Blätter*, April, 310–317.

——. (1990b). "Tribute to Wolfgang Stolper on the Fiftieth Anniversary of the Stolper-Samuelson Theorem," in Alan V. Deardorff and Robert M. Stern (eds), *The Stolper-Samuelson Theorem: A Golden Jubilee*. Ann Arbor, MI: University of Michigan Press.

——. (1993). "Foreword," in Horst Herberg and Ngo Van Long (eds), *Trade, welfare, and economic policies: essays in honor of Murray C. Kemp*, Ann Arbor, MI: University of Michigan Press.

——. (1994). "Facets of Balassa-Samuelson thirty years later," *Review of International Economics*, 2 (October), 201–226.

——. (1995). "The past and future of international trade theory," in A. Deardorff, J. Levinsohn, and R.M. Stern (eds), *New Directions in Trade Theory*. Ann Arbor, MI: University of Michigan Press.

——. (2002). "My Bertil Ohlin," in Ronald Findlay, Lars Jonung, and Mats Lundahl (eds), *Bertil Ohlin: A Centennial Celebration*, Cambridge, MA: MIT Press.

——. (2004). "Where Ricardo and Mill Rebut and confirm arguments of mainstream economists supporting globalization," *Journal of Economic Perspectives*, 18 (Summer), 135–146.

Spector, David. (2001). "Is it possible to redistribute the gains from trade using income taxation?" *Journal of International Economics*, 55 (December), 441–460.

Stolper, Wolfgang F. and Paul A. Samuelson. (1941). "Protection and real wages," *Review of Economic Studies*, 9 (January), 58–73. Reprinted as item 66 in Joseph E. Stiglitz (ed.), *The Collected Scientific Papers of Paul Samuelson*, Cambridge, MA: MIT Press, Volume II, 1966.

14

Paul Samuelson's Contributions to International Economics

Kenneth Rogoff

14.1 Introduction

Paul Samuelson's contributions to trade theory and international economics are simply breathtaking. Virtually every undergraduate or graduate student, anywhere in the world, is asked to understand his Stolper–Samuelson and factor–price equalization theorems. These theorems tell us, of course, why trade liberalization tends to benefit the relatively abundant factor of production (skilled labor, in the case of the United States), and why trade in goods can, in many respects, equalize opportunities just as effectively as trade in people and capital. Indeed, it is a very safe bet that whoever the great economist of the twenty-second century turns out to be, he or she will be teaching and reinvigorating ideas Samuelson articulated during the middle part of the twentieth century.

Achieving eternal life in the pantheon of trade giants is already an extraordinary feat. What is perhaps even more remarkable about Samuelson's trade contributions is their vitality in today's globalization debate. Whereas few taxi drivers in Shanghai have ever been to college much less graduate school (something one cannot assume in Cambridge, Massachusetts), they will still understand that trade with the United States is raising the wages of Chinese workers, just as most Americans understand that the country's shrinking manufacturing base has more

I am grateful to Pol Antràs, Elhanan Helpman, and Kiminori Matsuyama for helpful discussions, to Brent Neiman, Karine Serfaty, and Jane Trahan for helpful comments on an earlier draft, and to Erkko Etula for compiling the references.

than a little to do with international trade. Indeed, the rising wage differential between skilled and unskilled workers in the United States (and throughout the advanced economies) stands as one of the most contentious and difficult economic and political issues of our day. There is still a great deal of disagreement about what drives this growing differential, and in particular how much is due to globalization, and how much is due to changing technologies that favor skilled labor. Regardless, Samuelson's ideas contributed greatly to building the framework that economists use for asking such questions and for quantifying potential answers.

In this chapter, I will not attempt a technical exposition of Samuelson's core trade theories, since one can find these (at various levels) in any economics textbook, from introductory to advanced (including, of course, the many generations of Samuelson's own celebrated book, first published in 1948). Rather, I will concentrate on highlighting a few main ideas in his work, and saying how they are influencing the contemporary policy debate. My discussion is necessarily selective and omits some areas others might have chosen to focus on. At the end of the chapter, I attach an extensive list of Samuelson's contributions to international economics and international finance.

14.2 International Trade

In his earliest work on trade, including (1), Samuelson used his theorem of revealed preference to show that in a representative agent economy (where everyone is the same), free trade must be welfare improving for all parties. If trade were not welfare improving, a country could choose to continue in autarky, ignoring the rest of the world. This may seem like a trivial result, but with it Samuelson began to lay the foundations of the general equilibrium approach he would ultimately use to prove many other trade theorems. For example, later in (14) he was able to show that whereas trade typically generates winners and losers, there is always, in principle, a way for winners to make sidepayments to compensate the losers so that everyone comes out ahead. (Viner and Lerner had earlier intuited this idea, while Kemp (1962) simultaneously published a closely related analysis.) Even today, this is really the core result around which all trade policy discussions take place. The modern conundrum, of course, is that in practice, it is very hard to find ways to pay off the losers in trade, at least not without creating incentive distortions almost as egregious as the tariff barriers being eliminated in the first place. So all too often, special interests will lobby for trade protection despite the fact that it is a hugely inefficient and expensive way for governments to buy off small groups (see for example Grossman and Helpman, 2002). The most spectacular example, really, has to be the agricultural supports that Organization for Economic Cooperation and Development (OECD) countries lavish on their farmers, making it far more difficult for poor developing countries to export farm products. (One calculation, from a 2003 IMF–World Bank study, showed that the $300 billion dollars rich countries lavish on farm subsidies would be enough to fly every cow in the OECD around the world first class each year, with lots of spending money left over.)

Perhaps the cornerstone of Samuelson's early trade work, however, is his widely celebrated paper (3) with Stolper. This paper was the first to demonstrate the "Heckscher–Ohlin theorem" in a two-good, two-country, two-factor (labor and capital) model. The H–O theorem, of course, shows that with identical technologies at home and abroad, the country with the larger endowment of labor relative to capital should export the labor-intensive good. Obvious? Hardly. Even today, it is amazing how many people seem convinced that China (which, with 1.3 billion people, is clearly a labor-rich country) is going to export everything to everybody as free trade opens up. Admittedly, demonstrating that the Heckscher–Ohlin theorem holds empirically has proven a lot trickier than anyone expected (see, for example, Trefler, 1995), but the bottom line is that it is extremely helpful for thinking about trade between countries with widely different capital-labor ratios. From a policy perspective, the major result of (3) was to confirm the intuitive analysis of Ohlin about who wins and who loses when a country opens up to trade. The answer, as we now well understand, is that the relatively abundant factor gains, and the relatively scarce factor loses, not only in absolute terms but in real terms. Thus if capital is the relatively abundant factor (compared to the trading partner), then an opening of trade will lead the return on capital to rise more than proportionately compared to the price of either good, whereas the wage rate will *fall* relative to the price of either good. Admittedly, many of the simple $2 \times 2 \times 2$ results do not generalize so easily where there are more factors and more goods but they do typically go through in a weaker sense (e.g. Deardorff, 1980), and the broad intuition remains critical to helping us understand how trade impacts welfare.

Whereas Stolper and Samuelson's paper laid the cornerstone of modern trade theory, and contains many of the core results we use today, the real show-stopper in Samuelson's trade contributions has to be his famous factor price equalization theorem (6). Before Samuelson, economists recognized, of course, that factor mobility would help equalize wage rates and returns on capital across countries, at least up to a point. During the latter 1800s as Britain poured money into the rest of the world (with current account surpluses often topping 9 or 10%), capitalists in Britain garnered higher returns on their wealth, while workers in the colonies saw their wage rates rise. Similarly, the great waves of migration from Europe to the Americas in the nineteenth and early twentieth centuries played a significant role in equalizing rates of return on capital between the old world and the new world. Indeed, at times, labor mobility has played a bigger role than capital mobility. But, as is still the case today, international labor and capital mobility is far from perfect, for a host of reasons (see Obstfeld and Rogoff, 1996 for an overview). But is factor mobility the only channel for helping equalize relative wages across countries? Again, leading trade economists understood the possibility that trade in goods might also play a role, if labor-poor countries export capital-intensive goods, and labor-rich countries export labor-intensive goods. Because free trade equalizes relative prices of various goods (up to trade costs, as Samuelson was always careful to emphasize), the result has to be to put equalizing pressure on relative factor returns as well (or so Ohlin and others conjectured). But could one prove this? Samuelson not only proved this result but much more; he developed conditions under which trade in goods could fully substitute for trade in factors themselves. That is, he demonstrated conditions under which trade in goods, and only trade in goods, could fully equalize wages and rates of return on capital across countries! (One important caveat is that the two countries' endowments of capital relative to labor cannot be too different. Otherwise, at least one country will specialize and the logic of the result would break down.) This is one of those rare but powerful insights that just knocks people's socks off when they see it; many were so incredulous they thought that there must be an error in Samuelson's mathematics. But his logic was flawless.

Of course, in practice, one does not typically see factor price equalization, or indeed anything close to it. The 1992 North American Free Trade Agreement between Mexico, Canada, and the United States did not fully equalize wages across the United States and Canada, much less between Mexico and the United States. Numerous factors, including different quality of institutions (Mexico is still a young state where the rule of law is progressively strengthening), different levels of technology and other factors still drive a wedge that keeps Mexican wages far below US levels (despite the fact that there are large immigration flows going on at the same time). One assumption of Samuelson's analysis that is perhaps strained in practice is that labor and capital are perfectly mobile across sectors; in practice, workers often require extensive retraining or relocation, and a great deal of capital is industry specific. Nevertheless, the result gives a critical benchmark for illustrating the extraordinary importance and power of free trade. All in all, Samuelson's results still guide the trade debate, and his results still provide the benchmark for the subsequent literature. Indeed, this author has no doubt that if and when interplanetary trade ever commences (say, via radio beam exchanges of technological blueprints and music), economists of the day will quickly find themselves trotting out expositions of Samuelson's 1948 paper (6).

Though the contribution is more methodological than practical, one can hardly survey Samuelson's contributions to trade without mentioning his clever (11) device of modeling trade costs as "iceberg costs" so that when a good is shipped from country X to country Y, a fraction of it dissipates in transit costs. This simple yet elegant device allows trade economists to introduce trade frictions while keeping their models simple and tractable. Virtually every other trade paper today uses it in some form, and the trick has been widely applied in other fields as well. A small thing, perhaps, but this is precisely the kind of clever device that helps propel whole new fields of inquiry.

Although Samuelson made many other critical contributions to trade theory, perhaps the next truly giant step was (31) his 1980 paper with (much junior) MIT colleagues Rudiger Dornbusch and Stanley Fischer, in which they (henceforth DFS) developed a so-called Ricardian model of trade with a continuum of goods. By "Ricardian" model, of course, they meant a model with only one factor of production (for Ricardo, that was usually labor), where differences in technology drive comparative advantage. This is in contrast to the Heckscher–Ohlin inspired framework developed in Stolper and Samuelson, where there are two factors (labor and capital) and (in the classic setup) countries have identical technologies. In a Ricardian model, one cannot think of countries as exporting, say, labor-intensive goods, because that is all any country has. Rather, trade arises due to different technologies (which could in turn be traced to different endowments of land or weather). Of course, a Ricardian model is all one needs to develop the theory of comparative advantage, which Samuelson famously quipped (including in his text) is one of the few results in economics that is simultaneously true and not obvious. The theory of comparative advantage also explains why xenophobic politicians should not worry that China will some day produce everything in the world. Rather, the theory tells us that China will only export what it is *relatively* good at even if, some day, it really does gain an absolute advantage in producing everything. People who have not taken trade theory often seem stunned when they hear the theory of comparative advantage. But, of course, most people in our highly specialized society have come to terms with the principle of comparative advantage in their daily lives (for example, even if a high-paid investment banker is very good at doing her shopping, she may find it advantageous to pay someone to do it in her stead, so as to be able to devote more time to highly paid investment banking activities).

Prior to DFS, the Ricardian approach had been dormant for years, not because the assumptions were so unreasonable, but because the model had been viewed as intractable for all but illustrative purposes. Through the brilliant device of introducing a continuum of goods, DFS were able to enormously simplify the standard Ricardian model, and allow one to do comparative statics exercises with an elegance that had previously seemed impossible. At first, the DFS model was greatly admired, but did not lead to any flowering of new research. In recent years, however, the research line following the DFS model has become an explosion. The DFS model has become the starting point for a number of applied papers (e.g. see Copeland and Taylor, 1994). In addition, the DFS model has formed the basis for an important and exciting resurgence of empirical work in trade (e.g. see Eaton and Kortum, 2002; Kehoe and Ruhl, 2002; and Kraay and Ventura, 2002; Yi, 2003; Ghironi and Melitz, 2005). One interesting application is Feenstra and Hanson (1996), who apply the continuum-of-goods model to show how direct foreign investment flows from a capital-abundant country to a labor-abundant economy may actually increase the skill premium in both countries. Whereas the migrating industries may be skill-intensive from the point of view of the recipient country, they might not be so from the point of view of the country losing the industries—a very Samuelson-like result!

14.3 International Finance

Samuelson has also made important contributions to the field of international finance. First and foremost, in (15) he is codeveloper of the famous Balassa–Samuelson theorem (Obstfeld and Rogoff, 1996, note Harrod's (1933) contribution as well, and I will follow their convention here). Simply put, the Harrod–Balassa–Samuelson (H–B–S) theorem predicts that fast-growing countries will tend to have appreciating real exchange rates, and that rich countries will have high real exchange rates relative to poor countries. Underlying the H–B–S model is a fact that Samuelson had emphasized throughout his early trade writings: trade is costly, and for some goods, it is prohibitively costly. Second, the analysis assumes that fast-growing countries tend to see faster rates of productivity improvement in their (highly) traded goods industries than in their (relatively) nontraded goods industries. Assuming that labor and capital are mobile across sectors, factor prices will get bid up by the fast-growing traded goods sector. But this, in turn, will make production in the nontraded goods more expensive, and bid up prices there. Then assuming (a third assumption) that traded goods prices tend to be equalized across countries, higher nontraded goods prices must translate into a higher real exchange rate. Simply put, as a poor country gets better at manufacturing, haircuts and hotels will have to become more expensive as the general level of wages in the economy starts to rise. The H–B–S model is useful because it gives a framework for say, trying to understand why the price of McDonald's Big Mac hamburger is five dollars in Switzerland but just over one dollar in China. Again, like the Heckscher–Ohlin theorem, the H–B–S theorem is at best a loose description of reality, since many complex forces work together to create price differentials, including pricing to market, slow adjustment of factors across sectors, sticky prices, etc. Also, in a world where many countries have a degree of monopoly power in the goods they produce, the H–B–S result can also become weaker or even be stood on its head (Fitzgerald, 2003). Nevertheless, it is a very useful benchmark.

Indeed, the logic of H–B–S is arguably the central idea behind the International Comparison of Prices project that began in the 1950s (see Rogoff, 1996) which later culminated in the celebrated Heston–Summers comparisons of incomes and prices across countries (see Summers and Heston, 1991). The Heston–Summers data base, of course, attempts to compare different countries' incomes in terms of a common relative price matrix (the United States). For example, if one measures the relative size of Japan and China using market exchange rates and national prices, then the Chinese economy is only 1/3 the size of Japan's. However, an alternative way to compare these economies uses "Purchasing Power Parity" exchange rates, which are constructed to set equal, on average, the values of identical goods in different countries (such as the Big Mac). Using Purchasing Power Parity exchange rates, rather than market rates, China is twice the size of Japan (in this case, arguably a better description of its influence in the world). The Heston–Summers data set has been very important in empirical research on growth since it allows much more meaningful comparisons across countries than do national income accounts. Increasingly, it has also become important in policy circles as well (e.g. the International Monetary Fund *World Economic Outlook* projections for global and regional growth are all based on purchasing power parity aggregations that are motivated by very similar considerations as H–B–S). (Robert Summers, of course, is Paul Samuelson's brother, having once changed his name.)

Another area of international finance where Samuelson's work remains widely cited and enormously influential is in studies of the "Transfer Problem," famously debated in the early 1920s by Keynes and Ohlin. The central question of the Keynes–Ohlin debate was whether the vast wartime reparations being demanded from Germany would lead to a secondary burden due to induced price effects. In (10) and (11), Samuelson basically settled the issue, showing that neither of them were quite right. On the one hand, Samuelson showed that from a policy perspective, Keynes was right in the sense that, under reasonable assumptions, the real cost of Germany's postwar reparations would likely be magnified by price effects. Lower wealth in Germany would reduce domestic demand for German goods, but higher wealth abroad would increase demand for its goods. However, since Germans tend to prefer their own tradeable goods to imports (a home bias), they consume a disproportionately large amount of them. So as Germany transferred money to the Allies, higher foreign demand for its goods would not fully substitute for reduced domestic demand and the relative price of German goods would fall. On the other hand, Samuelson showed that Ohlin was right from a methodological viewpoint, in that income effects are what matter most. To understand how the wealth transfer would impact prices, one needed to know who is giving money and who is receiving, and how, at the margin, the two groups will tend to adjust to these income changes. Samuelson's work on the transfer problem is enormously influential today in theory and policy. For example, transfer problem type analysis underlies the analysis of Obstfeld and Rogoff (2000, 2005). Their analysis strongly suggests that when the US trade deficit finally closes up from its astounding current 6 percent of GDP value, the real value of the trade-weighted dollar will almost surely plummet. Foreign demand for American goods will rise, but not by as much as American demand will fall, and foreign demand will not substitute at all in the case of nontraded goods. Hence, at least until factors can migrate across sectors (which will take years if not decades), large relative price movements are needed, which in turn implies large movements in exchange rates if central banks are stabilizing overall inflation rates.

14.4 Conclusions

It is impossible in this brief space to do justice to Paul Samuelson's stunning contributions to international economics, or to adequately characterize their profound policy impact. I trust, however, that the reader will at least gain a flavor of the remarkable span of ideas this man has generated, and the profound policy influence he has had. Finally, I have not even mentioned Samuelson's role as a teacher in trade; many of us in this volume have been his students.

Paul A. Samuelson's Main Articles on International Trade and Finance

1. "Welfare economics and international trade" (*The American Economic Review*, June 1938)
2. "The gains from international trade" (*Canadian Journal of Economics and Political Science*, May 1939)
3. "Protection and real wages," with W.F. Stolper (*The Review of Economic Studies*, November 1941)
4. Review of Jacob L. Mosak, *General Equilibrium Theory in International Trade* (*The American Economic Review*, December 1945)
5. "Disparity in postwar exchange rates" (Seymour Harris, ed., *Foreign Economic Policy for the United States*, Harvard University Press, 1948)
6. "International trade and equalization of factor prices" (*Economic Journal*, June 1948)
7. "International factor-price equalization once again" (*Economic Journal*, June 1949)
8. "A comment on factor-price equalization" (*The Review of Economic Studies*, February 1952)
9. "Spatial price equilibrium and linear programming" (*The American Economic Review*, June 1952)
10. "The transfer problem and the transport costs: the terms of trade when impediments are absent" (*Economic Journal*, June 1952)
11. "The transfer problem and the transport costs: analysis of effects of trade impediments" (*Economic Journal*, June 1952)
12. "Prices of factors and goods in general equilibrium" (*The Review of Economic Studies*, 1953–1954)
13. "Intertemporal price equilibrium: a prologue to the theory of speculation" (*Weltwirtschaftliches Archive*, December 1957)
14. "The gains from international trade once again" (*The Economic Journal*, December 1962)
15. "Theoretical notes on trade problems" (*The Review of Economics and Statistics*, May 1964)

16. "Equalization by trade of the interest rate along with the real wage" (*Trade, Growth and the Balance of Payments*, in honor of Gottfried Haberler, Rand McNally, 1965)
17. "Summary of factor-price equalization" (*International Economic Review*, October 1967)
18. "An exact Hume-Ricardo-Marshall model of international trade" (*Journal of International Economics*, February 1971)
19. "On the trail of conventional beliefs about the transfer problem" (J. Bhagwati et al. (eds), *Trade, Balance of Payments, and Growth: Papers in International Economics in Honor of Charles P. Kindleberger*, Amsterdam, North-Holland Publishing Co., 1971)
20. "Ohlin was right" (*Swedish Journal of Economics*, 73(4), 1971, 365–384)
21. "Heretical doubts about the international mechanisms" (*Journal of International Economics*, 2(4), 1972, 443–454)
22. "International trade for a rich country" (Lectures before the Swedish-American Chamber of Commerce, New York City, May 10, 1972)
23. "Deadweight loss in international trade from the profit motive?" (C. Fred Bergsten and William G. Tyler (eds), *Leading Issues in International Economic Policy: Essays in Honor of George N. Halm*, Lexington, Mass., D.C. Heath and Co., 1973)
24. "Equalization of factor prices by sufficiently diversified production under conditions of balanced demand" (*International Trade and Finance: Essays in Honor of Jan Tinbergen*, Willy Sellekaerts, ed., London, Macmillan, 1974)
25. "Trade pattern reversals in time-phased Ricardian systems and intertemporal efficiency" (*Journal of International Economics*, 5, 1974, 309–363)
26. "Illogic of Neo-Marxian doctrine of unequal exchange" (D. A. Belsley, E. J. Kane, Paul A. Samuelson, Robert M. Solow (eds), *Inflation, Trade and Taxes: Essays in Honor of Alice Bourneuf*, Columbus, Ohio State University Press, 1976)
27. "Interest rate equalization and nonequalization by trade in Leontief–Sraffa models" (*Journal of International Economics*, 8, 1978, 21–27)
28. "Free trade's intertemporal pareto-optimality" (*Journal of International Economics*, 8, 1978, 147–149)
29. "America's interest in international trade" (*New England Merchants Company, Inc.*, 1979 Annual, pp. 4–5)
30. "A corrected version of Hume's equilibrating mechanism for international trade" (John S. Chipman and Charles P. Kindleberger (eds), *Flexible Exchange Rates and the Balance of Payments: Essays in Memory of Egon Sohmen*, Amsterdam: North-Holland, 1980, pp. 141–158)
31. "Comparative advantage, trade and payments in a Ricardian model with a continuum of goods," with Rudiger Dornbusch and Stanley Fischer (*American Economic Review*, 95(2), 1980, 203–224)
32. "To protect manufacturing?" *Zeitschrift für die gesamte Staatswissenschaft* (*Journal of Institutional and Theoretical Economics*, Band 137, Heft 3, September 1981, 407–414)

33. "Summing up on the Australian case for protection" (*The Quarterly Journal of Economics*, 96(1), 1981, 147–160)
34. "Justice to the Australians" (*The Quarterly Journal of Economics*, 96(1), 1981, 169–170)
35. "Japan and the world at the century's end" (*NEXT Magazine*, August 1984, 4–15, Original English version provided for translation into Japanese)
36. "The future of American industry in a changing economy" (*The Journalist*, Fall 1984, 3–5, 19)
37. "Analytics of free-trade or protectionist response by America to Japan's growth spurt" (Toshio Shishido and Ryuzo Sato (eds), *Economic Policy and Development: New Perspectives*, Dover MA: Auburn House, 1985, pp. 3–18)
38. "US economic prospects and policy options: impact on Japan–US relations" (Ryuzo Sato, and John A. Rizzo (eds), *Unkept Promises, Unclear Consequences: US Economic Policy and the Japanese Response*, Cambridge University Press, 1989)
39. "Gottfried Haberler as economic sage and trade theory innovator" (*Wirtschaftspolitische Blätter*, No. 4, 1990, 310)
40. "Factor-price equalization by trade in joint and non-joint production" (*Review of International Economics*, 1(1), 1992, 1–9)
41. "Tribute to Wolfgang Stolper on the 50th anniversary of the Stolper-Samuelson theorem" (Alan V. Deardorff and Robert M. Stern (eds), *The Stolper-Samuelson Theorem: A Golden Jubilee*, Ann Arbor, MI: University of Michigan Press, 1994)
42. "The past and future of international trade theory" (Jim Levinsohn, Alan V. Deardorff, and Robert M. Stern (eds), *New Directions in Trade Theory*, Ann Arbor, MI: The University of Michigan Press, 1995, pp. 17–23)
43. "Economic science grapples with dilemmas of international finance"
44. "Recurring quandaries in international trade"
45. "A Ricardo-Sraffa paradigm comparing gains from trade in inputs and finished goods" (*Journal of Economic Literature*, 39 (4), 2001, 1204–1214)
46. "The state of the world economy" (Paul Zak, and Robert A. Mundell (eds), *Monetary Stability and Economic Growth: A Dialog Between Leading Economists*, Edward Elgar Publishing, 2003)
47. "Pure theory aspects of industrial organization and globalization" (*Japan and the World Economy*, 15 (1), 2003, 89–90)
48. "Where Ricardo and Mill rebut and confirm arguments of mainstream economists supporting globalization" (*Journal of Economic Perspectives*, 18 (3), Summer 2004, 135–146)

References (other than Samuelson)

Balassa, Bela. (1964). "The purchasing power parity doctrine: a reappraisal, " *Journal of Political Economy*, 72, 584–596.

Bergin, P. R. and R. Glick (2003). "Endogenous nontradability and macroeconomic implications," NBER WP 9739.

Copeland, Brian and M. Scott Taylor. (1994). "North-South trade and the environment," *The Quarterly Journal of Economics*, 109 (August), 755–787.

Deardorff, Alan. (1980). "The general validity of the law of comparative advantage," *Journal of Political Economy*, 88 (October), 941–957.

Eaton, Jonathan and Samuel Kortum. (2002). "Technology, geography, and trade," *Econometrica*, 70 (September), 1741–1779.

Feenstra, Robert and Gordon Hanson. (1996). "Globalization, outsourcing, and wage inequality," *American Economic Review*, 86, 2.

Fitzgerald, Doireann. (2003). "Terms-of-trade effects, interdependence and cross-country differences in price levels." Ph.D. dissertation, Harvard University.

Ghironi, Fabio and Marc J. Melitz. (2005). "International trade and macroeconomic dynamics with heterogeneous firms." Mimeo, Harvard University.

Grossman, Gene M. and Elhanan Helpman. (2002). *Interest Groups and Trade Policy*. Princeton and Oxford UK: Princeton University Press.

Harrod, Roy. (1933). *International Economics*. London: James Nisbet and Cambridge University Press.

Kehoe, Timothy J. and Kim J. Ruhl. (2002). "How important is the new goods margin in international trade?" Mimeo, University of Minnesota.

Kemp, Murray C. (1962). "The gain from international trade." *Economic Journal*, 72, 803–819.

Kraay, A. and Jaume Ventura. (2002). "Trade integration and risk sharing," *European Economic Review*, 46, 1023–1048.

Obstfeld, Maurice and Kenneth Rogoff. (1996). *Foundations of International Macroeconomics*. Cambridge: MIT Press.

—— and ——. (2000). "Perspectives on OECD capital market integration: Implications for U.S. current account adjustment," in Federal Reserve Bank of Kansas City, *Global Economic Integration: Opportunities and Challenges*, March 2001, pp. 169–208.

—— and ——. (2005). "Global current account imbalances and exchange rate adjustments," in William Brainard and George Perry (eds). *Brookings Papers on Economic Activity*, 1, 67–146.

Rogoff, Kenneth. (1996). "The purchasing power parity puzzle," *Journal of Economic Literature*, 34 (June), 647–668.

Summers, Robert and Alan Heston. (1991). "The Penn World Table (Mark 5): An expanded set of international comparisons, 1950–88," *Quarterly Journal of Economics*, 106 (May), 327–368.

Trefler, Daniel. (1995). "The case of the missing trade and (December) other mysteries," *The American Economic Review*, 85, 1029–1046.

Yi, Kei-Mu. (2003). "Can vertical specialization explain the growth of world trade?" *Journal of Political Economy*, 111, 52–102.

15

Protection and Real Wages: The Stolper–Samuelson Theorem

Rachel McCulloch

Second only in political appeal to the argument that tariffs increase employment is the popular notion that the standard of living of the American worker must be protected against the ruinous competition of cheap foreign labor. . . . Again and again economists have tried to show the fallaciousness of this argument.

Thus begins Stolper and Samuelson's (1941) analysis of the effect of protection on real wages, a landmark contribution to the modern theory of international trade. The central result, now known as the Stolper–Samuelson theorem, is that "international trade necessarily lowers the real wage of the scarce factor expressed in terms of any good." The paper signals a transition in the debate among international economists concerning the welfare consequences of free trade, from largely verbal reasoning toward the use of formal general-equilibrium models. Derived in a simple framework of two homogeneous factors, each freely mobile between two domestic industries, the Stolper–Samuelson theorem is striking because it demonstrates that a productive factor's ability to relocate from an import-competing to an export industry does not prevent a loss in real income due to expanded trade. Moreover, it shows that the sharp redistributive consequences of trade do not depend on tastes or expenditure patterns.

Chad Bown and Gary Chamberlain provided helpful comments.

15.1 Birth of a Theorem

According to Samuelson (1994), the collaboration arose from Wolfgang Stolper's efforts to reconcile the new general-equilibrium trade theory with the work of earlier economists: "How can Haberler and Taussig be right about the necessary harm to a versatile factor like labor from America's tariff, when the Ohlin theory entails that free trade must hurt the factor that is scarce relative to land?" Stolper's friend and junior colleague, first the sounding board, eventually became "the midwife, helping to deliver Wolfie's brain child." The infant prospered.

Earlier analyses of the effect of free trade on real wages had emphasized the implications of trade for productive efficiency. In the long run, free trade would increase demand for the country's comparative-advantage goods and thereby shift employment toward the domestic industries where labor is most productive. The classical economists had typically assumed a one-factor model or, equivalently, that productive factors were used in unvarying proportions both within and across industries. In either case, trade could have no redistributive consequences within a country. Although Stolper and Samuelson's teachers and contemporaries recognized the implications of changing factor proportions for income shares, their analyses were based on a partial-equilibrium model of a protected industry. While elimination of tariffs might cause the money wage to fall, the resulting reduction in the prices of the goods workers buy with their wages was presumed to be larger. The *real* wage was thus anticipated to rise, at least in terms of imported goods and most likely overall, though the effect would depend on the relative importance of imported and exported goods in workers' total expenditure.[1]

The general-equilibrium trade theory introduced by Eli Heckscher and Bertil Ohlin opened a new line of inquiry focusing on differences in relative factor intensity across industries and differences in relative factor abundance across countries.[2] Stolper and Samuelson adopted this approach and coined the now standard terminology "Heckscher-Ohlin theorem" to refer to the proposition that "each country will export those commodities which are produced with its relatively abundant factors of production, and will import those in the production of which its relatively scarce factors are important."

15.2 The Stolper–Samuelson Analysis

Formalizing the logic of the Heckscher–Ohlin model, Stolper and Samuelson assumed two homogeneous goods *A* and *B*, each produced under constant returns to scale using labor L and capital *K* , but with good *A* using more capital relative to labor than good *B*. The two factors were assumed fixed in total supply but freely mobile between the country's two industries:

$$L_A + L_B = \bar{L} \quad \text{and} \quad K_A + K_B = \bar{K}$$

The two full-employment conditions together imply that the economy's overall capital–labor ratio $\bar{k}$ can be expressed as the weighted average of the capital–labor ratios k_A and k_B used in the two industries:

$$\lambda_A k_A + \lambda_B k_B = \bar{k},$$

where $\lambda_A = L_A/\bar{L}$ and $\lambda_B = L_B/\bar{L}$ are the shares of the total labor supply used in the two industries, $\lambda_A + \lambda_B = 1$. Thus, as the production mix moves toward specialization in good *A* and λ_A approaches unity, the capital–labor ratio used in *A* production must fall toward $\bar{k}$. Factor mobility and perfect competition together imply that the equilibrium factor returns *w* and *r* are equal across industries, and the return to each factor is equal to the value of its marginal product in that industry:

$$w = p_A \frac{\partial A}{\partial L_A} = p_B \frac{\partial B}{\partial L_B}, \qquad r = p_A \frac{\partial A}{\partial K_A} = p_B \frac{\partial B}{\partial K_B}.$$

The ratio of the marginal physical products of the two factors must therefore be equal across industries:

$$\frac{\partial A/\partial K_A}{\partial A/\partial L_A} = \frac{\partial B/\partial K_B}{\partial B/\partial L_B}.$$

Stolper and Samuelson used an Edgeworth–Bowley box diagram to represent the model geometrically. Each point in the box represents a feasible full-employment allocation of the factors between the two industries.[3] Points along the contract curve indicate alternative efficient allocations of the two factors between industries and thus alternative efficient output combinations for the economy, with a one-to-one correspondence between points on the contract curve and points on the economy's production possibility frontier. At the corners of the box representing specialization in one of the two products, the capital–labor ratio in the industry of specialization must equal the country's overall capital–labor ratio. In between, where both goods are produced, the capital–labor ratios in the two industries change systematically, with both falling monotonically as the economy moves from production only of labor-intensive B toward production only of capital-intensive A. As a consequence of the changing capital–labor ratios in the two industries, the physical marginal product of labor must fall, and the physical marginal product of capital must rise, in both industries as the economy produces more A and less B.

The actual output combination produced depends on the relative price p_A / p_B. Although their original motivation was to shed new light on the effect of protection on wages, Stolper and Samuelson avoided further consideration of the details of trade by focusing on the resulting change in the domestic relative price of the goods.[4] Their result is thus applicable to a change in relative price that occurs for any other reason. Trade would reduce the relative price of the import-competing good, which by the Heckscher–Ohlin theorem was assumed to be labor-intensive B for the United States, a labor-scarce country.[5] The lower relative price of good B would cause a shift in the economy's production toward good A—a movement along the production possibility frontier and the contract curve in the Edgeworth–Bowley box. If each industry were to use the same factor proportions as before, the change in output mix would raise the country's total demand for capital and reduce its total demand for labor. Given fixed total factor supplies and full employment of both factors before and after the rise in relative price of good A, the new output mix would thus be feasible only if both industries were now to employ a lower capital–labor ratio, or equivalently, if there was a rise in the rental-wage ratio facing the firms in both industries. These lower capital–labor ratios imply a lower marginal physical product of labor in both industries and thus an unambiguously lower real wage (and higher real rental) measured in terms of *either* good. This outcome is independent of the pattern of consumption.

15.3 Stolper–Samuelson and the Simple General-Equilibrium Model

Although the Stolper–Samuelson argument based on varying factor demand and fixed factor supply is intuitively appealing, their key result does not actually require fixed factor supplies. An alternative proof hinges on the observation that with constant returns and perfect competition, both industries can maintain positive output only if both yield equal (zero) economic profits. As neatly laid out in Jones (1965),[6] the price of each good produced must in equilibrium be equal to its unit production cost:

$$p_A = a_{LA}(w/r)w + a_{KA}(w/r)r$$

$$p_B = a_{LB}(w/r)w + a_{KB}(w/r)r,$$

where $a_{ij}(w/r)$ indicates the cost-minimizing input of factor *i* in producing one unit of good *j*. With the assumption that the two industries differ in relative factor intensity, and given the money prices of the two goods, these two equations can be solved to obtain unique equilibrium factor rewards *r* and *w* consistent with production of both goods, as well as the real returns expressed in terms of either good.[7]

Jones derived corresponding "equations of change" that show the comparative statics of the model. To restore equilibrium, any change in the price of either good must be matched by an equal change in its unit cost of production. The proportional change in each good's production cost can be expressed as a weighted average of the proportional changes in the factor rewards, with a larger weight on the change in wages for the labor-intensive good:

$$\theta_{LA}\hat{w} + \theta_{KA}\hat{r} = \hat{p}_A$$

$$\theta_{LB}\hat{w} + \theta_{KB}\hat{r} = \hat{p}_B,$$

where θ_{ij} indicates factor *i*'s share in the total cost of producing good *j* and $\hat{x}$ is the proportional change in *x*. For the case considered by Stolper and Samuelson, where trade raises the relative price of capital-intensive good *A*, these conditions imply:

$$\bar{w} < \bar{p}_B < \bar{p}_A < \bar{r}.$$

Jones called this relationship the magnification effect—a rise in the relative price of a good is accompanied by a *magnified* increase in the equilibrium return to the factor used intensively in its production and a decrease in the real return to the other factor.

Jones's reformulation of the Stolper–Samuelson theorem highlights its broad applicability. In the context of the basic model of two goods, two factors freely mobile between industries, constant returns to scale, and diversified production, Jones's version shows the "magnified" consequences for equilibrium real factor prices of *any* change in the relative price of the goods. Regardless of its cause, and even in a closed economy, a fall in the relative price of the labor-intensive good must be accompanied by a decrease in the corresponding equilibrium real wage and a rise in the real return to the other factor. The redistributive effect of adding or removing a tariff, or of moving toward or away from autarky, is a special case.

The proof based on equality of cost and production price also shows that the theorem holds even when each industry uses factors in fixed proportions, that is, when the production isoquants are L-shaped rather than smoothly curved, as had been assumed by Stolper and Samuelson.[8] With additional assumptions (free trade, no factor-intensity reversal, a second country with the same production technology), Samuelson's factor-price equalization theorem follows directly from the same formulation of the model. When free trade equalizes product prices between countries, factor rewards in each country must satisfy the same set of equations (unit cost must equal price for each of the two goods). This argument is similar in spirit to Lerner's (1952) geometric proof of factor-price equalization.[9]

15.4 Stolper–Samuelson's Seminal Role

As with other path-breaking papers, "Protection and Real Wages" did not immediately find favor with journal editors. Howard Ellis and Paul Homan of the *American Economic Review* read the paper and agreed (as stated in Homan's rejection letter to Samuelson) that it "is a brilliant theoretical performance" but also "a very narrow study in formal theory, which adds practically nothing to the literature," not to mention "practically a complete 'sell-out' "—this no doubt because the key result might offer intellectual comfort to protectionists.[10] Still, a positive response from Ursula Hicks at the *Review of Economic Studies* came less than half a year later—and the rest is history.[11]

The huge literature built upon the Stolper–Samuelson theorem has proceeded in many directions, with contributors constituting a veritable Who's Who of international trade theory.[12] Theoretical papers, including several by Samuelson, have systematically explored the robustness of the result by relaxing each of the assumptions used in the original derivation.

One important strand focuses on a question that Stolper and Samuelson raised in their paper but did not subject to detailed analysis: how well does the theorem generalize beyond the special world of two goods and two factors? As summed up in Wilfred Ethier's (1984) survey of this literature, the Stolper–Samuelson theorem survives, but in a "nonexclusive" sense. With more goods and more factors, *at least one* factor stands to gain unambiguously from trade, and *at least one* factor stands to lose unambiguously. The basic message of the original theorem is thus maintained: even when free trade raises national income overall, some factors may lose in the absence of compensation. But identifying specific gainers and losers becomes more complex, and intuition based on the two-by-two case may prove to be an unreliable guide; Edward Leamer (1994) demonstrates the failure in a three-by-three world of several plausible generalizations of the two-by-two version of Stolper–Samuelson. For example, it is not necessarily true that a country's "scarce" factors will lose from trade.

Another direction of inquiry returns to the original sharp focus of the theorem and asks how well its predictions can explain observed behavior in the political sphere. In voting or lobbying, do factor owners act as if they believe the Stolper–Samuelson theorem? Stephen Magee (1980) showed that the rival "specific factors" model, with two immobile industry-specific factors and one mobile factor, is more consistent with the lobbying positions of labor and capital. In retrospect, this result should not be surprising. The Stolper–Samuelson theorem is based on perfect factor mobility within a country, and thus its implications are best understood as long-term tendencies. Even assuming that factor owners seek to maximize the present discounted value of their lifetime earnings, the more immediate impact is likely to dominate.[13] Later work with William Brock and Leslie Young (Magee, Brock, and Young, 1989), which modeled protection as endogenous, again found that the specific-factors model explains short-run lobbying (time series data), but that Stolper–Samuelson works better in explaining patterns of protection across countries (cross-national data).[14] A new generation of scholars has continued the debate, for example, Eugene Beaulieu and Christopher Magee (2004).[15]

15.5 An Essential Tool for Economists

Notwithstanding the hundreds or perhaps by now thousands of scholarly contributions that the Stolper–Samuelson paper has inspired,[16] its real significance may be somewhat different. By linking output prices to equilibrium factor rewards, Stolper and Samuelson filled an important gap in the general-equilibrium model. Together with the other key elements of the Heckscher–Ohlin model, the stripped-down basic version of Stolper and Samuelson has become an essential part of the intellectual toolkit of every international economist and is now found in every international trade textbook.[17] Like the supply and demand curves of partial-equilibrium analysis, the simple Heckscher–Ohlin model provides the first back-of-the-envelope attack on an endless variety of questions. The framework thus continues to be used to cast light on important policy issues relating to income distribution. For example, Lawrence and Slaughter (1993) chose the Stolper–Samuelson framework to contrast price changes due to increased international competition with biased technical change as alternative explanations of an increasing gap between the wages of skilled and unskilled workers. As long as economists maintain a lively interest in the division of national income among factors of production, Stolper and Samuelson will be there. The end is not in sight.

Notes

1. Stolper and Samuelson provide illustrative quotations and references. One quote from Haberler rejects the possibility of equalization of wages across countries unless labor is internationally mobile. As of 1941, Stolper and Samuelson agreed, noting that "there will be a tendency—necessarily incomplete—toward an equalisation of factor prices" due to trade. A few years later, however, Samuelson (1948, 1949) would show that, under stipulated conditions, free trade alone is sufficient to equalize factor prices. A footnote to Samuelson (1949) indicates that Abba Lerner presented essentially the same result in a 1933 paper prepared for a seminar at the London School of Economics. Perhaps due to Samuelson's acknowledgment, the paper was finally published as Lerner (1952).
2. Ohlin's landmark treatise was published by Harvard University Press in 1933. The basic work by Heckscher and by his student Ohlin had been available a decade earlier, but only in Swedish. Heckscher's seminal 1919 article finally appeared in English translation in 1950 in a collection of fundamental contributions to the theory of international trade published by the American Economic Association.
3. This appears to be the first use of the Edgeworth–Bowley box to analyze efficient production—earlier uses of the diagram had dealt with efficiency in exchange.
4. Samuelson (1939) used the same simplification in examining a country's gains from trade.
5. This was of course long prior to Leontief (1954) and illustrates the ready acceptance by international economists of the empirical validity of the Heckscher–Ohlin theory.

6. Ronald Jones was Stolper's student at Swarthmore and then Samuelson's student at MIT.
7. Factor supplies do enter by the back door. The required equilibrium condition that the price of each good must equal its production cost applies only if both goods are produced at home, that is, if the country's factor endowment lies within its "cone of diversification."
8. The production possibility frontier in this case is made up of two linear segments, and the output combination at their intersection is the only one consistent with full employment of both factors. This output combination is consistent with a range of relative prices and corresponding factor rewards, even though the capital–labor ratios used in producing the goods do not change.
9. Lerner's paper and a comment by I. F. Pearce in the same issue of *Economica* introduced the Lerner–Pearce diagram into general use. The Lerner–Pearce diagram can be used to prove the Stolper–Samuelson theorem, as demonstrated in Deardorff (1994). Because this proof does not require calculus, it is now used in some undergraduate textbooks. Although the proof appears in my 1967 lecture notes from Harry Johnson's course in international trade theory at the University of Chicago, I have been unable to track down its earliest appearance in the literature.
10. As published, the paper ends with an effort to defuse any potential "political ammunition for the protectionist" by noting that "it is always possible to bribe the suffering factor . . . so as to leave all factors better off." Does a bigger pie really allow everyone to enjoy a larger slice? It is difficult to identify even a single case in which losers from a government policy choice have received full compensation, and in fact proposed changes in trade policy are often rationalized in terms of their anticipated redistributive consequences.
11. Both letters are reproduced in Deardorff and Stern (1994). Young economists coping with today's publish-or-perish environment may take heart from the initial rejection of this iconic work but may weep with envy over the speed with which the paper went from inspiration to print.
12. Several key contributions are reprinted in Deardorff and Stern (1994). The volume's annotated bibliography lists many others.
13. Robert E. Baldwin (1984) examined an intermediate model in which sector-specific labor skills give rise to labor rents. As a consequence, workers may not find it worthwhile to move between industries when relative output prices change.
14. Magee (1994) provides a brief summary of the results.
15. In this case it is literally a new generation; Christopher Magee is the son of Stephen P. Magee. He is also the student and coauthor of Robert E. Baldwin, an early and influential contributor to the literature on the political economy of trade policy.
16. The inspiration has evidently continued into the twenty-first century. Econlit reports (as of March 14, 2005) mentions of Stolper–Samuelson in forty-one new

items published since 2000. This is an underestimate of continuing impact, as political scientists are making increasing use of the result.

17. Given its enduring influence on subsequent economic analysis, the Stolper–Samuelson theorem may be appropriately regarded as a Schumpeterian innovation. Stolper and Samuelson were both students of the legendary Joseph Schumpeter.

References

Baldwin, Robert E. (1984). "Rent-seeking and trade policy: an industry approach." *Weltwirtschaftliches Archiv*, 120(4), 662–677.

Beaulieu, Eugene, and Christopher Magee. (2004). "Campaign contributions and trade policy: new tests of Stolper-Samuelson." *Economics and Politics*, 16(2), 163–187.

Deardorff, Alan V. and Robert M. Stern (1994). "Overview of the Stolper-Samuelson theorem," in Deardorff and Stern, (eds.), 3–6.

—— and Robert M. Stern (eds.) (1994). *The Stolper-Samuelson Theorem: A Golden Jubilee*. Ann Arbor, MI: University of Michigan Press.

Ethier, Wilfred J. (1984). "Higher dimensional issues in trade theory," in Ronald W. Jones and Peter B. Kenen (eds.), *Handbook of International Economics*, Volume 1. Amsterdam: North-Holland, 131–184.

Jones, Ronald W. (1965). "The structure of simple general equilibrium models." *Journal of Political Economy*, 73(6), 557–572.

Lawrence, Robert A. and Matthew J. Slaughter. (1993). "International trade and American wages in the (1980)s: giant sucking sound or small hiccup?" *Brookings Papers on Economic Activity: Microeconomics*, 2, 161–210.

Leamer, Edward E. (1994). "Commemorating the fiftieth birthday of the Stolper–Samuelson Theorem," in Alan V. Deardorff and Robert M. Stern (eds.), *The Stolper-Samuelson Theorem: A Golden Jubilee*. Ann Arbor, MI: University of Michigan Press.

Leontief, Wassily W. (1954). "Domestic production and foreign trade: The American capital position re-examined," *Economia Internationale*, 7(1), 3–32.

Lerner, Abba P. (1952). "International trade and factor prices," *Economica*, 19(73), 1–15.

Magee, Stephen P. (1980). "Three simple tests of the Stolper-Samuelson theorem," in Peter Oppenheimer (ed.), *Issues in International Economics: Essays in Honor of Harry G. Johnson*. London: Oriel.

——. (1994). "Endogenous protection and real wages," in Alan V. Deardorff and Robert M. Stern (eds.), *The Stolper-Samuelson Theorem: A Golden Jubilee*. Ann Arbor, MI: University of Michigan Press, 279–288.

——, William Brock, and Leslie Young. (1989). *Black Hole Tariffs and Endogenous Policy Theory*. New York: Cambridge University Press.

Pearce, I. F. (1952). "A note on Mr. Lerner's paper," *Economica*, 19(73), 16–18.

Samuelson, Paul A. (1939). "The gains from international trade," *Canadian Journal of Economics and Political Science*, 5(2), 195–205.

——. (1948). "International trade and the equalisation of factor prices," *Economic Journal*, 58(230), 163–184.

——. (1949). "International factor-price equalisation once again," *Economic Journal*, 59(234), 181–197.

——. (1994). "Tribute to Wolfgang Stolper on the fiftieth anniversary of the Stolper-Samuelson theorem," in Alan V. Deardorff and Robert M. Stern (eds.), *The Stolper-Samuelson Theorem: A Golden Jubilee.* Ann Arbor, MI: University of Michigan Press. 339–342.

Stolper, Wolfgang, and Paul A. Samuelson. (1941). "Protection and real wages," *Review of Economic Studies*, 9(1), 58–73.

16

Samuelson and the Factor Bias of Technological Change: Toward a Unified Theory of Growth and Unemployment

Joseph E. Stiglitz

It is a great pleasure for me to be able to write this chapter in honor of Paul's ninetieth birthday. On such occasions, one's students traditionally write an essay inspired by one's work. Paul's long and prolific career—which continues almost unabated—makes this both an easy and a difficult task: easy, because on almost any subject one reflects upon, Paul has made seminal contributions; all of MIT's students—indeed, much of the economic profession for the past half century—has been simply elaborating on Paul's ideas. But by the same token, the task is difficult: there are so many of his ideas the elaboration of which remain on my research agenda, forty two years after leaving MIT, it is hard to make a choice.

Take, for instance, his development of the overlapping generations model, which has played such a central role in macroeconomics. Social security is one of the central issues facing American public policy, and his model remains the central model for analyzing theoretically the consequences of various proposals. Obviously, the results obtained in that

This essay was written on the occasion of Paul Samuelson's ninetieth birthday. I had the good fortune of being asked to write a preface for a book in honor of Paul Samuelson (*Paul Samuelson: On Being an Economist*, by Michael Szenberg, Aron Gottesman, and Lall Ramrattan. Jorge Pinto Books: New York, 2005), in which I describe my days as a student of Paul Samuelson and my huge indebtedness to Paul—and the indebtedness of my fellow students and the entire economics profession. I will not repeat here what I said there. The research on which this essay is based was supported by the Ford, Mott, and MacArthur Foundations, to which I am greatly indebted. The influence of my teachers, Paul Samuelson, Robert Solow, and Hirofumi Uzawa, as well as those with whom I discussed many of these ideas more than forty years ago, including Karl Shell, David Cass, and George Akerlof, should be evident. I am indebted to Stephan Litschig for excellent assistance. I am also indebted to Luminita Stevens for the final review of the manuscript.

model are markedly different from—and far more relevant than—those in an infinitely lived representative agent model.

Recently, I used the model in a quite different context,[1] to study the impact of capital market liberalization, one of the central issues under debate in the international arena. Again, the results are markedly different from those obtained in the perfect information, perfect capital markets, representative agent models, where liberalization allows a country facing a shock to smooth consumption: it helps stabilize the economy. The evidence, of course, was overwhelmingly that that was not the case, and using a variant of the overlapping generations model, one can understand why. Without capital market liberalization, a technology shock, say, to one generation is shared with succeeding generations, as savings increase, wages of successive generations increase, and interest rates fall (in response to the increased capital stock). But with capital market liberalization, the productivity shock may simply be translated into increased income in the period, and increased consumption of the lucky generation. By the same token, capital market liberalization exposes countries to external shocks from the global capital market. I had thought of using this occasion to elaborate on the life-cycle model in a rather different direction: a central feature of the standard life-cycle model and some of the subsequent elaborations (such as Diamond[2]) is the possibility of oversaving: if capital is the only store of value, then the demand for savings by households may be such that the equilibrium interest rate is *beyond* the golden rule, and the economy is dynamically inefficient. Introducing a life-cycle model with land, however, can have profound implications. Take the case, for instance, with no labor force growth and no technological change; being beyond the golden rule would imply a negative real interest rate, which would, in turn, mean an infinite value to land. Obviously, this cannot be an equilibrium. The problems of oversaving, on which so much intellectual energy was spent in the 1960s, simply cannot occur when there is land (and obviously, land does exist). Samuelson was the master of simple models that provided enormous insights, but the result shows the care that must be exercised in the use of such models: sometimes, small and realistic changes may change some of the central conclusions in important ways.

But I have chosen in this chapter to focus on another topic on which I remember so vividly Paul lecturing: endogenous technological change. Long—some two decades—before the subject of endogenous growth theory (which really focuses on growth theory where the rate of technological change is endogenous) became fashionable, Paul Samuelson, Hirofumi

Uzawa, and Ken Arrow and their students were actively engaged in analyzing growth models with endogenous technological progress, either as a result of learning by doing[3] or research.[4]

Of particular interest to Paul was the work of Kennedy[5] and Weizacker[6] (and others) on the *bias* of technological progress—whether it was labor or capital augmenting. Earlier, Kaldor[7] had set forth a set of stylized facts, one of which was the constancy of the capital output ratio. It was easy to show that that implied that technological change was labor augmenting. But what ensured that technological change was labor augmenting—if entrepreneurs had a choice between labor and capital augmentation? These authors had posited a trade-off between rates of capital and labor augmentation, and shown an equilibrium with pure labor augmentation.

Contemporaneously, economic historians, such as Salter[8] and Habakkuk,[9] had discussed economic growth arguing that it was a *shortage* of labor that motivated labor saving innovations, for example, in America. Of course, in standard neoclassical economics, there is no such thing as a shortage—demand equals supply. One might be tempted to say what they meant to say was "high" wages. But how do we know that wages are high? What does that even mean? Of course, with productivity increases, wages are high, but not relative to productivity.

Once we get out of the neoclassical paradigm, of course, markets may be characterized by "tightness" or "looseness." There can be unemployment. Firms may have a hard time finding employees. Moreover, if the unemployment rate is low, workers are more likely to leave, so firms face high turnover costs; what matters is not just the wage, but total labor costs.[10] Worse still, if the unemployment rate is low, workers may shirk—the penalty for getting caught is low.[11] Some economies are plagued by labor strife, again increasing the total cost of labor. One of the motivations for the model below was to try to capture (even if imperfectly) some aspects of this as affecting the *endogenous direction* of technological progress.

There is another motivation for this chapter. The early beginnings of growth theory derive from the basic model of Harrod and Domar, where there was a fixed capital-output ratio, a. With savings, s, a fixed fraction of output (income), Y,

$$I = sY = \mathrm{d}K/\mathrm{d}t \qquad (16.1)$$

where K is the capital stock, so the rate of growth of capital is

$$\mathrm{dln}\, \mathrm{K}/\mathrm{d}t = sY/K = s/a. \qquad (16.2)$$

Moreover, as machines become more efficient, each machine requires less labor, so the number of jobs created goes up more slowly than the capital stock. If

$$L/Y = b \tag{16.3}$$

is the labor requirement per unit output, then b/a is the labor required per unit capital, and job growth is

$$\mathrm{dln}\, L/\mathrm{d}t = s/a - \beta - \alpha \tag{16.4}$$

where

$$-\mathrm{dln}\, b/\mathrm{d}t = \beta \tag{16.5}$$

$$\mathrm{dln}\, a/\mathrm{d}t = \alpha \tag{16.6}$$

s/a was sometimes referred to as the warranted rate of growth, what the system would support. Once technological change was incorporated, the warranted rate of growth is modified to $s/a - \beta - \alpha$.

By contrast, labor was assumed to grow at an exogenous rate, n. The problem was that, in general, n was not equal to $s/a - \beta - \alpha$.[12]

If (in the model without technological change), $s/a < n$, unemployment would grow continually; and if $s/a > n$, eventually the economy reached full employment—after which it would be profitable to invest only enough to keep full employment, an amount less than s/a.

The "dilemma" was resolved by Solow (1956), who proposed that the capital output ratio depended on the capital labor ratio, k: $a(k)$; and technological change was purely labor augmenting, so in equilibrium

$$s/a(k^*) = n + \beta \tag{16.7}$$

There is a capital labor ratio such that capital and *effective* labor (the demand for jobs and the supply of labor) grow precisely at the same rate.

The problem with Solow's "solution" is that it does away with the very concept of a job; alternatively, if there were ever a job shortage, simply by lowering the wage, more jobs would be created until the economy reached full employment. In developing countries, this means there is never a capital shortage; if there is unemployment, it must simply be because wages are too high. By the same token, there is never "technological unemployment." Technology may reduce the demand for labor *at a particular wage*, but whatever technology does, wage adjustments can undo. In practice, of course, at least in the short run, there is not such flexibility.[13]

In this short note, we take seriously the notion of jobs (perhaps more seriously than the concept should be taken). Given today's technology and capital stock, wage adjustments will not lead to full employment. There is a maximum employment which they can support.

In the model here, it is the combination of changes in capital stock and technology which drive changes in employment. Wages make a difference, through their effects on technology (and possibly capital accumulation). In short, we construct a model where, over time, technological change leads to either increases or decreases in the capital output ratio, so that *eventually*

$$s/a^* = n + \beta \tag{16.8}$$

That is,

$$a = a^* = s/(n+\beta). \tag{16.9}$$

It is technological change that ensures that jobs grow at the same rate as the labor force.

The problem with standard versions of the fixed coefficients model (where, at any moment of time, a and b are fixed) is that the distribution of income is very fragile: if N is the supply of labor and L is the demand,

$$L = (L/Y)\,(Y/K)\,K = (b/a)\,K \tag{16.10}$$

$$\text{If } (b/a)\,K < N, \quad \text{then } w = 0$$

$$\text{If } (b/a)\,K > N, \quad \text{then } r = 0$$

where w = (real) wage, r = (real) return on capital. If $(b/a)K = N$, the distribution of income is indeterminate.

Here, however, we present an alternative version, based on agency theory (Shapiro and Stiglitz, 1984). If workers are paid too low a wage, they prefer to shirk; there is the lowest wage which firms can pay at any unemployment rate to induce them not to shirk. That wage depends on the payment an unemployed worker receives. We write this as

$$w = f(v)w_{\min} \tag{16.11}$$

where v is the employment ratio,

$$v = L/N = (b/a)(K/N) \tag{16.12}$$

So

$$\mathrm{dln}\, v/\mathrm{dt} = s/a - n - \beta - \alpha \tag{16.13}$$

Finally, firms have a choice of innovations. Total cost of production per unit output is

$$c = ar + bw \tag{16.14}$$

The firm has a given technology today $\{a_0, b_0\}$. It can, however, decide on the nature of the technology by which it can produce next period (Figure 16.1).

Technology defines next year's feasibility locus. Taking for a moment r and w as given, the firm can reduce (next year's) cost by balancing out changes in a and b:

$$\mathrm{dc}/\mathrm{dt} = \alpha m - \beta(1 - m) \tag{16.15}$$

where m is the share of capital in costs, or the share of capital in income:

$$m = ar = rK/Y \tag{16.16}$$

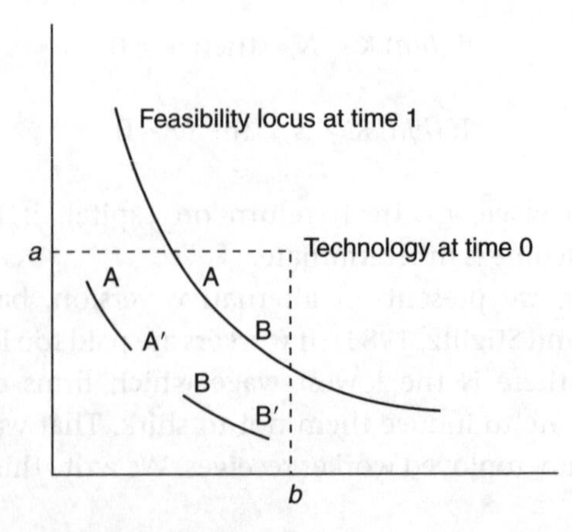

Figure 16.1 Technology feasibility locus.

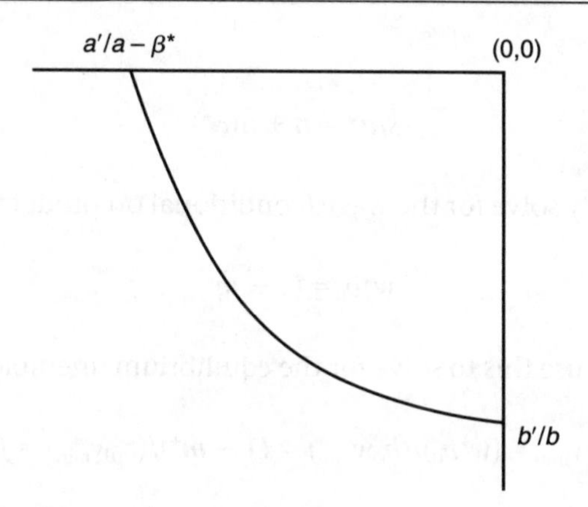

Figure 16.2 Labor vs. capital augmentation.

Assume that there is a trade-off between labor and capital augmenting progress, so that

$$\beta = \beta(\alpha). \quad \beta' > 0 \quad \beta'' < 0 \tag{16.17}$$

depicted in Figure 16.2.

Then cost reductions are maximized when

$$\beta'(\alpha) = m/(1 - m) \tag{16.18}$$

16.1 Steady State Equilibrium

We can now fully describe the steady state equilibrium. In the long run, we have argued that a must converge to a^*, which means that

$$\alpha^* = 0, \tag{16.19}$$

which in turn means that

$$m^*/(1 - m^*) = \beta'(0) \equiv \beta^* \tag{16.20}$$

or

$$r^* = m^*/a^*. \tag{16.21}$$

a^*, in turn, solves

$$s/a^* = n + \beta(\alpha^*) \tag{16.22}$$

We can similarly solve for the wage (conditional on productivity):

$$w^* b_0 = (1 - m^*) \tag{16.23}$$

Finally, we can use this to solve for the equilibrium unemployment rate:

$$w^*/w_{\min} = (w^* b_0)/(b_0 w_{\min}) = (1 - m^*)/(b_0 w_{\min}) = f(v^*) \tag{16.24}$$

That is, once we set the unemployment compensation ($w_{\min}$) relative to labor market productivity, then we know what the unemployment rate is.

16.2 Heuristic Dynamics

In this model, there is a simple adjustment process. If the capital output ratio is too high, too few jobs will be created (given the savings rate) and unemployment grows. Growing unemployment means that wages will become depressed—in the story told here, firms can pay a lower wage without workers' shirking, but there are other stories (such as bargaining models) which yield much the same outcome. Lower wages mean, of course, that the return to capital is increased. As wages get depressed, and labor becomes easier to hire, and the return (cost) of capital increases, firms seek ways of economizing on capital, and pay less attention to economizing on labor. The new technologies that are developed are capital saving and labor using. The capital output ratio falls, and the labor output ratio increases. Given the savings rate, more jobs are created, and the unemployment rate starts to fall.

16.3 Formal Dynamics

The convergence to equilibrium, however, may neither be direct nor fast. Figure 16.3 depicts the phase diagram, in $\{a, v\}$ space.

The locus of points for which $da/dt = 0$ is a vertical line, given by

$$\alpha = 0, \text{ that is,} \tag{16.25}$$

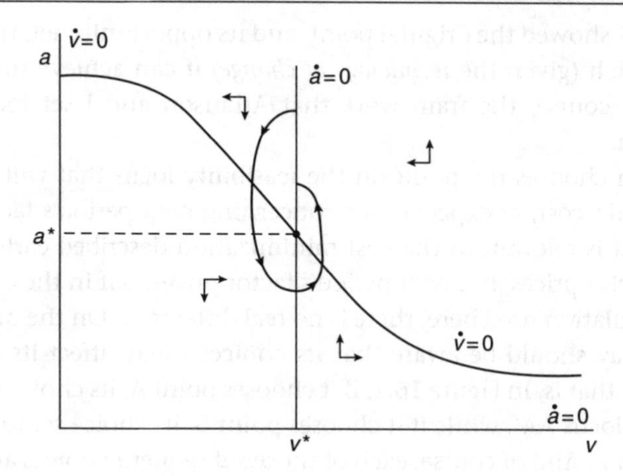

Figure 16.3

from Equations (16.24), (16.23) and (16.20), given $b_0 w_{\min}$ (which we will take as set), there is a unique value of v^* for which $\alpha = 0$, that is, a is constant; and if

$$v > v^*, \quad da/dt > 0$$

$$v < v^*, \quad da/dt < 0$$

when employment is high, wages are high; firms economize on labor, and the capital output ratio increases, and conversely when employment is low.

The locus of points for which $dv/dt = 0$ is the negatively sloped curve defined by

$$a = s/(n + \beta + \alpha) \tag{16.26}$$

and it is easy to show that below the curve, v is increasing, and above it, it is decreasing. We show a sample path converging through oscillations into the equilibrium.

In the appendix we provide sufficient conditions for this type of stability of the equilibrium.

16.4 Micro-economics

As noted earlier, at any point of time, the representative firm has a given technology, defined by $\{a, b\}$. Its choice is about its technology next period.

Figure 16.1 showed the original point, and its opportunity set, the locus of points which (given the *technology of change*) it can achieve next period. This is, of course, the framework that Atkinson and I set forth in our 1969 paper.

The firm chooses the point on the feasibility locus that will minimize next period's cost, at expectations concerning next period's factor prices. Thus, what is relevant in the cost minimization described earlier are not current factor prices, but next period's factor prices; but in the continuous time formulation used here, there is no real difference. On the other hand, a firm today should be aware that its choices today affect its choice set tomorrow, that is, in Figure 16.1, if it chooses point A, its choice set tomorrow is the locus AA′, while if it chooses point B, its choice set tomorrow is the locus BB′. And of course, each of those subsequent choices are affected by wages prevailing then and in the future. Hence, in reality, what should matter for a firm is not just tomorrow's wage, but the entire wage profile. The full solution of this complicated dynamic programming problem is beyond the scope of this brief note. The steady state *equilibrium* which emerges is identical to that described here, though the dynamics are somewhat more complicated.

16.5 A Generalization

Earlier, we set forth the notion that what mattered in the choice of technology was not just factor prices, but the total cost of labor, including turnover costs, how hard it was to hire workers, etc. These variables too will, in general, be related to the unemployment rate, so that the point along the feasibility set chosen by the firm will depend not only on relative shares, which depend on v, but also on v directly:

$$\alpha = \Phi(m(v), v). \tag{16.27}$$

Equilibrium still requires that

$$\alpha = 0, \beta = \beta^* = \beta(0) \tag{16.28}$$

and so $a = a^*$. Indeed, once we set the policy variable $(b_0 w_{\min})$, the analysis is changed little, except now, using Equation (16.24), m^* is defined by

$$0 = \Phi\,(m, v) = \Phi\,(m^*, f^{-1}(1 - m^*)/(b_0 w_{\min})) \tag{16.29}$$

16.6 A Kaldorian Variant

Kaldor provided an alternative approach to reconciling the "warranted" and "natural" rate of growth, the disparity between $s/a - \beta - \alpha$, the rate at which jobs are created, and n, the rate at which the labor force grows. He suggested that the average savings rate depends on the distribution of income, and by changing the distribution of income, s can be brought into line. Thus, he posited (in simplified form) that none of the wages are saved, but a fraction s_p of profits, so

$$\mathrm{d}K/\mathrm{d}t = s_p r K \tag{16.30}$$

Hence, we replace the differential equation for v, (16.13) with

$$\mathrm{dln}\, v/\mathrm{d}t = s_p r - n - \beta - \alpha \tag{16.13'}$$

$$= s_p(1/a - w(v)b/a) - n - \beta - \alpha$$

and the equilibrium Equation (16.8) defining a^* with

$$s_p r^* = n + \beta(0) \tag{16.8'}$$

defining the equilibrium interest rate. Before, given a, we used (16.21) to solve for r. Now, we use (16.21) to solve for a, given r:

$$a^* = m^*/r^* \tag{16.21'}$$

The dynamics are also modified only slightly. As (16.13′) makes clear, it is still the case that above the locus $\mathrm{d}v/\mathrm{d}t = 0$ (i.e. for higher values of a), the rate of growth of capital is lower (as before), so v (the employment rate) is falling; below the curve, it is rising. Hence, the qualitative dynamics remains unchanged.[14]

16.7 A Related Model

Some years ago, George Akerlof and I formulated a related model of the business cycle (another area in which Samuelson's contributions were seminal.)[15]

Real wages were portulated to depend positively on capital per worker, As here, an increase in capital accumulation led to increases in wages which reduced funds available for savings, which slowed growth and led to lower wages.[16] In that model, we again obtained oscillatory dynamic behavior.

16.8 Why it Matters: a Distinction with a Difference

At one level of analysis, the difference between this model and the standard Solow model is small. In the standard model, firms choose the *current* technology among a set of available technologies so that the capital output ratio adjusts and eventually the warranted and natural rate are equated. Here, firms choose *future technologies*, and again, eventually the warranted and natural rates are equated. In both models, at the microeconomic level, firms are choosing technologies in response to maximizing profits (minimizing costs), given factor prices.

There are, of course, important differences in dynamics: in the Solow model, convergence is monotonic. Here, the dynamics are far more complicated. Convergence may be oscillatory.

But there are some more profound differences, some of which relate to economic policy, to which I want to call attention. The first relates to the determination of the distribution of income and the choice of technique. In the Solow model, wages adjust *so that there is always full employment*. The choice of technique is, in effect, dictated by factor supplies. Though firms *choose* the technology to employ, factor prices always adjust so that the technology they choose is such that factors are fully employed. Thus, the distribution of income really plays no role—and in Solow's exposition, one could tell the entire dynamic story without reference to it, or without reference to firms "choosing" a technology. If there is unemployment, it is only because wages are too high and lowering wages would eliminate the unemployment (but increase growth only slightly and temporarily).

In the model here, the choice of (future) technology is central. Wages are not determined by marginal productivities, but by firms, as the lowest wage they can pay to avoid shirking on the part of workers. If minimum wages pushed wages above this level, they would result in increased unemployment; but for most workers, the minimum wage is set below that level so that lowering the minimum wage has little effect on wages actually paid, and hence on unemployment or growth. (An increase in unemployment compensation in this model does, however, increase the unemployment rate, by forcing firms to pay higher wages to avoid shirking.)

High wages do have an effect on unemployment, through the impact on the evolution of technology. This has two implications. First, it takes considerable time before any action to lower wages (even if it were successful) has any effect. The short-run effect on unemployment is nil.[17] Second, there are other ways by which the government could affect the evolution of the system and the creation of jobs. There are two ways by which this can be done in the medium run. First, policies which increase the national savings rate would be just as or more effective in increasing employment in the medium term. Second, marginal wage subsidies reduce the cost of labor, and it is the high cost of labor (at the margin) which induces firms to shift the direction of technological developments toward excessive labor savings and capital using technologies.

16.9 Concluding Remarks

For almost half a century, the Solow growth model, in which technological change was exogenous, has dominated discussions of growth theory. But almost half a century ago, Samuelson helped lay the foundations of an alternative approach to explaining the "stylized" facts of economic growth, based on endogenous technological change. What was needed, however, to close the model was a plausible theory of wage determination, which subsequent work in the economics of information (efficiency wage theory) has helped provide. By unifying these two disparate strands of literature, we have provided here a general theory of growth and employment which makes sense of discussions of technological unemployment or job shortages—concepts which have no meaning in Solow's formulation. We have suggested that the policy implications of this theory are markedly different from those arising from Solow's model.

It will be a long time before the fruit of the seeds which Paul sowed so many years ago are fully mature.

Notes

1. Stiglitz (2004)
2. Diamond (1965)
3. Arrow (1962a)
4. Here again, Arrow's (1962b) contribution was seminal. This is not the occasion to go into the large literature, except to mention Karl Shell's volume of essays (1967), Nordhaus' thesis (1969), and my own work with Tony Atkinson (1969).

5. Kennedy (1964)
6. Weizacker (1966)
7. Kaldor (1961)
8. Salter (1960)
9. Habbakuk (1962)
10. Stiglitz (1974)
11. Shapiro and Stiglitz (1984)
12. Harrod and Domar's original analysis did not include technological change. This is a slight generalization of their analysis.
13. Standard models have formalized this in the notion of putty-clay models.
14. The stability conditions are of course changed. See the appendix for details.
15. The accelerator-multiplier model has gone out of fashion, partly because the assumption of fixed coefficients on which it relied has become unfashionable, partly because it was not based on rational expectations (which has become fashionable). But one can obtain much the same results from a model in which investment increases not because sales have increased, but because profits have increased. Stiglitz and Greenwald (1993) have explained both why capital (equity) market imperfections exist and how they can lead to such a *financial accelerator*.
16. That model differed in the wage determination function (we used a real-Phillips curve) and, as in the Solow model, wages determined current choice of technique, as opposed to here, where it affects the evolution of future technology. In some cases, we showed that the economy could be characterized by a limit cycle.
17. Early students of growth theory recognized that this would be true even within the neoclassical model; they focused on putty-clay models in which after investments have been made, the ability to change its characteristics (the labor required to work it) is very limited. Dynamics of growth in putty-clay models are markedly different from those of standard neoclassical models. See Cass and Stiglitz (1969). Unfortunately, the models were not easy to work with, and the distinction seems to have been lost in discussions of growth in recent decades.

References

Ahmad, S. (1966). "On the Theory of induced invention," *The Economic Journal*, 76(302), 344–357.

Akerlof, G. and Joseph E. Stiglitz. (1969). "Capital, wages and structural unemployment," *Economic Journal*, 79(314), 269–281.

Arrow, Kenneth J. (1962a). "The economic implications of learning by doing," *Review of Economic Studies*, XXIX, 155–173.

——. (1962b). "Economic welfare and the allocation of resources for innovation," in Nelson (ed.), *The Rate and Direction of Inventive Activity*. Princeton, NJ: Princeton University Press. pp. 609-25

Atkinson, Anthony, and J. E. Stiglitz. (1969). "A new view of technological change," *Economic Journal*, 79, 573–578.

Cass, David, and J. E. Stiglitz. (1969). "The implications of alternative saving and expectations hypotheses for choices of technique and patterns of growth," *Journal of Political Economy*, 77, 586–627.

Diamond, Peter A. (1965). "National debt in a neoclassical growth model," *American Economic Review*, Part 1 of 2, 55(5), 1126.

Drandakis, E. M. and E. S. Phelps. (1966). "A model of induced invention, growth and distribution," *The Economic Journal*, 76(304), 823–840.

Habbakuk, H. J. (1962). *American and British Technology in the Nineteenth Century: the Search for Labour-Saving Inventions*. Cambridge, Cambridge University Press.

Kaldor, N. (1957). "A model of economic growth," *Economic Journal*, 67(268), 591–624.

——. (1961). "Capital accumulation and economic growth," in F. Lutz and V. Hague (eds.), *The Theory of Capital*, New York: St Martin's Press, 177–222.

Kennedy, C. (1964). "Induced bias in innovation and the theory of distribution," *Economic Journal*, LXXIV, 541–547.

Nordhaus, W. D. (1969). *Invention, Growth and Welfare: A Theoretical Treatment of Technological Change*. Cambridge, MA: MIT Press.

Salter Wilfred, E. J. (1960). *Productivity and Technical Change*, Cambridge, Cambridge University Press, 1996.

Samuelson, P. A. (1965). "A theory of induced innovation on Kennedy-von Weisacker Lines," *Review of Economics and Statistics*, 47(4), 343–356.

Shapiro, C. and J. E. Stiglitz. (1984). "Equilibrium unemployment as a worker discipline device," *American Economic Review*, 74(3), 433–444.

Shell, K. (1967). *Essays on the Theory of Optimal Economic Growth* (ed.), Cambridge, MA: MIT Press.

Stiglitz, Joseph E. (1974). "Alternative theories of wage determination and unemployment in L.D.C.'s: the labor turnover model," *Quarterly Journal of Economics*, 88(2), 194–227.

——. (2004), "Capital market liberalization globalization and the IMF," *Oxford Review of Economic Policy*, 20(1), 57–71.

—— and B. Greenwald. (1993). "Financial market imperfections and business cycles," *Quarterly Journal of Economics*, 108(1), 77–114.

Weizacker, Von, C. (1966). "Tentative notes on a two-sector model with induced technical progress," *Review of Economic Studies*, 33, 245–251.

Appendix: Stability Conditions

In order to analyze stability, we simplify by writing

$$\text{dln}\, a/\text{d}t = \alpha(v); \quad \alpha' > 0$$

$$-\text{dln}\, b/\text{d}t = \beta(\alpha); \quad \beta' > 0$$

The locus of points for which $dv/dt = 0$ is the negatively sloped curve defined by

$$a = s/(n + \beta(\alpha(v)) + \alpha(v)) \quad da/dv = -a^2(\beta'\alpha' + \alpha')/s \tag{16.27}$$

Below the $dv/dt = 0$ curve, v is increasing and above the curve, v is decreasing.

To evaluate the stability conditions of the pair of differential equations:

$$v' = v\,(s/a - n - \beta(\alpha(v)) - \alpha(v))$$

$$a' = a\,\alpha(v)$$

we look at the Jacobian evaluated at $\{v^*, a^*\}$ as follows:

$$J(v^*, a^*) = \begin{Bmatrix} -v^*(\beta'(0)\alpha'(v^*) + \alpha'(v^*)) & -v^*s/a^{*2} \\ a^*\alpha'(v^*) & 0 \end{Bmatrix}$$

The conditions for the steady state to be a stable spiral (converging to equilibrium through oscillations) is:

$$-v^*(\beta'(0)\alpha'(v^*) + \alpha'(v^*)) < 0$$

which is always satisfied; and

$$[v^*(\beta'(0)\alpha'(v^*) + \alpha'(v^*))]^2 - 4(v^*s/a^{*2})a^*\alpha'(v^*) < 0$$

which can be simplified to

$$v^*\alpha'(1 + \beta')^2 < 4(n + \beta(0)).$$

Provided the limit as α goes to zero of $d\ln\alpha/d\ln v$ is finite, then the limit of the LHS of the above condition is always satisfied.[1]

16A.1 Kaldorian Variant

For the Kaldorian variant, the dv/dt equation is now:

$$v' = v\,(s_p r - n - \beta - \alpha) \text{ from Eq. (13') in the text}$$

$$= v\,(s_p(1/a - w(v)b/a) - n - \beta(\alpha(v)) - \alpha(v)) \text{ from the fact that } Y = rK + wL$$

[1] If lim $d\ln\alpha/d\ln v$ is infinite, then the stability condition will be satisfied only if the derivatives of the technology functions with respect to employment are sufficiently small, that is in the limit, as α goes to zero

$$(1+\beta')^2\alpha' < 4(n + \beta(0))/v^*$$

The Jacobian under the Kaldorian variant becomes:

$$J(v^*, a^*) = \begin{Bmatrix} -v^*(s_p(b_0/a^*)w' + \beta'(0)\alpha'(v^*) + \alpha'(v^*)) & -v^*s_p(1 - w(v^*)b_o)/a^{*2} \\ a^*\alpha'(v^*) & 0 \end{Bmatrix}$$

The conditions for local stability with oscillations in this case are:

$$[v^*(s_p(b_0/a^*)w' + \beta'(0)\alpha'(v^*) + \alpha'(v^*))]^2 - 4(v^*s_p(1 - w(v^*)b_0)/a^{*2})a^*\alpha'(v^*) < 0$$

$$\text{and} - v^*(s_p(b_0/a^*)w' + \beta'(0)\alpha'(v^*) + \alpha'(v^*)) < 0$$

Again, the latter condition is always satisfied, but now if the limit as α goes to zero of dln α/dln v is finite, the former condition is never satisfied; but if the limit is finite, the former condition requires that real wages not be too sensitive to employment. To see this, we rewrite the former condition as

$$[v^*(s_p(b_0/a^*)w' + \beta'(0)\alpha'(v^*) + \alpha'(v^*))]^2 < \{(v^*s_pr^*\alpha' = 4v^*(n + \beta(0))\alpha'\}$$

$$\text{LHS} = [v^*s_p(b_0/a^*)w' + v^*\alpha'(1 + \beta')]^2$$

$$= [v^*s_pb_0/a^*w']^2 + [2(v^*s_p(b_0/a^*)w'(v^*\alpha(1 + \beta')] + [v^*\alpha(1 + \beta')]^2$$

It is apparent, first, that if dln α/dln v is finite, the condition for stable oscillations is never satisfied (in marked contrast to the standard case), because the LHS is strictly positive, the RHS is zero. If lim $\alpha'(v)$ is strictly positive, the condition can be satisfied only if w′ is not too large. If the condition is not satisfied, the equilibrium is locally stable and the approach is not oscillatory.

17

Samuelson and Investment for the Long Run

Harry M. Markowitz

When I was a student in the Economics Department of the University of Chicago, Karl Brunner and I diligently read through Paul Samuelson's *Foundations of Economics*. Karl and I found a bug in the book and wrote Professor Samuelson concerning it. Samuelson replied that several other people had called his attention to this bug, but we were the first non-Asians to do so. Years later, I was surprised and delighted to see Samuelson cite my work and write about portfolio theory, albeit sometimes critically as well as creatively.

Through the years, Paul and I have had one ongoing debate on the following topic. If an investor invests for the "long run" should she or he choose each period the portfolio which maximizes the expected logarithm of 1+ return for that period? I say yes; Paul says no. Our written works on the subject include Samuelson (1963, 1969, 1979) and Markowitz (1959, 1976). We also debated the matter at a meeting in Vale, Colorado many years ago. To this day both of us feel that our respective views have been completely vindicated. But, I must admit, Samuelson's (1979) article titled "Why We Should Not Make Mean Log of Wealth Big Though Years To Act Are Long" is a particularly remarkable expository achievement. As he explains in the last paragraph, "No need to say more. I've made my point. And, save for the last word, have done so in prose of but one syllable." It is hard not to feel intimidated in a debate with an opponent who is a combination of Albert Einstein and Dr Seuss.

In the present chapter I note the primary positions of the two sides and give one example that illustrates their differences. I chose an example which most simply supports my side of the debate. I believe that any other example will, upon close examination, also support my side but not necessarily as directly. I make no attempt to provide arguments on the other side since Paul, despite or because of his ninety years, is perfectly capable of doing so.

17.1 Background

The expected log criteria was proposed by Kelly (1956) and embraced by Latane (1957, 1959). Markowitz (1959) accepts the idea that the expected logarithm (of one plus return) of a portfolio is its rate of growth in the long run. Markowitz concludes that the cautious investor should not choose a mean-variance combination from the mean-variance efficient frontier with higher arithmetic mean (and therefore higher variance) than the mean-variance combination which approximately maximizes expected log, or, equivalently, geometric mean return. A portfolio higher on the frontier subjects the investor to more volatility in the short run and no greater return *in the long run*. The cautious investor, however, may choose a mean-variance combination lower on the frontier, giving up return in the long run for greater stability of return.

Breiman (1960, 1961) supplied a strong law of large numbers argument supporting the expected log rule. Samuelson (1963, 1969, 1979) provides an expected utility argument which contradicts the expected log rule. Markowitz (1976) provides an alternative expected utility argument which supports the expected log rule.

17.2 The Expected Log Rule in General and Particular

Throughout this chapter I consider an investor who starts with an initial wealth W_0 and allocates resources, without transaction costs, at discrete times 0, 1, 2, . . . separated by a day, month, year, or millisecond. The return on a portfolio P during time interval t—between time point $t-1$ and t—is denoted r_t^P. In general, as of time $t-1$, the probability distribution of r_t^P may depend on the values of state variables as of time $t-1$ and may be jointly distributed with the values of state variables as of t. The max E log rule says that, whatever this dependence on and joint distribution with state variables, as of time $t-1$ choose the portfolio P which maximizes current, single-period

$$E \log(1 + r_t^P) \qquad (17.1)$$

where E is the expected value operator.

The issues which separate the Kelly, Latané, Brieman, and Markowitz arguments *for* and the Samuelson arguments *against* are already present, and can be discussed more simply, in the special case wherein the returns r_t^P on a given portfolio are i.i.d. (independent and identically distributed) and the investor must rebalance to the same portfolio P (therefore the same probability distribution of r_t) at every point in time. We shall deal only with this special case in this chapter. See Markowitz (1976) for the more general case.

17.3 First Argument *For* Max *E* log

If an investor repeatedly draws from a rate of return distribution without adding or withdrawing funds beyond the initial W_0, then at time T the investor's wealth is

$$W^T = W_0 \prod_{t=1}^{T} (1 + r_t^P) \tag{17.2}$$

where r_t^P here represents the rate of return actually achieved on the portfolio at time t. The rate of return, g^P, achieved during the entire history from 0 to T satisfies

$$(1 + g^P) = (W_T^P / W_0)^{1/T}$$

$$= \left(\prod_{t=1}^{T} (1 + r_t^P) \right)^{1/T} \tag{17.3}$$

g^P is the rate of return which, if earned each period, would grow wealth from W_0 to W_T in T periods. Thus, wealth at time T is a strictly increasing function of

$$\log (1 + g^P) = (1/T) \left(\sum_{t=1}^{T} \log (1 + r_t^P) \right) \tag{17.4}$$

The assumption that r_t^P is i.i.d. implies that $\log (1 + r_t^P)$ is i.i.d. If $r_t^P = -1$ is possible then $\log (1 + r_t^P)$ is an "extended real" random variable defined on $[-\infty, \infty)$. If $\log (1 + r_t^P)$ has expected value

$$E \log (1 + r_t^P) = \mu \in [\infty, \infty] \tag{17.5}$$

then the strong law of large numbers says that—with probability 1—

$$\lim_{T\to\infty} \sum_{t=1}^{T} \left(\log\,(1 + r_t^P) \right) / T \to \mu. \tag{17.6}$$

In particular, if μ is finite then, with probability 1, for every positive ϵ there is a T_0 such that the difference between μ and the sample average of log $(1 + r_t^P)$ is less than ϵ, for all T greater than T_0:

$$\forall \varepsilon > 0\ \exists T_0 \quad \text{such that}\ \forall T > T_0$$

$$\sum_{t=1}^{T} \log\,(1 + r_t^P)/T - \mu| < \varepsilon \tag{17.7}$$

T_0 is random, and will typically vary from one randomly drawn sequence to the next (independently drawn) random sequence. If expected log $(1 + r_t^P) = \infty$ (or $-\infty$) then, with probability 1, for every $b>0$ there is a random time T_0 such that for all time thereafter average log $(1 + r_t^P)$ is greater than b (respectively, less than $-b$):

$$\forall b > 0\ \exists T_0 \quad \text{such that}\ \forall\, \mathrm{T} > T_0$$

$$\sum_{t=1}^{T} \log\,(1 + r_t^P)/T > b \tag{17.8}$$

$$(< -b, \text{ respectively})$$

One of the principal justifications for identifying max E log $(1 + r)$ with investment for the long run follows from the above. If r_1^P, r_2^P, . . . and r_1^Q, r_2^Q are two rate of return sequences, each i.i.d. but r_t^P may be correlated with r_t^Q, and the first has a higher E log $(1 + r)$ than the second, that is,

$$\mu_P = E \log\,(1 + r_t^P)$$

$$> E \log(1 + r_t^Q)$$

$$= \mu_Q \tag{17.9}$$

then (17.3), (17.4) and (17.7) or (17.8) imply that—with probability 1—there is a time T_0 such that $W_T{}^P$ exceeds $W_T{}^Q$ ever after

$$\exists T_0\ \forall\, T > T_0\ W_P^{\ T} > W_Q^{\ T}. \tag{17.10}$$

Since, with probability one, there comes a time such that forever after the wealth of the investor who rebalances to portfolio P exceeds that of the investor who rebalances to portfolio Q, surely one can say that P does better than Q in *the long run*. This does not necessarily imply that any particular investor, with a finite life and imminent consumption needs, should invest in P rather than Q. But it seems an unobjectionable use of language to summarize relationship (17.10) by saying that portfolio P does better than portfolio Q "in the long run."

17.4 Argument *Against* Max *E* log

Consider an investor who invests W_0 at time 0, and lets this investment "ride," without additional investments or withdrawals until some fixed, distant time T. At time T the investor, or his or her heirs, will "cash in" the investment. The investor must decide whether the trustees of this investment are to be instructed to rebalance each period to portfolio P or Q. We continue to assume that successive returns to a given portfolio are i.i.d., although the simultaneous returns r_t^P, r_t^Q may be correlated. Suppose that the investor seeks to maximize expected utility of final wealth, where the utility function is the form

$$U = \text{sgn}\,(\alpha)\, W_T^{\alpha} \tag{17.11}$$

for some $\alpha \neq 0$. Since returns to a given portfolio are i.i.d., expected utility equals

$$EU = \text{sgn}\,(\alpha)\, E\left(\prod_{t=1}^{T}(1 + r_t^P)\right)^{\alpha}$$

$$= \text{sgn}\,(\alpha)\left(E(1 + r^P)^{\alpha}\right)^{T} \tag{17.12}$$

Thus, the expected utility maximizing portfolio is whichever has greater $E(1 + r)^{\alpha}$. This is not necessarily the one with greater $E \log (1 + r)$.

Samuelson (1969) and Mossin (1968) show a much stronger result than shown above (in which it is *assumed* that the investor rebalances to the *same* portfolio each period). Even if the investor may switch portfolios, for example, choose one when there is a long way to go and another when the end is imminent, the optimum strategy for the utility function in (17.11) is to stay with the same portfolio from beginning to end, whether "time is long" or not.

Thus, no matter how distant the goal, the optimum strategy is not the max *E* log rule.

17.5 Example

Consider two portfolios *P* and *Q*. *P* provides 6 percent per year with certainty. *Q* provides, each year, a fifty-fifty chance of 200 percent gain or 100 percent loss. The expected return and expected log(1 + return) of *P* are 0.06 and $\log_e(1.06) = 0.058$, respectively. The expected return and expected log of *Q* are

$$\tfrac{1}{2}(2.00) + \tfrac{1}{2}(-1.00) = 0.50 \text{ (50 percent) and } \tfrac{1}{2}\log(3.00) + \tfrac{1}{2}\log(0.0) = -\infty.$$

An investor who followed the max *E* log rule would prefer *P*. For any fixed investment horizon *T*, the investor who maximized expected utility of form (11) with $\alpha = 1$, that is, an investor who maximized expected terminal wealth, would prefer *Q*.

The arguments for and against the max *E* log rule can be illustrated with this example. Imagine that the return on *Q* is determined by a flip of a fair coin, heads being favorable. If the coin is flipped repeatedly, with probability 1, eventually a tail will be tossed. From that time on $0 = W_T^Q < W_T^P = (1.06)^T$. Thus, in the particular case, as in general, with probability 1 there comes a time when the max *E* log strategy pulls ahead and stays ahead of the alternative strategy, forever.

On the other hand, pick some point in time, such as $T = 100$. At that time *P* provides $(1.06)^T$ with certainty. *Q* provides nothing if a tail has appeared in the first 100 tosses. If not, $W_T^Q = 3^T$. Since this has probability $(½)^T$ expected wealth (equals expected utility here) is

$$EW_T^Q = (\tfrac{1}{2})^T 3^T = (1.50)^T > (1.06)^T = W_T^P \qquad (17.13)$$

Thus, in the particular case as in general, the portfolio which maximizes *EU* for $T = 1$ also maximizes *EU* for arbitrarily large *T* fixed in advance.

17.6 Another Argument *For* Max *E* log

Markowitz (1976) argues that an assertion that something is best (or not best) in the long run should be an asymptotic statement that some policy or strategy does (or does not) approach optimality as $T \to \infty$. The Samuelson argument against Max *E* log is presented in terms of a (long) game of fixed length. Since this fixed length is arbitrarily long, the Samuelson argument can be transformed into an asymptotic argument as follows. Imagine a sequence of games $G_1, G_2, G_3, \ldots, G_{100}, \ldots$. The second game G_2 is "just like" the first except it is two periods long, $T = 2$, rather than one period long $T = 1$. The third game G_3 is just like the first two except that it is three periods long, $T = 3$, and so on.

In general, the notion that game G_T is "just like" game G_{T-1}, only longer, would require that the same opportunities be available in the first $T - 1$ moves of game G_T as were available in all of G_{T-1}. For the simple example in the last section, it implies that the same two probability distributions, *P* and *Q*, be used *T* times instead of $T - 1$. Let EU_T^P and EU_T^Q represent the expected utility of the *T*-period game, obtained by repeatedly investing in distribution *P* or *Q* respectively. Samuelson's complaint about identifying *P* as the better investment for the long run is that it is *not* true that

$$\lim_{T\to\infty} \mathrm{EU}_T^P \geq \lim_{T\to\infty} \mathrm{EU}_T^Q$$

even though *P* has greater $E\log(1 + r)$ on each spin of the wheel.

One way in which the Samuelson games stay the same as *T* varies is that each is scored by the expected value of *the same function* of *final wealth*. We could instead score the games by the same function of rate of return *g* defined in (17.3). In the example of the last section, *P* always supplies a rate of return of 0.06. The rate of return supplied by *Q* is

$$q^Q = \begin{cases} -1.0 & \text{with probability } 1-(\frac{1}{2})^T \\ 2.0 & \text{with probability } \quad (\frac{1}{2})^T \end{cases}$$

Let *f* be any strictly increasing function of *g*. Let us define a sequence of games, $H_1, H_2, \ldots, H_{100}, \ldots$ which are just like the Samuelson games except that they are each scored by expected value of the same function $V = f(g)$. Then

$$EV_T^P = f(0.06) \rightarrow f(0.06)$$

$$EV_T^Q = (1-(\tfrac{1}{2})^T)\, f(-1.0)$$

$$+(\tfrac{1}{2})^T f(2.0)$$

$$\rightarrow f(-1.0)$$

Thus, indeed,

$$EV_T^P > EV_T^Q \quad \text{as } T \rightarrow \infty.$$

If we score each game by the same function of g (rather than the same function of W_T) then the max E log rule *is* asymptotically optimal.

Suppose we wish to compare the performances of two investment strategies for varying horizons: for example, for a 5-year period, a 10-year period, . . . , a 50-year period, etc. How should we decide whether increasing time is more favorable to one than the other? No matter how long or short the horizon, there is *some* chance that one will do better, and *some* chance the other will do better. The question is how to "add up" these various possibilities. One way—the constant utility of final wealth way—assumes that the trade-offs should be the same between making a dollar grow to \$1.10 versus \$1.20 versus \$1.30 after 50 years as after 5 years. The other way—constant utility of rate of growth—assumes that the trade-offs should be the same between achieving a 3 percent, 6 percent and 9 percent rate of growth during the 5 or 50 years. For a fixed T, any utility of final wealth $U(W_t)$ can be expressed as a utility of growth $f(g) = U(W_0(1+g)^T)$. But, as our example illustrates, assuming that U remains the same versus assuming f remains the same as T increases has very different implications for the asymptotic optimality of the max E log rule.

17.7 Summary

One argument in favor of the *E* log rule is that (under broad assumptions) eventually the wealth of the investor who follows the rule will become greater than, and stay greater forever than, an investor who follows a distinctly different strategy. Samuelson's argument against the rule is that if the investor seeks to maximize the expected value of a certain kind of function of final wealth, for a long game of fixed length, then maximizing *E* log is *not* the optimal strategy. Indeed, if we let the length of the game increase, the utility supplied by the max *E* log strategy does not even approach that supplied by the optimum strategy. This assumes that utility of final wealth remains the same as game length varies. On the other hand, if we assume that it is the utility of rate-of-growth-achieved, rather than utility of final wealth, that remains the same as length of game varies, then the *E* log rule *is* asymptotically optimal.

As Keynes said, "In the long run we are all dead." Even if you buy the notion, for either reason, that the max *E* log rule is asymptotically optimal for the investor who lets her, his, or its money ride, it may not be optimal for the individual or institution with fixed or random cash flow needs. Perhaps this is a sufficient caveat to attach to the observation that the cautious investor should not select a mean-variance efficient portfolio higher on the frontier than the point which approximately maximizes expected log (1 + return); for a point higher on the frontier subjects the investor to greater volatility in the short run and, almost surely, no greater rate-of-growth in the long run.

References

Breiman, Leo (1960). "Investment policies for expanding businesses optimal in a long run sense," *Naval Research Logistics Quarterly*, 7(4), 647–651.

—— (1961). "Optimal gambling systems for favorable games," *Fourth Berkeley Symposium on Probability and Statistics*, I, 65–78.

Kelly, J. L., Jr (1956). "A new interpretation of information rate," *Bell System Technical Journal*, 917–926.

Latane, H. A. (1957). "Rational decision making in portfolio management," *Ph.D. dissertation, University of North Carolina*. Chapel Hill, NC.

——. (1959). "Criteria for choice among risky ventures," *Journal of Political Economy*, April. LXVII No. 2, pp. 144–155.

Markowitz, H. M. (1959). *Portfolio Selection: Efficient Diversification of Investments*. New York: John Wiley & Sons, Yale University Press, 1972.

——. (1976). "Investment for the long run: New evidence for an old rule," *The Journal of Finance*, XXXI (5), 1273–1286.

Mossin, Jan (1968). "Optimal multiperiod portfolio policies," *Journal of Business*, 41 (2), 215–229.

Samuelson, P. A. (1963). "Risk and uncertainty: a fallacy of large numbers," *Scientia*, 6th Series, 57th year, April–May. pp. 153–158.

——. (1969). "Lifetime portfolio selection by dynamic stochastic programming," *Review of Economics and Statistics*, August. Vol. 51, No. 3, pp. 239–246.

——. (1979). "Why we should not make mean log of wealth big through years to act are long." Journal of Banking and Finance 3, pp. 305–307, North-Holland Publishing Company.

18

Paul Samuelson and Financial Economics

Robert C. Merton

18.1 Introduction

It has been well said that Paul A. Samuelson is the last great general economist—never again will any one person make such foundational contributions to so many distinct areas of economics. His profound theoretical contributions over nearly seven decades of published research have been ecumenical and his ramified influence on the whole of economics has led economists in just about every branch of economics to claim him as one of their own. I am delighted to take part in this celebration of his life and work.

This volume provides a special opportunity to honor this universal man of economics as he enters his tenth decade. On such Festschrift occasions, the common practice is to write a substantive piece building upon the honoree's work. However, here I try my hand at a different format: synthesizing Samuelson's work in financial economics itself. As everyone knows, Paul Samuelson is his own best synthesizer and critic, and so the format as executed will only be at best second-best.[1] Synthesis, we know, involves abstraction from the complex original. With Samuelson, we must be severely selective since even with confinement to a single branch of economics, the wide-ranging scope and unflagging volume of his researches allows only a few elements of the work to be examined. Within that brute reality, I limit my discussion to just three of his chief contributions to the field of financial economics: (1) The Efficient Market Hypothesis; (2) Warrant and option pricing; and (3) Investing for the long run.

Happily, I had the great good fortune to explore this same synthesizing theme in print nearly a quarter century ago (Merton, 1983), covering early major contributions of Samuelson—a number of which are not discussed here—such as expected utility theory (from reconciling its axioms with nonstochastic theories of choice to its reconciliation with the ubiquitous and practical mean-variance criterion of choice), the foundations of diversification and optimal portfolio selection when facing fat-tailed, infinite-variance return distributions.[2] As we shall see, however, it is remarkable how much of Samuelson's early research remains in the mainstream of current financial economic thought decades later, having gained even greater significance to the field with the passage of time.[3] Samuelson's discoveries in finance theory, as in economic theory generally, constitute the manifest core of his multiform writings. His accomplishments in both the problem-finding and problem-solving domains of theory are legend. Another, latent but no less deep, theme of Samuelson's writings is trying to divert us away from the paths of error, whether in finance research, private-sector finance practice, or public finance policy.

Samuelson's attacks on error are not limited to engagements in the economics arena. He has, upon occasion, used the life works of other economists to discredit the widely held myth in the history of science that scientific productivity declines after a certain chronological age. The strongest debunking of this ill-founded belief would, of course, have been the self-exemplifying one. While my brief search of the literature produced neither an exact cutoff age where productivity is purported to decline nor whether this decline is to be measured by the flow of research output per unit time or by its rate of change, the data provided by Paul Samuelson's lifetime pattern of contributions are robust in rejecting this proposed result on all counts. Representing twenty-seven years of scientific writing from 1937 to the middle of 1964, the first two volumes of his Collected Scientific Papers contain 129 articles and 1772 pages. These were followed by the publication in 1972 of the 897-page third volume, which registers the succeeding seven years' product of seventy-eight articles published when he was between the ages of 49 and 56. A mere five years later, at the age of 61, Samuelson had published another eighty-six papers, which fill the 944 pages of the fourth volume. A decade later the fifth volume appeared with 108 articles and 1064 pages. Simple extrapolation (along with a glance at his list of publications since 1986) assures us that the sixth and even a seventh volume cannot be far away.

Nearly a quarter century ago, I presented Paul with a list of his then thirty articles in financial economics and asked him to select his favorite ones, leaving the criteria for choice purposely vague. By the not-so-tacit demanding criterion that was evidently applied, he was drastically selective, choosing only six. I list these below. Four of the six articles appear in journals not on the beaten path of most economists, but happily they are reproduced in Samuelson's Collected Scientific Papers.

18.1.1 Paul Samuelson's 1982 Selection of his Favorite Financial Economics Papers

1. "Probability, utility, and the independence axiom," *Econometrica,* 20 (4), 1952, 670–678; (1952b, I, Chap. 14).
2. "General proof that diversification pays," *Journal of Financial and Quantitative Analysis,* 2(1), 1967, 1–13; (1967a, III, Chap. 201).
3. "The fundamental approximation theorem of portfolio analysis in terms of means, variances, and higher moments," *Review of Economic Studies,* 37(4), 1970, 537–542; (1970a, III, Chap. 203).
4. "Stochastic speculative price," *Proceedings of the National Academy of Sciences, U.S.A.,* 68(2), 1971, 335–337; (1971a, III, Chap. 206).
5. "Proof that properly anticipated prices fluctuate randomly," *Industrial Management Review,* 6(2), 1965, 41–49; (1965a, III, Chap. 198).
6. "Rational theory of warrant pricing," *Industrial Management Review,* 6(2), 1965, 13–39; (1965b, III, Chap. 199).

Perhaps a bit selfishly, we in financial economics are especially thankful that Paul paid no heed to the myth of debilitating age in science. Five of the six articles he selected in 1982 as his most important papers in our branch of economics and all but six of his more than three-score contributions to our field to date were published after he had reached the age of fifty.

Along with his foundational research and important directives on avoiding the paths of error, there are the characteristic Samuelsonian observations in the history of economic science. Samuelson's writings on Smith, Ricardo, Marx, and his many essays on the evolution of more contemporary economic thought provide much grist for the mill-of-the-historian of science. But, to focus exclusively on those explicit undertakings in the history of economic science is to miss much. Part of an unmistakable stamp of a Paul Samuelson article is the interjections of anecdotes and stories around and between his substantive derivations, which serve to entertain and enlighten the reader on the developmental chain of thought underlying that substantive analysis.

One happy example in financial economics is Samuelson's brief description in the "Mathematics of Speculative Price" (1972a, IV, Chap. 240, p. 428) of the rediscovery of Bachelier's pioneering work on the pricing of options. In the text, he wrote:

In 1900 a French mathematician, Louis Bachelier, wrote a Sorbonne thesis on the *Theory of Speculation*. This was largely lost in the literature, even though Bachelier does receive occasional citation in standard works on probability. Twenty years ago a circular letter by L. J. Savage (now, sadly, lost to us), asking whether economists had any knowledge or interest in a 1914 popular exposition by Bachelier, led to his being rediscovered. Since the 1900 work deserves an honored place in the physics of Brownian motion as well as in the pioneering of stochastic processes, let me say a few words about the Bachelier Theory.*

The footnote elaborates

*Since illustrious French geometers almost never die, it is possible that Bachelier still survives in Paris supplementing his professional retirement pension by judicious arbitrage in puts and calls. But my widespread lecturing on him over the last 20 years has not elicited any information on the subject. How much Poincaré, to whom he dedicates the thesis, contributed to it, I have no knowledge. Finally, as Bachelier's cited life works suggest, he seems to have had something of a one-track mind. But what a track! The rather supercilious references to him, as an unrigorous pioneer in stochastic processes and stimulator of work in that area by more rigorous mathematicians such as Kolmogorov, hardly does Bachelier justice. His methods can hold their own in rigor with the best scientific work of his time, and his fertility was outstanding. Einstein is properly revered for his basic, and independent, discovery of the theory of Brownian motion 5 years after Bachelier. But years ago when I compared the two texts, I formed the judgment (which I have not checked back on) that Bachelier's methods dominated Einstein's in every element of the vector. Thus, the Einstein–Fokker–Planck–Fourier equation for diffusion of probabilities is already in Bachelier, along with subtle uses of the now-standard method of reflected images.

In addition to providing the facts on how Bachelier's seminal work found its way into the mainstream of financial economics after more than a half century of obscurity, Samuelson's compact description provides a prime example of multiple and independent discoveries across the fields of physics, mathematics, and economics.[4] On the issue of allocating the credit due to innovative scholars, he also provides an evaluation of the timing and relative quality of the independent discoveries. His mention of Poincaré provides a hint that there may be still more to the complete story. Furthermore, note his signature use of a chain of eponyms, the "Einstein–Fokker–Planck–Fourier equation," to compactly remind us of the sequence of scientists to whom we owe credit. And, of course, what economist would not relish this revelation of the great debt owed to this early financial economist by the mathematical physicists and probabilists to be added to the well-known debt owed to Malthus by the Darwinian biologists?

Although most would agree that finance, micro investment theory and much of the economics of uncertainty are within the sphere of modern financial economics, the boundaries of this sphere, like those of other specialties, are both permeable and flexible. It is enough to say here that the core of the subject is the study of the individual behavior of households in the intertemporal allocation of their resources in an environment of uncertainty and of the role of economic organizations in facilitating these allocations. It is the complexity of the interaction of time and uncertainty that provides intrinsic excitement to study of the subject, and, indeed, the mathematics of financial economics contains some of the most interesting applications of probability and optimization theory. Yet, for all its seemingly obtrusive mathematical complexity, the research has had a direct and significant influence on practice. The impact of efficient market theory, portfolio selection, risk analysis, and option pricing theory on asset management and capital budgeting procedures is evident from even a casual comparison of current practices with, for example, those of the early 1960s when Paul Samuelson was just publishing his early foundational papers in finance.

New financial product and market designs, improved computer and telecommunications technology, and advances in the science of finance during the past four decades have led to dramatic and rapid changes in the structure of global financial markets and institutions. The scientific breakthroughs in financial economics in this period both shaped and were shaped by the extraordinary flow of financial innovation, which coincided with those changes. The cumulative impact has significantly affected all of us—as users, producers, or overseers of the financial system.

The extraordinary growth in size and scope of financial markets and financial institutions including the creation of the enormous national mortgage market in the United States were significantly influenced by the models developed in financial economic research. The effects of that research have also been observed in legal proceedings such as appraisal cases, rate of return hearings for regulated industries, and revisions of the "prudent person" laws governing behavior for fiduciaries. Evidence that this influence on practice will continue can be found in the curricula of the best-known schools of management where the fundamental financial research papers (often with their mathematics included) are routinely assigned to MBA students. Although not unique, this conjoining of intrinsic intellectual interest with extrinsic application is a prevailing theme of research in financial economics. Samuelson, once again, did much to establish this theme as a commonplace and to exemplify it in his substantive writings.

It was not always thus. Fifty years ago, before the birth of the economics of uncertainty and before the rediscovery of Bachelier, finance was essentially a collection of anecdotes, rules of thumb, and manipulations of accounting data with an almost exclusive focus on corporate financial management. The most sophisticated technique was discounted value and the central intellectual controversy centered on whether to use present value or internal rate of return to rank corporate investment projects. The subsequent evolution from this conceptual potpourri to a rigorous economic theory subjected to systematic empirical examination was the work of many and, of course, the many included Paul Samuelson.

After this brief overview of Samuelson's multifaceted influence on the ethos of financial economic research, I turn now to that promised discussion of three of his chief contributions to the field.

18.2 The Efficient Market Hypothesis

A question repeatedly arises in both financial economic theory and practice: When are the market prices *of* securities traded in capital markets equal to the best estimate *of* their values? I need hardly point *out* that if value is defined as "that price at which *one* can either buy or sell in the market," then the answer is trivially "always." But, of course, the question is rarely, if ever, asked in this tautological sense, although the distinction between value and price is often subtle. Moreover, as the following examples suggest, the answer to this question has important implications for a wide range of financial economic behavior.

In the fundamentalist approach of Graham and Dodd to security analysis, the distinction between value and price is made in terms of the (somewhat vague) notion of intrinsic value. Indeed, the belief that the market price of a security need not always equal its intrinsic value is essential to this approach because it is disparities such as these that provide meaningful content to the classic prescription for successful portfolio management: buy low (when intrinsic value is larger than market price) and sell high (when intrinsic value is smaller than market price).

In appraisal law, the question is phrased in terms of how much weight to give to market price in relation to other nonmarket measures of value in arriving at a fair value assessment to compensate those whose property has been involuntarily expropriated. In corporation finance, the answer to that question determines the extent to which corporate managers should rely upon capital market prices as the correct signals for the firm's production and financing decisions.

Characteristically, Samuelson's version provides both a clear distinction between value and price and a focus on the broadest and most important issue raised by this question: When are prices in a decentralized capital market system the best estimate of the corresponding shadow values of an idealized central planner who efficiently allocates society's resources? Thus, in "Mathematics of Speculative Price" (1972a, IV, Chap. 240, p. 425), he wrote

> A question, for theoretical and empirical research and not ideological polemics, is whether real life markets—the Chicago Board of Trade with its grain futures, the London Cocoa market, the New York Stock Exchange, and the less-formally organized markets (as for staple cotton goods), to say nothing of the large Galbraithian corporations possessed of some measure of unilateral economic power—do or do not achieve some degree of dynamic approximation to the idealized "scarcity" or shadow prices. In a well-known passage, Keynes has regarded speculative markets as mere casinos for transferring wealth between the lucky and unlucky. On the other hand, Holbrook Working has produced evidence over a lifetime that futures prices do vibrate randomly around paths that a technocrat might prescribe as optimal. (Thus, years of good crop were followed by heavier carryover than were years of bad, and this before government intervened in agricultural pricing.)

As we know, such theoretical shadow prices are "prices never seen on land or sea outside of economics libraries." However, testable hypotheses can be derived about the properties that real-life market prices must have if they are to be the best estimate of these idealized values. Because it is intertemporally different rather than spatially different prices that are of central interest in financial economics, most of Samuelson's analyses in this area are developed within the context of a futures market. In his 1957 "Intertemporal Price Equilibrium: A Prologue to the Theory of Speculation" (1957, II, Chap. 73), however, he does use spatial conditions of competitive pricing as tools to deduce the corresponding conditions on intertemporal prices in a certainty environment. From these local "no-arbitrage conditions," he proves that the current futures price must be equal to the future spot price for that date. In completing his analysis of the price behavior over time, he shows that the dynamics of "allocation-efficient" spot prices can be determined as the formal solution to a particular optimal control problem.[5]

Samuelson underscores his use of the word *Prologue* in the title by pointing out that "A theory of speculative markets under ideal conditions of certainty is Hamlet without the Prince," (p. 970). Indeed, his later papers, "Stochastic Speculative Price" (1971a, **III**, Chap. 206), "Proof That Properly Anticipated Prices Fluctuate Randomly" (1965a, **III**, Chap. 198), and "Rational Theory of Warrant Pricing" (1965b, **III**, Chap. 199), have in common their deriving the stochastic dynamic behavior of prices in properly functioning speculative markets. They also share the distinction of being important papers published in obscure places, which nevertheless found their way into the mainstream. Such occurrences suggest that high visibility of scientific authors may tend to offset low visibility of publication outlets.

Published in the same issue of the *Industrial Management Review*, "Proof That Properly Anticipated Prices Fluctuate Randomly" and "Rational Theory of Warrant Pricing" are perhaps the two most influential Samuelson papers for the field. During the decade before their printed publication in 1965, Samuelson had set down, in an unpublished manuscript, many of the results in these papers and had communicated them in lectures at MIT, Yale, Carnegie, the American Philosophical Society, and elsewhere. The sociologist or historian of science would undoubtedly be able to develop a rich case study of alternative paths for circulating scientific ideas by exploring the impact of this oral publication on research in rational expectations, efficient markets, geometric Brownian motion, and warrant pricing in the period between 1956 and 1965.

In "Proof That Properly Anticipated Prices Fluctuate Randomly," Samuelson provides the foundation of the efficient market theory that Eugene Fama independently and others have further developed into one of the most important concepts in modern financial economics. As indicated by its title, the principal conclusion of the paper is that in well-informed and competitive speculative markets, the intertemporal changes in prices will be essentially random. In a conversation with Samuelson, he described the reaction (presumably his own as well as that of others) to this conclusion as one of "initial shock—and then, upon reflection, that it is obvious." The time series of changes in most economic variables (GNP, inflation, unemployment, earnings, and even the weather) exhibit cyclical or serial dependencies. Furthermore, in a rational and well-informed capital market, it is reasonable to presume that the prices of common stocks, bonds, and commodity futures depend upon such economic variables. Thus, the shock comes from the seemingly inconsistent conclusion that in such well-functioning markets, the changes in speculative prices should exhibit no serial dependencies. However, once the problem is viewed from the perspective offered in the paper, this seeming inconsistency disappears and all becomes obvious.

Starting from the consideration that in a competitive market, if everyone *knew* that a speculative security was expected to rise in price by more (less) than the required or fair expected rate of return, it would *already* be bid up (down) to negate that possibility. Samuelson postulates that securities will be priced at each point in time so as to yield this fair expected rate of return. Using a backward-in-time induction argument, he proves that the changes in speculative prices around that fair return will form a martingale. And this follows no matter how much serial dependency there is in the underlying economic variables upon which such speculative prices are formed. Thus,

> We would expect people in the market place, in pursuit of avid and intelligent self-interest, to take account *of* those elements of future events that in a probability sense may be discerned to be casting their shadows before them. (Because past events cast "their" shadows after them, future events can be said to cast their shadows before them.) (1965a, III, Chap. 198, p. 785)

In an informed market, therefore, current speculative prices will already reflect anticipated or forecastable future changes in the underlying economic variables that are relevant to the formation of prices, and this leaves only the unanticipated or unforecastable changes in these variables as the sole source of fluctuations in speculative prices.

Samuelson is careful to warn the reader against interpreting his conclusions about markets as empirical statements:

> You never get something for nothing. From a nonempirical base of axioms, you never get empirical results. Deductive analysis cannot determine whether the empirical properties of the stochastic model I posit come close to resembling the empirical determinants of today's real-world markets. (1965a, III, Chap. 198, p. 783)

Nevertheless, his model is important to the understanding and interpretation of the empirical results observed in real-world markets.

Suppose that one observes that successive price changes are random (as empirically seems to be the case for many speculative markets). Without the benefit of Samuelson's theoretical analysis, one could easily interpret the fact that these prices wander like a drunken sailor as strong evidence in favor of the previously noted Keynes's view of speculative markets.

Whereas had it been observed that speculative markets were orderly with smooth and systematic intertemporal changes in prices, the corresponding interpretation (again, without Samuelson's analysis) could easily be that such sensible price behavior is (at least) consistent with that of the shadow prices of the idealized rational technocratic planner.

In the light of Samuelson's analysis, we all know that the correct interpretations of these cases are quite the reverse. For speculative market prices to correspond to their theoretical shadow values, they must reflect anticipated future changes in relevant economic variables. Thus, it is at least consistent with equality between these two sets of prices that changes in market prices be random. On the other hand, if changes in speculative prices are smooth and forecastable, then speculators who are quick to react to this known serial dependency and investors who are lucky to be transacting in the right direction will receive wealth transfers from those who are slow to react or who are unlucky enough to be transacting in the wrong direction. More important, under these conditions, current market prices are not the best estimate of values for the purposes of signaling the optimal intertemporal allocation of resources.

In studying the corpus of his contributions to the efficient market theory, one can only conclude that Paul Samuelson takes great care in what he writes. As is evident throughout his Proof paper and in his later discussion of the topic in "Mathematics of Speculative Price," (1972a, IV, Chap. 240) he is keenly aware of the ever present danger of banalization by those who fail to see the subtle character of the theory. Thus, having proved the general martingale theorem for speculative prices, he concludes

> The Theorem is so general that I must confess to having oscillated over the years in my own mind between regarding it as trivially obvious (and almost trivially vacuous) and regarding it as remarkably sweeping. Such perhaps is characteristic of basic results. (1965a, III, Chap. 198, p. 786)

Without Samuelson's careful exposition, the martingale property could easily be seen as either a simple deduction (whose truth follows from the very definition of competitive markets) or as a mere tautology. That is, subtract from any random variable, Y_t, its conditional expectation as of $t - 1$, $E_{t-1}[Y_t]$, and as a truism, the sum of the $\{Y_t - E_{t-1}[Y_t]\}$ will form a martingale. Indeed, in discussing the fair expected returns $\{\lambda_t\}$ around which speculative prices should exhibit the martingale property, Samuelson points out that

> Unless something useful can be said in advance about the $[\lambda_{T-i}]$– as for example, $\lambda_t - 1$ small, or λ_t a diminishing sequence in function of the diminishing variance

to be expected of a futures contract as its horizon shrinks, subject to perhaps a terminal jump in λ_1 as closing-date becomes crucial-the whole exercise, becomes an empty tautology. (1972a, IV, Chap. 240, p. 443)

But, of course, such restrictions can be reasonably imposed (using for example, the capital asset pricing model and the term structure of interest rates), and it is these restrictions that form the basis for testing the theory.

Many less precise discussions of the efficient market theory equate the theory with the property that speculative price changes exhibit a random walk around the fair expected return. However, Samuelson clearly distinguishes his derived martingale property from this much stronger one by showing that such changes need not be either independently or identically distributed for the theory to obtain. He is also careful to make the distinction between *speculative* prices that will satisfy the martingale property and *nonspeculative* prices (as well as other economic variables) that need not exhibit this property in a well-functioning market economy. In his "Stochastic Speculative Price" analysis, for example, the optimal stochastic path for the spot price of a commodity is shown not to satisfy the martingale condition for a speculative price. Indeed, only in periods of positive storage when the spot price also serves the function of a speculative price will the expected changes in the spot price provide a fair expected rate of return (including storage costs). "Thus," Samuelson remarks, "Maurice Kendall almost proves too much when he finds negligible serial correlation in spot grain prices" (1965a, III, Chap. 198, p. 783). I only allude to the import of this message for those in other areas of economics who posit and test models of rational expectations.

In preparing this chapter, I found in my files a 25-year-old unpublished manuscript of Samuelson's, "Nonlinear Predictability Though the Spectrum is White," which he had given to me with a kind invitation to once again become his coauthor and "revise as seems best."[6] As is clear from the title, Samuelson's intent was to provide a specific and empirically plausible model to underscore his point that "white noise" lack of (linear) serial correlation in stock returns is not sufficient to ensure the nonpredictability of those returns. As he describes it

The "efficient markets hypothesis" is sometimes overdramatized by the description that "speculative price behaves like a random walk." More exactly the correct hypothesis is that the speculative price is a *martingale* and therefore has a *zero* autocorrelelogram or "white spectrum" with a zero Pearsonian correlation coefficient between price changes in non-overlapping time periods.

Samuelson elaborates on the implications:

It follows from a zero autocorrelation that any "technical" or "chartist" method of prediction that depends on *linear* multiple correlation is doomed to failure. Econometricians commonly test, and often verify, the white-spectrum necessary condition for the efficient-market hypothesis. This *necessary* condition is *not*, however, *sufficient*. Zero autocorrelation would be equivalent to probabilistic independence (of "excess" returns) if the data were assuredly drawn from multivariate Gaussian distributions. However, for non-Gaussian distributions as with curvilinear functions of Gaussian variates, higher than second-moment tests must also be confirmed. Thus, the whiteness of spectrum with its guarantee of the *impotence of linear multiple regression prediction* is not at all a guarantee that *nonlinear* chartism will fail.

Although the file also contains some mathematical modeling of mine, apparently in anticipated acceptance of his invitation, the paper was neither completed nor circulated. I harbor the hope that with this rediscovery Paul will consider publishing it in full. In the meantime, I sketch out here a simplified version of his central thesis in an example from that modeling.

Let X_t denote the realized return on a stock minus its "fair" expected return between time $t-1$ and t. If the stock price satisfies the efficient market hypothesis, then the expected excess return on the stock will satisfy the martingale property that

$$E[X_t|X_{t-k}] = 0, \quad \text{for } k = 1, 2, 3, \ldots$$

Suppose however that the process for X_t is given by

$$X_t = a\varepsilon_{t-1}\left(\varepsilon^2_{t-1} - b\right) + \varepsilon_t$$

where the $\{\varepsilon_t\}$ are independently and identically distributed Gaussian random variables with zero mean and variance σ^2 and $a > 0$. Consider the linear serial correlation between the excess return from $t-1$ to t and the excess return from $t-k-1$ and $t-k$, given by

$$E\,[X_t X_{t-k}] = 0 \quad \text{for } k \geqslant 2 \text{ and all } a \text{ and } b$$

$$= a\left[E(\varepsilon^4_{t-1}) - bE(\varepsilon^2_{t-1})\right] \quad \text{for } k=1$$

$$= a\sigma^2\left[3\sigma^2 - b\right] \quad \text{for } k=1$$

If the stock price is efficient with respect to linear combinations of past returns, then we have that $E[X_t X_{t-k}] = 0$ for $k = 1, 2, 3\ldots$ and therefore

$b = 3\,\sigma^2$. Under that white-spectrum condition, we have that the conditional expected excess return is given by

$$E[X_t | \varepsilon_{t-1}] = a\varepsilon_{t-1}\left(\varepsilon_{t-1}^2 - 3\sigma^2\right)$$

By inspection,
$E[X_t | \varepsilon_{t-1}] > 0$ and one will earn a greater than fair expected return on the stock, that is, it is "undervalued" when either $\varepsilon_{t-1} > \sqrt{3}\sigma$ or $-\sqrt{3}\sigma < \varepsilon_{t-1} < 0$ and $E[X_t | \varepsilon_{t-1}] < 0$ and one will earn a less than fair expected return on the stock, that is, it is "overvalued" when either $0 < \varepsilon_{t-1} < \sqrt{3}\sigma$ or $\varepsilon_{t-1} < -\sqrt{3}\sigma$. Put in terms of the directly observable excess returns, we have that

$$E[X_t | X_{t-1}] = aX_{t-1}\left[X_{t-1}^2 + 18a^2\sigma^6 - 3\sigma^2\right],$$

which will not equal 0 in general and thus, the martingale test condition for the efficient market hypothesis fails.[7]

Thus, Samuelson concludes, "Despite the resulting impotence of *linear* prediction, the experienced eye will soon recognize that the example's white-spectrum series is anything but a random walk, instead being the archetype of a stationary time series that does lend itself to profitable *nonlinear* filtering." In a characteristically careful clarification, he goes on, "The point of this dramatic example is *not* to deny that numerous people in the marketplace may learn to recognize the predictability structure present in this time series—and, in so learning, may subsequently act to wipe out that structure. The point of the example is to illustrate how weak is the power of a test of mere *un*autocorrelation to appraise the efficiency and predictability of market prices."[8]

Samuelson not only exercises great theoretical care himself, but he also tries to induce such in his readers. On his derivation of the efficient market hypothesis, he warns, for example, against reading "too much into the established theorem:"

> It does not prove that actual competitive markets work well. It does not say that speculation is a good thing or that randomness of price changes would be a good thing. It does not prove that anyone who makes money in speculation is *ipso facto* deserving of the gain or even that he has accomplished something good for society or for anyone but himself. All or none *of* these may be true, but that would require a different investigation. (1965a, III, Chap. 198, p. 789)

Samuelson later undertook that investigation (1972b) and demonstrated that uninformed speculators (in later literature, also known as "noise traders") confer less benefit to society than their losses. In an extension of "Proof" (1973), he showed that the dynamics of properly discounted present values of assets must also exhibit the same martingale property.

In the last paragraph of "Proof," Samuelson concludes by raising a number of questions, all of which focus on an issue central to making operational his concept of properly anticipated prices. Namely, where are the basic probability distributions (for which the martingale property of speculative prices applies) to come from? Although he makes no pronouncements on this issue, by identifying it he opened gates to its resolution in the important later work by Fama (1970). Fama defines market efficiency in terms of a hierarchy of information sets that are the basis for forming the probability distributions. He shows that if changes in speculative prices (around their fair expected returns) form a martingale based upon the probability distribution generated by information set Φ then these price changes will also satisfy the martingale property for the distribution generated by any information set Φ' that is a subset of Φ. It therefore follows that if these prices do not satisfy the martingale property for information set Φ', they will not satisfy this property for any information set Φ that contains Φ' as a subset. Thus, Fama makes operational Samuelson's martingale requirement for properly anticipated prices by showing that it is possible to reject the martingale property (and hence, market efficiency) by using only a subset of the information available to any (or for that matter, all) investors. As Fama makes clear in his development of the strong, semi-strong, and weak versions of the efficient market theory, it is also possible for speculative prices to satisfy the martingale conditions for one information set but not to satisfy it for another.

The martingale property of speculative prices is the key element in Fama's development of procedures for testing market efficiency. Indeed, as Fama points out, virtually all empirical studies of speculative price returns (both pre- and post-"Proof") can be viewed as tests of this property and that remains the case to this day, which underscores further the significance of Samuelson's having established it as the crucial one for price behavior in an efficient market.

The early empirical studies focused on tests for serial correlation and comparisons of return performance between buy-and-hold and various simple filter-type trading strategies. While their results were on the whole consistent with market efficiency, these studies were, by necessity, limited to investigations of small numbers of securities and relatively short observation periods. This perhaps explains why the practicing financial community paid little attention to the results of those studies. However, with the development in the late 1960s of large-scale stock return data bases (principally at the University of Chicago Center for Research in Security Prices) and the availability of high-speed computers, there came an avalanche of tests of the efficient market theory, which were neither limited to a few securities nor to short observation periods.

Using return data on thousands of securities over more than forty years of history, some of the studies extended the earlier work comparing buy-and-hold with various mechanical trading strategies. Others, such as the Jensen (1968) study of mutual fund performance, broke new ground and analyzed the performance of real-life portfolio managers. In collectively echoing the findings of the earlier limited examinations, these large-scale studies put to final rest the myth that professional money managers can beat the market by miles, and indeed, cast doubt on whether they could even beat it by inches.

As the evidence in support of the efficient market theory mounted, the results and their implications for optimal strategy were widely disseminated to both the investing professional and the investing public in popular and semi-popular articles written by a number of academics. Included in this number is Paul Samuelson. With the widespread dissemination of this mountain of accumulated evidence, the practicing financial community could no longer ignore the efficient market theory although, as is perhaps not surprising, few (at least among the money managers in that community) accepted it. Here again, Samuelson exercises great care in his writings on this controversial issue by always keeping clear the distinction between "not rejecting" and "accepting" the efficient market theory. In discussing the controversy between practicing investment managers and academics in "Challenge to Judgment" (1974b, IV, Chap. 243, pp. 479–480), for example, he writes:

> Indeed, to reveal my bias, the ball is in the court of the practical men: it is the turn of the Mountain to take a first step toward the theoretical Mohammed,... If you oversimplify the debate, it can be put in the form of the question,
>
> Resolved, that the best of money managers cannot be demonstrated to be able to deliver the goods of superior portfolio-selection performance.
>
> Any jury that reviews the evidence, and there is a great deal of relevant evidence, must at least come out with the Scottish verdict:
>
> Superior investment performance is unproved.

With characteristic clarity, Samuelson provides a constructive perspective on the controversy by pointing out that while the existing evidence does not prove the validity of the efficient market theory, the burden of proof belongs to those who believe it to be invalid. In his final paragraph of

"Challenge to Judgment," (1974b, p. 485), he summarizes the point:

> What is interesting is the empirical fact that it is virtually impossible for academic researchers with access to the published records to identify any members of the subset with flair. This fact, although not an inevitable law, is a brute fact. The ball, as I have already noted, is in the court of those who doubt the random walk hypothesis. They can dispose of the uncomfortable brute fact in the only way that any fact is disposed of—by producing brute evidence to the contrary.

Later in the same journal, Samuelson revisits the question of market efficiency in real-world markets measured in terms of possible superior investment performance:

> Fifteen years have passed since my "challenge to judgment." What has been the further testimony of the 1970s and 1980s? What, in sum, is the judgment of 1989 economic science on the challenge to judgment?
>
> Broadly speaking, the case for efficient markets is a bit stronger in 1989 than it was in 1974, or in 1953 when Holbrook Working and Maurice Kendall were hypothesizing that stock and commodity price changes are pretty much a random walk (or a white-noise martingale). (1989b, p. 5)

5 years later, he reconfirms his position:

> To commemorate this Journal's fifteen years of success, I reviewed the cogency and accruing empirical verisimilitude of that agnostic questioning of activistic judgmental investing. By and large, the ball that was put in the court of the would-be judgment-mongers never did get returned with point-winning velocity. The jury of history did not find systematic inefficiency that exercisers of judgment could use to achieve excess risk-corrected returns.
>
> We can expect the debate to go on. And that tells you something about the approximate microefficiency of the organized markets where widely owned securities are traded. (1994, p. 15)

However, Samuelson is discriminating in his assessment of the efficient market hypothesis as it relates to real-world markets. He notes a list of the "few not-very-significant apparent exceptions" to microefficient markets (1989b, p. 5). He also expresses belief that there are exceptionally talented people who can probably garner superior risk-corrected returns... and names a few. He does not see them as offering a practical broad alternative investment prescription for active management since such talents are few and hard to identify. As Samuelson believes strongly in microefficiency of the markets, so he expresses doubt about *macro*-market efficiency, supporting the views of Franco Modigliani and Robert Shiller.

There is no doubt that the mainstream of the professional investment community has moved significantly in the direction of Paul Samuelson's position during the 30 years since he issued his challenge. Indexing as either a core investment strategy or a significant component of institutional portfolios is ubiquitous and even among those institutional investors who believe they can deliver superior performance, performance is typically measured incrementally relative to an index benchmark and the expected performance increment to the benchmark is generally small compared to the expected return on the benchmark itself. It is therefore with no little irony that as investment practice has moved in this direction these last 15 years, academic research has moved in the opposite direction, strongly questioning even the microefficiency case for the efficient market hypothesis. The conceptual basis of these challenges come from theories of asymmetric information and institutional rigidities that limit the arbitrage mechanisms which enforce microefficiency and of cognitive dissonance and other systematic behavioral dysfunctions among individual investors that purport to distort market prices away from rationally determined asset prices in identified ways. A substantial quantity of empirical evidence has been assembled, but there is considerable controversy over whether it does indeed make a strong case to reject market microefficiency in the Samuelsonian sense.[9] What is not controversial at all is that Paul Samuelson's efficient market hypothesis has had a deep and profound influence on finance research and practice for the past 40 years and all indications are that it will continue to do so well into the future.

18.3 Warrant and Option Pricing

If one were to describe the important research gains in financial economics during the 1960s as "the decade of capital asset pricing and market efficiency," then surely one would describe the corresponding research gains in the 1970s as "the decade of option and derivative security pricing." Once again, Samuelson was ahead of the field in recognizing the arcane topic of option pricing as a rich area for problem choice and solution. His research interest in options can be traced back at least to the early 1950s when he directed Richard Kruizenga's thesis on puts and calls (1956). As is evident from that thesis, Samuelson had already shown that the assumption of an absolute random walk for stock prices leads to absurd prices for long-lived options, and this before the rediscovery of Bachelier's work in which this very assumption is made. Although Samuelson lectured on option pricing at MIT and elsewhere throughout the 1950s and early 1960s, his first published paper on the subject, "Rational Theory of Warrant Pricing," appeared in 1965 (III, Chap. 199). In this paper, he resolves a number of apparent paradoxes that had plagued the existing theory of option pricing from the time of Bachelier. In the process (with the aid of a mathematical appendix provided by H. P. McKean, Jr), Samuelson also derives much of what has become the basic mathematical structure of option pricing theory today.[10]

Bachelier postulates that stock prices follow a random walk so that the expected change in the stock price over any interval of time is zero. The limit of this stochastic process in continuous time in modern terms is called a Wiener process or a Brownian motion. Bachelier also postulated that the price of a call option (or warrant) that gives its owner the right to buy the stock at time T in the future for an exercise price of *$a* must be such that the expected change in the option price is also zero. From these postulates, Bachelier deduced that the option price, $W(X;\,T,\,a)$ must satisfy the partial differential equation

$$1/2\sigma^2 W_{xx}\left(X;T,a\right) - W_T\left(X;T,a\right) = 0$$

subject to the boundary condition $W(X;0,a) = \mathrm{Max}[0,\, X - a]$ where X is the price of the stock and σ^2 is the variance rate on the stock. The solution of this equation is given by

$$W(X;T,a) = (X-a)\Phi\left(\frac{X-a}{\sigma\sqrt{T}}\right) + \frac{1}{\sqrt{2\pi}}\exp\left[\frac{(X-a)^2}{2\sigma^2 T}\right]\sigma\sqrt{T}$$

where Φ ( ) is the standard normal cumulative density function. For an at-the-money option (i.e. $X = a$) and relatively short times to expiration T, the Bachelier rule that the value of option grows as $\sqrt{T}$ is a reasonable approximation to observed option prices. However, as Samuelson points out, for long-lived options the formula implies that the option will sell for more than the stock itself, and indeed, for perpetual options, ($T = \infty$), the value of the option is unbounded.

Samuelson traces this result to the absolute Brownian motion assumption which for T large implies the possibility of large negative values for the stock prices with nontrivial probability. Noting that most financial instruments have limited liability and, therefore, cannot have a negative price, Samuelson introduces the idea of "geometric Brownian motion" to describe stock price returns. By postulating that the logarithmic price changes, $\log [X_{t+T}/X_t]$, follow a Brownian motion (with possibly a drift), he shows that prices themselves will have a lognormal distribution and, therefore, this ensures that they will always be nonnegative. Moreover, because lognormal distributions preserve themselves under multiplication, stock returns will have a lognormal distribution over any time interval. Indeed, this geometric Brownian motion has become the prototype stochastic process for stock returns in virtually all parts of financial economics.

Using much the same procedure of Bachelier, but modifying his postulates to include the geometric Brownian motion and the possibility of a nonzero expected rate of return on the stock, α, Samuelson derives a partial differential equation for the option price given by

$$1/2\sigma^2 X^2 W_{xx}(X;T,a) + \alpha X W_x(X;T,a) - \beta W(X;T,a) - W_T(X;T,a) = O$$

subject to $W(X;\,0,\,a) = \text{Max}[O,\,X - a]$ where β is the required expected return on the option. For the case corresponding to Bachelier's where the required expected return on the option is the same as on the stock (i.e. $\beta = \alpha$), the solution can be written as

$$W(X;T,a) = X\Phi(h_1) - ae^{-\alpha T}\Phi(h_2)$$

where $h_1 \equiv [\log (X/a) + (\alpha + 1/2\sigma^2)T]/\sigma\sqrt{T}$ and $h_2 \equiv h_1 - \sigma\sqrt{T}$.

Even when $a = 0$, Samuelson's solution satisfies $W(X;\,T,\,a) \leq X$ for all X and T. Hence, the substitution of the geometric Brownian motion for the arithmetic one eliminates the Bachelier paradox. However, as the reader can readily verify for $X = a$ and T small, $W(X;\,T,\,a) \sim \sigma\sqrt{T}$ as in the Bachelier case.

Bachelier considered options that could only be exercised on the expiration date. In modern times, the standard terms for options and warrants permit the option holder to exercise on or before the expiration date. Samuelson coined the terms "European" option to refer to the former and "American" option to refer to the latter.[11] Although real-world options are almost always of the American type, published analyses of option pricing prior to his "Rational Theory" paper focused exclusively on the evaluation of European options and therefore did not include the extra value to the option from the right to exercise early.

Because he only requires that the option price be equal to Max $[O,\,X - a]$ at the expiration date, Samuelson's ("$\beta = \alpha$") analysis formally applies only to a European type of option. However, he also proves that his solution satisfies the strict inequality $W(X; T, a) > \text{Max}\ [0, X - a]$ for $T > 0$ and $\beta = \alpha \geq 0$. Thus, under the posited conditions, it would never pay to exercise a call option prior to expiration, and the value of an American call option is equal to its European counterpart. In consequence, he views the special "$\beta = \alpha$" case of this theory as incomplete and unsatisfactory. It is incomplete because it provides no explanation of early exercise of options or warrants. Although it resolves the Bachelier paradox, the theory is unsatisfactory because it creates a new one; namely, the value of a perpetual call or warrant, $W(X; \infty, a)$ is equal to the stock price, X, independently of the exercise price. That is, according to the theory, the right to buy the stock at any finite price a (where this right can never be exercised in finite time) is equal to the price of the stock (which in effect is an option to buy the stock at a zero exercise price where the right can be exercised at any time).

Although he rejects the special case *of* his theory when $\beta = \alpha$, Samuelson resolves both its incompleteness and its paradox within the context of *his* general theory by simply requiring that $\beta > \alpha$. He does so by first formally solving his differential equation for the value *of* a European warrant. He then shows that for $\beta > \alpha \geq 0$ and any $T > 0$, there exists a number $C_T < \infty$ such that $W(X; T, a) < X - a$ for all $X \geq C_T$. Thus, for $\beta > \alpha$, there is always a finite price for the stock at which it pays to exercise prior to the expiration date, and hence, the American feature of an option has positive value. He also shows that $\beta > \alpha$, $W(X; T, a) < X$ for $a > 0$ and the value of a European perpetual call option, $W(X; \infty, a)$ is zero.

Having established that the early exercise provision has value when $\beta > \alpha$, Samuelson then proves that the correct formula for an American call option or warrant will satisfy his partial differential equation subject to the boundary conditions: (1) $W(O; T, a) = 0$; (2) $W(X; 0, a) = \text{Max}\ [0, X - a]$; (3) $W(C_T; T, a) = C_T - a$; (4) $W_X(C_T; T, a) = 1$, which he calls the "high-contact" condition.[12] For those familiar with parabolic partial differential equations *of* this type, it may appear that the boundary conditions are overspecified. However, C_T, which is the time boundary *of* stock prices where the option should be exercised, is not known, and it is precisely the overspecification that permits the simultaneous determination of the option price and the time boundary. Of course, closed-form solutions to such boundary value problems are not easy to derive although Samuelson does solve the perpetual call option case. He also develops a recursive integral technique that is a precursor to the numerical approximation methods used to this day to solve these equations.

While Samuelson mentions the greater riskiness of a warrant over the stock and different tax treatment, his principal argument for the $\beta > \alpha$ case and possible early exercise is that the stock is paying or may pay dividends during the life of the warrant. As formulated in his differential equation, α is the expected rate of price appreciation in the stock and, therefore, will be equal to the expected rate of return on the stock only if there are no cash dividends. In the example he discusses at length, where the dividend rate is a constant fraction, δ, *of* the stock price, he shows that for the expected rate of return on the warrant to just equal that of the stock $\beta = \alpha + \delta$, and therefore, $\beta > \alpha$. This analysis also makes it clear why a perpetual warrant on a currently nondividend-paying stock will not have a price equal to the stock price (as predicted by the $\beta = \alpha$ theory): namely, it could only do so if it were believed that the stock would never pay a dividend.

As Samuelson would be the first to say, his 1965 warrant pricing theory is incomplete in the sense that it simply postulates the first-moment relations between the warrant and stock. Yet, the basic intuitions provided by his theory have been sustained by later, more complete, analyses. For example, his focus on dividends as the principal reason for early exercise of call options and warrants was later justified in his 1969 "A Complete Model of Warrant Pricing That Maximizes Utility" (III, Chap. 200) (He brought me along as his junior coauthor), where it was shown that dividends are the only reason for such early exercise. Still later, an arbitrage argument presented in Merton (1973) proves that this result holds in general. Earlier warrant pricing theories uniformly neglected the possibility of early exercise in the development of their evaluation formulas. Samuelson, in addition to proving that early exercise was a possibility, shows that the effect of this possibility on value can be quite significant especially for long-lived options and warrants. Furthermore, his demonstration that the schedule of stock prices at which the warrant should be exercised can be endogenously determined as part of a simultaneous solution for the warrant price provides one of the cornerstones of modern option pricing theory and its application to the evaluation of more complex securities.[13]

In a subsequent conversation with me, Samuelson contrasted the "Rational Theory" with its companion piece "Proof That Properly Anticipated Prices Fluctuate Randomly" by noting that "the results of the paper were not obvious," and that he "was not sure how they would come out until the work was done." Despite his obvious delight with the paper (I do not doubt that this is his favorite among his contributions to financial economics) and despite the many important contributions it contains, discussion of the paper led Paul to remark that "Too little is written about the 'near misses' in science." While far from unique in the history of science, Samuelson's "Rational Theory" is surely a prime example of such a near miss by an eminent scientist.

Open the financial section of a major newspaper almost anywhere in the world and you will find pages devoted to reporting the prices of exchange-traded derivative securities, futures, warrants and options. Along with the vast over-the-counter derivatives market, these exchange markets trade options and futures on individual stocks, stock index and mutual-fund portfolios, on bonds and other fixed-income securities of every maturity, on currencies, and on commodities including agricultural products, metals, crude oil and refined products, natural gas, and even, electricity. The volume of transactions in these markets is often multiple times larger than the volume in the underlying cash-market assets.[14] Options have traditionally been used in the purchase of real estate and the acquisition of publishing and movie rights. Employee stock options have long been granted to key employees.

In all these markets, the same option-pricing methodology is used both to price and to measure the risk exposure from these derivatives. However, financial options represent only one of several categories of applications for the option-pricing technology. "Option-like" structures are lurking everywhere.[15]

Virtually everyone would agree that the Black–Scholes option pricing model published in 1973 was the breakthrough that led to an explosion in option and derivative security pricing research in the 1970s that has had widespread impact on finance research and practice to the current time. I focus here only upon the development of the Black–Scholes option pricing formula and its relation to Samuelson's "Rational Theory" formula.

The foundation of the Black–Scholes model is that, at least in principle, a dynamic hedging strategy can be derived to form a riskless portfolio of the option, the stock, and riskless bonds. Moreover, if such a portfolio can be created, then to avoid the opportunity for arbitrage, it must yield a return exactly equal to that earned on a riskless bond. From this condition, it follows that there must be a unique relation among the option price, the stock price, and the riskless interest rate.

Of course, hedge strategies using a warrant or other convertible securities and the stock were not uncommon undertakings by practitioners long before 1973. Thorp and Kasouff's *Beat the Market* (1967) is devoted entirely to such hedging strategies. In his "Rational Theory" paper, Samuelson discusses at length (including numerical examples) the use of hedge positions between the warrant and the stock as a means for deriving bounds on the discrepancies between β and α. These bounds translate through his warrant pricing equation into bounds on the range of rational warrant prices. In this discussion, he goes on to mention that the opportunity cost or carrying charges for the hedge should be included and therefore, the riskless rate of interest would enter into the bounds. Thus, Samuelson had in his paper the hedging idea for restricting prices and the possibility that the interest rate would enter into the evaluation, both of them key elements in the Black and Scholes analysis. Yet, neither he nor the others pushed their ideas in this area the extra distance required to arrive at what became the Black–Scholes formula. As Samuelson later wrote in "Mathematics of Speculative Price" (1972a, IV, Chap. 240, p. 438),

> My 1965 paper had noted that the possibility of hedging, by buying the warrant and selling the common stock short, should give you low variance and high mean return in the $\beta > \alpha$ case. Hence, for dividendless stocks, I argued that the $\beta - \alpha$ divergence is unlikely to be great. I should have explored this further!

The most striking comparison to make between the Black–Scholes analysis and Samuelson's "Rational Theory" is the formula for the option price. In their derivation, Black and Scholes assume a nondividend-paying stock whose price dynamics are described by a geometric Brownian motion with a resulting lognormal distribution for stock returns.[16]

This is, of course, the identical assumption about stock returns that Samuelson made. Under these conditions, the Black–Scholes no-arbitrage price for a European call option, $F(X;\, T,\, a)$, is shown to be the solution to the partial differential equation

$$1/2\sigma^2X^2F_{xx}(X;T,a) + rXF_x(X;T,a) - rF(X;t,a) - F_T(X;T,a) = 0$$

subject to the boundary condition $F(X;\, 0,\, a) = \text{Max}[0, X-a]$ and where r is the (instantaneous) riskless rate of interest that is assumed to be constant over the life of the option. By inspection, this equation is formally identical to the one derived in the "Rational Theory" for the special "$\beta = \alpha$" case if one substitutes for the value of "a" the interest rate "r." It follows, therefore, that the Black–Scholes option pricing formula, $F(X;\, T,\, a)$, is formally identical to the Samuelson option pricing formula, $W(X;\, T,\, a)$, if one sets $\beta = \alpha = r$ in the latter formula.

It should be underscored that the mathematical equivalence between the two formulas (with the redefinition of the parameter α) is purely a formal one. That is, the Black–Scholes analysis shows that the option price can be determined without specifying either the expected return on the stock, α, or the required expected return on the option, β. Therefore, the fact that the Black–Scholes option price satisfies the Samuelson formula with $\beta = \alpha = r$ implies neither that the expected returns on the stock and option are equal nor that they are equal to the riskless rate of interest. Indeed, Samuelson notes in his "Mathematics of Speculative Price" (1972a) that even if α is known and constant, β will not be for finite-level options priced according to the Black and Scholes methodology. It should also be noted that Black–Scholes pricing of options does not require knowledge of investors' preferences and endowments as is required, for example, in the Samuelson–Merton (1969) warrant pricing paper. The "Rational Theory" is clearly a "miss" with respect to the Black–Scholes analysis. However, as this analysis shows, it is just as clearly a "near miss."

This said, it may seem somewhat paradoxical to suggest that the Black–Scholes breakthrough actually added to the significance of Samuelson's "Rational Theory" for the field, yet I believe it did. Before Black–Scholes, there were a number of competing theories of warrant and convertible security pricing. Some, of course, were little more than rules of thumb based on empirical analyses with limited data. Others, however, like the "Rational Theory," were quite sophisticated. The Black–Scholes analysis provides a degree of closure for the field on this issue, and thus renders these earlier theories obsolete. However, as noted here and as shown in detail in the Appendix to "Mathematics of Speculative Price" (Merton, 1972), virtually all the mathematical analysis in the "Rational Theory" (including its formidable McKean appendix) can be used (with little more than a redefinition of parameters) to determine the prices of many types of options within the Black–Scholes methodology. For example, consider options where early exercise can occur. As is shown in Merton (1973), one can solve for the Black–Scholes price of either a European or an American call option on a proportional-dividend-paying stock simply by substituting $\beta = r$ and $\alpha = r-\delta$ into the "Rational Theory" analysis of the "$\beta > \alpha$" case. Similar results obtain for the evaluation of put options.

As a second example, there is the solution in the McKean appendix for the price of an option on a stock whose return is a Poisson-directed process that is discussed in Cox and Ross (1976) and Merton (1976). As still a third example, there is the Samuelson development in the "Rational Theory" of the partial differential equation for option pricing and its solution that uses a limiting process of discrete-time recursive difference equations and a local binomial process for stock price returns. This development is formally quite similar to the simplified procedure for Black–Scholes option pricing presented in Cox–Ross–Rubinstein (1979) and Sharpe (1978) as well as to the numerical evaluation procedure for options in Parkinson (1977). In light of these consequences, Samuelson's "Rational Theory of Warrant Pricing" is some near miss!

18.4 Investing for the Long Run

In so many branches of economics, Paul Samuelson is a kind of gatekeeper. When he is not busy opening gates to new research problems for himself and an army of other economists to attack, he is busy closing gates with his definitive solutions. And in between, he somehow finds the time to convey to both the professional practitioner and the general public those important research findings that have survived the rigors of both careful analytical and empirical examination.

Samuelson's new discoveries in finance are foundational. However, his diligence in trying to subvert error is also deeply important to the field. Just as in investing where the most gold goes to those who show us how to make money, so the most academic gold (or credit) goes to new discoveries. But in investments, as Samuelson's work in efficient markets and portfolio theory amply demonstrates, there is also considerable value to being shown how not to lose money by avoiding financial errors. Just so, there is also considerable value to those who divert us away from the paths of error in research.

By defanging the St Petersburg Paradox, Samuelson (1960, 1977) has taught us not to unduly fear unbounded utility and, thereby, he has left intact the important body of research into the economics of uncertainty that is based upon the Hyperbolic Absolute Risk Aversion (HARA) family of utility functions, most of whose members are unbounded functions. While defending the legitimacy of the HARA family, he has also kept us from becoming enthralled with the enticing geometric mean maximization hypothesis where log utility, a particular member of the family, is proclaimed to be the criterion function for "super" rational choice.[17] Samuelson discriminates among brain children, and his success in saving the profession from being drawn further along these paths of error has been due in no small part to his willingness to reaffirm basic beliefs whenever, like the phoenix, some new version of an old error arises. Disposing of one version in his "The 'Fallacy' of Maximizing the Geometric Mean in Long Sequences of Investing or Gambling" (1971b, III, Chap. 207), Samuelson returned to battle a second one (this time taking me along as coauthor) in

"Fallacy of the Lognormal Approximation to Optimal Portfolio Decision Making Over Many Periods" (1974, IV, Chap. 245). Still later in 1979, he countered a third with his paper of the monosyllabled title, "Why We Should Not Make Mean Log of Wealth Big Though Years to Act Are Long?"

Beginning sometime in the early 1980s, a new fallacy, also associated with long-horizon investing, arose that over the next two decades would have a far greater impact on real-world practice than the fallacy of investing so as to maximize the expected log return on one's portfolio. This new fallacy prescription is that "Stocks are not risky in the long run." That is, over a long enough investment horizon, stocks will outperform risk-free long-maturity bonds and so investors with long-term investment goals such as saving for retirement should invest their retirement savings in equities.

This prescription, like the max expected log strategy, is driven formally by an assessment that one investment strategy will outperform another (or all others) with increasingly greater probability the longer the investment horizon, until in the limit of an infinite horizon, the probability of superior performance approaches 100 percent. As a matter of mere mathematics, it can indeed be shown that under relatively mild assumptions about the expected return on the stock market and its volatility, the probability that stocks will *underperform* bonds goes to zero as the horizon becomes infinite and that indeed over a 25–35 year horizon the estimated probability of such a "shortfall" is in low single digits. The apparent (asymptotic long run) dominance of stocks over bonds permits nearly universal and uniform advocacy for this investment policy, independently of individual economic status. Hence, it is argued that investors with a long-horizon goal should invest in stocks over bonds, *without regard to their risk-tolerance preferences*. Further "practical" support for this prescription was provided by observing that historical returns on the US stock market outperformed bonds over every (or nearly every) 15- or 20-year time period in the last century. Nearly every advice engine on the Internet offers this same age-dependent strategy as a fundamental principle of retirement saving. The same principle is central to asset allocation advice to corporate pension funds.

Characteristically, Samuelson recognized early on that the question of the effect of age on risk-taking and optimal portfolio selection was an important issue, worthy of careful scientific analysis. And so, in 1969, Samuelson published a paper on the optimal intertemporal portfolio selection and consumption problem, which applied the method of stochastic dynamic programming together with the Expected Utility criterion.

Although others studied the problem,[18] it was Samuelson who focused his analytical modeling on the substantive issue of age-dependent influences on portfolio allocations and often-discussed-but-not-well-defined related concepts such as "businessman's risk." He shows that risk-averse investors with constant-relative-risk-aversion (CRRA) utility functions (which includes the heralded log function) and facing the same investment opportunities each period of their investment life, would allocate the same fractions of their optimal portfolio between risky equities and safe short-term debt, *independently of their age*. And while this surely does not rule out age-dependent portfolio behavior for some preferences, it just as surely demonstrates that growing investment conservatism with age is not a robust optimization principle which obtains universally. And in particular, the Samuelson finding provides absolute counter-evidence against the claimed absolute dominance of investing in equities over bonds when the investment horizon becomes very long. And this is so even though the temporally independently and identically distributed returns for equities posited in the Samuelson model also satisfy the probability condition that as investment horizon increases, the probability that equities underperform bonds decreases, asymptotically approaching zero.

The period 1969–82 just after the publication of Samuelson's paper shows no widespread adoption of this prescription for long-horizon investors to allocate a large fraction of their portfolios to equities, perhaps because it was a very poor one for stock performance in the United States. The creation of ERISA and with it, the corporate pension fund industry in 1974 thus did not cause equities to become a significant part of pension fund portfolios immediately. However, by the late 1980s after some strong performing years, institutional pension-fund investors had moved their allocation to equities increasingly to the point of their dominating the typical portfolio. The large shift to equities was encouraged by the actuarial treatment of pension expenses that applied the traditional Law of Large Numbers approach to argue that expected returns on the pension asset portfolio could be treated as virtually sure-thing returns over the long horizon of pension liabilities and so projected pension expense would be reduced by holding larger expected return (and larger risk) equities instead of bonds. This "institutionalization" of the principle that "Stocks are not risky in the long run" was completed when the pension accounting rules were adopted that called for firms to use the *projected* pension expense in computing accounting earnings for the firm instead of the *realized* pension expense based on the actual performance of the pension fund portfolio, with any reconciliation of deviations between the two smoothly amortized over a 10-year period.

In a series of papers, Samuelson (1989b, c, 1990, 1994, 1997a, b) was quick and clear to define the issue: Investing in equities may well be part of an optimal investing strategy for pensions as elsewhere, so long as the risk that goes with the higher expected return on equities is properly accounted for in the decision. What is fallacious . . . and therefore dangerous . . . reasoning is the misapplication of the Law of Large Numbers to argue that these higher expected returns will turn into higher realized returns almost certainly, if one has a long enough horizon, and thus with a long horizon one need pay *no* attention to the risk component. Samuelson presented his position both in intuitive fashion and in very formal mathematical terms why the exclusive focus on diminishing probability of a shortfall from equities as horizon lengthens is not sufficient for dominance because it does not take into account the growing magnitude of the present value of the expected shortfall that occurs as horizon increases. That is, what matters is the product of the probability of stocks underperforming times the present value of the conditional expected shortfall when they do, and while the probability is declining, the present value of that expected shortfall is growing and so one needs to consider the net growth or decline of their product with horizon. Furthermore, it turns out that the product grows with longer horizon and thus, the shortfall risk in that sense is not declining at all but increasing.[19]

Samuelson along with others also highlighted the fallacy in simply taking the realized stock returns in the United States for the last century or more as statistically significant empirical proof of the dominance principle by pointing out that from a statistical perspective that long history is only a single sample. He then goes on constructively to specify the proper representation which uses the historical data in what is formally a "bootstrap" process to generate by Monte Carlo techniques the prospective distributions from the past. These distributions demonstrate that a significant shortfall risk does exist, even with a long horizon. Samuelson and others also noted that the data themselves are subject to selection bias in that the United States stock market performance over the twentieth century may not be an unbiased estimate of the future for it or any other country's. Had the focus instead been on the investment history over the same period in other countries, Argentina, Russia, and Japan for instance, the "obvious" empirical evidence for nearly sure-thing outperformance of stocks over bonds in the long run would hardly be so obvious.

Despite the cautioning writings of Samuelson and others on the subject, the influence of the "Stocks are not risky in the long run" principle actually expanded and grew enormously with the creation of

Define–Contribution 401k pension plans in the beginning of the 1990s, in which individuals are directly responsible for allocating their retirement savings. Every advice engine, whether on the Internet or at a mutual fund complex, had this as one of its foundational principles. The extraordinary performance of the US stock market in the 1990s only served to confirm the validity of the principle, even in the not so long run.[20] The related argument for age-dependent growing conservatism exemplified by the rule of thumb "Invest fraction 100 minus your age in stocks" was institutionalized by the mutual fund industry that offers life-cycle funds that adjust the stock-bond mix toward more bonds as one gets older. Having correctly educated investors on the power of diversification among assets as an efficient means for managing risk, intuitive explanations by analogy were put forward claiming that diversification across time works in a similar way to justify the principle of more stock allocation the longer the horizon. Indeed, the principle that one can earn high equity expected returns with virtually no risk if one has a long horizon is tailor-made for arguing that Social Security should consider funding with investments in equities whether in private accounts or the government-controlled fund.[21]

Throughout this period, Samuelson was steadfast in making the case that there are no shortcuts to taking into account risk. Because the performance of 401k plans go directly to individuals, he reiterated the points made by his 1969 paper that sensible preference functions for evaluating the risk-return trade-off do not necessarily lead to ever increasing allocations to stock as one has longer time until retirement. He demonstrated formally and in simple illustrations the fallacy of time diversification (1997b).

Characteristically, Samuelson having made the strong multidimensional case against universal age-dependent arguments for holding a larger fraction in stocks the longer the horizon until retirement, then goes on to investigate what characteristics of the return distribution would cause those counter-example CRRA-utility investors of his 1969 paper to hold more equities the longer the time until retirement. In Samuelson (1989a, 1991, 1997b), he shows that such age-dependent behavior will obtain if one replaces intertemporally independently and identically distributed stock returns (a "white noise" process) posited in his 1969 paper with stock returns that exhibit mean-reversion or negative serial correlation (what he calls a "red noise" process). However, he also shows that the age-dependent behavior can go in the opposite direction with a larger fraction of the portfolio allocated to risky equities the *shorter* the time left before retirement, if stock returns exhibit momentum or positive serial correlation (what he calls a "blue noise" process). Having made these affirmative cases when age-dependent portfolio allocation is optimal, he points out that the evidence for either mean-reversion or momentum in stock returns is hardly overwhelming. He concludes by reaffirming his position that stocks are risky in the short, intermediate, and long runs and that arguments for holding stocks based on a contrary belief are fundamentally flawed.

After the large three-year decline in equity markets and interest rates between 2000 and 2002, there were widespread, deep losses in corporate pension fund portfolios and in individual retirement accounts. Together with the fall in interest rates which caused pension liabilities to increase at the same time, the effect was to cause enormous shifts toward large underfunding of corporate pension plans, which in weakened industries such as steels, airlines, and automobiles has caused, or at least accelerated, bankruptcies. These failures in turn have caused the government insurer of corporate pensions, Pension Benefit Guarantee Corporation (PBGC), to incur enormous losses, going from a large reserve surplus to a huge negative shortfall on its balance sheet, raising the specter of another taxpayer-bailout as was experienced with deposit insurance and the thrift institutions in the 1980s. The ceiling on PBGC insurance coverage has in turn led to large losses in accrued pension benefits by higher-paid workers in these industries.

With these events, corporate plan sponsors, pension regulators, and other overseers have taken notice: Rating agencies are already taking into account pension underfunding on setting credit ratings and it is a safe prediction that they will move from there to recognizing that the risk as well as the expected return of pension fund assets, like any other risky asset of the corporation, needs to be taken into account in assessing the creditworthiness of the firm. The Financial Accounting Standards Board in the United States is currently studying widespread pension accounting reforms with focus on the use of projected pension expenses instead of actual expenses for determining earnings of the firm. Similar reforms are already further underway in the United Kingdom and in the setting of international accounting standards.

Today, 36 years after the publication of Samuelson's paper identifying and analyzing age-dependent optimal rules for long-horizon investing, we thus find that work at the center of some of the most important private- and public-sector finance-related policy issues around the world.

18.5 Afterword

As noted at the outset of my remarks, a prevailing theme of research in financial economics is the conjoining of intrinsic intellectual interest with extrinsic practical application. This research has significantly influenced the practice of finance whether it be on Wall Street, LaSalle Street, or in corporate headquarters throughout the world. In this regard, Paul Samuelson provides a sterling counterexample to the well-known dictum of Keynes that "practical men, who believe themselves to be quite exempt from intellectual influences, are usually the slaves of some defunct economist." Any attempt to trace *all* the paths of influence that Samuelson has had on finance practice is, of course, doomed to failure—we need only remember the seemingly countless editions of his basic textbook on which so many practitioners were reared.[22]

As in all fields where the research is closely connected with practical application, in financial economics, conflicts in problem choice are not uncommon between those that have the most immediate consequences for practice and those that are more basic. As is evident from the following excerpt from his Foreword to *Investment Portfolio Decision-Making* (1974c, IV, Chap. 244, p. 488), there is surely no doubt how Paul Samuelson resolves such conflicts in his own research.

My pitch in this Foreword is not exclusively or even primarily aimed at practical men. Let them take care of themselves. The less of them who become sophisticated the better for us happy few! It is to the economist, the statistician, the philosopher, and to the general reader that I commend the analysis contained herein. Not all of science is beautiful. Only a zoologist could enjoy some parts of that subject; only a mathematician could enjoy vast areas of that terrain. But mathematics as applied to classical thermodynamics is beautiful: if you can't see that, you were born color-blind and are to be pitied. Similarly, in all the branches of pure and applied mathematics, the subject of probability is undoubtedly one of the most fascinating. As my colleague Professor Robert Solow once put it when he was a young man just appointed to the MIT staff: "Either you think that probability is the most exciting subject in the world, or you don't. And if you don't, I feel sorry for you."

Well, here in the mathematics of investment under uncertainty, some of the most interesting applications of probability occur. Elsewhere, in my 1971 von Neumann Lecture before the Society for Industrial and Applied Mathematics, I have referred to the 1900 work on the economic Brownian motion by an unknown French professor, Louis Bachelier. Five years before the similar work by Albert Einstein, we see growing out of economic observations all that Einstein was able to deduce and more. Here, we see the birth of the theory of stochastic processes. Here we see, if you can picture it, radiation of probabilities according to Fourier's partial differential equations. And finally, as an anti-climax, here we see a way of making money from warrants and options or, better still, a way of understanding how they must be priced so that no easy pickings remain.

In short, *first things first.*

There is no need to dwell on the prolific and profound accomplishments of Paul Samuelson, which have become legend—especially when the legend is a brute fact. Rather I close with a few observations (drawn as his student, colleague, and coresearcher over nearly four decades) on some of Paul's modes of thought that perhaps make such super achievement possible. First, there is his seemingly infinite capacity for problem finding and his supersaturated knowledge of just about every special sphere of economics. Second, there is his speed of problem solving together with the ability to put the solution quickly to paper with great skill, great verve, and lack of hesitation. Third, strong opinions and decisive language are characteristic of Samuelson writings, and yet it is his willingness to change his views and admit errors that makes his steadfastness on some issues so credible. Finally, although often masked by the apparent ease with which he produces, there is his diligence. Paul has always worked hard.

On the matter of sustained hard work of this particular kind, Paul is fond of a story (and so, he repeated it in his Presidential Address to the International Economics Association) about the University of Chicago mathematician Leonard Dickson, who was to be found playing bridge all afternoon every afternoon. When a colleague asked how he could afford to spend so much of his time playing, Dickson is said to have replied: "If you worked as hard at mathematics as I do from 8–12, you too could play bridge in the afternoon." As Paul also notes in that address, the same story holds for the mathematician G. H. Hardy, who watched cricket rather than play bridge. I can improve on these yarns with one about Paul from the glorious days when as his research assistant I lived in his office. I was working (not very successfully) on the solution to an equation in warrant pricing that was needed for some research Paul was doing when he left for the tennis courts (as he often did). Sometime later, the phone rang. It was Paul calling from the courts (presumably between sets) to tell me exactly how that equation could be solved. Dickson and Hardy segregated creative work and well-earned play, and so, it appears, does Paul, but with a finite and significant difference. Even at play, he is at work.[23]

Notes

1. Samuelson offers us some brief synthesizing observations on foundational developments in the field in his recent "Modern Finance Theory Within One Lifetime (2002)," but characteristically he confines his remarks only to the contributions of others.
2. See Samuelson (1950, 1952a, b, 1967a, b, 1970a).
3. The explicit content of Samuelson's early work reviewed here, of course, has not changed but its subsequent application and impact on the field, both in breadth and depth, surely has. Hence, even when overlaps with my past writings occur, the substance of Samuelson's work warrants repeating here, especially when the originals appear in obscure places. Thus, when applicable, the text draws heavily on my 1983 essay.
4. See Taqqu (2001) for more on the Bachelier story.
5. As Samuelson notes with his typical great care, without the tranversality or other terminal boundary condition, these local arbitrage conditions are necessary but not sufficient to ensure an optimal path.
6. Samuelson's draft is not dated but I would estimate 1980. The acknowledgment helped pin it down: "We owe thanks to the National Science Foundation for financial aid and to Aase Hugins for editorial assistance. Hal Stern, an MIT senior, kindly tested the data to verify its conformity with theoretical expectations." Hal Stern graduated from MIT in 1981.
7. Note that within this model, excess returns exhibit both mean-reversion and momentum, depending on their size: mean-reversion behavior for small-in-magnitude excess returns and momentum behavior for large-in-magnitude returns. Thus, we have in this early Samuelson work a conditional combination of both his "red noise" and "blue noise" processes for stock returns that he introduces in later work (1989a, 1991, 1997b) to demonstrate possible properties of age-dependent optimal portfolio selection rules.
8. It can be shown that if investor learning is sufficient to wipe out the profitable trading structure, the resulting new excess return process for the model of the example will be $X_t = \varepsilon_t[1 + a(\varepsilon_t^2 - b)]$ for which the martingale property obtains.
9. See Lo and MacKinlay (1999). Merton and Bodie (2005, especially p. 4, footnotes 8 and 9) provide extensive references on both sides of the controversy.
10. Samuelson uses warrants instead of call options as the specific instrument examined in his paper, perhaps because at that time, warrants were listed and traded on exchanges and so price data were available whereas options were only traded through dealers with opaque pricing. Indeed, I tested the Samuelson pricing model in the late 1960s using prices of listed perpetual warrants [Merton, 1969]. Although there is a slight difference between the two in terms of dilution effects depending on whether the company is the issuer or not, the pricing models for warrants and call options are essentially the same and the terms are used interchangeably for purposes of the discussion here.

11. Samuelson started to formulate his theory of warrant and option pricing in the mid-late 1950s. As he often did, and still does, with a new area of research, he began then by talking to those in practice to get a sense of how it all works institutionally before proceeding with the formal model specification and theory development. So he went to New York to see a well-known put and call dealer (there were no traded options exchanges until 1973) who happened to be Swiss. After identifying himself and explaining what he had in mind, Samuelson was quickly told, "You are wasting your time—it takes a *European* mind to understand options." Later on, Samuelson understandably chose the term "European" for the relatively simple(-minded)-to-value option contract that can only be exercised at expiration and "American" for the considerably more-complex-to-value option contract that could be exercised early, any time on or before its expiration date.
12. Later authors refer to this as the "smooth-pasting" condition.
13. Merton (1972, 1973) proves that the Samuelson-posited "high-contact" condition is implied by the unique value-maximizing early-exercise strategy that rules out arbitrage possibilities.
14. A recent Federal Reserve estimate is that $270 trillion notational amount of derivatives are outstanding worldwide.
15. Examples are insurance contracts including deposit and pension insurance, loan guarantees, privatization of Social Security, prepayment of mortgages, farm price supports, oil-drilling and automobile leases, quotas on taxis and fishing, patents, tax and market timing, tenure, labor-force training, health plans, pay-per-view television, retail store shelf space, modularity and flexibility in production processes, drug discovery phasing, and movie sequel timing. See Merton (1992, 1998) for references. Jin *et al.* (1997) provide a live website with an extensive and growing listing of applications.
16. In a 1968 critique of the Thorp–Kasouff book, Samuelson quite correctly warns the reader that their reverse-hedge techniques in expiring warrants are no "sure-thing" arbitrage. Later (1972a, IV, Chap. 240, p. 438, n. 6), he reiterates a similar valid warning in his discussion of the Black–Scholes arbitrage argument. If, however, Samuelson had not discovered this overstatement in the Thorp–Kasouff analysis so quickly, then he might have used the occasion to pursue further his own earlier work in using hedge strategies to restrict the range of rational warrant prices. Perhaps this thought was in his mind when Paul commented to me on his 1968 review as one in which "I won farthings and lost pounds."
17. Cf. Kelly (1956), Latane (1959), Markowitz (1976), and Thorp (2004).
18. Other early developers of this problem include Edmund Phelps, Nils Hakansson, Hayne Leland, and Jan Mossin. I developed a continuous-time version.
19. Bodie (1995) provides an elegant demonstration of this point when he shows that the cost of buying "shortfall insurance" which is structurally a put option on equities with strike price equal to the forward price of the current value of

the portfolio, is an increasing function of the investment horizon. Through his foundational work on options, Samuelson contributed, albeit indirectly, to the Bodie demonstration as well.

20. Unfortunately the experience in Japan, the second largest economy in the world, during this period was quite the opposite: In 1989, the Japanese stock market hit a peak of over 39,000 and today, 16 years later, it is 14,700.
21. It has been noted by a number of observers including Paul Samuelson that the government has an even longer horizon than any pension plan and furthermore, with a central bank it has no short-term liquidity problems, and so if the no-long-term-risk-to-stock-returns principle applies validly to retirement savings, why not apply it to funding *all* government expenditures?
22. Bernstein (1992) nevertheless provides a rich description of the many paths of Samuelson's influence on modern Wall Street.
23. Happily, some things do not change. A few days ago, Paul called me (this time I was on a cell phone in a taxi cab) to discuss a certainty–equivalent calculation he was doing to demonstrate in still another enlightening way why the Kelly Criterion is not even near-optimal for those with nonlog preferences that also do not risk ruin. After he painstakingly described the detailed calculations he was performing in the mere two-period case, he asked whether they were correct. I responded that perhaps I could check them with pencil and paper after reaching my destination. Paul then reminded me that Student was (reputed to be) able to compute Pearsonian correlation coefficients in his head. The message was clear. After my later checking, Paul's calculations were indeed correct.

References

Bachelier, L. (1900). "Theorie de la Speculation," Paris: Gauthier-Villars, Cf. English translation in P. Cootner (ed.), *The Random Character of Stock Market Prices*, Cambridge, MA: MIT Press.

Bernstein, L. (2005). *Capital Ideas: The Improbable Origins of Modern Wall Street*. Hoboken, New Jersey: John Wiley & Sons, Inc..

Black, F. and M. Scholes (1973). "The pricing of options and corporate liabilities," *Journal of Political Economy*, 81, 637–659.

Bodie, Z. (1995). "On the Risk of Stocks in the Long Run," *Financial Analysts Journal*, Vol. 51 May–June, 18–22.

Cox, J., and S. Ross (1976), "The Valuation of Options for Alternative Stochastic Processes", *Journal of Financial Economics*, 3(January–March), 145–166.

Cox, J., S. Ross, and M. Rubinstein (1979). "Option pricing: A Simplified Approach," *Journal of Financial Economics*, 7, 229–263.

Fama, E. (1970). "Efficient capital markets: a review of theory and empirical work," *Journal of Finance*, 25, 383–417.

Jensen, M. (1968). "The performance of mutual funds in the period 1945–1964," *Journal of Finance*, 23, 389–416.

Jin, L., L. Kogan, T. Lim, J. Taylor, and A. Lo (1997). "The derivatives source book: a bibliography of applications of the Black-Scholes/Merton option-pricing model," MIT Sloan School of Management Laboratory for Financial Engineering Working Paper, Website: http://lfe.mit.edu/dsp/index.htm.

Kelly, J. L., Jr (1956). "A new interpretation of information rate," *Bell System Technical Journal*, 917–926.

Kruizenga, R. (1956). "Put and call options: a theoretical and market analysis," doctoral dissertation, MIT, Cambridge, Massachusetts.

Latane, H. A. (1959). "Criteria for choice among risky ventures," *Journal of Political Economy*, 67, 144–155.

Lo, A. and A. C. MacKinlay (1999). *A Non-Random Walk Down Wall Street*. Princeton University Press Princeton, New Jersey.

Markowitz, H. M. (1976). "Investment for the long run: new evidence for an old rule," *The Journal of Finance*, XXXI(5), 1273–1286.

Merton, R. C. (1969). "An Empirical Investigation of the Samuelson Rational Warrant Pricing Theory." Class paper, Massachusetts Institute of Technology, spring 1969, Chapter V in *Analytical Optimal Control Theory as Applied to Stochastic and Non-Stochastic Economics*, MIT Ph.D. dissertation, 1970.

—— (1972). " 'Continuous-time speculative processes': Appendix to P. A. Samuelson's 'Mathematics of Speculative Price'," in R.H. Day and S.M. Robinson (eds), *Mathematical Topics in Economic Theory and Computation*. Philadelphia; Society for Industrial and Applied Mathematics, reprinted in *SIAM Review*, 15, 1973, pp. 1–42.

—— (1973). "Theory of rational option pricing," *Bell Journal of Economics and Management Science*, 4, 141–183. R.C. Merton (1992), Chap. 8.

—— (1976). "Option pricing when underlying stock returns are discontinuous," *Journal of Financial Economics*, 3 (January–February) 125–144. R.C. Merton (1992), Chap. 9.

—— (1983). "Financial Economics," in *Paul Samuelson and Modern Economic Theory*, edited by E. C. Brown and R. M. Solow. New York: McGraw-Hill.

—— (1992). *Continuous-Time Finance*. Oxford, UK: Basil Blackwell, Revised Edition.

—— (1998). "Applications of option-pricing theory: twenty-five years later," *American Economic Review*, 88(3), 323–349.

—— and Z. Bodie (2005). "The design of financial systems: towards a synthesis of function and structure," *Journal of Investment Management*, 3(1), 1–23.

Parkinson, M. (1977): "Option pricing: the American put," *Journal of Business*, 50, 21–36.

Samuelson, P. A. (1966). *The Collected Scientific Papers of Paul A. Samuelson*, vols. I and II, J. E. Stiglitz (ed.), Cambridge: MIT Press.

——. (1972). *The Collected Scientific Papers of Paul A. Samuelson*, vol. III, R. C. Merton (ed.), Cambridge: MIT Press.

——. (1977). *The Collected Scientific Papers of Paul A. Samuelson*, vol. IV, H. Nagatani and K. Crowley (eds), Cambridge: MIT Press.

Samuelson, P. A. (1950). "Probability and the attempts to measure utility," *The Economic Review*, I, 167–173; *Collected Scientific Papers*, I, Chap. 12.

——. (1952a). "Utility, preference and probability," Conference on "Les fondements et applications de la theorie du risque en econometrie," Paris; *Collected Scientific Papers*, I, Chap. 13.

——. (1952b). "Probability, Utility, and the Independence Axiom," *Econometrica*, 20, 670–678; *Collected Scientific Papers*, I, Chap. 14.

——. (1957). "Intertemporal price equilibrium: a prologue to the theory of speculation," *Weltwirtschaftliches Archiv*, 79, 181–219; *Collected Scientific Papers*, II, Chap. 73.

——. (1960). "The St. Petersburg paradox as a divergent double limit," *International Economic Review*, I, 31–37; *Collected Scientific Papers*, I, Chap. 15.

——. (1963). "Risk and uncertainty: a fallacy of large numbers," *Scientia*, 57, 1–6; *Collected Scientific Papers*, I, Chap. 16.

——. (1965a). "Proof that properly anticipated prices fluctuate randomly," *Industrial Management Review*, 6, 41–49; *Collected Scientific Papers*, III, Chap. 198.

——. (1965b). "Rational theory of warrant pricing," *Industrial Management Review*, 6, 13–39; *Collected Scientific Papers*, III, Chap. 199.

——. (1967a). "General proof that diversification pays," *Journal of Financial and Quantitative Analysis*, 2, 1–13; *Collected Scientific Papers*, III, Chap. 201.

——. (1967b). "Efficient portfolio selection for pareto-levy investments," *Journal of Financial and Quantitative Analysis*, 2, 107–122; *Collected Scientific Papers*, III, Chap. 202.

——. (1968). "Book review of E.D. Thorp, and S. T. Kasouff *Beat the Market*," *Journal of American Statistical Association*, 10, 1049–1051.

——. (1969). "Lifetime portfolio selection by dynamic stochastic programming," *Review of Economics and Statistics*, 51, 239–246; *Collected Scientific Papers*, III, Chap. 204.

——. and R. C. Merton (1969). "A complete model of warrant pricing that maximizes utility," *Industrial Management Review*, 10, 17–46; *Collected Scientific Papers*, III, Chap. 200, and R. C. Merton (1992), Chap. 7.

——. (1970a). "The fundamental approximation theorem of portfolio analysis in terms of means, variances and higher moments," *Review of Economic Studies*, 37, 537–542; *Collected Scientific Papers*, III, Chap. 203.

——. (1970b). "Foreword," in R. Roll: *The Behavior of Interest Rates: An Application of the Efficient Market Model to U.S. Treasury Bills*. New York: Basic Books, Inc., pp. ix–xi; *Collected Scientific Papers*, III, Chap. 205.

——. (1971a). "Stochastic speculative price," *Proceedings of the National Academy of Sciences*, 68, 335–337; *Collected Scientific Papers*, III, Chap. 206.

——. (1971b). "The 'Fallacy' of maximizing the geometric mean in long sequences of investing or gambling," *Proceedings of the National Academy of Sciences*, 68, 2493–2496; *Collected Scientific Papers*, III, Chap. 207.

——. (1972a). "Mathematics of speculative price," in R. H. Day and S. M. Robinson (eds), *Mathematical Topics in Economic Theory and Computation*. Philadelphia: Society for Industrial and Applied Mathematics, reprinted in *SIAM Review*, 15, 1973, 1–42; *Collected Scientific Papers*, IV, Chap. 240.

——. (1972b). "Proof that unsuccessful speculators confer less benefit to society than their losses," *Proceedings of the National Academy of Sciences*, 69, 1230–1233; *Collected Scientific Papers*, IV, Chap. 260.

——. (1973). "Proof that properly discounted present values of assets vibrate randomly," *Bell Journal of Economics and Management Science*, 4, 369–374; *Collected Scientific Papers*, IV, Chap. 241.

——. and R. C. Merton (1974). "Fallacy of the log-normal approximation to optimal portfolio decision making over many periods," *Journal of Financial Economics*, I, 67–94; *Collected Scientific Papers*, IV, Chap. 245.

——. (1974a). "Comments on the favorable-bet theorem," *Economic Inquiry*, 12, 345–355; *Collected Scientific Papers*, IV, Chap. 248.

——. (1974b). "Challenge to judgment," *Journal of Portfolio Management*, 1, 17–19; *Collected Scientific Papers*, IV, Chap. 243.

——. (1974c). "Foreword," in J. L. Bicksler and P. A. Samuelson (eds), *Investment Portfolio Decision Making*, Lexington, D. C. Heath; *Collected Scientific Papers*, IV, Chap. 244.

——. (1976). "Is real-world price a tale told by the idiot of chance?" *Review of Economics and Statistics*, 58, 120–123; *Collected Scientific Papers*, IV, Chap. 242.

——. (1977). "St Petersburg paradoxes: defanged, dissected and historically described," *Journal of Economic Literature*, 15, 24–55.

——. (1979). "Why we should not make mean log of wealth big though years to act are long," *Journal of Banking and Finance*, 3, 305–307.

——. (1987). "Paradise lost & refound: The Harvard ABC barometers," *Journal of Portfolio Management*, Spring, 4–9.

——. (1989a). "A case at last for age-phased reduction in equity," *Proceedings of the National Academy of Science*, November, 9048–9051.

——. (1989b). "The judgment of economic science on rational portfolio management: indexing, timing, and long-horizon effects," *Journal of Portfolio Management*, Fall, 4–12.

——. (1989c). "The $\sqrt{N}$ law and repeated risktaking," in T.W. Anderson (ed.), *Probability, Statistics and Mathematics: Papers in Honor of Samuel Karlin*. San Diego, CA: The Academic Press, pp. 291–306.

——. (1990). "Asset allocation could be dangerous to your health," *Journal of Portfolio Management*, Spring, 508.

——. (1991). "Long-run risk tolerance when equity returns are mean regressing: pseudoparadoxes and vindication of 'Businessman's Risk'," in W. C. Brainard, W. D. Nordhaus, and H. W. Watts (eds), *Money, Macroeconomics, and Economic Policy*. Cambridge, MA: The MIT Press, pp. 181–200.

Samuelson, P. A. (1992). "At last a rational case for long horizon risk tolerance and for asset-allocation timing?," in Robert D. Arnott and Frank J. Fabozzi (eds), *Active Asset Allocation*. Chicago, IL: Probus Publishing Co.

——. (1994). "The long-term case of equities and how it can be oversold," *Journal of Portfolio Management*, Fall, 15–24.

——. (1997a). "Dogma of the day," *Bloomberg Personal Magazine*, January/February, 33–34.

——. (1997b). "Proof by certainty equivalents that diversification-across-time does worse, risk-corrected, than diversification-throughout-time," *Journal of Risk and Uncertainty*, 14(2), 129–142.

——. (2002). "Modern finance theory within one lifetime," in H. Geman, D. Madan, S. R. Pliska, and T. Vorst (eds), *Mathematical Finance Bachelier Congress 2000*. Berlin, Heidelberg, New York: Springer-Verlag, pp. 41–45.

Sharpe, W. F. (1978). *Investments*. Englewood Cliffs, NJ: Prentice Hall.

Taqqu, M. S. (2001). "Bachelier and his times: a conversation with Bernard Bru," *Finance and Stochastics*, 5(1), 3–32.

Thorp, E. O. and S. T. Kasouff (1967). *Beat the Market: A Scientific Stock Market System*. New York: Random House.

——.(2004). "A perspective on quantitative finance: models for beating the market," in Paul Wilmott (ed.), *The Best of Wilmott 1: Incorporating the Quantitative Finance Review*. New York: John Wiley & Sons.

Part II

Samuelson's Relevance

19

Multipliers and the LeChatelier Principle

Paul Milgrom

19.1 Introduction

Those studying modern economies often puzzle about how small causes are amplified to cause disproportionately large effects. A leading example that emerged even before Samuelson began his professional career is the Keynesian multiplier, according to which a small increase in government spending can have a much larger effect on economic output. Before Samuelson's LeChatelier principle, however, and the subsequent research that it inspired, the ways that multipliers arise in the economy had remained obscure.

In Samuelson's original formulation, the LeChatelier principle is a theorem of demand theory. It holds that, under certain conditions, fixing a consumer's consumption of a good X reduces the elasticity of the consumer's compensated demand for any other good Y. If there are multiple other goods, X^1 through X^N, then fixing each additional good further reduces the elasticity. When this conclusion applies, it can be significant both for economic policy and for guiding empirical work. On the policy side, for example, the principle tells us that in a wartime economy, with some goods rationed, the compensated demand for other goods will become less responsive to price changes. That changes the balance between the distributive and efficiency consequences of price changes, possibly favoring the choice of nonprice instruments to manage wartime demand. For empirical researchers, the same principle suggests caution in interpreting certain demand studies. For example, empirical studies of consumers' short-run responses to a gasoline price increase may underestimate their long-run response, since over the long run more consumers will be free to change choices about other economic decisions, such as the car models they drive, commute-sharing arrangements, uses of public transportation, and so on. However, the principle tells us those things only when its assumptions are satisfied, so Samuelson made repeated efforts during his career to weaken the assumptions needed for the principle to apply.[1]

Newer treatments of the LeChatelier principle differ in several important ways from Samuelson's original. First, while the original conclusion applies solely to the choices of an optimizing agent, the newer extensions apply also to many other equilibrium systems. Second, the original conclusion was a local principle that applied only to small parameter changes, while the modern extension is a global principle that applies to all parameter changes, large and small. Finally, the original principle gives at least the appearance of great generality, because it applies locally for any differentiable demand system, while the modern extension depends on a restriction. However, because the restriction always holds locally for differentiable demand systems, the modern principle actually subsumes the original.

All versions of the LeChatelier principle explain how the direct effect of a parameter change can be amplified by feedbacks in the systems in which they are embedded. Thus, the principles provide a foundation for understanding economic multipliers and, more generally, how it may be that small causes can have large effects.

19.2 A Local LeChatelier Principle for Optimization Problems

To explain Samuelson's original LeChatelier principle and set a context for the modern extensions, we restrict attention to the simplest form of the principle—one governing the choices of a profit-maximizing firm with just two inputs. Define the firm's unrestricted and restricted choice functions as follows:

$$x^U(w) \text{ solves } \max_x f(x) - w \cdot x \tag{19.1}$$

$$x^R(w, \bar{x}_2) \text{ solves } \max_x f(x) - w \cdot x \text{ subject to } x_2 = \bar{x}_2 \tag{19.2}$$

In the unrestricted problem (19.1), the firm maximizes profits over a set such as $\Re^2_+$, choosing quantities of both inputs. In the restricted problem (19.2), the firm maximizes profits subject to the additional constraint that its "choice" for input 2 is exogenously given. Clearly, if the maximum is unique at the prices $\bar{w}$ and $\bar{x}_2 = x_2^U(\bar{w})$, then $x^U(\bar{w}) = x^R(\bar{w},\bar{x}_2)$. Then, the traditional LeChatelier principle is the following result.

Theorem 19.1. Suppose that the functions $x^U(w)$ and $x^R(w,\bar{x}_2)$ are well defined and continuously differentiable in w_1 in a neighborhood of $w = \bar{w}$ and that $\bar{x}_2 = x_2^U(\bar{w})$. Then, $(\partial x_1^U/\partial w_1)(\bar{w}) \leq (\partial x_1^R/\partial w_1)(\bar{w},\bar{x}_2) \leq 0$

Proof. Let $\pi^U(w) = \max f(x) - w{\cdot}x$ and $\pi^R(w,\bar{x}_2) = \max_x f(x) - w{\cdot}x$ subject to $x_2 = \bar{x}_2$ be the corresponding unrestricted and restricted profit functions. Since the value is always higher in a problem with fewer constraints, $\pi^U(w) \geq \pi^R(w,\bar{x}_2)$ and, by construction, $\pi^U(\bar{w}) = \pi^R(\bar{w},\bar{x}_2)$.

By the envelope theorem, the profit functions are differentiable at w and the derivatives satisfy $x_1^U(\bar{w}) = -(\partial\pi^U/\partial w_1)(\bar{w}) = -(\partial\pi^R/\partial w_1)(\bar{w},\bar{x}_2) = x_1^R(\bar{w})$. Then, by the results of the previous paragraph, $(\partial x_1^U/\partial w_1)(\bar{w}) = -(\partial^2\pi^U/(\partial w_1)^2)(\bar{w}) \leq -(\partial^2\pi^R/(\partial w_1)^2)(\bar{w},\bar{x}_2) = (\partial x_1^R/\partial w_1)(\bar{w},\bar{x}_2)$.

This is a "local" principle, because it allows comparative conclusions only for infinitesimal price changes. It cannot be directly extended to a global principle without extra assumptions. The following simple example, adapted from Milgrom and Roberts (1996), illustrates the problem.

Example. Suppose that a firm can produce one unit of output using two workers or using one worker and one unit of capital, or it can shut down and produce zero. It can also do any convex combination of these three activities. We represent the three extreme points of the firm's production possibility set by triples consisting of labor inputs, capital inputs, and output, as follows: (0, 0, 0), (−1,−1,1), and (−2,0,1). At an initial price vector of (0.7,0.8,2), the firm maximizes profits by choosing (−2,0,1), that is, it demands two units of labor and earns a profit of 0.6. If a wage increase leads to the new price vector (1.1,0.8,2), then the firm's new optimum is (−1,−1,0) that is, it demands one unit of labor and earns a profit of 0.1. If capital is fixed in the short run, however, then the firm must choose between its using two units of labor, which now earns −0.2 or shutting down and earning zero. So, the firm's short-run demand for labor is zero. The important point is that labor demand adjusts *more* when capital is held fixed, in contrast to the conclusion of the LeChatelier principle.

19.3 Positive Feedbacks

We now consider a much more general approach to the LeChatelier conclusion that is not founded in optimization theory at all, but treats the principle as a *global property* of positive feedback systems. We will show below how this theory specializes to yield a global LeChatelier principle for optimization models and how it implies Theorem 19.1.

For comparability with the preceding results, let us limit attention to a simple system of two equations, as follows:

$$x_1 = f_1(\theta, \bar{x}_2); \qquad x_2 = f_2(\theta) \tag{19.3}$$

The variables x_1, x_2, $\bar{x}_2$ and the parameter θ are all real numbers.

We need to assume that f_1 is monotonic in the parameter. Since our central example is one with an input price parameter and the corresponding input choice, let us assume that f_1 is nonincreasing in θ. Then, this system exhibits positive feedbacks if either of the following two conditions holds globally: (1) f_2 is nondecreasing and f_1 is nonincreasing in $\bar{x}_2$ or (2) f_2 is nonincreasing and f_2 is nondecreasing in $\bar{x}_2$. When (1) holds, let us say that "the choices are substitutes" and when (2) holds, that "the choices are complements."[2] This corresponds exactly to the use of these terms in the theory of the firm, subsuming the insight that the relation that two inputs are substitutes (complements) is a symmetric one.

Theorem 19.2. Suppose that (1) or (2) is satisfied (so the choices are substitutes or complements). If $\theta \geq \bar{\theta}$ then $f_1(\theta,f_2(\theta)) \leq f_1(\theta,f_2(\bar{\theta})) \leq f_1(\bar{\theta},f_2(\bar{\theta}))$ and if $\theta \leq \bar{\theta}$ then $f_1(\theta,f_2(\theta)) \geq f_1(\theta,f_2(\bar{\theta})) \geq f_1(\bar{\theta},f_2(\bar{\theta}))$.

According to the theorem, the unrestricted change is in the same direction as the restricted change and larger in magnitude, and this holds globally for any change in the parameter. The proof is quite trivial; it uses the fact that the composition of two nonincreasing functions (or of two nondecreasing functions) is nondecreasing.

To apply this theorem to the model of a firm's input choices analyzed above, fix the price w_2 of input 2 and treat the parameter as being the price of input 1: $\theta = w_1$. Let f_1 and f_2 denote the restricted and unrestricted demands for inputs 1 and 2, respectively. In symbols, this means that $x_1^R(w,\bar{x}_2) = f_1(\theta,\bar{x}_2)$ and $x_2^U(w) = f_2(\theta)$. The unrestricted choice for input 1 is the same as the restricted choice when input 2 is chosen at its unrestricted level, so $x_1^U(w) = f_1(\theta,f_2(\theta))$. With these specifications, the theorem says that, provided inputs are (globally) either substitutes or complements and the price of input 1 increases ($w_1 \geq \bar{w}_1$), demand will fall by more in the unrestricted case than in the restricted case: $x_1^U(w) \leq x_1^R(w,x_2^U(\bar{w})) \leq x_1^U(\bar{w})$. The inequalities are all reversed for the case of a price decrease, so in that case demand rises by more in the unrestricted case. In both cases, unrestricted responses are larger.

The counterexample presented earlier, in which the conclusion of the LeChatelier principle fails, is a case where the positive feedbacks condition does not apply globally. In that example, the two inputs (capital and labor) are sometimes complements and sometimes substitutes. When the output price is 2 and capital costs 0.8 per unit, an increase in the wage rate from 0.7 to 1.1 causes the profit-maximizing firm to substitute capital for labor, switching from the production plan $(-2,0,1)$ to the plan $(-1,-1,1)$. For that range of prices, inputs are substitutes. When the wage further increases beyond 1.3, the firm switches to the plan $(0,0,0)$, reducing its use of capital and revealing the inputs to be complements on that portion of the price domain. The pattern displayed in this example is not pathological and represents an economically significant restriction on the scope of the LeChatelier principle.

How can one check whether the complements or substitutes conditions are satisfied? Recall that a smooth function $f(x_1,x_2)$ is *supermodular* if the mixed partial derivative $\partial^2 f/\partial x_1 \partial x_2 \geq 0$ everywhere and is *submodular* if $-f$ is supermodular.

Theorem 19.3. Suppose there are *just two* choice variables. If $f(x_1,x_2)$ is supermodular and the optimal choices are unique, then the choices are complements. If $f(x_1,x_2)$ is submodular and the optimal choices are unique, then the choices are substitutes.

Theorem 19.3 also lends insight into the original Samuelson–LeChatelier principle. In a differentiable demand system, the production function f is twice differentiable. There are three cases, according to whether $(\partial^2 f/\partial x_1 \partial x_2)(\bar{x})$ is positive, negative, or zero. If the mixed partial derivative is positive, it is positive in a neighborhood of $\bar{x}$. In that case, inputs are complements in a neighborhood and, restricting attention to choices in the neighborhood, Theorem 19.2 applies. Similarly, if the mixed partial derivative is negative, then the inputs are substitutes and Theorem 19.2 applies. By continuity, the theorem also applies when the mixed partial derivative is zero although in that case, the inequality of Theorem 19.1 holds as an equality:

$$\frac{\partial x_1^U}{\partial w_1}(\overline{w}) = \frac{\partial x_1^R}{\partial w_1}(\overline{w},\bar{x}_2).$$

The positive feedbacks approach to the LeChatelier principle can be extended to a much richer array of problems. Within optimization models, one can drop the assumption that optimal choices are unique at the cost of a slightly subtler statement about how the *set* of optima changes. One can also drop the assumptions that the objective is smooth and/or that there are just two choice variables. Milgrom and Roberts (1996) develop these generalizations and others.

The LeChatelier conclusion, however, is not limited to optimization problems. One can also apply the positive feedbacks approach to study the behavior of fixed points of systems such as the following one:

$$x_1 = f_1(x_1, x_2, \theta) \tag{19.4}$$

$$x_2 = f_2(x_1, x_2, \theta) \tag{19.5}$$

Suppose that the relevant domain is some product set, say $f:[0,1]^3 \to [0,1]^2$. If f is nondecreasing in all its arguments, then, by Tarski's theorem, there exist a maximum fixed point and a minimum fixed point and those are given by $x^{\max}(\theta) = \max\{x | f(x,\theta) \geq x\}$ and $x^{\min}(\theta) = \min\{x | f(x,\theta) \leqslant x\}$, and these are nondecreasing functions of θ.[3]

Positive feedback systems like (19.4)–(19.5) arise frequently in economic analysis and game theory (see Milgrom and Roberts, 1990). To simplify our study of the LeChatelier effect in such systems, we focus on the *largest* fixed points of the system (a similar analysis applies to the *smallest* fixed points of the system). Thus, let $\bar{x}_2 = x_2^{\max}(\theta)$. Our goal is to compare changes in $x_1^{\max}(\theta)$ when the parameter changes with the corresponding changes in x_1 in the *restricted* system in which (19.5) is replaced by $x_2 = \bar{x}_2$. By the logic of the preceding paragraph, in the restricted system, the maximum fixed point for x_1 is $g_1(\theta, \bar{x}_2) \equiv \max\{x_1 | f_1(x_1, \bar{x}_2, \theta) \geq x_1\}$, which is a nondecreasing function of both arguments. Let us define $g_2(\theta) \equiv x_2^{\max}(\theta)$. By a direct application of Theorem 2 to the pair of functions (g_1, g_2) , we get the LeChatelier conclusion, as follows:

Theorem 19.4. Suppose that f_1 and f_2 are nondecreasing, $\theta \geqslant \bar{\theta}$, and $x_1^{\max}$, g_1 and g_2 are defined as above. Then, $x_1^{\max}(\theta) \geqslant g_1(\theta, g_2(\bar{\theta})) \geqslant x_1^{\max}(\bar{\theta})$

The conclusion, again, is that the change in the endogenous variable x_1 is larger when x_2 is free to change than when x_2 is restricted. The key is the positive feedback: the change in x_1 pushes x_2 up, and that in turn pushes x_1 up further.

19.4 Conclusion

In modern theory, Samuelson's LeChatelier principle has evolved into a principle for understanding multipliers. The original principle was limited to demand theory applications and reflects the symmetry of the substitution matrix, which implies that the relations of being substitutes or complements are symmetric relations. That symmetry creates a positive feedback system. For example, if capital and labor are complements, then an increase in the wage not only directly reduces the hiring of labor but also reduces the use of capital which leads to a further reduction in the hiring of labor. Alternatively, if capital and labor are substitutes, then an increase in the wage not only directly reduces the hiring of labor but also increases the use of capital which leads to a further reduction in the hiring of labor. Including capital in the model can attenuate the direct effect of the wage increase only when capital is sometimes a substitute and sometimes a complement for labor.

To a modeler who finds that the direct effect of a parameter change cannot explain an observed effect, the LeChatelier principle analysis suggests a line of further analysis. It may be that the variable in question is part of a positive feedback system. Such systems amplify the direct effect of parameter changes. This reasoning is not limited to demand systems, nor to small parameter changes, nor to models with divisible choice variables.

This knowledge is helpful not only for new applications, but also for thinking about the policy and empirical consequences ascribed, only sometimes correctly, to the original LeChatelier principle.

Notes

1. Samuelson (1947, 1949, 1960a, 1960b, 1972).
2. If f_1 is nondecreasing in θ, then the conditions change. In that case, we need that either (1) f_2 is nonincreasing and f_1 is nonincreasing in $\bar{x}_2$ ("decisions are substitutes") or (2) f_2 is nondecreasing and f_1 is nondecreasing in $\bar{x}_2$ ("decisions are complements").
3. For a more complete analysis, see Milgrom and Roberts (1994) and references therein.

References

Milgrom, Paul and John Roberts. (1990). "Rationalizability, learning and equilibrium in games with strategic complementarities," *Econometrica*, 58(3), 155–1278.

—— and ——. (1994). "Comparing equilibria," *American Economic Review*, 84(3), 441–459.

—— and ——. (1996). "The LeChatelier Principle," *American Economic Review*, 86(1), 173–179.

Samuelson, Paul. (1947). *Foundations of Economic Analysis*. Cambridge, MA: Cambridge University Press.

Samuelson, Paul. (1949). "The Lechatelier principle in linear programming," Santa Monica, CA: The RAND Corporation.
——. (1960a). "An extension of the Lechatelier principle," *Econometrica*, 28, 368–379.
——. (1960b). "Structure of a minimum equilibrium system," *Essays in Economics and Econometrics: A Volume in Honor of Harold Hotelling*. R. Pfouts. Chapel Hill: University of North Carolina Press, pp. 1–33.
——. (1972). "Maximum principles in analytical economics," *American Economic Review*, 62(3), 249–262.

20

The Surprising Ubiquity of the Samuelson Configuration: Paul Samuelson and the Natural Sciences

James B. Cooper and Thomas Russell

Dedicated to Professor Paul A. Samuelson on the occasion of his ninetieth birthday, this chapter is inspired by the principle made clear throughout Professor Samuelson's writings, that a deep unity of mathematical method underlies the study of optimizing systems, be they drawn from the natural, life, or social sciences.

20.1 Introduction

In his 1972 Nobel Prize acceptance speech, Professor Samuelson (1972) summarized the idea that is now associated with his name: that meaningful theorems in economics are often naturally obtained by framing the issue as a problem in constrained optimization. To illustrate the power of this optimization principle, several analogies were made to the natural sciences, attention being given to a geometrical condition (Figure 20.1).

Figure 20.1 gives a criterion for when a set of equilibria are constrained optima. The axes of this diagram are labeled P_1 for the price of input 1 and V_1 for its quantity. Shown are the level curves of the quantities of input 1 demanded at various own prices by a monopolist who hires two inputs, input 1 (shown) and input 2 (not shown), in two regimes of constraint. In constraint regime 1, the quantity of input 2 is held fixed and the

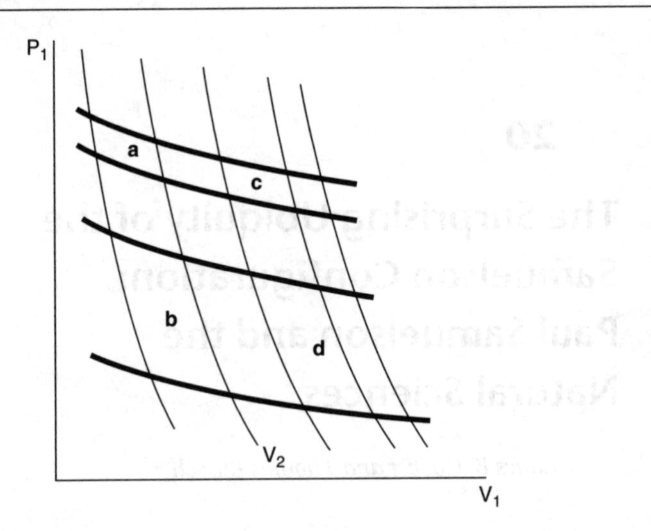

Figure 20.1 The Samuelson configuration

level curves are given by the steeper curves. In regime 2, the price of input 2 is fixed, the level curves being given by the flatter curves shown in bold.

The remarkable property of this diagram is this. If the ratio of the area of any "parallelogram" such as **a** to any area such as **b** is everywhere equal to the ratio of any other "parallelogram" such as **c** to any area such as **d**, the firm hires input 1 to maximize constrained profits. Where does such an unexpected result come from?

Samuelson recalls that in classical thermodynamics, labeling the axes *p* for pressure and *v* for volume, the same level curves represent the equilibrium positions of a heat engine also in two regimes of constraint. In regime 1, shown by the flatter curves, the engine is allowed to equalize its temperature with its surroundings, these curves being called isotherms. In regime 2 the engine is insulated, the steeper level curves being called adiabats.

He then states:

> While reading Clerk Maxwell's charming introduction to thermodynamics, I found that his explanation of the existence of the same absolute temperature scale in every body could be true only if on the p-v diagram that I earlier referred to in connection with LeChatelier's Principle, the two families of curves—steep and light or less-steep and heavy—formed parallelograms like a, b, c, d . . . which everywhere have the property area a/ area b = area c/ area d. And so it is with the two different economic curves.

A casual reader of the lecture might be forgiven for thinking that were they to open Maxwell's classic work (1872), they would find there a clear discussion of the area condition as providing the foundation for classical energy minimizing thermodynamics. Such a casual reader, however, would be wrong. It may well be true that Samuelson's Figure 20.1 is lurking in Maxwell's geometry, but Maxwell's treatment is viewed by contemporary physicists as "little used" and "amazingly obscure"[1] and it seems to have had very little influence on the development of modern thermodynamics.

Given this, and recognizing, of course, the inspiration provided by Maxwell, we will now define the area ratio condition embedded in Figure 20.1 as the Samuelson (*S*) area ratio condition. When two families of curves (more precisely a pair of foliations in the plane in general position) satisfy this property, we will say they are a Samuelson (*S*) configuration. This deceptively simple geometric structure does indeed provide a foundation for constrained optimization in both economics and the natural sciences, but reasons for this are far from transparent. In this paper we repay some of the debt which maximizing economics owes to physics by considering the role of the (*S*) condition in a number of physical applications. We begin with that part of physics that is closest to economics, classical thermodynamics.

20.2 The Samuelson Area Condition and Classical Thermodynamics

The history of thermodynamics shows uncanny parallels with the history of economics.[2] In thermodynamics, for example, as much ink was spilled over the meaning of terms such as temperature and entropy as was spilled by economists over the meaning of the term utility. In fact on this issue, economics, remarkably, can claim to have reached the high ground of enlightenment before thermodynamics. In economics it was clear after the contributions of Debreu in the 1950s (Debreu, 1954) that utility, the consumer's maximand, was a numerical representation of a preference ordering.

In thermodynamics it was realized very early of course that temperature was an ordering, the classic Fahrenheit and Celsius scales being just alternative representations. But understanding that the mysterious quantity entropy was also just a representation of an ordering, though certainly glimpsed by Caratheodory (1909), does not seem to have been fully grasped till the work of Giles (1964), and continues to be rediscovered today. There is no indication that mathematical physicists had any awareness of the highly relevant work of Debreu.

Since both temperature and entropy are representations of orderings, just as with the scaling of the economist's utility, these representations will not be unique. Indeed the necessity of a canonical choice of temperature[3] independent of the particular type of thermometer used (absolute temperature versus empirical temperature) was recognized very early and was the subject of one of William Thomson's (Lord Kelvin) most famous contributions (Thomson, 1851).

But now we need to be careful. It is true that we can relabel the temperature and entropy level curves separately in any order preserving the way we please, but, taken together,[4] we must make sure that such recalibrations satisfy whatever equilibrium restrictions of a thermodynamic nature are imposed by constrained energy minimization.

What exactly are these restrictions? In modern thermodynamics it is recognized that this question can be given a very elegant geometric answer. When energy is being minimized, there is a special representation of the two orderings called T (absolute temperature) and S (absolute entropy) for which the mapping from pressure p and volume v to T and S is area preserving.[5] All of the classical laws of thermodynamics follow from this restriction.

However, this area preserving restriction applies only when the underlying orders are represented by the very special coordinates T and S. The workaday experimentalist who plots these level curves can give them perfectly legitimate labels (so-called empirical temperature t and empirical entropy s) but these would correspond to T and S only if the Gods of physics were feeling particularly generous. So what restriction would the workaday empiricist expect to find if indeed energy were being minimized?

As we have shown elsewhere, the answer to this question is precisely the (S) area ratio condition. Indeed, we have the following propositions. (Note that here, and throughout the paper, all statements of equivalence are to be interpreted as local statements. Global statements of equivalence require more delicate analysis.)

Proposition 1. The (S) area ratio condition is necessary and sufficient for the existence of a recalibration of the pair of orderings, $T \to \phi(t)$ $S \to \psi(s)$ such that the map from p, v to T, S is area preserving. We will call these recalibrations (S) recalibrations. Clearly in this case the map has Jacobian matrix with determinant equal to 1. This renumbering gives the isotherms and adiabats a canonical[6] calibration.

Proposition 2. When the temperature and entropy functions are canonically calibrated, then the classical relations known as Maxwell's equations hold, and there exists an energy function E from which these equations can be derived by constrained minimization.

These two propositions are proved in Cooper *et al.* (2001).

The (*S*) area condition is thus the key geometric test for the presence of an energy function. However, although geometric tests are easy to state, they may be difficult to apply. It is therefore of some interest to give the condition in analytic form.

There are several ways to do this.

1. We can think of the foliations as the level curves of two scalar functions f and g. In this case, in our earlier paper, Cooper *et al.* (2001) we obtained a lengthy nonlinear third order PDE on the functions f and g which is equivalent to the area ratio condition.
2. We can also think of the level curves as the flow lines of vector fields **v** and **w**. In this case we have shown (Cooper *et al.*, 2005) that the area ratio condition is equivalent to the existence of strictly positive scalar functions which we can assume to be of the form $e^{\phi(p,\,v)}$, $e^{\psi(p,v)}$, and which are such that
   (a) div $e^{\phi}\,\mathbf{v}$ = div $e^{\psi}\,\mathbf{w} = 0$ and
   (b) $[e^{\phi}\,\mathbf{v}, e^{\psi}\,\mathbf{w}] = 0$, where [ ] is the Poisson bracket.

   Once again this can be shown to be equivalent to a third order nonlinear PDE in the components of the vector fields.
3. Both approaches (1) and (2) require that the level curves be calibrated in some arbitrary way. This calibration, however, is not intrinsic to the problem, and often goes beyond the data provided to the experimentalist. Experiments produce level curves with some specific shape, but they do not provide a numbering. Ideally, then, an analytical test should be in terms of the direction fields along the level curves (what economists think of as the marginal rates of transformations), not in terms of the vector fields themselves.[7] As part of a larger study of classical thermodynamics with Professor Samuelson, we have specialized 2a and 2b to direction fields.

So let $(1, a\,(p, v))$ and $(1, b\,(p, v))$ be two direction fields in the plane: that is, $a\,(p, v)$ and $b\,(p, v)$ are the slope functions of the families. We ask, when do the two families of foliations generated as solutions to the equations

$$\frac{dp}{dv} = a\,(p, v), \text{ respectively, } \frac{dp}{dv} = b\,(p, v),$$

satisfy the Samuelson area ratio condition?

The equation is[8]

$$b^3a_{vv}+a^3b_{vv}+2(a_p-b_p)^2+b^2(2a_v^2-aa_{vv}+2a_{pv})+2a^2(b_v^2+b_{pv})-a(b_v(3a_p-4b_p)$$
$$+a_v b_p+a_{pp}-b_{pp})-b(a^2b_{vv}+(-4a_v+b_v)a_p+3a_v b_p$$
$$+2a(2a_v b_v+a_{pv}+b_{pv})-a_{pp}+b_{pp}=0 \quad (20.1)$$

It is useful to contrast the treatment of thermodynamics given here with another interesting geometric approach, due to Hermann (1973) and Arnold (1990), noted in footnote 4. In that approach, energy E is added to the system as (initially) an independent variable so that their configuration space M is five-dimensional, measuring energy, pressure, volume, temperature, and entropy. Equilibrium considerations are then captured by adding to this space a contact form. The fundamental equations of state are then incorporated in this form and a thermodynamical substance is what is called a Legendre submanifold of M (see Arnold for details).

Our treatment differs from this one, first due to the fact that we do not presuppose the existence of an energy function. We work with the four quantities that one can, in principle, measure directly, pressure, volume, temperature, and entropy. Second we assume that, for the two latter variables, we can only observe their level curves, that is, the isotherms and adiabats. As mentioned above we can then define empirical temperature and entropy but these are only determined initially up to recalibrations. Thus our mathematical system consists of a four-dimensional configuration manifold (which is just ordinary four space with coordinates (p,v,t,s)). Any thermodynamical substance is then obtained by imposing two restraints on these quantities and is thus described by a two-dimensional submanifold, or more precisely, an equivalence class of such submanifolds (under the actions of recalibrations on the t and s coordinates). Our task is then to determine which (equivalence classes of) submanifolds actually correspond to thermodynamical substances, that is, have representatives that can be embedded as Legendre submanifolds of a suitable five-dimensional contact manifold. We call these Samuelson submanifolds.

We can illustrate the variety of approaches to this question noted above by considering one of the simplest examples of a nontrivial (*S*) configuration, namely the ideal gas $t = pv$, $s = pv^{\gamma}$. In this case we can compute the various cases explicitly.

In terms of set up 1, above, the manifold can be regarded as the graph of the above pair of functions t and s (and these, of course, satisfy the appropriate PDE).

In terms of set up 2, the curves are the flow lines of the vector fields

$$\mathbf{v} = (-p, v), \quad \mathbf{w} = (-\gamma p v^{\gamma-1}, v^{\gamma})$$

and these can be shown to satisfy the vector equations mentioned there.

In terms of set up 3, the slope functions are given by

$$a(p, v) = -v/p, \quad b(p, v) = -v/\gamma p$$

and these can be shown to satisfy Equation 20.1.

Hence we can compute the recalibrated versions which for t and s are

$$T = pv, \quad e^{(\gamma-1)}S = pv^{\gamma}$$

The recalibrated vector fields are

$$\mathbf{v} = (-p, v) \ \mathbf{w} = \left(\frac{-\gamma}{(\gamma-1)v}, \frac{p}{v-1} \right)$$

We can also calculate the relevant energy functions. Finally we remark that when the (S) area ratio condition is satisfied, the families of curves are given by a Lie group representation as discussed below. Lie groups are still somewhat unfamiliar to economists, though they have been used extensively by Sato (1999). Accordingly this approach will not be pursued here.

This characterization of the ideal gas clearly privileges p and v as independent variables. In general, from a purely mathematical point of view, this assignment cannot always be made. All we know is that locally the submanifold is the graph of a function which arises from one of the possible six choices of a pair of independent variables. Hence we require further PDE's to use for the various possible choices.

We call these equations the uncalibrated Maxwell relations. The choices (t, p), (t, v), (s, p) or (s, v) as independent variables give four possibilities. (For example, for the ideal gas one alternative description is $t = sv^{(-\gamma+1)}$, $p = sv^{-\gamma}$.) Then, in addition to the standard case, we have its inverse—independent variables t and s—giving a total of six possible cases.

The need to model the manifold in this way is physically important, since examples of empirical data for suitable substances (e.g. water at high pressures, the van der Waals gas) show that there is no choice of a pair of independent variable that allows a universally valid model for thermodynamical substances, a fact that has led to some polemics among those interested in the foundations of thermodynamics (see Truesdell and Bharatha, 1977).

As an example of this complication, consider the low temperature generalization of the ideal gas. In particular let isotherms be given by $p{\cdot}v = k$ (a constant) and adiabats by $S = p{\cdot}v^{\gamma} = l$ (a constant), but now, unlike the ideal gas for which γ is a constant, let γ depend on temperature t (see e.g. Feynman *et al.* (1963) 40.8 and 40.9).

In this case, of six possible choices of independent variable, only three can be computed explicitly, but it is still possible to verify that the submanifold given by $t = pv$, $s = pv^{\gamma(pv)}$ satisfies the (*S*) area condition. The recalibrations in this case are given by

$$T = t = \phi(pv) \quad S = \ln\,(pv^{(\gamma\,(pv))})$$

where ϕ is a primitive of the function $1/(\gamma - 1)$.

Remark: Because of the area ratio condition, complete knowledge of both families (isotherms and adiabats) overdetermines the system. It can be shown (Cooper and Russell, (2005)) that if the (*S*) condition is satisfied, knowledge of the first system of uncalibrated curves (say the isotherms) and just two uncalibrated level curves of the other family (say the adiabats) determines the whole system of curves and the canonical calibration. Put differently, it is possible in principle to reject the energy minimization hypothesis if one has knowledge of the shapes of the level curves of one of the families and just three uncalibrated level curves from the other family. This fact also plays an important role in the theory of equal area map projections discussed below.

20.3 The Samuelson Area Condition and Celestial Mechanics

The intimate connection between area conditions and minimizing systems is not confined to thermodynamics. It occurs in many parts of classical mechanics, most famously in the problem of characterizing planetary motion, the problem that may be said to have given birth to modern physics. In this section we show how the ability to transform an area ratio condition into an equal area condition sheds light on the classical Newtonian problem of explaining planetary motion by the presence of a central gravitational force that follows a power law.[9]

Suppose that we are given an observed orbit of planetary motion that we write in polar coordinates in the rather unusual form $rf(\theta) = 1$ (rather than the more standard $r = g(\theta)$). This simplifies the expressions, which we will obtain below. As is standard with polar coordinates we assume that the origin is the sun, r the radial distance of the orbit from the sun, and θ the angle made by the planet with respect to some given horizon. See Figure 20.2.

Now consider two families of foliations. One family consists of blowups of the given curve, that is, curves described by $rf(\theta) = k$. Note that we are not assuming that these are orbits, although, in the power law case, in fact, they are. The other family consists of rays through the origin. Again, see Figure 20.2. Trivially these two foliations satisfy the Samuelson area ratio condition. Thus we have canonical recalibrations that satisfy the equal area condition and it is easy to see that they are $s = r^2 f^2(\theta)/2$ and ν where ν is a primitive of $1/f^2(u)$.

If we use the new variable ν as time, and write it as t, we see that we have now arranged that our initial arbitrary orbit satisfies the property that, relative to the sun, it traces out equal areas in equal times. This, of course, is Kepler's famous second law, the law from which Newton derived the principle of a central force field with the sun as the center. Changing back to Cartesian coordinates, we can see that the equations of motion of all central force field systems must have the form

$$x(t) = \frac{\cos\theta(t)}{f(\theta(t))} \quad \text{and} \quad y(t) = \frac{\sin\theta(t)}{f(\theta(t))} \text{ where}$$

$$\frac{d\theta}{dt} = f^2(\theta)$$

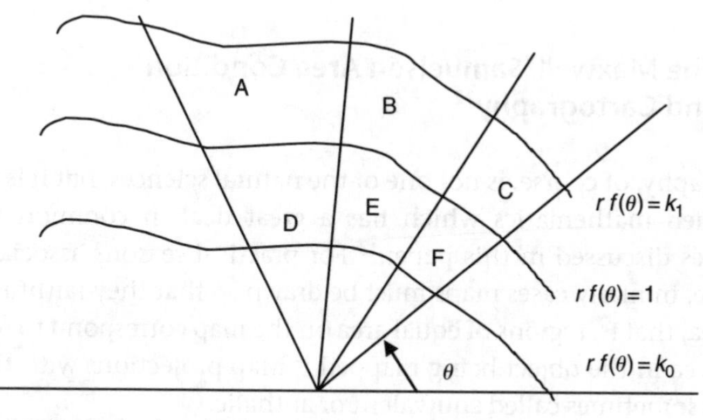

Figure 20.2 Dilations of an arbitrary orbit

Thus, via the Samuelson condition,[10] for any orbit, we have now gained a great deal of information about the underlying dynamics of the path of the planet around this orbit assuming it satisfies Kepler's second law. For example, all derivatives of x and y with respect to time can now be expressed in terms of f and its derivatives. In particular we have

(a) acceleration is given by

$$x''(t) = -\frac{\cos\theta(t) f^2(\theta)}{(f(\theta) + f''(\theta))}, \quad y''(t) = -\frac{\sin\theta(t) f^2(\theta)}{(f(\theta) + f''(\theta))},$$

(b) The curvature, κ_h, of the hodograph[11] is given by

$$\kappa_h = \frac{1}{f(\theta) + f''(\theta)}$$

(c) The curvature, κ, of the curve itself is given by

$$\kappa = f(\theta)^3 \frac{f(\theta) + f''(\theta)}{f(\theta)^2 + f'(\theta)^2}$$

From this we can deduce a wealth of results (some known, even to Newton, some new) in a very quick manner. These include a differential equation for f that characterizes whether the planet is moving under a power law, an explicit formula for the ensuing power, Hamilton's characterization of Keplerian motion by the fact that the hodograph is a circle and a refinement of the so-called duality theory (see Arnold, 1990 b) for power laws (see also Cooper, 2005).

20.4 The Maxwell/Samuelson Area Condition and Cartography[12]

Cartography, of course, is not one of the natural sciences, but it is a branch of applied mathematics which has a great deal in common with the examples discussed in this paper.[13] For practical reasons associated with land use, in many cases maps must be drawn so that they faithfully represent area, that is, regions of equal area on the map correspond to regions of equal area in the object being mapped.[14] Map projections with this property are sometimes called equivalent or authalic.

Many standard projections have the equal area property, see, for example, the list on the United States Geological Survey (no date) web page. The relevance of the (*S*) configuration to mathematical cartography can be summed up as follows. Any system of curves which satisfies the (*S*) area ratio condition leads automatically (by recalibration) to an area preserving mapping of the plane (or a part thereof). Since any equal-area projection can be obtained by composing one of the standard ones (e.g. the famous Lambert projection, see Figure 20.3) with an area preserving map of the plane, we can confine our attention to the latter.

In terms of cartography this means that any suitable family of curves can be the parallels (meridians) of an equivalent projection and that two further transversal curves (i.e. arbitrarily chosen meridians (parallels)) determinethe entire family and the calibrations (i.e. assignment of longitude andlatitude).[15]

The recipe for producing area preserving projection maps is therefore simple. Find an (*S*) transformation and recalibrate. Hence the theory of Samuelson configurations can potentially create all possible equal area projections.

Staying within the class of equivalent maps, for obvious reasons cartographers gave special attention to the class of projections with the property that the parallels and meridians are straight lines or circles. Since the parallels and meridians for the Lambert projection are just the usual Cartesian coordinate system, investigation of this restricted set of projections leads to the problem of characterizing all equal area transformations of the plane which map the parallels to the coordinate axes into circles or lines. This problem was solved by Grave[16] (1896), but his solution is somewhat analytically cumbersome, making it difficult to disentangle the underlying geometry.

What is needed is a unifying principle. This is provided by the fact that all (*S*) configurations consisting of circles and lines, and therefore all area

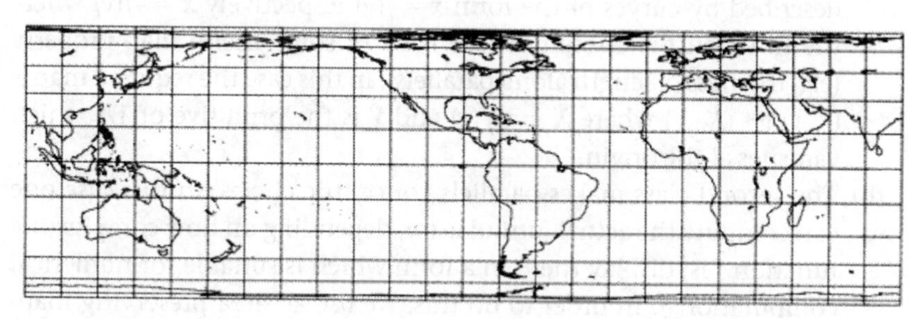

Figure 20.3 Lambert's cylindrical equal area map 1772

preserving map projections with straight lines and circles as meridians and parallels, can be constructed in the same simple way.

Take an arbitrary line or circle. Consider one parameter Lie group actions on the plane[17] whose orbits are circles and lines and which preserve circles and lines. There are three obvious candidates, the translations, the dilations, and the rotations and these generate all the Grave projections in an intuitive geometric manner. In particular it can be shown that every (*S*) circle/ line configuration can be generated by combining

(a) the orbits of the group and
(b) the images of the line or circle under the group.

Once we have the (*S*) configuration we can then recalibrate to obtain an equal area map. Specifically the combinations producing Grave's forms are

(i) translation group and line;
(ii) translation group and circle;
(iii) rotation group and line;
(iv) rotation group and circle;
(v) rotation group and line;
(vi) rotation group and circle.

We now return to the problem of describing the most general form of an equal area projection. The practical question, of course, is to choose suitable families of curves for the meridians and parallels. As we have seen we have no restrictions on the choice of parallels, and having chosen these wisely, we can still choose two meridians at will. To be an (*S*) configuration the geometric form of the other meridians is now specified and all that remains is to recalibrate.

Again from a practical point of view two choices of parallels dominate.

(a) Cylindrical projections in which the parallels are straight lines parallel to the x-axis. In the standard examples, the two extreme meridians are described by curves of the form $x = f(y)$ respectively $x = -f(y)$ where the function f is chosen on the basis of some useful map property (e.g. trueness of length along parallels). In this case the required map is $(x, y) \mapsto (X, Y)$ where $X = x/f(y)$ and Y is the primitive of $1/f$ which vanishes at the origin.
(b) The second class makes parallels concentric circles. In this case one can compute the actual formulae (or, depending on how complex the function f is, display them in a form which is suitable for numerical computations). In order to do this, we use an area preserving mapping of the plane that maps these concentric circles onto the parallels to the x axis and note that this reduces the problem to case a).

For an example of an exotic choice of configuration see Figure 20.4, the classical Stab equal area projection. The presence of the (*S*) configuration is clear to the eye.

20.5 Samuelson Area Condition, Growth and Form

As a final, albeit highly speculative example, we tentatively suggest that the (*S*) configuration can also play a role in the life sciences. In particular, in this section we consider how the (*S*) recalibration can be used to describe the evolution of biological shapes and forms. The section is motivated by observing the diagrams in D'Arcy Thompson's classic work "On Growth and Form" (1942), Chapter 17. The majority of these cases appear to arise as (*S*) transforms of the verticals and horizontals. For example, consider Figure 20.5, taken from Thompson, in which he shows how coordinate transforms, verticals into circles, horizontals into hyperbolae, render the porcupine fish as the otherwise very different looking sunfish. This is one of many examples used by Thompson to show that transformations of form between related species can often be displayed as mathematical transformations between coordinate systems adapted to the individual species. For further discussion see O'Connor and Robertson (no date).

The presence of the (*S*) configuration, of course, could be complete happenstance. D'Arcy Thompson himself, however, believed strongly that the

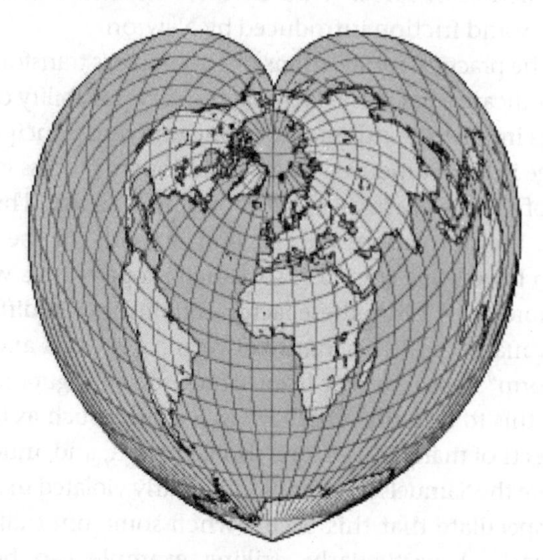

Figure 20.4 The Stab equal area projection

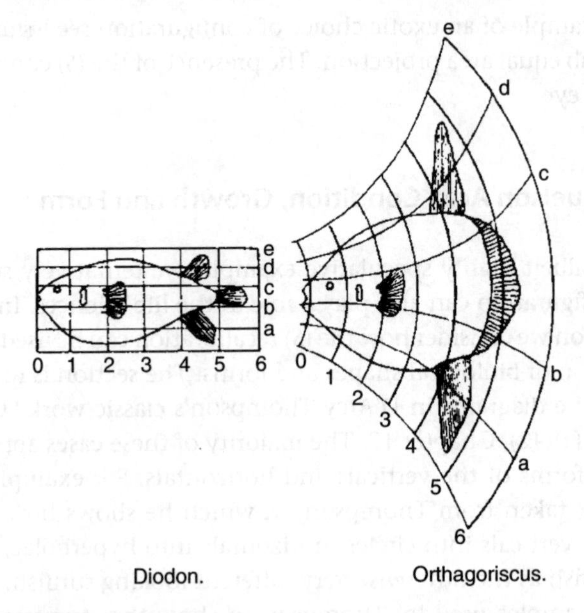

Figure 20.5 Porcupine fish (Diodon) becomes sunfish (Orthagoriscus Mola)

shape of living things was as much conditioned by mechanical forces as was the shape of planetary orbits. As he stated, "The form of any particle of matter, whether it be living or dead, and the changes in form which are apparent in its movements and in its growth, may in all cases be described as due to the action of force." And by force he meant exactly the same forces of gravity and friction introduced by Newton.

Apart from the practical implications of Thompson's transformations, their theoretical significance lies in the fact that the very possibility of constructing such mappings implies the existence of some unifying principle to the effect that the change in form produced by an evolutionary process is the result of a coordination of a relatively small number of genetic factors. Thus if one could show that the transformations are not only smooth (in the mathematical sense) but also have some common structural property, this would presumably lead to more insight into these factors. But just as it is difficult not to be struck by how many of the diagrams between pages 1054 and 1086 of "On Growth and Form" appear to arise from Samuelson configurations, one could hardly expect this to be a universal law. In a subject such as biology, which studies the effects of many causes, one should expect, and, indeed, one finds, examples where the Samuelson condition is clearly violated in subregions.

We would speculate that this occurs when some unusual evolutionary force is at work. A particularly striking example can be found[18] on pp. 1078, 1079 that illustrates the evolutionary development of the modern horse. Here it is tempting to relate the violation of the Samuelson condition which occurs in the region in front of the eye with the well-known transition of the position of this organ from the middle to the back region of the skull (presumably as an evolutionary tactic of combining all-round vision and speed as a defense against predators).

In this respect we note that one way to describe intuitively the transformations of the plane which arise from Samuelson configurations is that they are composed of an area preserving transformation followed by nonuniform deformations along the curvilinear coordinate lines corresponding to the area-preserving transformation. A glance at the diagrams shows that examples of each of these two extreme cases, that is area preserving mappings and nonuniform deformations abound. A particularly striking example of the latter can be found on page 1052, which compares the tibia of an ox, a sheep, and a giraffe. Further remarks on p. 1089 on volume preserving properties (more precisely, conservation of the areas of sections) during the transition between fish which are as distinct as haddock and plaice supports this speculative view.

What D'Arcy Thompson lacked and what geometric morphometrics (as the field is now called) in general lacks is an optimizing principle akin to those derived from Hamiltonians. As Bookstein has noted (1989), more general coordinate transformations, so-called thin plate splines, can be introduced to link two given shapes. These splines can be thought of as energy minimizing, but this is just a statistical analogy akin to the distance minimizing of least squares regressions. It remains to be seen whether or not there exists in nature a true optimizing principle which can be captured by the Samuelson grid.

20.6 Conclusion

One of the fascinating aspects of the Samuelson configuration is the variety of guises in which it appears. The basic geometry is, of course, the simple area ratio condition shown in Figure 20.1. In the applications discussed in that section, as Samuelson pointed out, the configuration is equivalent to the fact that the foliations arise from a constrained optimization problem.

In the thermodynamics case the foliations given by experiment (so-called empirical temperature and empirical entropy) are the level curves of orderings which can be represented by classes of functions in ways familiar to students of preference and utility. Whenever the Maxwell/Samuelson condition is satisfied, however, there is an essentially unique (and so canonical) choice of the calibrations of the scalar functions representing the orders, so-called absolute temperature and absolute entropy. By analogy, in the Newtonian case of planetary motion there is a canonical recalibration of the speed of the velocity vector field tangent to the orbit (absolute time).

When a Samuelson configuration is recognized it will often be useful to compute this canonical recalibration because then on we will have a canonical area preserving map of the plane (or suitable subset) and area preserving maps play a crucial role in modern physics. As we have seen, area preserving maps of the plane also play a major role in cartography where we have discussed the theory and practice of equivalent (equal area) projections. Indeed it has been our experience that (*S*) manifolds are ubiquitous and the above principle—given an (S) configuration compute the canonical recalibration—usually leads to interesting consequences.

What is the general structure underlying these configurations? As we have seen in Section 20.5, we can derive any Samuelson configuration from the usual system of parallels to the coordinate axes. These derive from a Lie group action[19] (the translations parallel to the coordinates which have this system as orbits). And so we get the most sophisticated interpretation. Samuelson configurations are representations of two-dimensional commutative Lie groups in the infinite-dimensional Lie group of area preserving diffeomorphisms of the plane. This fact seems to open the door to a more profound investigation of minimizing systems both in the natural sciences and in economics.

Notes

1. "Interestingly, Maxwell also uses the above-mentioned equality of areas to derive his relations. But he seems not to have cared for or known about Jacobians, and instead uses Euclidean geometry in the tradition of Newton to get his four identities in an amazingly obscure way." V. Ambegaokar and Mermin N.D. (2002) *American Journal of Physics*, 70(2), 2002.
2. For an interesting discussion of this issue see Candeal *et al*. (2001).
3. Alluded to by Samuelson in the Maxwell quote given earlier.
4. The need to consider temperature and entropy together once led Tisza to state that "If someone claims to understand temperature while being mystified by entropy, then his statements may be presumed to be 50 percent accurate," Tisza (1966) p. 75.
5. That dynamic flows are area preserving (or in the higher dimensional generalization, symplectic) is today the central geometric characterization of all Hamiltonian systems. When the thermodynamic model is extended to include energy E, it becomes five-dimensional, p, v, T, S, and E. The mathematically equivalent characterization for what is now an odd dimensional system is the preservation of a contact form (see Hermann, 1973, Arnold, 1990, Samuelson, 1990).

6. This recalibration is unique up to choice of origin for one of the variables and related choice of scale for both.
7. A direction field is related to a geometric object (sometimes confusingly called a line element) defined as an equivalence class of vectors $a\mathbf{v}$, $a > 0$. These objects are the natural differential tool for studying the local behavior of uncalibrated foliations and perhaps should be better known to economists.
8. Here subscripts denote partial differentiation.
9. Remarkably, after 300 years, Newton's work remains controversial and continues to inspire interesting applied mathematical questions (see V. Arnold, 1990, S. Chandrasekar, 1995, and Mittag, L. and M. J. Stephen, 1992).
10. Of course we are not claiming that this is the only way in which these classic results can be obtained. It is simply that starting with the uncalibrated curves then moving to the calibrated version, as in the case of thermodynamics, gives a very general analytical description of the system. For celestial mechanics this means that we have an analytical expression for all central force fields. This makes it easy to ask questions about those central force fields which are given by power or any other special laws.
11. The hodograph, a construction due to Hamilton, is the curve $(x'(t), y'(t))$ traced out by the velocity vector.
12. This section borrows from Cooper and Russell (mimeo).
13. The German artist Dürer, for example, maintained an interest in both form altering transformations (Section 20.4) and cartography.
14. Map projections come in many forms depending on their purpose, but most fit into one of two disjoint classes: conformal ones, which preserve angle and therefore direction (useful for navigation), and the equivalent (area preserving) ones discussed here.
15. Recall from the remark in Section 20.1 that an (*S*) configuration is determined by one family of curves and any two members of the other family.
16. The problem of the straight line and circle conformal maps (i.e. maps which preserve angles) had been solved earlier by Lagrange (1779).
17. For an accessible introduction to Lie groups in the plane, see Hydon (2000).
18. All page references here are to D'Arcy Thompson.
19. The importance of Lie groups in economics has been frequently noted by R. Sato (1999).

References

Ambegaokar, V. and N. D. Mermin. (2002). "Reply," *American Journal Physics*, 70(2), 105.

Arnold, V. (1990a). "Contact geometry: the geometrical method of Gibbs' thermodynamics," in D. Caldi and G. Mostow (eds), *Proceedings of the Gibbs Symposium*. Providence: American Mathematical Society, pp. 163–179.

Arnold, V. (1990b). *Huygens and Barrow, Newton and Hooke*, Boston: Birkhauser.

Bookstein, F. L. (1989). "Principal Warps: Thin Plate Splines and the Decomposition of Deformations." *IEEE Transactions Pattern Analysis and Machine Intelligence* 11, 567–585.

Candeal, J. C., J. R. De Miguel, E. Induráin, and G. B. Mehta. (2001). "Utility and entropy," *Economic Theory*, 17(1), 233–238.

Caratheodory, C. (1909). "Untersuchung über die Grundlagen der Thermodynamik," *Math. Ann.* 67, 355–386.

Chandrasekhar, S. (1995). *Newton's Principia for the Common Reader*. Oxford: Clarendon Press.

Cooper, J. B. (2005). "Notes on power law duality" (mimeo).

——, and T. Russell. (2005)"One parameter groups of affine transformations and area-preserving map projections" (mimeo).

——, T. Russell. and Samuelson, P. A. (2001). "Characterizing an area condition associated with minimizing systems," in T. Negishi, R.V. Ramachandran, and K. Mino (eds), *Economic Theory, Dynamics and Markets: Essays in honor of Ryuzo Sato,* Norwell, Ma: Kluwer, pp. 391–403.

Debreu, G. (1954). *"Representation of a preference ordering by a numerical function,"* in Thrall, Davis and Coombs (eds), *Decision Processes*. John Wiley & Sons.

Feynman, R., R. B. Leighton, and M. Sands. (1963). *The Feynman Lectures on Physics*, Vol. 1. Addison Wesley Longman.

Giles, R. (1964). *Mathematical Foundations of Thermodynamics*. Oxford: Pergamon.

Grave, D. A. (1896). "Sur la construction des cartes géographiques," *Journal de Mathematiques Pures et Appliqués*, series 5, 2, 317–361. [Doctoral dissertation, St. Petersburg University.]

Hermann, R. (1973). *Geometry, Physics, and Systems*. New York: Dekker.

Hydon, P. E. (2000). *Symmetry Methods for Differential Equations*. Cambridge: Cambridge University Press.

Lagrange, J. L. de. (1779). "Sur la construction des cartes géographiques, Nouveaux Mémoires de l'Académie Royale des Sciences et Belles Lettres de Berlin, pp. 161–210.

Mittag, L. and M. J. Stephen. (1992)."Conformal transformations and the application of complex variables in mechanics and quantum mechanics," *American Journal of Physics*, 60(3), 207–211.

O Connor, J. J. and E. F. Robertson http://www.history.mcs.standrews.ac.uk/history/Miscellaneous/darcy.html

Samuelson, P. A. (1972). *"Maximum principles in analytical economics,"* Nobel Lecture, *American Economic Review*, Vol. 62(3), pp. 249–262.

——. (1990). "Gibbs in economics," in D. Caldi and G. Mostow (eds), *Proceedings of the Gibbs Symposium*, (Providence: American Mathematical Society), pp. 255–267.

Sato, R. (1999). Theory of Technical Change and Economic Invariance, Cheltenham, UK: Edward Elgar Publishing Inc., reprint, with amendments of 1981 edition.

Thompson, D'Arcy Wentworth (1942). *On Growth and Form*. Cambridge University Press.

Thomson, W. (1851). Dynamical Theory of Heat, *Trans. R. Soc.* Edinburgh.

Tisza, L. (1966). *Generalized Thermodynamics*, MIT Press.

Truesdell, C. and S. Baratha. (1977). *Classical Thermodynamics as a Theory of Heat Engines*. Springer.

USGS Map Projections http://www.3dsoftware.com/Cartography/USGS/MapProjections/ (no date)

21

Paul Samuelson's Mach

Rod Cross

Methodology involves words about methods. At the cognitive level these words can reflect some automatic, reflexive neural processes running parallel to the methods being pursued to address some problem. This is methodology with a small m. Or these words can reflect some controlled, serial, effortful introspection about methods, almost as though they could exist as things in themselves. This is Methodology with a big M. Then there is the affective response. The automatic, or controlled, response to liking or disliking is to embrace or avoid. There are various ways to respond, such as embracing methodology and avoiding Methodology.

In the brave new world of neuroscience it might be possible to use imaging techniques, scale electrodes and the like to track the role of the little m and the big M in experimental and control tasks performed by eminent scientists such as Paul Samuelson. In the absence of such neural evidence, and leaving deconstruction aside, the evidence from the horse's mouth is that Paul Samuelson has embraced methodology but, with the occasional lapse, has avoided Methodology. "I rather shy away from discussions of Methodology with a capital M. To paraphrase Shaw, those who can, do science, those who can't, prattle about its methodology. Of course I cannot deny that I have a methodology. It is just that there seems little appeal in making it explicit to an outsider. Or, for that matter, in spelling it out to my own consciousness" (Samuelson, 1992, p. 240). To paraphrase poet Browning, do science, shall breed the science, nor wrong the science, missing the mediate word.

The author would like to take this opportunity to thank Paul Samuelson for the assistance he provided in the author's work on hysteresis. This was a mark of the man, as well as of the scientist.

It is tempting to finish an account of Paul Samuelson's relationship with Methodology at this point. The autobiography of the British football player Len Shackleton (1955) contained a chapter titled "The Average Director's Knowledge of Football"—the page was blank. We would thus obey Wittgenstein's injunction to remain silent, wherewithon we cannot speak. Fortunately, or unfortunately as the case may be, there have been lapses. In his voyages of discovery to the lesser known realms of the economic world, this Odysseus has not always remained sufficiently bound to the mast of doing science to avoid the Siren calls of Methodology. Also, as is evident in the writings of Paul Feyerabend, saying no to Methodology can be a Methodological stance.

21.1 Big M

It is evident from Paul Samuelson's still-accumulating collected works that our nonagenarian has read widely outside the boundaries of economics. Given the breadth of the reading, it would have been surprising if Paul Samuelson had not read some writings on the philosophy of science. Amongst such writings mentioned by Samuelson (1992) are those of Ernst Mach, Willard van Orman Quine, a friend and one-time colleague when they were Junior Fellows at Harvard, Karl Popper, and Thomas Kuhn. Pride of place, in relation to Methodology, goes to Mach. "Unpopular these days are the positivists, who deem good theories to be merely economical descriptions of the complex facts that tolerably well replicate those already-observed or still-to-be-observed facts. Not for philosophical reasons but purely out of long experience in doing economics that other people will like and that I myself will like, I find myself in the minority that take the Machian view" (Samuelson, 1992, p. 242). So the big M is that to be found in Mach.

It is interesting that Mach was an eminent physicist, and a psychologist working on the physiology of the senses, as well as a philosopher. Thus he did science, as well as "prattle" about it. And the science done encompassed the nonrepeated worlds of sensations as well as the recurrent patterns of phenomena postulated in the laws of physics. Psychology was central to economic behavior in Adam Smith's *Theory of Moral Sentiments* account of the way the passions have a direct control, but one that can be overridden by individuals scrutinizing their behavior the way an impartial spectator might. In recent work on behavioral economics, and even neuroeconomics, psychology shows signs of coming in from the cold. Physics has long had a place in the economics tent, at least as a source of illustrative metaphors, at most as a constitutive form of borrowing and carrying over of properties. Read Irving Fisher's Ph.D. thesis (1891, 1925) if you want an extreme example. So an account of Methodology that covers psychology as well as physics could well be of interest to economists. As Mach put it in *The Analysis of Sensations*, "only by alternate studies in physics and in the physiology of the senses . . . have I attained to any considerable stability in my views. I make no pretensions to the title of philosopher. I only seek to adopt in physics a point of view that need not be changed the moment our glance is carried over into the domain of another science; for, ultimately, all must form one whole" (1897, 1959, p. 15).

21.2 Ontological Economy

The view attributed to Heraclitus in Plato's *Cratylus* dialogue was that "you don't put your foot into the same river more than once." Such a Heraclitean view of the world as a nonrepeating flux was the starting point for Mach. This world is made up of elemental qualities, such as sounds, colors, and pressures, that are individually unique and nonrepeatable. The mosaic of such qualities appears, then vanishes never to recur in the same form. The elemental qualities exhibit a reciprocal functional dependence on each other, in the form of actions and reactions, but the relationships are instantaneous ones such as $F[a, b, c, \ldots] = 0$, where a, b, c . . . are the elemental qualities, pertaining to the instant between which the qualities appear and vanish.

The key to constructing some ordered account of this flux is memory. "The images of earlier times are tied to the images of present states. States in the memory field are bound to other states in the perceptual field. That which was, we see at the same time with that which is" (Mach notebook 1881, cited in Banks, 2004, p. 28). With memory it is possible to perceive some elemental qualities as recurring facets of past instances. This is a first, ontological, role for "economy" in Mach. Instead of keeping a separate record of each nonrepeating elemental quality, the memory invents element types such as a "red" color that seem to recur in the flux of "fading" "light" in a "cloudless" "sky." The memory applies such ontological economy principles to what come to be taken to be recurring complexes of the world and associations or causal connections, such as a "red sunset." In doing so the memory does injustice to the historically unique, nonrecurrent nature of the underlying elemental qualities. By using conventions to construct recurrent regularities from nonrecurrent elemental qualities, memory paves the way for science. But this still means that the only ultimate reality is one of instantaneous appearances. "If we intended to ascribe the property to nature, that under equal conditions she produces the same effects, we would not know how to find these equal conditions. Nature is but *once* there. Only our reflection produces equal cases. The dependency of certain properties on one another exists only in this. All of our toil to mirror the world were fruitless were it not possible to find something enduring in this brightly coloured flux" (Mach, 1882, 1910, cited in Banks, 2004, p. 29).

"I am primarily a theorist. But my first and last allegiance is to the facts" (Samuelson, 1992, p. 240). Samuelson goes on to explain that, as a student at Chicago, "Frank Knight and Aaron Director planted in me the false notion that somehow deduction was more important than induction" (p. 240). He "grew out of this phase fast. Once Lionel Robbins explained lucidly in the first edition of his *An Essay on the Nature and Significance of Economic Science* his claims for a Kantian a priorism in economics, his case was lost" (p. 241). But escaping from the clutches of the devil of deductive syllogism primacy did not mark a conversion to the deep blue sea of untrammelled induction.

> Wesley Mitchell's empiricisms on the business cycle do seem to me to have been overrated—not because they are empirical, but rather because his was an eclecticism that never had much luck in discovering anything very interesting. Some of the scepticisms of Knight and Jacob Viner regarding the empirical statistical studies that their colleagues Paul Douglas and Henry Schulz were attempting, I readily admit, were well taken—just as some of Keynes's corrosive criticisms of Jan Tinbergen's econometric macromodels were. But it is on *empirical* grounds that these empirical attempts have to be rejected or accepted, and not because deductive syllogisms can claim a primacy to vulgar fact grabbing (p. 241).

In Mach's account of ontological economy the dichotomy between theory and facts is blurred. Inertia was in one manifestation a law of Newton, but in another guise appears as a fact. "What facts one will allow to rank as fundamental facts, at which one rests, depends on custom and on history" (Mach, 1910, p. 56). Quine demolished the theory–fact guillotine that Mach had blurred. Samuelson is aware of Quine's contribution, in this respect. "I am aware that my old friend Willard van Orman Quine, one of this age's greatest logicians, has cast doubt that anyone can in every case distinguish between "analytic" a priorisms and the "synthetic" propositions that positivists take to be empirical facts" (1992, p. 241). Or as Quine put it,

"My present suggestion is that it is nonsense, and the root of much nonsense, to speak of a linguistic component and factual component in the truth of any individual statement. Taken collectively, science has its double dependence on language and experience; but this duality is not significantly traceable into the statements of science taken one by one" (Quine, 1980, p. 42).

Among the popular criticisms of economics as a science are that the subject deals with a social world in which events are historically unique, whereas the physical sciences deal with a natural world where phenomena recur; and that in economics the facts are "soft," subject to different subjective interpretations and definitions, whereas in the natural world the facts are "hard" and objective. Mach, as far as I am aware, did not discuss political economy, but in his account of ontological economy these criticisms fail, certainly in terms of differences of substance, though maybe not in terms of degree. In Mach the natural world is also historically unique, and the fact–theory distinction is often a matter of custom, of history. Thus, at the very least, Mach's ontology does not take the economist into unfamiliar territory.

21.3 Epistemological Economy

Ask a philosopher who has not read Mach, and the answer is likely to be that Mach's distinctive contribution to the philosophy of science was to follow Bishop George Berkeley in rebutting the realist or essentialist view of science—that the concepts and relations correspond to, and have real counterparts in, nature—and proposing instead that there is only the world of appearances, with scientific concepts and equations being constructions, conventions, or instruments designed to explain the appearances. Ask an economist who has not read Mach the same question and the answer is likely to be "who?" or "wasn't he an instrumentalist who believed that realism in assumptions doesn't really matter so long as the predictions of a theory are OK?" Ask those trained in the arts of the pub quiz and the answer is likely to be "named the ratio between the velocity of a projectile and the ambient speed of sound." The philosopher's answer is incomplete—no mention of economy principles; the economist's answer is wrong—appearances are to be described, or "saved," not assumed away; only the pub quiz fan would have been right—if the quizmaster had asked about physics.

Mach's actual philosophy of science involves an extension of ontological economy to epistemology. This is stated concisely, obeying his own economy principle, in *The Science of Mechanics*: "it is the object of science to replace, or *save*, experiences, by the reproduction and anticipation of facts in thought . . . science itself . . . may be regarded as a minimal problem, consisting of the completest possible presentment of facts with the *least possible expenditure* of thought" (Mach, 1883, 1960, pp. 577, 586). So, for example, light refraction is an elemental quality that can be sensed in the nonrecurrent instances that constitute nature. Ontological economy in memory allows the variegated instances of refraction to be classified into refraction types and associations. Epistemological economy occurs at a further stage where a scientific law is a "compendious rule" for the mental reconstruction of the refraction types and associations that are now regarded as facts, as in Snel's law of refraction for example. The economizing principle involves explaining a lot from a little, so obeying the common sense of Ockham's razor dictum that "entities are not to be multiplied without need."

Good theories are thus those that provide an economical, or "minimal," description of the facts. Bad theories do not. "What was wrong with the German Historical School was not that it was historical, but rather that its sampling of the facts was incomplete and incoherent. The facts don't tell their own story. You can't enunciate all the facts. And if you could, the job of the scientists would just begin—to organize those facts into useful and meaningful gestalts, into patterns that are less multifarious than the data themselves and which provide economical *descriptions* of the data that afford tolerable accurate extrapolations and interpolations" (Samuelson, 1992, p. 243).

21.4 Some Objections

One line of criticism is that Mach has dispensed with explanation in science, replacing it with description. This problem is sometimes raised by those who favor a hypothetico-deductive model of science. This is partly a matter of semantics, as Samuelson points out: "'Understanding' of classical thermodynamics (the archetype of a successful scientific theory) I find to be the capacity to 'describe' how fluids and solids will actually behave under various specifiable conditions. When we are able to give a pleasingly satisfactory 'HOW' for the way of the world, that gives the only approach to 'WHY' that we shall ever attain" (Samuelson, 1992, p. 242). In Mach's account the theory–fact distinction is partly a matter of convention, of history, as his early resistance to the treatment of atoms as facts demonstrated.

So the notion that the explanans is *completely* independent of the explanandum does not hold in Mach.

Another objection is that Mach's position would eventually involve the abandonment of theoretical terms in science. Mach did propose a reformulation of Newtonian mechanics to eliminate the absolute concepts of motion, space, and time, but the point of the exercise was to produce a more economical description (read explanation if you like). Einstein, indeed, paid Mach a generous obituary tribute for having dispensed with the absolute motion concept. "It is not improbable that Mach would have found the theory of relativity if, at a time when his mind was still young, the problem of the constancy of the velocity of light had agitated the physicists" (Einstein, 1916, cited in Popper 1963, p. 232).

A third objection is the curious argument that surfaced in the debate surrounding what was meant in Milton Friedman's *The Methodology of Positive Economics* (1953). The claim was that instrumentalists, such as Mach, argued that theories were merely instruments for generating predictions about facts, and that whether or not the theories were unrealistic or contained unrealistic assumptions was a matter of no consequence. This is how many economists have taken Friedman's Methodology essay. Samuelson called this the F-Twist, impishly "avoiding his name because this may be, and I hope it is, a misinterpretation of his intention" (Samuelson, 1963, p. 232). The irony here is obvious. The problem is that the "unrealism in assumptions is OK" claim has nothing to do with Mach's instrumentalism, or Berkeley's for that matter. Mach was an instrumentalist in the sense that he rebutted the idea that there are real entities corresponding to the concepts and relationships involved in theories. The task of science is to provide an economical description of the facts. If a theory cannot explain the facts associated with its assumptions it is the worse for that. It is implausible to suppose that a theory could describe or explain everything, but that is another matter.

> A hypothesis's full set of predictions includes its own descriptive contents: so, literally understood, an unrealistic hypothesis entails some unrealistic predictions and is all the worse for those false predictions—albeit it is all the better for its (other) empirically correct predictions. We are left then validly with only the prosaic reminder that few theories have all their consequences exactly correct; and it can be the case that a scientific theory is deemed valuable because we have reason to give great weight to those of its predictions that happen to be true and to give little weight to those that are found to be false. In no case is unrealistic falsity a virtue; and there is danger of self-serving Humpty-Dumptyism in letting the theorist judge for himself which of his errors he is going to extenuate or ignore. (Samuelson, 1992, p. 242)

A related objection is that Mach's instrumentalism (read antirealism, not unrealism in content) is a form of conventionalism which says that theories are human constructions or conventions for explaining facts, rather than being provably true or false in themselves. This is the case, but invites the retort "so what?" If you take a hypothetico-deductive model, the $T \rightarrow I.$ $O \rightarrow T$ argument is invalid, where T is theory, I is implications and O is observational evidence or facts. The error would be in "affirming the consequent," so it is not possible to infer that, because the implications of a theory are true, the theory is true. So we are left with Popper's falsificationism: $T \rightarrow I.\ {\sim} O \rightarrow {\sim} T$. But the problem is that the arrow of falsity strikes the theory as a whole, and does not isolate which one or more of the constituent hypotheses is responsible for the falsification. As Pierre Duhem, and later Quine, pointed out, which hypothesis or hypotheses are dispensed with or amended in response to a refutation is a matter of convention.

> Total science is like a field of force whose boundary conditions are experience. A conflict with experience at the periphery occasions readjustments in the interior of the field. Truth values have to be redistributed over some of our statements. . . . Even a statement very close to the periphery can be held true in the face of recalcitrant experience by pleading hallucination or by amending certain statements of the kind called logical laws. Conversely, by the same token, no statement is immune to revision. Revision even of the logical law of the excluded middle has been proposed as a means of simplifying quantum mechanics; and what difference is there in principle between such a shift, and the shift whereby Kepler superseded Ptolemy, or Einstein Newton, or Darwin Aristotle? (Quine, 1980, pp. 42–43)

Popper's solution was to propose that some hypotheses or parts of the "background knowledge" should be regarded as not open to question, leaving target hypotheses open to falsification. But that is yet another knot on the master's whip, another form of conventionalism, as is the Lakatos typology of scientific research programmes.

21.5 Socratic Misgivings

Some issues still nag in relation to Mach's philosophy of science. One is whether this is a Methodology that is too open to be abused by scientists who want to defend their theories from empirical criticism. To one exposed to Popper and Lakatos whilst at the London School of Economics, the Machian account can appear to be lacking in critical safeguards such as that theories are bold, in the sense that they expose themselves to a wide array of falsifying instances, that they predict novel facts, or that they are revised in a nonadhoc manner, so allowing themselves to be more exposed to empirical criticism. Such safeguards can be seen as applying the Socratic ideal of questioning, of exposing arguments to a wide array of criticism, to science. Is this ideal captured in Mach? This misgiving is maybe more down to the language used by Mach, or the translation there of, than to the substance of the Methodology. The term "description" is usually used to refer to what has happened, not to what might have happened or to what will happen. The connotation is that science just describes what is already known, rather than also anticipates what is still to be known. The language is misleading. Mach does talk about the task of science being "to replace, or *save*, experiences" but also includes "the reproduction, and anticipation, of facts in thought." Similarly, Samuelson talks both of "already-observed" and "still-to-be-observed" facts. The term "economical" also raises doubts. Could it not also be taken to apply to the facts? Once it is made clear that the facts are not to be ignored, however inconvenient, and are to be anticipated, an "economical description" is difficult to distinguish from the falsificationist's excess empirical content. Popper's falsificationist precepts are indeed mentioned by Samuelson. "Long before knowing of Karl Popper's writings, I sought to be my own strictest critic. Why give that fun to the other chap?"(Samuelson, 1992, p. 242).

21.6 Simplicity

Mach's *Denkökonomie* principle suggests that it is possible, at least in certain cases, not only to discard unnecessary theoretical terms, such as absolute motion, but also to distinguish between competing theories in terms of their simplicity. An early criticism, from Herbert Buzello and Edmund Husserl (see Banks, 2004), was that Mach's principle takes the facts as given when discussing what a more economical or simpler theory is. If the theories differ in terms of the implied "still-to-be observed" facts, there is a problem.

It is surprisingly difficult to articulate in general terms what is meant by a simpler theory. A linear relationship has two parameters, a cubic three, so the linear is in one sense simpler. But the linear relationship may require a more complicated correction for error in order to fit the data. One can use an Akaike-type information criterion, such as the encompassing principle advocated in econometrics by Grayham Mizon, David Hendry, and Jean-François Richard, that weights the data likelihoods against the number of parameters. This yields an encapsulation of the Machian economy principle for given data sets. But this leaves open the question of what will happen in the not-yet-observed data sets, and hence "gruesome" paradoxes of the Goodman type.

Then there is the problem of incommensurability. The fruits of theories are multifaceted. There are implications about already-observed facts that have been found to be true or false. There are implications about still-to-be-observed facts that may be found to be true or false. Some of the facts implied are novel, some bring no news; some are bold conjectures, others innocuous; some are qualitative implications, some quantitative; and so on. Then there is silence, neither a yeah nor a nay. There has to be some weighting scheme if an economy principle is to be implemented, as in the size and power trade-off in the Neyman–Pearson account of statistical inference.

The freshwater economist might give you an economical description of what happens in the rivers and lakes. The seawater economist might tell of what happens in the oceans and estuaries. Of course a comprehensively economical description would tell you about both fresh and seawater, about the voluntarily at leisure fish in the one medium and their involuntarily unemployed counterparts in the other, about whether the media are comparable in terms of pollution, and so on. But how do you judge before the "compendious rule" is invented?

Samuelson understands that these are matters of judgment.

> Precision in deterministic facts or in their probability laws can at best be only partial and approximate. Which of the objective facts out there are worthy of study and description or explanation depends admittedly on subjective properties of scientists. Admittedly, a given field of data can be described in terms of alternative patterns of description, particularly by disputing authorities who differ in the error tolerances they display toward different aspects of the data. Admittedly, observations are not merely seen or sensed but rather often are perceived in gestalt patterns that impose themselves on the data and even distort those data. (Samuelson, 1992, p. 244)

21.7 Is Mach Done?

It is quite brave of one who has an aversion to Methodology to adhere to a particular account of scientific method, for this immediately raises questions about whether the preaching or "prattling" is practiced. This leaves Paul Samuelson open to critical commentaries on whether he has done his science the Mach way. In one sense this does not matter too much. Fish can swim without seemingly knowing too much about hydrodynamics, billiard players are not all well versed in Newtonian mechanics. Maybe, though, if the Methodology chorus reacts in a different way to what is happening on the stage, the audience will change its view.

Methodologists such as Stanley Wong (1978), E. Roy Weintraub (1991), and Philip Mirowski (1989) have assessed aspects of the way Samuelson has done his science, but not through Machian spectacles (see also Samuelson's (1998) response). Wong, for example, analyzed the development of Samuelson's revealed preference theory by way of a Popper–Lakatos rational reconstruction. The Google hit count on Mach. Samuelson will no doubt rise at an alarming rate.

Is it necessarily the case that the perception of science, and what scientists have achieved, depends on the Methodological spectacles used? One way out of this is to say no to Methodology: "science at its most advanced and general returns to the individual (scientist) a freedom he seems to lose in its more pedestrian parts" (Feyerabend, 1975, p. 285, my addition in brackets). Otherwise the reader's preferred big M will color the perception of what a great scientist such as Paul Samuelson has done. This is an aspect of Mach's world of appearances.

Samuelson acknowledges that Methodology can make some sort of difference. "When Thomas Kuhn's book, *The Structure of Scientific Revolutions*, came out in 1962, I made two lucky predictions: one, that in the physical and life sciences its thesis would have to be modified to recognize that there is a cumulative property of knowledge that makes later paradigms ultimately dominate earlier ones, however differently the struggle may transiently look; second, that Kuhn's doctrine of incommensurability of alternative paradigms would cater to a strong desire on the part of polemical social scientists who will be delighted to be able to say "That's all very well in your paradigm, but your white is black in my paradigm—and who's to say that we'uns have to agree with you'uns" (Samuelson, 1992, p. 244). Paul Samuelson is right, though, to stress the need for perspective: "Kuhn has correctly discerned the warts on the countenance of evolving science. His readers must not lose the face for the warts" (p. 244).

References

Banks, E. C. (2004). "The philosophical roots of Ernst Mach's economy of thought," *Synthese*, 139, 23–53.

Feyerabend, Paul K. (1975). *Against Method: Outline of an Anarchist Theory of Knowledge*. London: New Left Books.

Fisher, Irving. (1891). *Mathematical Investigations in the Theory of Value and Prices.* New Haven; CT: Yale University Press, thesis published in 1925.

Friedman, Milton. (1953). "The methodology of positive economics," in Milton Friedman, *Essays in Positive Economics*, Chicago, IL: Chicago University Press.

Kuhn, Thomas S. (1962). *The Structure of Scientific Revolutions.* Chicago, IL: University of Chicago Press.

Mach, Ernst. (1883). *The Science of Mechanics*, trans. T.J. McCormack. La Salle: Open Court Publishing, 1960.

——. (1897). *The Analysis of Sensations*, trans. C.M. Williams and S. Waterlow. New York: Dover Books, 1959.

——. (1910). *History and Root of the Principle of the Conservation of Energy.* Chicago, IL: Open Court.

Mirowski Philip. (1989). *More Heat than Light.* New York: Cambridge University Press.

Popper, Karl. (1963). *Conjectures and Refutations.* London: Routledge.

Quine, Willard van Orman. (1980). *From a Logical Point of View.* Cambridge, MA: Harvard University Press.

Samuelson, Paul. (1963). "Problems of methodology—discussion," *American Economic Review*, 53, 231–236.

——. (1992). "My life philosophy: policy credos and working ways," in Michael Szenberg (ed.), *Eminent Economists: Their Life Philosophies.* New York: Cambridge University Press.

——. (1998). "How foundations came to be," *Journal of Economic Literature*, 36, 1375–1386.

Shackleton, Len. (1955). *The Clown Prince of Football.* London: Nicholas Kaye.

Weintraub, E. Roy. (1991). *Stabilising Dynamics: Constructing Economic Knowledge.* New York: Cambridge University Press.

Wong, Stanley. (1978). *The Foundations of Paul Samuelson's Revealed Preference Theory: a Study in the Method of Rational Reconstruction.* London: Routledge and Kegan Paul.

Index

accounting:
  fiscal gap 48
  generational 47–8
additive technologies:
  efficient provision 94
  global public goods 93–4
Afriat's approach, revealed preference 101
AIDS 96
Akerlof, George:
  business cycle model 245
Allais, Maurice 35
altruism, intergenerational transfer 42, 44–5
American Economic Review 167, 229
'An Exact Consumption-Loan Model of Interest with or without the Social Contrivance of Money' 35, 42
anti-inflation policy 166
antirecession policy 166
Arrow, Kenneth 54, 118, 143–4, 192
Arrow-Debreu securities 203–4, 206
Arrow-Debreu theory 206
autarky 199, 213
Azariadis, Costa 44
  'Self-Fulfilling Prophecies' 40

baby-boomers 50, 55, 63
  pension overhang and 72
Bachelier, Louis 265,
  Theory of Speculation 267, 278–81
Balasko, Yves 44
Balassa-Samuelson effect 206
Balassa-Samuelson theorem *see* Harrod-Balassa-Samuelson theorem
Bank of Italy address '1997' 127, 135, 137, 139
bankruptcy 191
Barro, Robert 44
Baumol, William 130, 134
Becker, family economics 118–21
behavioral economics 55
Bentham 42
Bergson-Samuelson social welfare function 54, 117
best-shot technologies:
  efficient provision 95
  global public goods 94
  noncooperative provision 95
Beaulieu, Eugene 230
biological stocks, global public goods 91
'biological theory of interest' 37
biology 42
Black-Scholes option pricing model 283–5
Blanchard, Olivier 71
'blue noise' process 291
Böhm-Bawerk 42
  circularity charge 138
  overlapping generations 39
Bohn 63
Bogle, John 80
Branson, William 71
Brown 122
Brownian motion 269, 279–80
Bryce, Robert 181
Buckley, William, *God and Man at Yale* 179
budget:
  non social security 59
  social security 59
Buffet, Warren 169
Bush tax cuts 63
business cycle, model of 245–6

Capital, see *Das Kapital*
capital:
  intergenerational transfer 49
  national 60, 61–62
  social security 57, 62
capital market liberalization 236
capitalist accumulation, Ricardo-Marx-Solow model of, 135
cartography, Maxwell/Samuelson area condition 320–23
Cass, David 40
Cassel 68
Catchings 170

celestial mechanics, Samuelson area condition 318–20
CES intertemporal preference 46
CES production 46
Chiappori:
  methodological individualism 120–1
  see also family economics
chocolate bar metaphor 43–5, 49
classical economics 150, 188
  theory 146, 149, 161
Cohen 130
Colander 179–82
cold war 76
Coming of Keynesianism to America 179
competitive capitalism 132
competitive economies 42, 144
competitive equilibrium theory 78
computers 55
Congress 55
constant-relative-risk-aversion (CRRA) 288, 290
consumer behavior, basic theory 100
consumption rate 57, 59–62
  household 50
  sharing 45
Cowles Commission 171–2, 174–5

D'Arcy Thompson, *On Growth and Form* 323–5
Das Kapital 128, 130, 131, 136, 139
Deaton 102
Debreu 313–14
debt 63
'debt bombs' 70, 71–3; *see also* pension overhang
Define-Contribution 401k pension plans 290
deforestation 93
demand function, revealed preference 101
demand theory 303, 308
Denkökonomie principle 338
depreciation rate, global public goods 91
depression economics 166
Diamond, Peter 39, 44, 46, 57
Diamond-Mirrlees condition 200–1
Diewert 102
discretionary spending, federal 48
Dixit, Avinash 197–207
Dobb, Maurice 130, 137
Dobell 104
'doctrine of increasing misery' 138
dominant economics 146
'Dr Jekyll and Mrs Jeykell' problem 117–18, 123
duality, international trade theory 197, 204
dynamic economies 42
dynamic efficiency 44, *see also* Pareto inefficiency
dynamic general equilibrium 46
  interest rates 46
  wage rates 46

earnings 69
Econometric Society 170–1, 173–4
Economic Journal 147
economic theory, trade theory and 198
Economics 135, 169, 170
Economics An Introductory Analysis 179–80
economics of state intervention *see* depression economics
Edgeworth-Bowley box diagram 226–7
efficient market hypothesis, financial economics 262, 267–78
efficient provision:
  best-shot technology 95
  global public goods 94–5
Einstein-Fokker-Planck Fourier equation 265–6
Elmendorf 56
endogenous growth theory 236–41
endogenous technological change 236–7, 247
Engel curve 108–9
Engles, Friedrich 42, 128, 130
entrepreneurs 67, 68, 83, 188, 191
ERISA 288
equilibrium 55, *see also* rational expectation equilibrium
ergodic economic world, axiom of 187, 190
  ergodic hypothesis 184–6
Ethier, Wilfred 230
expected log rule 253–4
Expected Utility criterion 287
Ezekiel, Dr Mordecai 167–8, 171, 173, 176

Fama 275
family economics:
  'altruist model' 118–21
  bargaining models 121–2, 124
  'collective model' 123
  cooperative bargaining models of marriage 121
  divorce threat model 122
  'Dr. Jekyll and Mrs. Jekyll' problem 117–18, 123
  husband and wife 119
  income pooling 122–4
  Nash bargaining model 121–2
  North Holland Handbook 124
  resource pooling 122

revealed preference 122
Rotten Kid Theorem 119
'unitary models' 120, 122–4
Feenstra 201
Feldstein, Martin 44–5
Fellner 83
Festschrift 128, '1983' 54
Income, Employment, and Public Policy, essays in Honor of Alvin H Hansen 176
Financial Accounting Standards Board 291
financial economics:
Black-Scholes option pricing model 283–5
efficient market hypothesis 262, 267–78
investing for the long run 286–91
martingale theorem 271–2, 275
option pricing 262, 266, 278–85
uncertainty 266
warrant pricing 262, 269, 278–85
financiers 67, 83
fiscal gap accounting, 48–9
Fisher 144
First Welfare Theorem 142
formal dynamics 242
Foster 170
Foundations of Economic Analysis 122, 149–50, 159, 167, 180, 184, 189, 252
Frydman 83
free trade 199, 213, 214, 224–5, 229
Friedman's Monetarism 179
Frisch, Ragnar 170, 171
future:
asset prices 69
'debt bombs', 70, 71–3
earnings 69
prospects, mutability of 77–82
inferential movements in shadow values 77–9
Knightian uncertainty 68, 83
macroeconomics and the 67–8
productivity surges, 73–5
prospects 69–70
radical uncertainty 68
share prices and 79–82
war prospects 71, 75–6
futures market 268

GDP function 48, 72–3, 76, 80, 197, 205
Geanakoplos, John 35, 40, 57
General Theory of Interest, Employment and Money 144, 166, 170, 175, 178–9, 181–4, 186, 190, 193
general equilibrium:
dynamic 46–7
First Welfare Theorem 142
Hicks Conditions 143, 145
Invisible Hand 142, 145
monopoly power 144
Rational Expectations school of thought 142
Second Welfare Theorem 142
stability of 142–5
*'tatonnement'*143–4
trade theory and 198
Walrasian, competitive equilibrium 144, 182–3, 185
general equilibrium trade theory *see* Heckscher-Ohlin-Samuelson model
general theory revolution 186–90
Generalized Axiom of Revealed Preference 103–10
generational accounting, neoclassical model, 47–8
genetic stocks, global public goods 91
German School 68
Gesell 170
Gibbs, J. Willard 150
global inverse function theorem 203
global public goods:
additive technologies 93–4
best-shot technologies 94
character of 89–90
depreciation rate of stock 91
efficient provision 94–5
examples of 88, 91
federalism 92–3
historical notes 97
noncooperative provision 95–6
production technology for 93–6
'stock externalities' 90–1
time dimension in 91
weakest-link technologies 94
Westphalian dilemma 92–3
global warming 89, 90, 92, 93–4
God and Man at Yale 179
Goldberg 83
Golden Age of capitalism 135
golden rule 44, 236
government bonds 49
Grandmont Jean-Michel 39, 44, 200
Great Depression 69, 78, 166, 169, 170
Greenspan, Alan 75
gross substitution axiom 187, 189

Haavelmo, Trygve 170–2
Habakkuk 237
Hahn 143, 188, 192
Hammond 200
Hansen, Alvin H, 176–7

HARA family of utility functions 286
Harcourt, Geoff 127–39
Harris, Donald 135
Harrod, Roy 42, 136, 169
Harrod-Balassa-Samuelson theorem 217–9
Heckscher-Ohlin-Samuelson model 197, 202, 204–6, 213–4, 218, 225–6, 231
Hegel 130
Heston-Summers comparisons 218
heuristic dynamics 66, 242
Hicks Conditions 143, 145
Hicks, John 100, 142, 171
Hicks, Ursula 229
Hilferding 138
Hirshleifer 94
Homothetic Axiom of Revealed Preference (HARP) 107, 111
Horney 122
Hoson 170
Houthakker 100, 101, 103
Hurwicz 143

ignoration elenchi 183
income tax:
  distribution of 63
  national savings 60
  payroll tax rates and 56–7
individual choice 55
Industrial Revolution 149–50
infinity, economics of 44
institutional stocks 91
intergenerational transfer 42–51
Intergovernmental Panel on Climate Change 93
International Comparison of Prices project 218
International Economic review 122
international economics, *see also* international trade theory
  finance 217–19
  North American Free Trade Agreement '1992' 215
  trade 213–17
  'transfer problem' 219
international law, critical global public goods 92–3
International Maritime Organization 93
international trade 213–7
international trade theory:
  'beyond two by two' 205–6
  Dornbusch-Fischer-Samuelson model 197, 206, 216–7
  economic theory and 198
  factor endowment models of trade 202–7
  gains from trade 199–201
  Heckscher-Ohlin-Samuelson model 197, 202, 204–6, 214, 216–8, 225, 231
  Ricardian models of trade 201–2, 216
  Ricardo-Viner-Samuelson model 197, 205
  Rybczynski theorem 204
  two-by-two model 197
  see also Stolper-Samuelson theorem
intertemporal budget constraint 38
intertemporal general-equilibrium 35, 38, 39
  Arrow-Debreu theory 206
Intertemporal Price Equilibrium: A Prologue to the Theory of Speculation 268
intra-family human capital transfer 44
investment boom 69
  1920, 69, 74
  1990 US 74
investment for long run 286–91
  background 253
  expected log rule 253–4
  max E log, argument against 256–7
  max E log, argument for 254–6, 258–9
Invisible Hand 142, 145

Jones, Ronald:
  magnification effect 228–9
  Samuelson's impact on trade theory, 198, 202, 206
  Stolper-Samuelson analysis 228–9
Journal of Economic Literature 129, 134
Journal of International Economics 205

Kahn, Richard 166
Kaldor 237
Kaldorian variant 244
Kalecki, Keynesian economics and 170–1
Kant 42
Kelly 253–4
Kemp 199, 201, 213
Kepler's second law 319–20
Kerr, Prue 128, 130
Keynes, John Maynard 68–9, 147, 165, 183
  General Theory of Interest, Employment and Money 144, 166, 170, 175, 178–9, 181, 183, 186, 190
  investor 169–70
Keynes/post-Keynesian revolution 178–93
  differences between neoclassical Keynesianism and 184–6
  overthrow of Samuelson's Keynesian axioms 186–90
Keynesian 'animal spirits', future prospects 69, 135

Keynesian economics 193
early post war period 176–7
Kalecki 170–1
meaning of 165–7, 169
multiplier 303
Neoclassical Keynesian Synthesis 165, 167
policy 173–4
Ragnar Frisch 170–1
unemployment ahead 174–6
unemployment equilibrium 171–3
Keynesians 44
Keynes's Circus 166–7, 171, 177
Klein, L.R. 165–77
Knight 68
Knightian uncertainty 68, 83
knowledge, stock character nature of 91
Kotlikoff 47
Kuhn, Thomas 157–8, 160, 331, 340
Korean War 76

labor theory of value 128–31, 133, 136, 138, 155–6
Landreth 179–82
Lange 171
Latane 253–4
Lavoisier, Antoine Laurent 158
Law of Large Numbers 288–9
Leaner, Edward 230
LeChatelier principle 312
introduction 303–4
optimization problems 304–5
positive feedback systems 305–8
Lerner, Abba 37–8, 213, 229
Levhari, David 151–2
Levine 147, 150
Lewis 201
Liebman 56
life sciences, Samuelson area condition 323–5
Little 100
liquidity 190–3
liquidity preference theory 187
long-horizon investing 287, 288, 291
Loury, Glenn 44
low-carbon fuels 96
Lucas 66
Lundberg 122–3

McCarthyism 179, 193
McElroy 122
McFadden 200
Mach, Ernst 331–40
Denkökonomie principle 338
see also methodology

macroeconomics 82–3, 235
dynamic recursive models 66, 68
future expectations 68
Magee, Christopher 230
malaria 96
Malinvaud, article of 206
Malthus 170
Manara, Carlo Felice 155
Manser 122
marginal ecomonic theory 146, 149
Markowitz 253–4
markups, staggered 66
Marschak, Jacob 173
martingale theorem 271–2, 275
Marx, Karl:
capitalism 131–2, 139
capitalist accumulation 135
'doctrine of increasing misery' 138
feudalism 131
labor theory of value 129–31, 133, 135–6, 138, 153, 155–6
'transformation of algorithm' 129–30, 133
reserve army of labor 128, 132–3
surplus 131–2, 137
MasColell 203
Mathematics of Speculative Price, 265, 268, 271, 284
max E log, 287
argument against 256–7
arguments for 254–6, 258–9
Maxwell/Samuelson area condition, cartography 320–23, 325
Meade, James 136
Meckling, W.J. 38, 39, 43, 47
Medicare benefits, cuts in 48
Meek, Ronald 130, 134–5, 137–8
methodology:
big M 330, 331–2
epistemological economy 334–5
ontological economy 332–4
simplicity 338–9
socratic misgivings 337–8
Metzler 143
micro-economics 243–4
micro-economic theory, stability analysis 142
model structure, two types
Monetarists 44
money contracts 190–3
money laundering 94
Moscow School of Probability 190
multipliers 303, 308; *see also* LeChatelier principle
Musgrave, Richard 54
Mulligan, Casey 77

Index

national capital, *see* capital
national mortgage market 266
national public goods 92
national savings, permanent fund increase 60–1, 63
natural sciences:
  optimization principle 311
  Samuelson area condition 313–25
neoclassical economics 146
neoclassical Keynesian Synthesis 165, 167, 171, 176, 179–80
  differences between Keynes/post Keynesian theory and 184–6
neoclassical theory of consumer behavior 117
Nerlove 118
net national saving rate 49–50
neutrality of money axiom 187, 192
New Palgrave Dictionary 155
Newman 101
Newton 318, 319, 324
noncooperative provision:
  best-shot technologies 95
  global public goods 95–6
  weakest-link technologies 95
non-Euclidean economics 187, 189, 190
Non-Proliferation Treaty 93
nonstationarity 68
Norman 200
North American Free Trade Agreement '1992' 215
North Holland Handbook 124
nuclear proliferation 89, 94
nuclear weapons 93

OECD economies 73, 214
O'Neill, Paul, Treasury Secretary 48
optimization principle, natural sciences and 311
option pricing:
  financial economics 262, 266, 278–85
outsourcing, international trade theory and 198
overlapping generations model 35–40, 235–6
  public economics 54–5

PPP exchange rates 218
Palgrave Dictionary 35
'paradigm' concept 157
  'exchange paradigm' 161
  'production paradigm' 161
'paradox of thrift' 171
Pareto efficient:
  equilibrium 123, 203–4
  Nash bargaining model 121
  outcomes 123, 199, 201
  sharing rule 123
Pareto improvement 43, 54
Pareto inefficient, competitive economies 42–3
Pasinetti, Luigi 133, 146–161
Patinkin, Don 172
payroll tax 55, 59
  income tax cut and 56–7
  increase in rate 59
  national savings 60
Pension Benefit Guarantee Corporation 291
pensions 287–91
  corporate pension fund industry 288
  overhang 71–3
permanent fund, *see* trust fund
Perron-Frobenius theorems on nonnegative matrices 154–5
personalized lump-sum tranfers 200
Phelps, Edmund 44, 66–83
Pigou, A.C. 70,
Pigou effect 172–3, 175
Plutonium-239, stock externalities 90
Pollak 119, 122–3
pollution, stock character of 91
Poor 500 index 79
Popper, Karl 331, 336, 337, 338, 340
Prelude to a critique of economic theory 150
Prescott 66
Presidential Address to the American Economic Association '1961' 128, 201
price-earnings ratio 80–1
prices 69
Priestley, Joseph 158
private goods 88
probabilities, diffusion of:
  Einstein-Fokker-Planck Fourier equation 265–6
Production of Commodities by means of Commodities 134, 147, 149, 151, 156, 160–1
production, zero elasticity 188
productivity surges, future 73–5
public economics:
  introduction 54–5
  model structure 57–9
  permanent fund increase 59–62
  social security 55–7
public goods *see* global public goods
pure capital theory of value 156–7

Quine, Wilard van Orman 331, 333

radioactive waste, stock character 91
Ramsey, Frank 177
Ramsey model, overlapping generations 39
rational expectations equilibrium 66–70
  convergence of 45
  microfoundations and 67
  share prices 69
recursive dynamic models, *see* rational expectations equilibrium
'red noise' process 290
reputational stocks 91
reserve army of labor 128, 132–3
re-switching of techniques debate 151–2
  non-switching theorem 151
retirement:
  public economics 58
  see also pensions
revealed preference:
  Afriat's approach to 100, 101
  consistency 103–6
  empirical analysis 104
  family economics 122
  forecasting 109
  form 106–7
  goodness-of-fit measure 106
  international trade 213–17
  pure theory of 99–101
  recoverability 110–11
Ricardian Equivalence 44
Ricardo 130, 132, 136, 153–4
  labor theory of value 155–6
Richter 101
Robinson, Austin 148
Robinson, Joan 135, 136, 151, 166
Rotten Kid Theorem 119
Rowthorn, Bob 135, 138
Rybczynski theorem 204

Salter 237
Samuelson area condition:
  celestial mechanics 318–20
  growth and form 323–4
  thermodynamics and 312–18
Samuelson configuration 311–3, 321, 325, 326
Samuelson, Paul:
  architect of modern mathematical economics 167–9
  investor 169–70
  Keynes' theory, 180–4
Samuelson submanifolds 316–18
'Samuelsonian Economics' 160–1
Samuelson's Relativity Theory 47, 48
Sardoni, Claudio 136
SARS 94
savings, retirement 58
savers 57–9, 60, 63
  lifetime budget constraint 62
savings-investment cross 171, 173
Schrager 73
Schultz, Henry 167
Schumpeter 68
Second Welfare Theorem 142
Second World War 78–9
security analysis 267
shadow prices 76, 78, 80
shadow values, inferential movements in 77–9
share prices 69, 76–7
  future prospects and 79–82
Shell, Karl 44
Skidelsky, Lord 182
Slutsky equation 100, 122
social contracts, sale of 46
social security 38, 48, 235
  1983 reform 55–7
  benefits, cuts in 48
  budgets 56, 58–9
  capital 57, 62
  pay-as-you-go 44, 55
  savings, impact on national savings 56
  taxes 63
Socialists 44
Solow growth model 238, 246–7
Solow, Robert 136, 151,
Sondermann 101
space statistics 185
Spector 201
speculative markets 270–2
Spiethoff 68
Sraffa, Piero 133–4, 137, 146–7, 166
  Paul Samuelson and 148–50
  Prelude to a critique of economic theory 150
  price system 153
  Production of Commodities by means of Commodities 134, 147, 149, 151, 156, 160–1
  reswitching of techniques debate 151–2
  'Sraffian economics' 160–1
  standard commodity 152–7, 158
stability of general equilibrium, *see* general equilibrium; *Value and Capital*
standard commodity 152–7, 158
Standard Share Index 79
steady state equilibrium 241–2
Stigum 101
Strong Axiom of Revealed Preference (SARP) 100, 102, 103, 104, 112
stock externalities, meaning of 90–1
Stolper, Wolfgang 202, 225

Stolper- Samuelson effect 202, 204
Stolper-Samuelson theorem 212
  analysis of 226–7
  birth of 225
  essential tool for economists 230–1
  seminal role 229–30
  simple general equilibrium model and 227–9
Strict Constructionists 44
substitution, zero elasticity of 188
'sunspots', economics of 40, 44
surrogate production function 151
Swan, Trevor 135–6, 151
Szenberg, Michael xxiii

Tarshis, Lori 179–81, 183–4, 193
Teck Hoon, Hian 71, 72, 77, 78
'temporary equilibrium' 45
theoretical behavioral economics:
  individual choice 55
  equilibrium models 55
Theory of Capital 148
thermodynamics:
  Samuelson area condition and 312–18
  Samuelson submanifolds 316–18
three-period-long consumption sequences 36
time statistics 185
Tinbergen, Jan 175
Tinbergen model 174, 190
The Road since Structure 158
Tobin 54
'Tobin Q ratio' 78, 80, 82, 83
trade theory, economic theory 198
Treaty of Westphalia 92
trust fund:
  building of 55–6
  increase in, 59–62
  national savings and, 60
turnover-training model 71, 72, 79
  open economy version 72

uncertainty, economics of 266–7
unemployment 69, 171, 235–47
  ahead 174–6
  early post war period 176–7
  equilibrium 171–3, 183
United States:
  net national saving rate 49, 50
  Treasury 48
utility function:
  constant-relative-risk-aversion (CRRA) 288, 290
  HARA family 286
  family economics 121
  revealed preference 101–2
utility possibility function 199–200
Uzawa 101

Value and Capital:
  stability of general equilibrium 142
Varian 106, 109–11
von Neumann output composition 154, 157

wages 49
  effect of protection on real 225–31
  dependent on capital 49
  high 247
  staggered 66
Wales 122
Walrasian economics 149, 182, 185, 188, 191–2
Wan 201
war prospects 71, 75–6
Ward-Batts 123
warrant pricing:
  financial economics 262, 269, 278–85
Weak Axiom of Revealed Preference 99–100, 102
weakest-link technologies:
  global public goods 94
  noncooperative provision 95
Westphalian dilemma:
  global public goods 92–3, 95
'white noise' process 290
workers 57–9, 60, 63, 132
Works and Correspondence of David Ricardo 147
White House 50

Yokoyama 100

DATE DUE
